DICKENS STUDIES ANNUAL
Essays on Victorian Fiction

DICKENS STUDIES ANNUAL
Essays on Victorian Fiction

EDITORS

Michael Timko
Edward Guiliano

DICKENS STUDIES ANNUAL

Essays on Victorian Fiction

VOLUME
25

Edited by
Michael Timko and Edward Guiliano

AMS PRESS
NEW YORK

DICKENS STUDIES ANNUAL
ISSN 0084-9812

Dickens Studies Annual: Essays on Victorian Fiction is published in cooperation with Queens College and the Graduate Center, CUNY.

International Standard Book Number
Series: 0-404-18520-7
Vol. 25:0-404-18545-2

Dickens Studies Annual: Essays on Victorian Fiction welcomes essay and monograph-length contributions on Dickens as well as other Victorian novelists and on the history of aesthetics of Victorian fiction. All manuscripts should be double-spaced, including footnotes, which should be grouped at the end of the submission, and should be prepared according to the format used in this journal. An editorial decision can usually be reached more quickly if two copies are submitted. The preferred editions for citations from Dickens' works are the Clarendon and the Norton Critical when available, otherwise the Oxford Illustrated or the Penguin.

Please send submissions to the Editors, *Dickens Studies Annual,* Room 1522, Graduate School and University Center, City University of New York, 33 West 42nd Street, New York, N.Y. 10036; please send subscription inquiries to AMS Press, Inc., 56 East 13th Street, New York, N.Y. 10003.

Contents

Preface

Volume 25 continues the commitment of the editors of *DSA* to present a variety of approaches to Dickens studies and Victorian fiction and to publish substantial review articles on the major novelists and important categories of critical inquiry into Victorian fiction. Our ability to publish fresh volumes of *DSA*, to stimulate new thought (we hope some of the best that is being thought, said, and done in the world of Victorian fiction) is testimony to the strong commitment from general readers and the academic world our focus and approach holds. Perhaps even more significantly, it is testimony to the generous services and commitments of the many people who enable us to bring out this annual volume.

The editors welcome the collegiality and appreciate the expertise and cooperation of the members of our editorial and advisory boards. We acknowledge our now long, fruitful and engaging association with the California Dickens Project, and once again repeat our very special thanks to the members of our profession who serve as readers. The principle of peer-evaluation is at the heart of maintaining standards of excellence in research and publication.

Once more we note and express our gratitude to those in administrative posts in different institutions who provide support and encouragement of various kinds—people at the CUNY Graduate Center, Queens College, and the New York Institute of Technology, especially the Executive Office, Ph.D. Program in English, the Graduate Center and University Center, CUNY. We thank AMS President, Gabriel Hornstein, and our valued AMS editor, Jack Hopper, and we thank our DSA editorial assistant, Ann Kincaid, for this volume.

Notes on Contributors

LAURA C. BERRY is assistant professor of English at the University of Arizona. Her essays are forthcoming in *Novel* and in *Victorian Literature and Culture*. She is currently completing a book on social welfare and the social work of the nineteenth-century novel.

JOEL J. BRATTIN associate professor of English at Worcester Polytechic Institute, has served for five years as secretary and treasurer of the Dickens Society. He is on the editorial boards of *Nineteenth-Century Prose* and the California Carlyle edition, is a contributing editor for *UniVibes*, and is an advisory editor for the *Charles Dickens* volume in the Oxford Author Companions series. He has recently published on Carlyle, Dickens, Emerson, Hendrix, and Nabokov, and he coordinated the International Dickens Symposium 1996 in Worcester.

BRIAN CHEADLE is professor of English at the University of the Witwatersrand, Johannesburg. He has previously published an article on *Great Expectations* in this annual.

JOSEPH E. CHILDERS is an associate professor of English at the University of California at Riverside. He is the author of *Novel Possibilities: Fiction and the Formation of Early Victorian Culture* (University of Pennsylvania Press, 1995) and is co-editor of *The Columbia Dictionary of Modern Literary and Cultural Criticism* (1995).

LUANN MCCRACKEN FLETCHER is assistant professor of English at Cedar Crest College. She has published articles on Charlotte Brontë and Virginia Woolf; her encyclopedia entries on Anne Brontë and Elizabeth Rigby, Lady Eastlake are forthcoming in the second edition of *An Encyclopedia of British Women Writers*. She is currently at work on an anthology of Victorian prose.

GILIAN GANE has worked for many years as a part-timer at the University of Massachusetts at Boston, teaching mainly composition courses. She is assistant editor of *College English*. Her scholarly interests are now largely postcolonial, although she retains an enduring interest in Dickens; in September

1996 she presented a paper on the Native in *Dombey and Son* at a conference on Dickens, Empire, and Children at Rhodes University in her native South Africa.

ELIZABETH GITTER is professor of English at John Jay College, City University of New York. She has written on numerous Victorian subjects, and her work has been published in a variety of journals, including *Victorian Poetry, Dickens Quarterly, PMLA,* and *Victorian Literature and Culture.*

ANN GRIGSBY received her PhD from the University of New Mexico. She is currently employed as a technical editor and also teaches at Pima Community College and Park College in Tucson, Arizona.

WINIFRED HUGHES is book review editor of *Victorian Literature and Culture* and author of *The Maniac in the Cellar: Sensation Novels of the 1860s.* Recent articles on the silver fork novel and Mrs. Gore have appeared in *Novel* (1992) and *Nineteenth-Century Literature* (1995).

ANN HUMPHERYS is professor of English at Lehman College and the Graduate School of the City University of New York. She is the author of *Travels into the Poor Man's Country: The Work of Henry Mayhew* and articles and chapters on Dickens, G. W. M. Reynolds, Victorian popular culture and the press. She is currently writing a book on the Victorian divorce novel.

WENDY S. JACOBSON was educated at the University of Rhodesia (now Zimbabwe) and at The Shakespeare Institute in Birmingham. She is the author of *The Companion to the Mystery of Edwin Drood* and of several articles on Dickens. She teaches at Rhodes University in South Africa.

JAMES R. KINCAID, Aerol Arnold Professor at the University of Southern California, is author of books (old ones, outmoded) on Dickens, Tennyson, and Trollope, and of recent (hip) studies entitled *Child-Loving: The Erotic Child and Victorian Culture, Annoying the Victorians,* and (forthcoming) *Manufacturing Virtue: The Culture of Child-Molesting.*

JOHN B. LAMB is an associate professor of English at West Virginia University and the assistant editor of *Victorian Poetry.* His essay ''Turning the Inside Out: Morals, Modes of Living, and the Condition of England Question'' is forthcoming in *Victorian Literature and Culture.*

BRIAN W. MCCUSKEY is an assistant professor of English at Utah State University, where he teaches nineteenth-century British literature, literary theory, and cultural studies. He is currently working on a book entitled "Servants' Characters: Below Stairs in Victorian Culture."

TORE REM is a doctoral candidate and junior research fellow at Christ Church, Oxford University. He has published in *English Studies* and on Dickens and film in *Word & Image*. He has an article on Dickens and the supernatural appearing in *The Dickensian*.

SHIRLEY S. STAVE is an assistant professor of English at the University of Wisconsin Center—Waukesha County. She is the author of *The Decline of the Goddess: Women, Nature, and Culture in Thomas Hardy's Fiction*.

JOHN WATSON lectures and publishes in the fields of Victorian and New Zealand literature at the University of Otago. Dimedin, New Zealand. From time to time he indulges in amateur dramatics.

In the Bosom of the Family:
The Wet-Nurse, The Railroad,
and *Dombey and Son*

Laura C. Berry

Wanting to appear capricious, one could hardly do better than to suggest a necessary relationship between the wet-nurse and the railroad laborer in the mid-nineteenth century. Of course, Dickens made this connection first, in *Dombey and Son*, but there the necessary relation between the rails and the nursing mother is defined, in the Toodle union, as marriage. Suppose you wanted to insist on such a relationship outside the boundaries of the novel. There is, first of all, John Francis's 1851 *History of the English Railway, Its Social Relations and Revelations*. Francis views the railway worker as instigator of an especially poisonous social epidemic, fatal to family life. The worker is a literal and figurative appetite out of control:

> . . . impetuous, impulsive, and brute-like; regarded as the pariahs of private life, herding together like beasts of the field, owning no moral law and feeling no social tie, [the railroad labourer] increased with an increased demand, and from thousands grew to hundreds of thousands . . . There were many women, but few wives; loathsome forms of disease were universal.
> . . . The waste of power which their daily labour necessitated, was supplied by an absorption of stimulant and nourishment perfectly astounding. Bread, beef, bacon, and beer, were the staple of their food . . . They devoured as earnestly as they worked . . If they caught a fever, they died; if they took an infectious complaint, they wandered in the open air, spreading the disease wherever they went . . . Their presence spread like a pestilence . . .   (Francis 67).

Situate this portrait alongside medical man C. H. F. Routh's *Infant Feeding and Its Influence on Life*, in which a poor woman, it is said, may be unable to properly nourish her upper-class charge because of "hyperoemia or plethora":

1

This is a variety [of lactation problem] which I have chiefly observed among *hired wet nurses* selected from among the poorer classes, and admitted into wealthier families. It is a peculiarity that many of our London poor, indeed of domestic servants generally, that when obliged to support themselves, or put upon board-wages, they live as it were upon the smallest quantity of food possible; but when feeding at the expense of a master or mistress, the amount they devour often surpasses all moderate imagination. They, in fact, gormandize. If . . . a wet-nurse is given all she asks for, she will be found to eat quite as much as any two men with large appetites; and as a result she becomes gross, turgid, often covered with blotches or pimples, and generally too plethoric to fulfill the duties of her position   (Routh, *Infant* 56).[1]

Both the railroad laborer and the wet-nurse are classed among the vexing social problems of contemporary life. Laboring men and servant women alike are dangerously hungry, eating their betters out of house and home. Their overeating signals either a dangerous accumulation of power, or a seriously harmful enervation—either one of which might make them unfit for duty, even render them dangerous. Gender plays a role in these fears, too, in that it is uncontrolled ("brute-like") power that threatens anyone who falls in the rail man's way, while an unacceptable passivity is dramatized in the "turgid" and "plethoric" wet-nurse.

The wet-nurse and the railroad laborer are in these passages enrolled among the numbers of the devouring Victorian poor, where they no doubt join countless others. But these two figures are particular in that they foreground not just class, but fluidity within the body politic as a social issue. The trouble with the wet-nurse is the circulation of her internal fluids as they flow into the body of her wealthier charge, flowing always with the threat of contamination. And the trouble with the railroad laborer is that he represents the socially levelling tendencies of the expanding railway system, and is himself pictured in John Francis's *History* as a roving, primitive brute. Each portrayal is tensely poised over a fissure both necessary and dangerous. It is critically necessary that there be milk for an ailing child; the alternative, artificial feeding, represents a grave risk for the infant. And the increased traffic in goods and in people that the railroad makes possible is certainly desirable, even necessary from a certain economic vista, but the necessity brings with it an uncomfortable social proximity. In the railroad, the bourgeois passenger comes into tangible contact with the machine, not to mention an all-too casual contact with third and fourth class passengers. And in hiring the wet-nurse, the employer must take up a daily association with, even turn his child over to, a poor servant who may not be reassuringly relegated to the scullery or the outdoors.

The association of gender and class that is achieved in linking the railroad worker and the wet-nurse may ease anxieties of increased social mobility in the period of railway expansion. In *Dombey and Son*, Dickens, conjoining two of the more troubling modes through which the classes intermix, employs one of them—the wet-nurse—to occlude the problems of the other—the rails. Working-class contamination may be imaginatively transformed, tolerated—finally, even championed—under the class-effacing sign of feminine "influence."

This movement in *Dombey*, from contamination to influence, is a sophisticated and literary version of a medical debate. Even as Dickens was serializing *Dombey*, and for some years afterward, the medical journals engaged in vigorous argument over breast-feeding practices and, even more specifically, the wet-nurse's body fluids. In their interchange doctors fluctuate between rejecting and sentimentalizing the poor, always fallen, wet-nurse. The wet-nursing debates appear to focus on the woman's body, but the ultimate object, we shall see, is one rooted in class concerns.

The wet-nursing debate was carried on during the 1850s, primarily in a dispute between William Acton and C. H. F. Routh.[2] The debate turns on the question of whether the wet-nurse is a victim of the upper classes, being "eaten" by those with money, literally milked for her vital fluids, as Acton would have it; or whether, alternately, this corrupt servant is feeding grossly off the riches of her betters, her immoral behavior crudely turned into the basis of an undeserved financial gain. In the discourse of the medical texts, although not in *Dombey*, the wet nurse is always understood to be the mother of an illegitimate child, a fallen woman. Her fallen nature is critical for both sides. Not all women who chose to offer their services as wet-nurses, of course, were necessarily the mothers of bastards, but both Acton and Routh locate the stain of illegitimacy at the center of their arguments. Should society, they ask, extend "an avenue back to the world from which they are cast out to those who have fallen[,] through the very functions by which that fault has originated;" that is, should "organized means . . . be used to employ women of this class as wet-nurses"?[3] Routh's response is swift and unequivocal: "I believe these benevolent intentions, if fully carried out, would be attended with some of the worst consequences that could be conceived, both socially and morally" (Routh, "Selection" 580). He offers an organized, if not always medically defensible, set of reasons. First, fallen women are by definition corrupt. "I know from experience," Routh says, "that where you have to do with a woman of bad character (particularly if she has been confirmed in her vicious habits—if she be a harlot in taste and habit), do what you will, you cannot obtain from her reliable information . . . " (Routh, *Infant* 119).

Secondly, there is a concern that her own child will suffer. Often it is made to seem as if that child's death is not only certain but willful. "*We are, perhaps, encouraging murder, at least authorizing the death of the nurse's child*" (Routh, *Infant* 112). And, third, wet-nursing is said to encourage vice and promote a course of sin: "If fallen women are preferred to married . . . if we pass over their fault lightly . . . we are favoring the passions of the frail sisterhood . . . (Routh, *Infant* 111).

Routh's wet-nurse is duplicitous and dangerous, and the reader is forced to consider the inevitable fact that she must maintain such intimate contact with the household. Routh hints, if only by insisting so vigorously upon the opposite view, that a wife's mind might be poisoned, even her chastity assailed:

> As to the effect upon a mistress of a household in a country where the purity of our wives is unimpeachable, and their virtue proverbial, the tendency to corruption by conversation with such women is fortunately very rare, and I believe that it seldom, if ever, occurs. To dwell on this point is therefore unnecessary. Still all will admit that too frequent association and companionship of the better classes, even with virtuous domestic servants, is nearly always prejudicial.   (Routh, *Infant* 110).

And we are not allowed to forget the lure that the fallen woman must present even to the most faithful husband. "She is generally attractive. Her attractions have been her snare; and the vanity which has caused her to fall once, and the difficulty of curbing strong passions once roused, make her an easier prey" (Routh, *Infant* 110). The more comfortable, and therefore dominant, danger is that the wet-nurse will encourage other servants in a life of rewarding vice, for it is

> chiefly among the women servants in an establishment . . . that the danger is greatest . . . "What a difference in wages! what superior food is given her! She rides in the carriage as a lady visitor. She is more considered than any other servant in the establishment. What prevents my doing likewise?"
>   (Routh, *Infant* 110–11).

Everyone in a household, it is very clear, stands to be corrupted.

But no one is more at risk than the infant, most threatened because he receives such unmediated and intimate contact. If the wet-nurse's speech might destroy her mistress or her fellow servants, if her body might lead to her master's destruction, it is her most interior self, the fluids of her body, that threaten to contaminate her infant charge. The risk is not just to health, but to the moral fiber of the child, for "if a nurse of confirmed vicious and passionate habits suckles a child, that child is in danger of having its own morality tainted likewise (Routh, "Selection" 580). The contagion of the wet nurse is longlasting—lifelong, in fact: "[O]nce the morbid cell has been developed, it will impart its nature to surrounding parts, and poison the whole blood . . . it is possible to sow a seed in the infant which shall contaminate the life of the man, taint his whole constitution, and influence his psychical power" (Routh, "Selection" 581).

Routh's aim is to encourage a woman to nurse her own child or, if that is not possible, methods of artificial feeding must be employed. To this end, Routh eventually invented and patented the "Mamma" bottle, one of the first reasonably safe infant feeding bottles. The servant's bodily fluids should be avoided not only because they are filthy, but because to use them would be to relieve a mother of her duty to nurse her child. Routh's polemic distinguishes between classes of women, and insists that the working-class woman be left to her servant status, and the middle-class family made to fulfill its own domestic duties. Prominent in Routh's discussion is the troubling status of the wet-nurse in the household. Like the governess, she cannot be secured above or below stairs. But unlike the governess, whose wages signify servant status, but whose education provides her with an ambiguating superiority, the wet-nurse is unambiguously lower-class. It is the resulting potential for contagion that most troubles Routh.[4]

There is, however, a significant minority view promulgated simultaneously by William Acton, in which Routh's easy rejection is powerfully countered. Acton establishes a new liberal position that depends upon writing a discourse of reform, and an almost Benthamite argument for greater "use" of the poor. But first, Acton assaults the tenuous nature of Routh's medical assertions, in pointing out that:

> a cry was attempted to be got about the influence of *immoral* milk. I thought this had been forever silenced by the many recorded instances of children having been reared on asses' milk, without manifesting any of the stubbornness of their foster mothers   (Acton, "Child-Murder" 184).

Acton thus presents himself as the modern and medically advanced voice, claiming both reason and science as his supports. But perhaps his most modern role comes in his quick adoption of social reform as a goal. Taking precisely the position opposite to that of Routh, Acton views the working-class woman with a sentimental fondness. She is, in his vocabulary, "falling" and not "fallen." To employ her as wet nurse is first of all to help her, he claims. Acton constructs a tale as novelistic as it is medical:

> Remember, it is not street-walkers nor professional prostitutes we are speaking of. We are speaking of the young house-maid or pretty parlour-maid in the same street in which the sickly lady has given birth to a sickly child, to whom healthy milk is life, and anything else death. With shame and horror the girl bears a child to the butler, or the policeman, or her master's son. Of course she is discharged; of course her seducer is somewhere else; of course, when her savings are spent, she will have to take, with shame and loathing, to a life of prostitution. Now, she is healthy and strong, and there is a little life six doors off, crying out for what she can give, and wasting away for want of it, and in the nursing of that baby is a chance, humanly speaking, of her salvation from

the pit of harlotry   (Acton, "Unmarried" 175).

Acton embraces the proximity of the working class; the fallen woman is a victim, in spirit "our poor erring sister (183)." She is the house-maid, just a few doors away from the needy family who should be eager to take her in. Proximity is no longer a horror; on the contrary, it conveniently makes the working-class girl's services more readily accessible. This woman is invested with a certain psychology ("shame and loathing"). Acton invites readers to join him in a paternal benevolence, and constructs those readers as middle-class professional men with a social conscience.

But these must be men, also, with a sense of business efficiency—with an understanding of the exigencies of supply and demand. The language of the market soon merges with Acton's vocabulary of reform:

> No accoucheur in extensive practice can shut his eyes to the demand for wet-nurses. He has to meet that requirement every day; and I ask him . . . if he has ever been able to supply it from the ranks of married women?
> There is the demand, already largely supplied by the very class that most wants help. We only ask that the supply be enlarged and regulated.
> (Acton, "Unmarried" 175).

To reform the servant woman is to identify with, and indeed to depend upon, the marketing of the fluids of her body. Acton thus merges the portrayal of the sentimentalized female body with a representation of the enlargement and regulation of the market. To put it another way, the commodification of the servant-class woman's milk is effectively masked by the sentimental psychologizing of her plight, at the same time that it is made available in the market-place.

This interchange between social conscience and the market makes it as necessary for Acton that the wet-nurse be a *fallen* woman as it is for Routh. Acton relies upon associating the social reform of the fallen with the demands of the market. This leads the doctor to a curious reversal in which he must, and actually does, recreate purity in the defiled body of the fallen woman, and simultaneously represent moral corruption in the "conjugal solicitude" that is sanctioned in marriage. Acton elevates his "honest" fallen wet-nurse over the married one, for "[a] married woman who voluntarily

> leaves her own child for money may not be much better than the girl accidentally seduced, who nurses another's child for bread . . . It is not wise to be too acute in your inquiries about the husband, and the nature of the conjugal solicitude that keeps him eternally lounging about your area steps, or lounging in the back kitchen . . . You certainly know the best of the married wet-nurse, who hawks about her breast of milk . . . but you know little else
> (Acton, "Unmarried" 175).

That is, the married vendor of milk seeks profit, and for that reason may be reviled. Meanwhile, the hawking of milk among the lower classes can be tolerated so long as it is associated with the rhetoric of reform.

Acton reserves for himself the powerful voice of the "liberal father," the moderate paternal figure that we will encounter formidably in Dickens. The sentimentalizing of the fallen wet-nurse serves just as firmly to discursively separate classes as does Routh's anxious fears of contamination. Two rhetorical modes—Acton's reformist stance and Routh's rejection—contend in the medical journals. While these models may superficially oppose one another, ultimately they are eminently compatible. On its own, Routh's rhetorical extremity is self-betraying, often medically illogical, even in 1859. The reader is unlikely to see himself as the husband tempted by a dirty servant girl's meager charms, and his wife is not likely to imagine herself in tender companionship with her child's nurse. Routh's text merely sets up an absolute boundary; it imagines an extreme—a syphilitic drunken nurse destroying a household; a weak family that cannot control its impulses or its servants—that is hardly cautionary. If anything, Routh is reassuring, in that he offers a narrative tale from which the bourgeois reader may easily distance himself.

And Routh's discourse has a special function in relation to Acton's more "balanced" or "liberal" view: it reinforces Acton's position as socially responsive. Acton's liberal stance, bolstered by the hysteria of extremism, becomes the reasonable and moderate voice. It can invite the danger to approach, and assure us that proximity is harmless, negated by the reformative generosity of the liberal father as it is mirrored in ourselves. This gesture of inclusion works, of course, to distinguish and exclude, as such paternal gestures almost always do. Routh and Acton busily feed on the "wet-nursing dilemma," debating the perils and profits of social fluidity. Meanwhile, the debate as a whole reinscribes the social differences between classes, and reinforces the necessity of avoiding the need to rely on the fallen woman. This is the implicit lesson in the second chapter heading of *Dombey and Son*, "In which Timely Provision is made for an Emergency that will sometimes arise in the best-regulated Families." While dire need will make itself felt, the best defense is an ordered family. More pertinently, to imagine and maintain class distinctions is crucial. If Acton represents an eruption of the liberal father's voice in medicine, it must be said that the novel adopts this voice first and most forcefully. Not only in Dickens, but perhaps in Dickens especially, a grand space is created for a simultaneous reform and use of the family, for a complex, and literary, formulation of class and gender issues.

Dickens reverses the portrait of the hungry poor; indeed, the novel pictures them as edible, literally food for the rich. The railroad laborer and the nursing mother are viewed as solidly useful members of society, joined together in a marriage not only happy, but extraordinarily fruitful; the Toodle brood, in its numbers and outrageous vigor, contrasts sharply with Mr. Dombey's meager reproductive output. Dickens reads the railway worker not only as socially palatable, but as—well, edible. *Dombey and Son*'s Toodle family tempts with its

> plump rosy-cheeked wholesome apple-faced young woman, with an infant in her arms; a younger woman not so plump, but apple-faced also, who led a plump and apple-faced child in each hand; another plump and also apple-faced boy who walked by himself; and finally, a plump and apple-faced man, who carried in his arms another plump and apple-faced boy, whom he stood down on the floor and admonished, in a husky whisper, to 'kitch hold of his brother Johnny.'   (63–4).

Indeed, Miss Tox parades the family before Mr. Dombey as if they are candidates for his table; and it almost makes one hungry just to hear of them. Disease is out of the question entirely: as Miss Tox tells us of the Toodle's home, "the cleanest place my dear! You might eat your dinner off the floor" (64). Mr. Toodle is no home-wrecker; in fact he is a solid, if simple-minded, bulwark of the family. Far from spreading pestilence, the railway laborer and his kin exude the kind of health only possible in Victorian novels among those whose morals are as clean as their kitchen floors. The emphasis, in *Dombey*, on the wet-nurse and the railroad, puts a unique spin on a much-debated Victorian worry: who is being fed, and who is being eaten alive?

Circulation, across class lines as well as within social categories, structures the world of this novel, first of all in a universal insistence that social circulation is unavoidable. When Sir Barnet Skettles urges Florence, "My dear Miss Dombey, are you sure you can remember no one whom your good Papa . . . might wish you to know?" (418), he is expressing a fact of the novel no less true for its baleful consequences or cliched tiredness: people must mingle. London society demands fluidity, both in the social and in the business worlds. Sir Barnet Skettles, in his call to mingle, comically underscores the urge to circulate. Edith Dombey introduces the importance of coupling in its more realistic, and most malevolent, manifestation. On the prowl for a suitable mate for her daughter, Mrs. Skewton has brought her "to a great many places. To Harrogate [sic] and Scarborough, and into Devonshire. We have been visiting, and resting here and there" (362). Edith's refusal to put herself into active circulation does not stop her being "hawked and vended here and there" (473) on the marriage market. Mr. Dombey, pacing on the railway platform as he awaits the train upon which he will try to escape his unpleasant memories and (above all) his daughter, demonstrates how, in modern life, there is no escape from what he sees as the "vulgar herd" (351). However eagerly they might try, characters in this novel discover that it is impossible to go it alone.

Further, lest we imagine that the potential dangers of social circulation might be avoided by seeking refuge in a purely financial, and therefore less complicated, exchange of currency, the novel insists that the financial cannot function without the social. That is, Mr. Dombey's perfect economic plan is profitless in the face of his sterile home life, where he is unable to produce an heir. His best efforts gain him only little Paul, a son too sick to inherit, and too "old-fashioned" to care about the proper distribution of property. And there is Florence: "merely a piece of base coin that couldn't be invested—a bad Boy—nothing more" (51). Meanwhile, the abundant fantasies of social mobility that issue from Sol Gills's shop, and the social transgressions of which Captain Cuttle is so blithely capable, cannot pump up an obviously hopeless economy within this otherwise thriving family: "competition, competition—new invention, new invention—alteration, alteration—the world's gone past me," Sol says, and then astutely identifies his problem as lacking a proper inheritance to offer his very proper heir, Walter. These opposing worlds—one financially solvent but morally bankrupt and without heir, the other boasting the model youth, but economically moribund and outside the capitalist loop—of course must merge, and in doing so at the novel's end enact one of its chief messages: be morally scrupulous (defined in part as playing the good family man), but at the same time be absolutely certain your business is ship-shape.[5]

The isolation for which these characters yearn is made a virtual impossibility, reiterated when Mrs. Chick clucks of Mr. Dombey, "It's no use remaining shut up in his own rooms. Business won't come to him. No. He must go to it" (930–31). The need to traffic in goods, of course, is most aptly proven in the Firm itself, which hinges upon continual circulation in that the business of import and export is responsible for circulating goods all over the world. And of course, Mrs. Skewton's circulation of her daughter's body qualifies as a necessary economic move, as much as it is a socially strategic one.

Having established the critical impossibility of avoiding either social or economic circulation, the novel goes about demonstrating that such contact always carries with it the threat of danger, particularly the possibility of infection. Almost any traffic between people is a scary thing, liable to result in a violent collision or supreme personal discomfort. Physical contact can be disconcerting, as when Mr. Chick gives "Mr. Dombey his hand, as if he feared it might electrify him," and Mr. Dombey takes it "as if it were a fish, or seaweed, or some such clammy substance . . . " (110). These fears are not confined to interactions across class lines, and often hint at contagion or infectious contact. "There may be such contagion in me; I don't know," Carker the Junior says (248), fearful of infecting Walter Gay. When Edith imagines that her mother bears infectious malice toward Florence, and Mrs. Skewton shrieks, " . . . am I to be told . . . that there is corruption and contagion in me, and that I am not fit company for a girl" (514), Edith anticipates

her own anxious avoidance of Florence's touch. This avoidance is manifest
later, when Edith, in flight, "crawl[s] by[Florence] like some lower animal"
(754). That physical proximity might prove infectious, or at any rate abhorrent, is implied in Harriet Carker's "recoiling" from Alice Marwood: "Remove your hand! . . . Go away! Your touch is dreadful to me!" (848). The
most objectionable, and therefore memorable, scene of dangerous contact
occurs in Florence's abduction by "Good Mrs. Brown." The episode enacts
the fears of working-class contamination Mr. Dombey had concerning Polly's
nearness to little Paul, which had led him to believe that "a great temptation
was being placed in this woman's way. Her infant was a boy too. Now, would
it be possible for her to change them? (71)."[6] It is not Paul, however, who is
altered or contaminated by contact with the poor. Mrs. Brown, releasing
Florence after her ordeal, "conducted her changed and ragged little friend
through a labyrinth of narrow streets and lanes and alleys" (131). Florence
emerges from this maze of slums the perfect picture of a street urchin. Florence odyssey takes her across class lines, but whether or not there is a mingling between classes, the idea of contagion permeates the novel's notion of
physical contact.

And physical proximity is all too likely to spell trouble. Bunsby, failing to
take careful note of Captain Cuttle's warnings, is ensnared in Mrs. MacStinger's matrimonial net. It is in part Edith's nearness to Carker, his tracking of
her—"not a footprint did she mark [upon her "dangerous way"], but he set
his own there, straight" (736)—that ensures her fall. Mr. Dombey's stiff
reserve might reflect an anxiety about getting too near. Mr. Toots comically
reverses that stance; his passive aggressive behavior toward Florence brings
him into a constant contact with her that only pries them farther apart. Susan
Nipper—and perhaps this is what makes her the perfect foil for Toots—
charges forth with enviable strength of purpose. But her assertive conviction
leads to violent and inevitable eruptions, typified in her "struggles with
boys . . . [F]or, between that grade of human kind and herself, there was some
natural animosity that invariably broke out, whenever they came together"
(401).

Things break out when people come together, yet in *Dombey* isolation, no
matter how often attempted, it is just as often interrupted or radically impedes
progress.[7] Having created this drama of necessary-but-dangerous circulation,
the novel takes matters further, and enters into a specifically class-oriented
arena, when it imagines the rich as painfully dependent upon the poor. For
all his riches and power, Mr.Dombey's finances are never the thing that can
rescue him in his need. While the novel defines personal and professional
relationships of all kinds as crucially necessary, by far the most dangerous
and most necessary forms of circulation in the novel are those which take
place between the classes, particularly between the Dombey and the Toodle

families. It is no shock to learn that the working class is utterly dependent upon the upper class; we readily accept this familiar condition. But, surprisingly in this novel, the wealthy are powerless in the face of a soiling, humiliating need to seek out the assistance of the poorer classes, either in ways that are demeaning (such as augmenting a child's nutrition with hired milk), or in places that degrade (as in Good Mrs. Brown's den). Mr. Dombey reels with disgust in discovering that his hopes "should be endangered . . . by so mean a want; that Dombey and Son should be tottering for a nurse, was a sore humiliation." He views with "bitterness the thought of being dependent . . . on a hired serving-woman . . . " (67). Polly and her family, of course, have much less complicated feelings about the financial interactions here; dependency, or at lease economic exchange, and the lofty behavior of the better-off, is old news.

An even more horrible (and filthy) reliance on the poor comes much later in the novel when Mr. Dombey must descend into the slums to receive "secret intelligence." Good Mrs. Brown relates Dombey's initial abhorrence, followed by eagerness: "T'other day when I touched his coat in the street, he looked round as if I was a toad. But Lord, to see him when I said their names, and asked him if he'd like to find out where they was!"(817–18). Once again Dombey is humiliated to find that all his power has failed him, and it is the poor and dirty alone who can help him:

> "Woman! I believe that I am weak and forgetful of my station in coming here . . .
> how does it happen that I can find voluntary intelligence in a hovel like this,
> 'with a disdainful glance about him,' when I have exerted my power and means
> to obtain it in vain?"   (818–19)

The traffic between the Toodle and the Dombey family, as I have already suggested, is also significant, and more troubling, in that Polly and her husband exemplify unmediated encounters between classes. In the employment of each, consumption and production are unavoidably simultaneous. The importance of "simultaneity of production" derives from Marx's discussion of spatial relations and capitalism: "This locational movement—the bringing of the product of the market, which is a necessary condition of its circulation, except when the point of production is itself a market—could be more precisely regarded as the transformation of the product *into a commodity*."[8] Spatial movement, Marx claims, creates in part the strictly economic value a product has at market.

There is no factory or slum separating social groups in *Dombey*'s representation of the Toodle family. Because in the wet-nurse and the train the "point of production" *does* happen to be the "market" itself, contact is nearer, and more painful. When Mr. Dombey makes use of Polly's services, he must have *Polly* as well, since her body is the factory from which her tangible self cannot easily be separated. The prospect of sending Paul out to nurse, to the slum itself—the Continental solution, and one which may account for the greater endurance of wet-nursing there, as opposed to England—is more abhorrent because it raises even scarier prospects of social proximity.[9] The best Mr. Dombey can do is to re-name Polly "Richards," remove her from her working-class surroundings, and redefine the maternal role as "a question of wages altogether." Needless to say, Mr. Dombey would prefer that the relationship between Polly and her charge be contained as merely financial, and thus he tries to enforce Polly's breast milk as a commodity in spite of her presence in the house. Of course, Mr. Dombey's insistence on the language of the market, and his attempt thereby to impose control on the nursing relationship can only convince the reader of the impossibility of his project. It has the effect of reinforcing the intimacy of the very connection Mr. Dombey hopes to deny.

The rails, like Polly, are a particularly threatening site for inter-class relations. Even as the railroad was a place where the gap between the bourgeois subject and the machine were narrowed, the railroad even more controversially limited the distance between the middle-class passenger and the working class as a social group.[10] Most obviously, the railroad tangibly represents the demise of the aristocratic coach, and the rise of more egalitarian transport. To mediate this misfortune, first- and second-class coaches were made to seem as rich as possible, and unlike the American railroad cars, the English compartments were modeled on coaches rather than canal boats. But however elaborate the furnishings, the truth of the matter was only reinforced by the lavish appointments: third- and fourth-class passengers were simply in the next car, or down the line. As Constantin Pecquer rather gleefully pointed out, "It is the *same convoy,* the *same power* that carries the great and the small, the rich and the poor; thus the railroads most generally provide a continuous lesson in equality and fraternity."[11]

The more vigorously Mr. Dombey tries to separate himself, the more proximity arises as an issue. The more firmly he works to insist upon a financial basis for relations between classes, the more that financial relation is denied. While Dombey tries hard to reduce matters to economic exchange, the poor keep insisting on an intimacy that transgresses purely financial limits. "Do you know of nothing more powerful than money?" Alice Marwood asks Dombey (819) and then makes sure he knows that anger and revenge—not his monetary reward—are her motivation in giving him her "secret intelligence." Mr. Toodle denies the strictly financial basis of his relationship to the family when he meets Mr. Dombey at the train station. Dombey is enraged to note that "this presumptuous raker among coals and ashes" wears mourning crape to memorialize the death of little Paul Dombey (353). And at the close of the novel Polly arrives to nurse the father, as she had done the child, and this time offers her services, if not her body, without any pecuniary consideration:

> In the dusk of the evening Mr. Toodle . . . arrives with Polly and a box, and leaves them, with a sounding kiss, in the hall of the empty house. . . . 'I tell you what, Polly, me dear,' says Mr. Toodle, 'being now an ingine-driver, and well to do in the world, I shouldn't allow of your coming here . . . if it warn't for favours past . . . To them which is in adversity, besides, your face is a cord 'l'
>   (932).

In the novel's treatment of class relations there is always the troubling fact of social proximity. But more, the rich are made to seem humiliatingly in need of the poor, who refuse to allow that dependency to be reduced to a strictly financial arrangement.

Dombey and Son sets up, deliberately, a troubling account of class relations: people and things must circulate, but the more they do the greater the risk undertaken. Proximity most troubles, as in the scenes we have just examined, when circulation requires that there be extended personal intercourse between classes. And yet Dickens goes out of his way to render Mr. Dombey indebted to the poorer classes, and in continual intercourse with them. Thus, *Dombey and Son* would seem to make matters impossibly complicated in constructing socio-economic circulation as absolutely necessary—and deeply degrading for the well-to-do. The novel insists on asking a provocative question, and that is, how to maintain profitable circulation while avoiding personal pollution—a question familiarly central to Victorian socio-economic debate. Dickens insists on the question by persisting in representing the rich as needing the poor. The novel restages the problem, virtually obsesses on it, in fact, in order to suggest a powerful answer, one found in embryo in the medical rhetoric of Acton that we have already examined.

The novel focuses on and returns repeatedly to the Toodle family as the center of circulation problems; like the railroad itself, the Toodles turn up everywhere. In Dombey's first need, to ensure Paul's survival, it is Polly and her family who arrive to fill the gap. It is Polly for whom Paul asks as he nears death, and for whom the mad search about London for Staggs's Gardens proceeds. At the train station, it is Mr. Toodle who intrudes on Mr. Dombey's grief. And in Mr. Dombey's dismal hours of repentance, it is Polly who comes to nurse him. And finally, Rob the Grinder's peripatetic and almost sinister presence, showing up, through his own blundering or by someone else's design, at most of the central encounters in the text, is a hyper-realized circulatory body. He is the working-class auditor to events in the novel great and small.

If the Toodle family seems too freely to circulate toward the Dombey family, they also seem a bit too dramatically to represent circulation problems between classes.[12] Literally marrying the railroad laborer and the wet-nurse, two figures (as we have seen in Francis and Routh) viewed with some suspicion by Victorians, allows Dickens to structure his portrayal of the working-class family, and from thence his portrait of inter-class conflict, along the lines of circulation. The novel stages the dilemma of proximity by way of a working-class family that emblematizes, not to say overdetermines, anxieties about Victorian social fluidity. The railroad and the wet-nurse, as Dickens styles them, but also as they are represented in cultural discourse outside the novel, are signally about the circulation of necessary commodities.

The railroad, represented in *Dombey* both in the locomotive itself and in Mr. Toodle, emphasizes the increased circulation of commodities and bodies at mid-century; very likely it was the most visible and powerful sign for the increase in traffic between people and in goods. The "impact of this railway development is beyond dispute," says one historian, for "[t]he railway accomplished a transportation revolution by reducing transportation costs and by broadening local markets. Even as it produced these economic changes, the railway stimulated social change, resulting in the interpenetration of town and country, and the blurring of social distinctions" (Lubenow 109). But we need go no farther than *Dombey* itself to perceive the railroad as evidence of a new, mobile society:

> To and from the heart of this great change, all day and night, throbbing currents rushed and returned incessantly like its life's blood. Crowds of people and mountains of goods, departing and arriving scores upon scores of times in every four-and-twenty hours, produced a fermentation in the place that was always in action. The very houses seemed disposed to pack up and take trips.   (290)

Yet, the railroad is seen as too-great a social leveller. The perceived social threat is exemplified in the fact that the traditional bastions of upscale England worked to (literally) distance themselves from the new technology. Eton, for example, along with Oxford, obtained special clauses in the railway acts establishing their lines which forbade a station within three miles of their property, and required the railroad company to provide a police patrol to safeguard the boys (Jackson 503). Some of the landed saw the new lines as symbols of the vulgar, and feared that "bad elements" would pass through or too near their estates. In an 1825 letter to the *Leeds Intelligencer* one landowner complained:

> On the very line of this railway, I have built a comfortable house; it enjoys a pleasing view of the country. Now judge, my friend, of my mortification, whilst I am sitting comfortably at breakfast with my family, enjoying the purity of the summer air, in a moment my dwelling, once consecrated to peace and retirement, is filled with dense smoke or foetid gas; my homely, though cleanly, table covered with dirt; and the features of my wife and family almost obscured

by a polluted atmosphere. Nothing is heard but the clanking iron, the blasphe-
mous song, or the appalling curses of the directors of these infernal machines
(Jackman 148).

Both the working-class woman who nurses her upper-class charge, and the
railroad laborer who serves as emblem for the newly established railroad,
represent the circulation of necessary commodities, and the threat that that
greater circulation implicitly holds. However, if I began by saying that the
railroad and wet-nurse both signal social fluidity, it must also be acknowledged that, no matter how closely they might be linked in Dickens' text, the
discourses surrounding the two of them have, if not different meaning, then
rather different cultural weight. For the railroad and the railroad laborer were
likely to have been far more focal in the average Victorian mind than the
largely medical debate over the wet-nurse. As interesting, as ideologically
useful, as is the wet-nursing debate, as important as the debate was in medical
circles, it could not hold the kind of regular fascination, nor could it be so
much a part of daily experience in England, and particularly London, as
the railroad.

In addition to the constant Parliamentary debate authorizing new rail lines,
the economic fervor and anxiety over "railway mania," and the relatively
rapid change in temporal and spatial relationships within England, the railroad
represented a fundamental and *visible* change in the Victorian landscape—literally so, in the massive street clearances of London. In *Curiosities of London
Life* (1853), Charles Mowbray Smith speaks of " . . . the deep gorge of a
railway cutting, which has ploughed its way right through the centre of the
market-gardens, and burrowing beneath the carriage-road, and knocking a
thousand houses out of its path, pursues its circuitous course to the city (Dyos
12). These street clearances connected the railroad with the opening of a
social wound, for they revealed to the middle-class eye the centuries-old slums
that had been obscured in small alleyways and tiny streets.[13] The "pestilential
alleys" were described by social reformers as "ill-ventilated culs de sac and
dens of wretchedness in the vicinity of Shoe Lane and Saffron Hill—the
nurseries of vice, the nuclei of filth and disease" (Dyos 13). The clearances
were a horrifying spectacle to better-off Londoners. They contributed to a
notion of the railroad as, if not the agent, then at least the revealer, of filth
and poverty. The railroad was thus imagined, and to a certain extent held
responsible for, bringing lower classes closer, insofar as they presented the
filth and dirt into open view. For "much of the rest of the century, the opinion
persisted that morality was intimately connected with the free circulation of
air and exposure to 'public gaze' " (Jones 180). Meanwhile, of course, this
sense of the railway as ruthlessly anatomizing social ills was in competition
with the economic gains it also made real, and also made visible.

The visibility of the railroad, and its importance during the period in which *Dombey* was being serialized, raises a question about its relationship to the wet-nursing debate. The two social issues are linked in an emphasis on circulation, in their tendency toward social levelling, but they had entirely different effects on the lives of Londoners. Why, then, does Dickens bind them so securely, indeed formally, in *Dombey and Son?* One answer may be precisely *because* the railroad is the greater, or at least more palpable, social force. In linking the rails to Polly, Dickens can emphasize the contaminating potential of one (female) Toodle, and diminish the presence of the other (male) one. Equating the circulation troubles imaged in the wet-nurse and the railroad laborer may be strategic in obscuring the power of the rails.

Dombey and Son does not ignore the levelling aspect of the train, or completely avoid the subject of street clearance. But in Staggs's Gardens, the social anatomizing is not handled by being made the subject of a renewing reform, a strategy frequently in use outside the novel. Instead, the novel rather weirdly offers only two possibilities. There is, on the one hand, a dirty and distressing slum, the only alternative to which is an antiseptic terrain rewritten by the railroad. All sense of community—except the thematic unity suggested in calling every business the "Railway" something-or-other—is thoroughly erased. The first effect of what is described as the "earthquake" of railway intervention is a domestic chaos that competes with the industrial: "... frowzy fields, and cow-houses, and dunghills, and dustheaps, and ditches" sit at the "very door of the Railway" (121).

Dickens views the railway's "mighty course of civilization and improvement" with suspicion and remarks that "[n]othing was the better for it, or thought of being so" (122). Dickens artfully ignores, in Staggs's Gardens, the fact of the many who would have been made homeless by this construction, and gives us a slum transmuted into a characterless appendage of industrialism. "Where the old rotten summer-houses once had stood, palaces now reared their heads, and granite columns of gigantic girth opened a vista to the railway world beyond" (289):

> The miserable waste ground, where the refuse-matter had been heaped of yore, was swallowed up and gone; and in its frowsy stead were tiers of warehouses, crammed with rich goods and costly merchandise. The old by-streets now swarmed with passengers and vehicles of every kind: the new streets that had stopped disheartened in the mud and waggon-ruts, formed towns within themselves, originating wholesome comforts and conveniences belonging to themselves . . .   (289)

The neighborhood is now clean, and it quite firmly supports an increase in circulation. But the cost of massive renewal is in its absolute loss of "individual" character. In place of the slums and filth that had been its meager identity before, Staggs's Gardens no longer has a name, no longer properly exists. Instead it is a series of "railway hotels, office-houses, lodging-houses, boarding-houses; railway plans, maps, views, wrappers, bottles, sandwich-boxes, and time-tables; railway hackney-coach and cab-stands . . . " There is even "railway time observed in clocks . . . " (290).

The loss of identity the rails produce in Dickens makes sense if we consider the effect of the train on the middle-class passenger, for he, too, suffers a disorienting dislocation of self at the hands of the train. Mr. Dombey's famous train ride is the signal for a potentially fatal equalizing and loss of self. The equalizing properties of the train are associated with death and monotony, which are to some extent identified with one another. The train is pictured as socially levelling, "dragging living creatures of all classes, ages, and degrees behind it" (354). It equalizes the landscape itself, for "onward and onward ever: glimpses of cottage-homes, of houses, mansions, rich estates, of husbandry and handicraft, of people, of old roads and paths that look deserted . . . " (354). And as it rushes onward, fearless and invincible, it brings Mr. Dombey to a monotonizing sameness that is associated with death.[14]

The train anatomizes the slums, and Mr. Dombey holds it responsible, for "as Mr. Dombey looks out of his carriage window, it is never in his thoughts that the monster who has brought him there has let the light of day in on these things: not made or caused them" (355). The progress of the train, of industrialism, is a force that cannot be controlled, which "rolls and roars, fierce and rapid, smooth and certain;" (354) it is "resistless to the goal" (355). The train becomes inextricably confused with the equalizing force going on everywhere around it and in it. The train station is the territory of the vulgar herd, the place where, encountering Mr. Toodle, Mr. Dombey is horrified at the suggestion of any sympathy between himself and this raker among coals: "To think that this lost child [little Paul] . . . should have let in such a herd to insult him with their knowledge of his defeated hopes, and their boasts of claiming community of feeling with himself, so far removed: if not of having crept into the place wherein he would have lorded it, alone!" (353)

In the face of the train's equalizing force there is nothing but "monotony" (354). The locomotive travels "not through a rich and varied country, but a wilderness of blighted plans and gnawing jealousies" (354). Mr. Dombey's internal state is pathetically reflected in a landscape that greets him from the window. He is "pursuing the one course of thought" and finds "a likeness to his misfortune everywhere" (355). In the train, as it is represented in *Dombey*, dislocation and loss of self are the inevitable result of a levelling circulation.

Similar anxieties are reflected in Carker's mad fugitive ride. Although he is propelled by coach, he is pursued in his thoughts, more urgently pushed forward, by the train, for even as he rushes away there is "[s]ome visionary terror, unintelligible and inexplicable, associated with a trembling of the ground,—a rush and a sweep of something through the air, like Death upon the wing" (863). The railroad is the avenging agent that avenges without passion, and ends Carker's life. If Mr. Dombey's thought is reduced to one thought, a thought that pursues him as insistently as the railroad pursues Carker, then Carker is reduced to being unable to think at all. He is "tormented with thinking to no purpose," troubled by the "monotonous ringing of the bells and tramping of the horses; the monotony of his anxiety . . . the monotonous wheel of fear, regret, and passion . . . " (867). A waiter, when Carker does at last arrive at the railway, mistakes him for a railway traveler, and he does not correct him, presumably to maintain his anonymity. [B]ut the waiter is right: he has as good as been traveling by rail. "Very confusing, Sir," the waiter says. "Not much in the habit of travelling by rail myself, Sir, but gentlemen frequently say so" (871). The train represents the most frightening, and least resolved, threat of the text—that one's self will be lost entirely in the disorienting, equalizing, monotonizing world of public travel.

Dombey and Son radically obscures this unresolved threat in representing the railroad in Mr. Toodle, and linking him to Polly. And the text doubly seeks to ensure against the troubling, terrifying properties of the train by emphasizing that it is Mr. Toodle, and not Mr. Dombey, who becomes so closely identified with the machine that he loses himself. We see him "in the bosom of his family," "shovelling in his bread and butter with a clasp knife, as if he were stoking himself . . . " (619). His speech is given over entirely to the locomotive: "If you find yourselves in cuttings or in tunnels, don't you play no secret games. Keep your whistles going, and let's know where you are" (619). His thoughts, as Mr Dombey's threatened to do, are governed by the movement of the train: "I comes to a branch; I takes on what I finds there; and a whole train of ideas get coupled on to him, afore I knows where I am, or where they comes from. What a Junction a man's thoughts is,' said Mr. Toodle, 'to-be-sure!'" Mr. Toodle becomes the train, just as his son, Rob the Grinder, is named after it ("The Steamingine was a'most as good as a godfather to him, and so we called him Biler, don't you see!" (70)).

The novel's first step toward assuaging the anxieties imaged in the train is carefully to position Mr. Toodle in the shadow of Polly. The brutish appetite of John Francis's *History*, with which we began, is antithetical to the almost charmingly benign Toodle.[15] Mr. Toodle is weak, "with an air of perfect confidence in his better half" (69), ceding all intelligence to his wife. No male threat is possible: Mr.Toodle turns all eyes in the direction of Polly's capable self.[16] In *Dombey*, male aggression is the special province of the younger Carker. Whatever social threat the male laborer in the period of Chartism might have been said to hold is obscured in an obsession with his destructive tendencies. Carker's scheming is no less vile for its almost total inexplicability, and it overpowers concern for any other male in the novel. "Carker the Manager" can be managed, it turns out, perhaps because he is an understandable evil, and therefore a more tolerable enemy by far than a pestilential menace roving the countryside.

Male contagion, or working-class appetite, is transformed into Carker's negative "influence," and defines Carker's power in the novel. That power extends to everyone, but works with special energy upon Dombey. Carker influences Mr. Dombey to do his will, and of course he attempts to manipulate Edith, in order to advance his own complicated plot. His influence extends even to Florence, for he "had assumed a confidence between himself and her . . . a kind of mildly restrained power and authority over her—that made her wonder and caused her great uneasiness" (476–77). Wherever Carker goes, he demonstrates a masterful control over others. And in his deployment of Rob the Grinder, Carker achieves an almost supernatural power over the working class male just coming of age:

> . . . Rob had no more doubt that Mr. Carker read his secret thoughts . . . than he had that Mr. Carker saw him when he looked at him. The ascendancy was so complete, and held him in such enthralment, that, hardly daring to think at all, but with his mind filled with a constantly dilating impression of his patron's irresistible command over him . . . he would stand watching his pleasure . . .
> (676–77)

Thus aggression, displaced onto a bourgeois character, is translated into a matter of influence. Carker's power lies on his ability to cunningly manipulate others, not in his physical force.

Carker also becomes the repository for the appetitive picture of the poor that operates outside the novel; it is Carker who devours all in a powerful oral aggression that rivals any hunger of the working class. He is an influential appetite out of control—or, rather, in too much control. It is Carker, and not Toodle, who is seen as the underling who wants to "gormandize," to take (to eat) everything his master has put away. Those prominent teeth signal his voracious desires, as he "approaches Edith, more as if he meant to bite her, than to taste the sweets that linger on her lips" (525). He is ever displaying his " . . . two unbroken rows of glistening teeth, whose regularity and whiteness were quite distressing. It was impossible to escape the observation of them, for he showed them whenever he spoke; and bore so wide a smile upon his countenance . . . that there was something in it like the snarl of a cat . . . " (239).

Carker's unprovoked and excessive cruelty (particularly his treatment of Alice Marwood) is only matched in its intensity by Florence's unprovoked and excessive beneficence. In the domestic realm, contagion becomes influence, and the "bad" circulation of the railroad is at last eased by a "good" circulation of milk. The most successful way by far that *Dombey and Son* "manages" class, and the one to which we shall now turn, is in re-imagining a (working-class) threat of contagion, transforming that threat in the novel in embracing a positive (female/middle-class) value of "influence." Put another way, the veiled threat of the Toodles is filtered through Polly's body. Polly translates working-class danger into working-class service, and in turn, the (maternal) services Polly provides become the basis of Florence's encompassing—not to say smothering—sympathy. Florence takes over as the novel's most important governing force. If the masculine dangers Mr. Toodle might pose are grafted on to Carker, the feminine values Polly embodies are gradually incorporated into the representation of Florence.

In their first meeting Polly and Florence establish a correspondence:

> In the simple passage that had taken place between herself and the motherless little girl, her own motherly heart had been touched no less than the child's; and she felt, as the child did, that there was something of confidence and interest between them from that moment (81).

And, indeed, there is, for the best of Polly is soon passed on to Florence. Florence replaces Polly as Paul's surrogate mother: "We'll go home together, and I'll nurse you, love" (267), Florence tells Paul. She becomes his world and all after Polly's dismissal, and repeatedly in the scenes between the siblings, Florence appears more mother than sister. She is seen, in fact, at least by Mr. Dombey, as the new wet-nurse, and one who has overstepped her limits: "Florence would remain at the Castle, that she might receive her brother there, on Saturdays. This would wean him by degrees, Mr. Dombey said; possibly with a recollection of his not having been weaned by degrees on a former occasion" (205).[17]

It is Florence, with her limitless good will and gentle charity, who gradually becomes the governing influence of the novel. "Influence" was, of course, a loaded word in this period, central to the separation of spheres. A woman's "influence," carefully used within her domestic circle, was said to be as important as any governmental controls. Sarah Stickney Ellis voiced the most popular version of this idea, arguing that wives have the power to curb men's minds in a noble direction:

> The first thing to be done in the attainment of this high object is to use what influence you have so as not to lower or degrade the habitual train of your husband's thoughts; and the next is, to watch every eligible opportunity, and to use every suitable means, of leading him to view his favourite subjects in their broadest and most expansive light (Ellis 101–02)[18]

Florence becomes just such an influential trainer of the thoughts of others, conversant as she is in the authoritative arts of the nurturer. Walter "preserve[s] her image in his mind," and it "restrain[s] him like an angel's hand from anything unworthy" (288). Florence maintains a special influence over Paul, as Carker does over Rob the Grinder; only she, with a mother's skills, can truly reassure him. And she is the only one who touches Edith's heart. Everywhere we look in the novel, particularly as Florence grows older, testimony to her selfless devotion is brought to the fore—so much so that nothing less is asked of the reader than that he, too, must cling like Diogenes in helpless canine devotion:

> Di, the rough and gruff . . . his dog's heart melted . . . put his nose up to her face, and swore fidelity. . . . When he had eaten and drunk his fill, he went to the window where Florence was sitting . . . rose up on his hind legs . . . licked her face and hands, nestled his great head against her heart, and wagged his tail till he was tired.   (324)

So we, too, come to worship at Florence's feet.[19]

Florence becomes her brother Paul's nurse, and by the end of the novel she has also become her father's.[20] It is Florence who officiates alone at Mr. Dombey's moment of redemption, and she holds him as a mother comforts her child:

> Upon the breast that he had bruised, against the heart that he had almost broken, she laid his face, now covered with his hands, and said, sobbing: "Papa, love, I am a mother."   (939–40)

The important transformation by this point (and even in this passage), is not the emotional reconstruction of Mr. Dombey, the narrowing of his pride, but rather the gradual but sure canonization of Florence as the nursing mother. The more thoroughly her "influence" governs events, the more possible it is for any threat from elsewhere to be reduced. The emphasis in the novel has shifted from the work place (where economic and social disputes ignite), to the family (where the milk of human kindness drowns all fires before they can explode).

The possibility of a beneficent domestic sympathy that can overcome all with its love is first suggested in the representation of Polly Toodle. As the novel progresses, that positive influence becomes the defining property of Florence Dombey. The focus shifts radically from the laborer and the incendiary possibilities of the work place. The important sphere of influence is not Mr. Dombey's office, but his home. The very idea of economic exchange is transformed: value will not refer to consumables and the price the market will bear. Rather, value refers to the interiority of the subject—to Florence's inner being.[21] The importance of redefining female worth in this way has, of course, been emphasized in the representation of Edith, whose "value" has been so carefully defined according to "false" values.

No longer merely a piece of useless coin, Florence's very presence is remunerative: the Skettleses "would have valuable consideration, for their kindness, in the company of Florence" (398). Or, more pertinently, as Susan Nipper later says to Mr. Dombey:

> . . . there ain't no gentleman, no Sir, though as great and rich as all the greatest and richest of England put together, but might be proud of her and would and ought. If he knew her value right, he'd rather lose his greatness and fortune piece by piece and beg his way in rags from door to door . . . than bring the sorrow on her tender heart that I have seen it suffer in this house!   (704).

Florence is elevated from a useless currency that can never be invested, to embodying the true "value" of the novel.[22] That value is in part her soothing influence, and partly her reproductive function. Overtly, Florence's body becomes, as she produces a new little Paul, a factory for the future of business, a business now to be presided over by the enterprising Walter Gay. Florence's covert value lies in the power of her middle-class motherhood to obscure social conflicts outside the family. Her domestic sphere becomes a locus for power, by novel's end it has become the center stage for novelistic struggles, while the slums, the poor, and the work place are kept at a distance. Into Florence's ready lap the moral center of the novel has arrived; thus we come to value her sphere of influence above all else, to rest our trust in the bosom of the family.

In *Dombey and Son*, the narrative voice of the liberal father guides us across the mine field of social relations, across class lines in order to obscure them at last in a reliance on Florence Dombey's motherhood. *Dombey* uses Polly Toodle just as Acton uses his pretty house maid who resides just down the street; each sentimentalizes the working wet-nurse as a rich and necessary subject for their separate narratives. And those narratives, in their turn, serve to stabilize a bourgeois identity. In enshrining the nursing mother by way of Polly Toodle, *Dombey and Son* reassures that the devouring working class can be devoured.

Notes

1. This is the third (American) edition of Routh's text. I have not located the first London edition of this text, but I believe that it was published, in substantially the same form as quoted here, in 1860. The book-length text is largely a compilation of articles Routh wrote for *The Lancet* and the *British Medical Journal* during

the late 1850s, and in many cases the text of *Infant Feeding* is a verbatim reprint of articles written in 1858 and 1859, some of which are examined in this essay.

2. Acton was a urologist who is best known for his interest in other medical issues, particularly for his 1857 *The Functions and Disorders of the Reproductive Organs*, and for his interest in questions of prostitution. Routh's involvement with the question of wet-nursing is more readily understandable. Routh authored a text specifically on nursing, *Infant Feeding and Its Influence on Life*.

3. *The Lancet* (1859) 1, p. 113, "Medical Annotations."

4. On the subject of the governess's "status incongruence," see M. Jeanne Peterson.

5. The merger at the close of the novel also underlines, as David Musselwhite hints, the essential sameness of the two worlds from the very start of the novel.

6. An astute reading of the fears of exchanging children associated with the working-class nurse is offered by Gerhard Joseph. Although his essay is more centrally concerned with the nature of change as Victorians saw it, he regards the entrance of the wet-nurse into the family as an event likely to awaken fears of contamination, and he points out that "the fear of the substituting powers of the nurse or governess is the 'realistic' upper- and middle-class version of the despised 'Irish,' lower-class superstition concerning the child stolen by fairies."

7. For a provocative account of the terrain I have just been covering—and one which heads in a different direction—see Jeff Nunokawa's reading of Dombey's, and the novel's, isolation as "an antagonism between the concept of ownership as exclusive access, and the workings of commodity exchange" (139). In other words, Nunokawa also interprets the circulatory failures of the novel as critical. He goes on to solve the problem as he poses it by introducing into the argument the instrumentality of the Oriental body.

8. As quoted, from Marx's *Grundrisse*, in Wolfgang Schivelbusch (46).

9. In France, during the nineteenth century, the practice of sending middle- and upper-class children out to nurse was thoroughly institutionalized. See George D. Sussman. On the history of wet-nursing and breast-feeding, see Valerie A. Fildes's excellent books.

10. Schivelbusch comments that typically the "nineteenth-century English bourgeoisie gains no authentic experience of the reality of the great industries of Manchester and Sheffield. It becomes aware of them only indirectly, by means of the displays of world exhibitions and humanitarian fiction. Yet the railroad, the industrial process in transportation, does become an actual industrial experience for the bourgeois, who sees and feels his own body being transformed into an object of production" (p. 123).

11. Quoted in Schivelbusch, p. 74–75. And Leonore Davidoff offers an anecdote of the 1830s concerning the "wife of a country gentleman [who] had her own coach put on the railway car as it was impossible for her to travel in a railroad carriage as she might find herself sitting opposite someone with whom she was not acquainted" (22).

12. The sense of the working class as contaminating is embodied largely in Mr. Dombey, and to that extent it is limited by the reader's conception of Mr. Dombey as a far from sympathetic figure. Yet Mr. Dombey represents a familiar mid-Victorian voice; indeed, he very closely resembles the voice of C. H. F. Routh.

It is one with which, I suggest, the reader is simultaneously invited to identify, and to reject—thus enacting the training in class relations that the novel presses. Mr. Dombey occupies a relatively extreme position, but one we may perhaps sympathize with, only to ultimately reject it in adopting the more complicated negotiation of class relations offered in the text's representation of gender. Thus the novel incorporates the same strategic action we examined in the rhetorical interplay between Acton and Routh.

13. See Gareth Stedman Jones on the street clearances (180). Dickens himself discusses railway construction in, among other places, "Railway Dreaming," *Household Words*, 10 May 1856; "An Unsettled Neighborhood," *Household Words*, 11 November 1854; "Rustic Townsmen," *Household Words* 19 (1859); and especially in "Attila in London," *All the Year Round*, 8 September 1866.

14. The remarkable passage in which Dickens describes Dombey's trip, and in fact the representation of the railroad in the entire novel, is extensively discussed by Murray Baumgarten. For Baumgarten, as for me, the railroad functions somewhat ambivalently, although ultimately the negative aspects of advancing technology are contained, in Baumgarten's view, since they appear in Dombey's "stunted imagination." Baumgarten argues that " . . . Dickens evokes not only the positive force of the railroad but the new possibilities provided by the expanding cities of Victorian England. His novels provide us with examples of the achievements of industry and commerce as well as the self-alienation of the underground man . . . " (84). Other important accounts of the railroad in *Dombey* include that of Harland Nelson, and of course Steven Marcus's originating argument in *From Pickwich to Dombey*.

    Jonathan Arac explores (as I do) the ambivalent representation of the railway, and he points out the need to diminish the potential dangers of Mr. Toodle (105–10).

15. Francis's concern, it should be pointed out, is specific to the navvy, a distinct and isolated role in Victorian economic terms, and in relation to Victorian life. Mr. Toodle is not, of course, a navvy. I would suggest that Francis's "brute" lurks, albeit at some distance, behind Mr. Toodle. The fears concerning the railroad represented in this essay—the social proximity enabled as well as emblematized by increased mobility, and contamination anxieties—are structurally similar to those of Francis, as portrayed in his *History*.

16. Of particular interest is Julian Moynahan's now classic discussion of the dichotomy between "firmness" and "wetness" in the novel.

17. Other critics have noted the smothering or near-malevolent nature of Florence's care. See, for example, Nina Auerbach (115). Using *Dombey and Son* to address issues of feminist theory and scholarship, Helene Moglen has pointed out how the "solution" Dickens engineers to the problem of separate spheres as the novel constructs it mirrors one strand of feminist criticism. Moglen would have us focus on the subversive elements in Charles Dickens' fiction—to take up Edith's melodramatic (and therefore, Moglen argues, subversive) performance, rather than Florence's sentimental one. In adapting *Dombey* to this use, Moglen acknowledges critics like Auerbach, Dianne Sadoff, and Louise Yelin, recognizing the ways in which these feminist readings of the family in Dickens enable later

discussion. My own interpretation is obviously critically influenced by these essays as well, particularly insofar as they insist, though in different ways, on the complex power relations of familial connections.

18. An important, and very useful, discussion of the early Victorian idea of influence, and of *Dombey and Son* (one which intersects at some points with my own), is that by Judith Newton; see especially pp. 127–34. Newton argues that the development of an ideal of female influence within a specialized domestic sphere took place in the 1830s and 1840s at least partly in response to economic stresses which exacerbated the evident distance between the classes. This, in turn, necessitated an ideological reformulation of middle-class identity. More particularly, the "ideology of woman's proper sphere . . . helped . . . on one level, to consolidate a larger class strategy, a strategy according to which class division, profit, and free enterprise were to be maintained while class conflict was softened by the creation of a more communal order" (128–29). She notes, significantly, that while the notion of a domestic sphere might assuage some concerns, it also produced a measure of sexual horror at the possibility of female power.

19. While Florence is aligned, as the nursing mother, with Polly Toodle, she is opposed to two other nursing mothers in the novel. Alice Marwood received no benefit from her mother's poisonous milk, for she was "born, among poverty and neglect, and nursed in it." Mrs. Skewton reminds Edith, just before dying, "For I nursed you"; but her body fluids, while they contain no tangible pollution, are implicitly as poisonous as that of her lower-class double.

Florence's ability to nurture and to nurse Paul is aligned with Polly and her world—that is, with the world of the good caretaking mother. She stands in opposition to Mrs. Pipchin who, compared to Polly Toodle, is a bitter apple, for "all her waters of gladness and milk of human kindness, had been pumped out dry . . ." (160). Like the mean Dickensian mother substitute who has preceded her in *Oliver Twist*, Mrs. Mann, and one who will come after her in *Great Expectations*, Mrs. Joe (note their masculine names), Mrs. Pipchin makes certain she gets fed, while the children may go hungry.

20. For a subtle rendering of the threats that Florence's position as daughter (mother, lover) pose, here and throughout the novel, see Lynda Zwinger.

21. Judith Newton argues that *Dombey* actually derides the idea of female influence in its depiction of Florence, whose feminine sympathy and influence she sees as "entirely self-referential . . . unheroic, enclosed and threatening . . ." (132). Newton reads the novel as substituting benign male capitalists (Captain Cuttle and Sol Gills) for women caretakers. She feels that Dombey's submission to Florence is no solution in the novel; rather, it merely gains him access to a fairytale, autumnal existence (133). Further, referring to the positive conclusion to Cuttle's and Gills's travails, Newton says that "[i]n a world where male capitalists cook, weep, sympathize, and form families together, womanly influence and womanly skills have little place" (134). This reading tends to diminish, I think, Florence's instrumentality in the happy outcomes of the book.

22. See Jonathan Loesberg, who explores the economic implications of Dickens' construction of Florence's "value" as everything but economic. His focus, however, in reading *Dombey*, is necessarily directed toward the marriage of Edith and Dombey.

WORKS CITED

Acton, William. "Child-Murder and Wet-Nursing." *British Medical Journal* 16 February 1861:183–84.

Acton, William. "Unmarried Wet-nurses." *The Lancet* Vol. 1, 1859:175–76.

Anonymous. "Medical Annotations: Wet-nurses from the Fallen." *The Lancet* Vol. 1, 1859:113–14.

Arac, Jonathan. *Commissioned Spirits: The Shaping of Social Motion in Dickens, Carlyle, Melville and Hawthorne.* New Brunswick, NJ: Rutgers UP, 1979.

Auerbach, Nina. *Romantic Imprisonment.* New York: Columbia UP, 1986.

Baumgarten, Murray. "Railway/Reading/Time: *Dombey and Son* and the Industrial World." *Dickens Studies Annual* 19 (1990): 65–89.

Clark, Robert. "Riddling the Family Firm: The Sexual Economy in *Dombey and Son.*" *ELH* 51:1 (1984): 69–84.

Davidoff, Leonore. *The Best Circles: Society, Etiquette and the Season.* London: Croom Helm, 1973.

Dickens, Charles. *Dombey and Son.* 1846–48. New York: Penguin, 1988.

Dyos, H. J. "Railways and Housing in Victorian London." *Journal of Transport History* 2.1 (1955): 11–21.

Ellis, Sarah Stickney. *The Wives of England.* London: Fisher, Son, & Co., 1843.

Fildes, Valerie A. *Breasts, Bottles and Babies: A History of Infant Feeding.* Edinburgh: Edinburgh UP, 1986.

Fildes, Valerie A. *Wet Nursing: A History from Antiquity to the Present.* New York: Blackwell, 1988.

Francis, John. *A History of the English Railway, Its Social Relations and Revelations 1820-1845.* Vol. 2. London: Longman, Brown, Green & Longmans, 1851.

Jackman, William T. *The Development of Transportation in Modern England.* Cambridge: Cambridge UP, 1917.

Jones, Gareth Stedman. *Outcast London: A Study in the Relationship Between Classes in Victorian Society.* New York: Pantheon, 1984.

Joseph, Gerhard. "*Dombey*, Change and the Changeling." *Dickens Studies Annual* 18 (1989): 179–96.

Loesberg, Jonathan. "Deconstruction, Historicism and Overdetermination: Dislocations of the Marriage Plot in *Robert Elsmere* and *Dombey and Son*." *Victorian Studies* 33:3 (1990): 441–64.

Lubenow, William C. *The Politics of Government Growth: Early Victorian Attitudes Toward State Intervention, 1833–1848*. Hamden, CT: Archon Books, 1971.

Marcus, Steven. *Dickens: From Pickwick to Dombey*. New York: Basic Books, 1965.

Moglen, Helene. "Theorizing Fiction/Fictionalizing Theory: The Case of *Dombey and Son*." *Victorian Studies* 35.2 (1992): 159–84.

Moynahan, Julian. "Dealings with the Firm of *Dombey and Son*: Firmness versus Wetness." *Dickens and the Twentieth Century*. Eds. John Gross and G. Pearson. Toronto, University of Toronto Press, 1962:121–32.

Musselwhite, David. "The Novel as Narcotic." *1848: The Sociology of Literature*. Eds. Francis Barker, et. al. Colchester, England: University of Essex, 1978:207–24.

Nelson, Harland S. "Staggs's Gardens: The Railway Through Dickens' World." *Dickens Studies Annual* 3 (1974): 41–53.

Newton, Judith Lowder. "Making—and Remaking—History: Another Look at 'Patriarchy'." *Feminist Issues in Literary Scholarship*. Ed. Shari Benstock. Bloomington: Indiana UP, 1987.

Nunokawa, Jeff. "For Your Eyes Only: Private Property and the Oriental Body in *Dombey and Son*." *Macropolitics of Nineteenth Century Literature: Nationalism, Exoticism, Imperialism*. Eds. Jonathan Arac and Harriet Ritvo. Philadelphia: U of Pennsylvania P, 1991.

Peterson, M. Jeanne. "The Victorian Governess: Status Incongruence in Family and Society." *Suffer and Be Still: Women in the Victorian Age*. Ed. Martha Vicinus. Bloomington: Indiana UP, 1972:3–19.

Routh, C.H.F. *Infant Feeding and Its Influence on Life*. Third Edition. New York: William Wood and Co., 1879.

Routh, C.H.F. "On the Selection of Wet Nurses from Among Fallen Women." *The Lancet*. Vol. 1, 1859:580–82.

Sadoff, Diane F. *Monsters of Affection: Dickens, Eliot and Bronte on Fatherhood*. Baltimore: Johns Hopkins UP, 1982.

Schivelbusch, Wolfgang. *The Railway Journey: Trains and Travel in the Nineteenth Century*. Trans. Anselm Hollo. New York: Urizen, 1979.

Sussman, George D. *Selling Mother's Milk: The Wet-Nursing Business in France 1715–1914* Urbana: U of Illinois P, 1982.

Watt, Ian. "Oral Dickens." *Dickens Studies Annual* 3 (1974): 165–81.

Yelin, Louise. "Strategies for Survival: Florence and Edith in *Dombey and Son*." *Victorian Studies* 22.3 (1979): 297–320.

Zwinger, Lynda. *Daughters, Fathers and the Novel: The Sentimental Romance of Heterosexuality*. Madison: U of Wisconsin P, 1991.

Mystification and the Mystery of Origins in *Bleak House*

Brian Cheadle

An unnamed, dark surgeon is mysteriously encountered at Nemo's deathbed in *Bleak House*, silently attendant when a quite different member of the profession pronounces Nemo's death (11.190).[1] The incident has two features which are typical of the mysteries in Dickens' later work. First, it seems clumsily gratuitous, like the never-solved murder of George Radfoot or the mechanism of Boffin's descent into miserhood in *Our Mutual Friend*. Secondly, it is part of a seemingly endless imbrication of further mysteries: What *were* the circumstances of Nemo's death? Who is this nameless Nemo the law writer? Is he linked to Lady Dedlock, as Tulkinghorn seems to suspect? Then too, is the dark surgeon, on his part, linked to Esther, for at the very end of the number in which Nemo's death occurs (13.233) she all too casually admits, in a telling collusion of phrasing between the two narratives, to having met a surgeon of dark complexion at a dinner party? And so on.

Because such mysteries are gratuitously proliferating the temptation is to write them off as mystification—creaking enigmas within what Roland Barthes calls the hermeneutic code, tedious features which finally tell only of the needs of serialization and keeping up sales. But even though, as Barthes suggests, *all* narrative exploits enigmas, and serial narratives by a popular author even more so, and even though there is not really anything intrinsically mysterious about Alan Woodcourt, the nagging question remains, "why was the *aura* of mystery so extraordinarily pronounced in Dickens' later fiction?"

A favored answer is that Dickens' preoccupation with mystery was his response to the new and threatening quality of large cities and the institutions they bred. In at least three crucial respects the mid-nineteenth-century experience of city life involved an encounter with mysterious *secrets* which opened the way to narrative exploitation. First there was the secret life of the slums; then there was the secret life of city institutions which became bureaucratic

29

enclaves of expertise and intricate documentation, closely guarding privilege with obfuscation. Finally there was the secret life of scandalous transgressions, fostered by the Victorian emphasis on maintaining a respectable front, by the separation of the public and private self which city experience encouraged, by the urban economy of reserving one's emotional capital, and by the fluid relationships of city life in which one frequently has to do with strangers. All these features of the metropolis encouraged the likelihood of hypocrisy, deceit and guilty secrets—secrets which those addicted to the will to power were eager to exploit.

At the same time, these secret aspects of city life provided narrative opportunities which were capitalized on by generic innovations. The new turns of narrative such as the extension of Gothic motifs to the urban milieu, the development of the novel of urban mysteries, and the emergence of the detective novel have had much recent and valuable attention; and *Bleak House* has been taken as a key example of all of them.[2] Indeed all of them can be seen as impinging on the nodal moment of Nemo's death: in an exotically Gothic touch, famine is imagined staring through the shutters of Nemo's room like "the Banshee of the man upon the bed" (10.188); Nemo himself has played his part in proliferating institutional mysteries by operating as a law writer, and his death will be formally processed through what the uncomprehending Jo calls an "Inkwhich" (16.276); Tulkinghorn invades the room of death in search of documented secrets, and this initiates a long series of amateurish probings into Nemo's antecedents which will finally be crowned by the detective professionalism of Inspector Bucket.

What is most striking, however, is the fact that these new generic possibilities exhaust themselves in *Bleak House*, certainly in so far as they belong to the project of *clarification* of which realism itself is so important a part. Consider, for example, the detective element. It soon becomes clear that the whole web of mystification in the novel converges on Esther and the facts of her origins; but the characters such as Tulkinghorn and Guppy who approach her secret aggressively as a means to social empowerment end up confounded. Moreover, the secret of her origins is very soon revealed (and even sooner guessed by any astute reader), and the mere revelation settles nothing—except perhaps for Tulkinghorn's hash, for he might seem, initially, to have been murdered for trying to exploit the secret. The question of who killed Tulkinghorn looms menacingly and by a sort of inner logic the need to read the signs correctly gives a new status to Bucket who emerges as a figure like the novelist himself, one whose Asmodean surveillance seems specially empowered to clear up mystery. But Bucket's unmasking of the murderess turns out to be oddly incidental to the subsequent action. With the flight of Lady Dedlock, pursued by "her enemy" Tulkinghorn even in death (55.815), the sense of guilt is intensified, not dispelled, mystification centering afresh on the question of where she is to be found; and Bucket is finally unable to prevent her death—though he does suppress public scandal so effectively that the supposedly "omniscient" narrator knows only that her death "is all mystery" (66.928). Even the seemingly climactic discovery of her body turns out to be strangely inconclusive and bereft of clarificatory release, for Esther's narrative is oddly reticent about analyzing or even commenting on the significance of the moment when she is reunited with her origins.[3]

Nor does a consideration of new urban conditions and new novelistic forms throw light on the scene of Nemo's deathbed, for the origins of Nemo's particular state of anomie and estrangement do not lie in the circumstances of urban life. His name reminds us that his fall had quite different origins in thwarted love: Nemo or "Nobody," in a traditional pairing, stands opposed to the influential "Somebody," figured in this instance by Sir Leicester who could offer status and wealth to a young wife whom it was whispered "had not even family" (2.57).[4] It is thus necessary to leave behind mystification gratifyingly clarified, as a reflex of urban circumstances, and to focus on the novel's concern with the more fundamental mystery of origins.

The quest for origins can be related generically to the romance quest for a mysteriously misplaced redemptive principle—a Holy Grail, a faultless love, "home," or some other transcendental signified. There is a strong residual pressure of this romance plot in *Bleak House*. Within this schema, the process of reuniting Esther with her origins is one of restoring her to health: when she discovers her mother finally reunited with her father at the gates of death the broken family is symbolically re-established. The discovery is a testimony that Esther was conceived in a lasting love, as is the fact that Lady Dedlock, in her two visits to the grave of her lover, wears the garb of passion (Hortense's clothes) and of maternity (Jenny's clothes). The death of what Esther takes at first to be "the mother of the dead child" (59.868) amid images of melting snow and ice signals release for the "child." It is thus fitting that the dark surgeon whom Esther is freed to marry should prove his rightness of heart by ministering solicitously to her father before his death, and to the desolate Esther herself when she finds her lost mother. Jarndyce underlines the special prerogative that goes with these circumstances, saying, in bestowing the new Bleak House upon Esther, "My dearest, Allan Woodcourt stood beside your father when he was dead—stood beside your mother" (64:914).

If the romance plot had this unqualified form it would be neatly consistent with the fact that Dickens' aesthetic retained to the end the belief in moral sentiment, the conviction that the only solution to all social ills was for each individual to rediscover the inner wellspring of a caring love and sympathy. But the simple romance plot is strangely obfuscated. Indeed it would seem that at the deep imaginative level at which plot is defined Dickens had come to doubt the principle of any such wellspring, for the novel is built upon the central structural irony that Esther comes "home" to be reunited with her lost parents only at the iron gates of death in the depths of the defiled city, the point of origin of the deadly contagion which spreads throughout this society.

Roland Barthes has observed that western thinking requires an urban space to have a center, a site of truth where value is condensed (be it in the form of churches, offices, banks, department stores, or cafés), "a complete site to dream of and in relation to which . . . to invent oneself" (Barthes 1982, 30). If *Bleak House* begins by moving inwards towards the Court of Chancery at "the very heart of the fog" (1.50), it soon discards this emptied center, replacing it with the polluted graveyard in which Nemo is buried, a center which spatialises the idea of origins by giving it all the ironic potency of a dead, and a deadly, end. In consequence, the main enigma of the novel is the problem of how Esther, after finding her parents, will "invent" herself—the question to which we will finally return.

Dickens' sense of the contingency of urban and social "pollution" intensified in his work from *Bleak House* onwards. Mrs Oliphant, reviewing *David Copperfield* in *Blackwood's* in 1855 wrote, "Into those dens of vice, and unknown mysteries, whither the lordly Pelham may penetrate without harm, and which Messrs Pendennis and Warrington frequent, that they may see 'life,' David Copperfield could not enter without pollution" (quoted Collins 327). The comment makes one aware of the extent to which Bulwer Lytton and Thackeray, by contrast with Dickens, were *secure* in their sense of social apartness from the low-life "mysteries of London," mysteries which they contained within the comfortable conventions of the urban picturesque; but the reminder that David Copperfield experiences the city with the intensity of inner contamination suggests that for Dickens too, the threat of pollution went deeper than concern for the condition of cities. In *Oliver Twist* Dickens had worked blithely enough within the notion that Oliver's restoration to the lost origin of the bourgeois bosom was a happy enough ending of his exposure to the city's worst "dens of vice, and unknown mysteries," but by the time of *Bleak House* Dickens' vision had darkened: both Nemo and Lady Dedlock are deeply ambivalent figures in whom respectability and delinquency, decency and dereliction, are almost impossible to disentangle. This is obviously so with Nemo, more subtly true of Lady Dedlock. For all her avowal of motherly love, she abandons Esther after finding her, "murdering within her breast the only love and truth of which it is capable" (36.568); and for all her conviction that her prior responsibility is to preserve the good name of the husband she cannot love, her sense of physical guilt leads her to replicate her sister's hysterical attitude towards her sexual transgression. It is thus hardly surprising that the revelation of Esther's origins produces no miraculous release. At the origin there is, it would seem, not plenitude but continuing lack, and a pollution of the generative principle.

The mystery of what I am calling Esther's return to origins is thus no more than a means of engaging with a deeper problematic: it opens up a space for Dickens to interrogate his originary assumption of innate goodness and health, and to probe his growing uncertainty about the *source* of, and *remedies* for, the "evil" spreading "pollutingly" across classes, and making victims of the innocent. This condition is the mystery which the novel seeks to plumb, a mystery whose dimensions are not simply institutional and urban but ethical and ontological.[5]

The problem of origins can be conveniently explored under the aegis of Derrida's extended essay, "Plato's Pharmacy," which takes off from Plato's reflections in the final section of *Phaedrus* on the origin and value of writing. For Plato, the Good (figured as father, origin, speech, health) is the *hidden* "blinding source of *logos*;" but because the transcendental signified is hidden it provides no control, and any substitutive representation can be "falsified, adulterated, mendacious, deceptive, equivocal" (82). Derrida observes that often in myths of origins, in Egyptian, Babylonian, and Assyrian mythology no less than in Plato, what he calls the "filial inscription" (84) involves the coming into being of a seemingly unnecessary supplement to the original godhead, a supplement who is also a supplanter. This equivocal supplanter figures as the god of writing who substitutes "the breathless sign for the living voice" of the absent origin (92): not surprisingly, this god figures also as the god of death, but he features too as the god of medicine who dispenses the *pharmakon*, the drug which is both a remedy and a poison. Within what Derrida punningly calls "Plato's pharmacy," the *pharmakon* of writing is perforce as ambivalent as the remedial drug. What Derrida's argument pushes towards is the deconstructive claim that the filial inscription as a myth of origin produces an "internal structural necessity" (84) whereby all oppositions are maintained only in consequence of "the movement and the play that links them among themselves, reverses them, or makes one side cross over into the other" (127). The assumption of an absent origin thus initiates and problematizes a set of unstable binaries (such as *logos*/writing, father/son, life/death, inside/outside, remedy/poison) in terms of which moral value will perforce have to be negotiated.

Whether or not one accepts Derrida's claim for a deconstructive necessity, his essay highlights the dilemma of the Victorian writer struggling to come to terms with the disappearance of God.[6] In Plato's consideration of the status of writing it is, as Derrida reminds us, "truly *morality* that is at stake" (74); and for Dickens, though he did not share Plato's qualms about the moral value of imitations, morality is equally the central issue. What Dickens seeks in his work is essentially a moral remedy for, and within, a polluted time. His work is sited at the point of cultural transition from a debate conducted largely in the religious language of salvation to one preoccupied with health;

and if salvation looks ultimately to the other world, finding a remedy for what has become polluted and diseased entails an urgent application within this world. With the retreat of the origin, however, the search for remedy is bounded by a context of finitude and death, and the status of the searcher becomes as problematic as that of the proferred remedy.

If the solicitous Woodcourt is fittingly present at Nemo's deathbed, and if he is fittingly designated the "dark" surgeon, it is because he provided what Miss Flite calls the "poison" (14.251), the opium intended as remedial which was the instrument of Nemo's death. Thus it is that the central concerns of *Bleak House* can be most opportunely explored by focusing on the dark surgeon and on the way that his presentation highlights the intrinsicately knotted opposites of poison and remedy, within a context of repeated deaths.

At his first appearance the dark surgeon might truly seem to be a spectator ab extra, gratuitously inscribed into the reader's encounter with the death of the father; but if he is intelligently detached, with a properly "professional interest in death," he is also intimately involved, not merely because he provided the deadly drug but in that he shows a "not unfeeling" regard for Nemo, recognizing that he "must have been a good figure when a youth" (11.191). If the surgeon's detachment enables him to be a dispassionate witness, his benevolence leaves him with a frustrated sense of helplessness, and even of guilt. A similar ambivalence attaches to Dickens' treatment of the surgeon's antecedents. Mrs. Woodcourt's absurd boast that her son has mythical origins, an access to the source provided by the heroic line of Morgan ap-Kerrig (17.292), wins only embarrassment from her son and mockery from the author. Dickens, however, tries himself to invest Woodcourt with heroic properties by sending him outside the realm of pollution to do valorous deeds of mythical proportions when his ship founders in distant seas. His triumphant survival of his encounter with death at sea is presumably meant to be seen as a rite of passage from the standard social self with its unquestioning conformity; and henceforth Dickensian "heroes" will all have to endure a ritual separation from society by way of a sea voyage or near drowning (or by both), though this experience hardly leaves them more equipped than Odysseus or Hamlet to set to rights a time which is sadly "out of joint." The point to make though is that both in his stance towards the action and in his striving to provide remedy, the dark surgeon is an analogue of the caring and compassionate author. Certainly both are caught within the same predicament.If there is no access to an original life-giving source, to hold out a remedy is to labor under a sense of inadequate supplementarity. Then again, if there is no privileged outside position, it is hardly possible to avoid the sense of an encircling entrapment and even of obscure guilt, the sense that, as Auden would later put it, "The situation of our time / Surrounds us like a baffling crime" (86).

In his essay on the *pharmakon*, Derrida points out that in Plato's account of the Good, God's perfection has no allergies, and comparably health and virtue are always thought of as proceeding from within. The *pharmakon*, on the other hand, is a remedy administered from without, which is why it has no unequivocal virtue of its own, and why the possibility of death is inscribed within its structure. Dickens' work shows a comparable uncertainty as to whether health must be sought within, or remedy be provided from without.

Raymond Williams has argued that the essential "structure of feeling" in Dickens' work issues from the presence of "two incompatible ideological positions . . . first, that environment influences and in some sense determines character; second, that some virtues and vices are original and both triumph over and in some cases can change any environment" (169–70). In crass terms, the issue is whether we are socially conditioned or free and creative souls; whether in seeking health we must look for social reform or a change of hearts. The problem with Dickens is that the alternatives are not as clear cut as Raymond Williams supposes. Believing as Dickens did in goodness of heart and the efficacy of moral sentiment, nothing was more of an anathema to him than the Calvinist doctrine of depravity and original sin—epitomised in Miss Barbary's monstrous indication to Esther that she was not born like others simply "in common sinfulness and wrath" (3.65). Yet at the same time, and quite inconsistently with the idea of an innate moral sense, Dickens believed in evil as an absolute. On the other hand, much as Dickens was committed to the cause of social reform, he had by the time of writing *Bleak House* seemingly lost his belief in the social will—if the apocalyptic overtones of the book are anything to go by. Small wonder then that Williams finds the "structure of feeling" in Dickens' work generous and indignant, but anxious and divided.

A carefully sequenced repetition of four wasteful deaths—those of Nemo, Jo, Richard and Lady Dedlock, each of which is presided over by the dark surgeon, allows us to see Dickens grappling with the problems of health and remedy, the intensity of his involvement clear from the concentration of so much of the book's iconic and rhetorical energy in the depiction of these deaths.

The death of Nemo in vividly imagined conditions of poverty, filth, and neglect opens the central issues, for through it *both* the remedial option of social reform *and* that of a change of heart are called in question. Nemo's death amid the "bitter, vapid taste of opium" (10.188), "with no more track behind him . . . than a deserted infant" (11.196), shows that the abandoned individual may reach the point where social intervention can be at best no more than an opiate, or even destructive, if those to be helped are unwilling to be helped or bent on misusing any proferred remedy. The recalcitrant brickmakers mark the limits of social reform in the same way in a different context. For those, on the other hand, who would change hearts, it is clear that though Nemo has been kind to Jo, his condition is finally one of perverse self-abandonment, making him an example of the book's most troubling insight: the realization that oppression can be self-oppression. The fear that what lies within is not the authentic self but simply the exhaustible will pervades the novel, most apparent in such major instances as Esther's state of near paralysis in respect of her own desires and Lady Dedlock's blankness and despair. Nemo's death in abjection, however, goes even deeper in mirroring this, the deepest of all middle-class fears, for in a society where one's origins are not aristocratically guaranteed, the fall from grace is to be imagined as a total loss of status and selfhood—the condition Lady Dedlock commits herself to in finally seeking out Nemo's grave with nothing about her by which she could be recognized. The dark surgeon's laconic reminder, as he leaves the room in which Nemo is lying, that it "won't do" (11.194) to leave the cat with the body grotesquely underlines Nemo's degradation; and nothing conveys the appalling nature of his total loss of dignity more powerfully than the casual factualness of Jo's later comment, flaunting decorum in its slippage of pronouns: "They put him wery nigh the top. They was obliged to stamp upon it to git it in" (16.278). Such touches are terminal bad manners. They are also important reminders that the "movement and play" within Dickens' verbal crossing of oppositions verges, at its most intense moments, on an anarchic relish, as though only a wild and terrible humor could ultimately contain the worst of fears.

As though to stabilize fears about the heart's capacity to rise above its circumstances, Dickens couples Nemo's death with that of Jo, who asks to be buried alongside him. Dickens underlines the connection between the two deaths, saying of the dark surgeon, solicitous for Jo: "He softly seats himself upon the bedside with his face towards him—just as he sat in the law-writer's room" (4.703). Jo's death allows Dickens to speak with unequivocal compassion and indignation as a social reformer.

Announcing Jo's death the narrator's voice almost seamlessly annexes the voice of the surgeon, as though speaking out his anger in the most impassioned paragraph in the whole novel:

> Dead, your Majesty. Dead, my lords and gentlemen. Dead, Right Reverend and Wrong Reverends of every order. Dead, men and women, born with Heavenly compassion in your hearts. And dying thus around us every day.   (47.705)

Nothing is more shattering than the shift in pronoun from "your" to "us" which makes it clear that the object of the despairing contempt is not simply others, in their collective and unfeeling guilt, but ourselves. As Steven Marcus has said, we are forced to recognize that the homeless exist—"a nuisance, an eyesore, an offense, a bother, and an expense" but also "an inseparable part of us" (106), our responsibility, not just that of authorities beyond us. Jo is as he is not because the system made him but because our neglect has allowed the system to get away with it; and underlying Dickens' anger and indignation is the hope that if one could only change sufficient hearts by reopening them to the "Heavenly compassion" they were born with, the changed hearts would surely change the system.

But the death of Richard, also presided over by the dark surgeon, enforces the opposite judgment—that an efficacious change of heart is rarely achieved. The dark surgeon ultimately finds Richard abandoned in the court of Chancery in a state of collapse, his fierce outburst against the outcome of the case "stopped by his mouth being full of blood" (65.924). Jo too was finally run to ground in "a court without access" (46.687), and the deaths of the two orphans, Richard and Jo, are pointedly linked, not merely by such uncanny verbal echoes and by the presiding presence of the dark surgeon, but by a careful repetition of details: the surgeon buys "restorative medicines" (47.697) for Jo and at the death of Richard there are again "restoratives on the table" (65.924); both die with blood in their mouths (when Phil Squod takes away his hammer from Jo's bedside it has a speck of rust on it); both clutch hold of the surgeon's hand in their last moments; Richard's life is "worn away" (65.925) just as Jo's cart is "shaken all to pieces" (47.705).

The difference between these last two metaphors, however, should give one pause. Where the image of Jo's cart implicitly protests against the brutal infliction of rough use, the image of the dying Richard as depleted and "destitute of colour" though still surprisingly handsome, invokes the pathos of waste. And pathos is what Dickens does worst. Richard is of course in every respect intended to be seen as the obverse of Jo. Where Jo is unloved and perpetually "moved on," Richard is taken into a home full of affection and benevolence; where Jo is an unwitting spreader of pollution and has the only paternal solicitude he knows taken from him,[7] Richard perversely believes Jarndyce's paternal affection to be poisonous, and wilfully elects to "move on," poisoning in consequence, through his inner weakness and disordered will, even his relationship with Ada. Richard, in short, thoroughly earns his final state of exhausted abandon. John Ruskin took strongly against what he saw as the morbidity of *Bleak House*, deploring the novel's obsession with "the reaction of moral disease upon itself, and the conditions of languidly monstrous character developed in an atmosphere of low vitality" (268). Ruskin was horribly wrong about *Bleak House*, but he rightly defined the specter which most deeply troubled Dickens' imagination in the book, and his words provide the most pertinent epitaph on Richard, the boy who believed he could rely upon great expectations. Richard's heart is broken, significantly enough, not by remorse but by chagrin at the news that the whole estate, to which he and Ada are now the confirmed heirs, has "been absorbed in costs" (65.923).

Despite this touch of hard-eyed realism, the treatment of Richard's death is sentimental as Jo's is not. This is most apparent in the chapter heading under whose aegis the whole death is presented, "Beginning the world." The phrase points to the notion of a radical change of heart and a new start, but its effect is to highlight the limits of sentimental morality as an ultimate remedy: for Richard is allowed to "begin the world" only in "The world that sets this right" (65.927). The unspoken assessment that Richard is incapable of seriously changing reflects the ill-concealed irritation with fecklessness of an author whose own salvation had been very much a matter of taking responsibility for himself: perhaps Richard's heart was simply not worth saving. But the implicit admission that things will never be put to rights in this world is papered over in the gesture of sentimental piety. In the representation of Richard's death then, Dickens finally retreats from ideological contradiction into mystification, precisely in the sense used earlier of a device too readily prefiguring clarification and release.

Before considering the last of the deaths at which the surgeon presides, it is apposite to explore more fully the question of how far the book retreats from mystery into mystification, for mystification is sometimes taken to be dominant in the novel's final remedy for the ills of the time, the marriage of Esther and Woodcourt. In bringing together the surgeon who ministers to the poorest sections of the community and the angel of the hearth, Dickens is clearly attempting to invest active social intervention with benevolent (and almost religious) impulse. Woodcourt strives humanely to eschew the disciplining officiousness of the medical police; nevertheless, even he finds it difficult to overcome a repugnance to Jo which is only partly explained by the recognition that it was Jo who infected Esther. When trying to find somewhere for the sick boy to sleep he thinks to himself: "It surely is a strange fact . . . that in the heart of a civilized world this creature in human form should be more difficult to dispose of than an unowned dog." (47.691) The difficulty of the disposal is an indictment of a heartless society, but the language of disposal, and the sense of Jo as a "creature in human form," suggest that there are "strange" reservations in Woodcourt's heart regarding those who might seem to be beyond what Foucault called "normalization." In a famous impassioned passage later in the same chapter, making ironic play with the idea of Jo as a "home-grown" savage, Dickens' own indignation has to struggle towards purity by pillorying his sense of distaste and by deleting a phrase in which Jo, rather than the condition which produced him, comes very close to being categorized, at least by implication, as one of the "*evil* things at hand" (47.696)[8]—a phrase in which "at hand" is as revealing as "evil," catching up as it does an irritation at the insistent contingency of placeless deviants, offensive to the respectable.

But it would be wrong to stop with this kind of analysis.[9] Dickens did not hesitate to hold up Woodcourt's voluntarily entering the infected haunts as heroic, a commitment against which are to be measured Skimpole's reneging on his training as a doctor and Richard's half-hearted toying with the practice of medicine which he found to be "rather jog-trotty and humdrum" (17.283). The inquest categorizes Jo as a case of "terrible depravity" (11.200) and moves him out of sight as firmly as Bucket does, but this is *not* what Woodcourt and Esther do; and it is not what Dickens does. The attempt to enter imaginatively into the "degenerate" life of Jo is something new and painful in literature. Nietzsche, In *Human, All-Too-Human*, albeit in an uncharacteristic vein, resorted to precisely the image of the *pharmakon*, the remedy which infects, in positing the process of change to a higher culture as an "ennoblement through degeneration." In this Nietzschean view of progress it is "precisely in [the] sore and weakened place [that] the community is *inoculated* with something new," by "deviant natures," in such a way that the body, if it is strong enough, will be able "to absorb the infection of what is new and incorporate it to its advantage" (I.V.v.208–09). The process may justly be seen as analogous to Dickens' attempting to implant in the reader a creatively reactive imagining of Jo's "deviant nature."

It is also all too easy to find in Esther's busy Dame Durdening, keys clanking at her side, the book's prime example of disciplinary practices. David Miller more subtly presents Esther's endless modesty as operating in an ideologically "useful" way to inscribe the insecurity of the family subject as "indispensable to counter the instability of the family structure, of which it is an effect"(102). But comments of this kind fail to do justice to the *panic* which impels Esther; and this sort of clarificatory placing of Esther's efforts might seem truly definitive only if it were possible to imagine a system beyond all crossing oppositions or the inscriptions of power, a system in which unselfish care had no part to play. And such an end is as mythical as the notion of a pristine origin. Though Dickens' later novels are annealed by scepticism, he was not ultimately a sceptic; and for all that *Bleak House* is beset by the most sapping fears and littered with dead bodies (nine by Ruskin's count), there was nothing morbid about his vision. Dickens, on the contrary, strove to take his own cue from Esther's care and commitment, in part by making her a co-narrator. The critique of benevolence and false sentiment in *Bleak House* is merciless, but this did not stop Dickens from seeing that the caring heart is the only basis on which a concatenation of small resistances can be forged. Indeed his insistence on the need to hold to a center of values is at one with Habermas's central objection to what are often taken to be the deeply sceptical tendencies in Foucault and Derrida—an objection in which might almost seem to have Esther specifically in mind—that to put oneself beyond such values as "the imperatives of work and usefulness" is to "step outside the modern world," and to have no basis on which to resist or condemn (Habermas 9).

In worrying away at the need for remedy, in expanding the area of concern for others, and even in rubbing up against its own contradictions, *Bleak House*, can be seen as a site of resistance and change; and Dicken's recourses are not mystification.[10] The same claim could be made for the implications of the book's climactic moment, Esther's discovery of her dead mother, the last of the deaths to be considered at which the dark surgeon looks on.

This death is difficult to take hold of because it is attended by many kinds of silence. First among these are the gaps in the story of Lady Dedlock and Nemo, and here one might begin with the recognition that gaps are often a sign of ideological slippage. In many ways *Bleak House*, with its inward drive to the iron gates of death at the heart of the great city (not to mention its final attempt to achieve a purely domestic closure), is the most centripetal of all Dickens' novels. But the moment of its writing, with Dickens attending gloomily to a succession of wasteful deaths, was the moment in which the culture at large was celebrating the *expansive* excesses of a commercial and imperialist economy in the plenty of the Great Exhibition. The book certainly reflects this economy vividly enough, and also with considerable subtlety. Lady Dedlock's conspicuous expenditure is shown to be dictated by her tradesmen, "deferential people, in a dozen callings, whom my Lady Dedlock suspects of nothing but prostration before her, who can tell you how to manage her as if she were a baby" (2.59). Again, though sir Leicester has refused to have the Chesney Wold portrait of Lady Dedlock engraved (7.138), another likeness of her is open to mass consumption as part of the Galaxy Gallery of British Beauty, and as such it adorns Tony Jobling's mantlepiece (32.503). Moreover, she is driven to her death by thoughts of what the threatened commodification of her scandal in the mass media would do to Sir Leicester no less than by a sense of guilt. Her enslavement to the economies of fashion is implicitly judged by being set against Esther's husbandry of her own image and guardianship of the keys of the cupboard. But apart from this kind of prudent denigration of excess (and the broad brushes with which greed is depicted), the novel avoids examining the premises of the economic imperium: indeed it takes a "telescopic" glance towards the unspoken Other on whom the wealth of the center depends not in order to comment on the moral (or material) exploitation of the natives of Borrioboola-Gha but only to afford an uneasy laugh at Mrs. Jellyby's avoidance of guilty secrets closer to home—secrets brought to sharp focus in the presentation of Jo and of the many other figures in the novel, from Caddy's deaf baby to Phil Squod, whose lives have been stunted.

Arguably, however, the most stunted figure of all is the great lady who courts death in the meanest of clothes. If we question the early affair between Honoria and Hawdon it would seem that prior to a young girl's ambition and "insolent resolve" (2.57) to invest herself beyond her station, lay the fact of the soldier abruptly consigned (for nine months at the very least) on some distant imperial task. From what Trooper George says to Smallwood it seems possible that Hawdon, despite the engagement to which Tulkinghorn refers (40.629), sought out a posting abroad and fled from England to avoid his debts (21.355); but his care in getting George to deliver a letter to the still unmarried girl (63,907), and his subsequent nurturing of the letters he received from her, suggest a lover unable rather than unwilling to return. The untold story, stirring in the silence of the lovers' deathly reunion is seemingly one in which the future of England's sons and daughters is sacrificed to financial exigencies and to the military exigencies of maintaining a commercial Empire.

But that is a romantic way of focusing on the crucial silence in a story which amounts to a refusal of romance. Woodcourt is sent off to be shipwrecked, as though pure and effective actions were possible only at the romantic margin, well away from the polluted center (where his mother is blind to Esther's virtues and hopes that he will find a rich wife in India). By contrast, Hawdon's being washed off the deck of a ship is not an opportunity for cleansing but an unremarkable erasure; and who knows what ineptitudes of colonial administration, or deliberate cutting loose from service might lie behind his being "officially reported drowned" (63.907)? In the end all that he gains from the margin is not a wife at all but an addiction to one of the empire's major imports. What such ironic contradictions effect is a disenchantement of "elsewhere" which intensifies the disenchantment with "here"—for within England (and in the register of realism) the Great House is under siege, Tom-all-Alone's is collapsing, and the northern factories, for all the energetic activity which fuels the whole enterprise, spawn "a great perplexity of iron" and "a Babel of iron sounds" (63.902). It is hardly surprising that the final relocation of a refurbished Bleak House (a synecdoche for all that remains hopeful in England) entails a geographical retreat into an unimagined no man's land.

Another dimension of the silence surrounding the lovers at the graveyard is the uncertainty that surrounds Lady Dedlock's motives in uniting herself with Nemo in death. It is of course possible to see the death of Lady Dedlock as straightforwardly endorsing the power of patriarchal society: her suffering and her death as an outcast are in such a view no more than the just retribution for transgression. On the other hand one might see her flight as a triumphant indication that she is no longer locked into her deadness, with her ultimate determination that Hawdon's grave is "the place where I shall lie down" (59.865) the mark of a subversive repudiation of a sterile marriage—a momentous repudiation, for in bourgeois society marriage is "the all-subsuming, all-organizing, all-containing contract" (Tanner 15). Both such views of Lady Dedlock's death would be wrong. The first is obtuse, and to see her return to Hawdon as a kind of flaunted posthumous adultery would be to ascribe to

Dickens the kind of openly adversarial stance he was not prepared to adopt. (Nor would an adversarial stance necessarily be subversive, for Foucault would encourage one to see the flagrant transgression of bourgeois norms as merely reinscribing the authority of marriage by the very frontality of the attack made on it.)

Nor has Lady Dedlock's original transgression anything of the sordid definitiveness of adultery; a fact which undercuts John Carey's provocative claim that what happened is deliberately mystified in deference to Victorian delicacy about sex, to the point that *Bleak House* is a novel Dickens could not write (177). On the contrary, the silence that surrounds all the phases of the relationship should ultimately be seen as deliberate in quite another way. It opens up a space for standing outside the oppositions in terms of which judgments are constructed within Victorian society. If we know neither the details of Lady Dedlock's transgression, nor what her real motives were in her restless return to Hawdon's grave, we are powerless to judge. We have to set aside the thinking bound by such opposites as blame and forgiveness, rebellion and conformity, even love and desire; and in doing so we are turned from the action of the parents, and from the clarification that judgment on those actions would afford. We are freed to enter into the experience of Esther.

Again, however, we meet a silence, for Esther tells us nothing about the significance of her return to origins. Her silence has its own kind of moving effectiveness: where more analytic novelists might have suffocated the character in their own understanding, Dickens does not try to arrogate, but defers to, Esther's private grief. Yet the silence *is* teasing. Some of the most interesting attempts to describe the significance of Esther's finding of her mother see it as symbolic of her coming to terms with physical desire, with much made of the fact that her pushing aside the veil of hair from her mother's face complements her pushing aside of her own hair to confront her ''fallen'' physical condition in the mirror after her illness.[11] But it would be wrong to see desire as a condition of pristine health in *Bleak House*, tempting though it is to discover the real radicalism of the novel in the release of destructive repressions. True ''health,'' in our reading of the book's economy, could be achieved only by a return beyond the crossing of such opposites as love and desire, to the lost origin.

But Derrida reminds us that that is an impossible return, and Dickens himself cancels out any mythical dimension implicit in the plot of romance by making the return ''a scene of horror'' (16.278), to borrow the words Lady Dedlock uses on her first visit to the iron gates. The recension of Esther's discovery must thus be a matter only of the utmost banality, as though all that could be said were hardly worth saying: ''these then were my parents—they are dead—whatever happened between them is forever unknowable and beyond judgment—I have to go on from here.'' None the less, these terms correspond exactly in their experiential simplicity to the necessary *form* of the mythical encounter: "I returned to the origin—it is a condition of absence—its mystery cannot be written—life flows on from here." This is why the discovery scene has the mysterious force, after all, of a kind of epiphany and release.

In the much earlier scene in which Lady Dedlock declared herself to Esther and parted from her for ever in this life, Esther was overtaken by "an augmented terror" of herself; but she wrenched herself out this state by defiantly telling herself that though the sins of the fathers are sometimes visited upon the children she was "as innocent of [her] birth as a queen of hers" (36.571). The incident pivots on the question whether we are conditioned or free to make ourselves; and we might well see Esther's protest as laudable but naive. Esther's return to her origins at the iron gates, on the other hand, presents a more chastened way of viewing the issue. Of course we cannot really stand outside the oppositions and contradictions which have made us what we are; but in order to go on we have no option but to act and believe as though we could. Foucault's discussion of "the retreat and return of the origin" in *The Order of Things* makes essentially the same point. "Origin, for man," he says (using man in the sense of the problematical entity produced by the passing of the classical *episteme*),

> is much more the way in which man in general, any man, articulates himself upon the already-begun of labour, life and language. . . . The origin, becoming what thought has yet to think, and always afresh, would be for ever promised in an immanence always nearer yet never accomplished.   (330. 332)

The book's final paragraphs would seem to indicate what is involved in such a paradoxical idea of freedom or immanence. Esther stands before the mirror and muses about the loss of her original beauty, only to have Woodcourt tell her, "you are prettier than you ever were" (67.935). This is anything but a coyly sentimental rendering of domestic "warmth," for all that it is natural and touching that Esther should want to be thought of as pretty. The point is not that Woodcourt is reassuring an Esther who still cannot believe in herself. It is not for her face that he loves Esther: the "prettiness" he recognizes is not something extrinsic, originally given and capable of being marred for ever like spoiled goods. Rather it is a matter of her urgent inclination to virtue, the generous selflessness which stems from the habit of being unable to believe that one should not be much better than one is. Where Oliver Twist's goodness is intrinsic and inviolable, Esther's is the product of a resilient set of the will that has survived the fevered weariness of toiling up "never-ending stairs" (35.544).[12] For Esther, no less than for those trapped in a Chancery suit, life is "an unfinished contention" (23.376). Correspondingly, the last sentence of one's narrative is unfinishable in a world where the scars of infection can never be left behind. Esther's narrative opens strangely: "I have a great deal of difficulty in beginning to write my portion of these pages" suggests that beyond the origin of her impulse to write lies not only her first remembered desire to tell the secrets of her desires to her doll, but also a mysteriously pre-existent discourse of which hers is only a portion. And behind the final unfinished sentence of her narrative which ends the book is endless supplementarity. Nevertheless, Esther's open anxiousness marks the efforts of goodness to inscribe itself and to survive in an unfriendly and disinherited world. And this capacity is arguably the oddest mystery of the Dickens universe.

Notes

This is a revised version of a paper delivered at the conference on Victorian Mystery held at the University of California, Santa Cruz in August 1993 under the aegis of The Dickens Project. My attendance at the conference was made possible by grants from the University of the Witwatersrand and from the Human Sciences Research Council.

1. It is only some sixty pages on (14.251) that any explanation is offered for the dark surgeon's presence, and the explanation raises more questions than it answers: Woodcourt says that Miss Flite brought him to Nemo's room, but he fails to account for her summoning of *two* doctors, and he does not explain how it was that he allowed the other to take charge though he himself might seem to have been there first.

2. On the urban Gothic see Pritchard and Herbert who is much more penetrating; on the novel of urban mysteries see Maxwell and Humphreys—all of whom use *Bleak House* as a prime instance.

3. In "Fictions of the Wolfman" Peter Brooks links the rise of both the detective novel and psychoanalytical investigation to nineteenth-century historicism and the premise that we can explain what we are only by plotting a story which derives effects from origins. Yet within both these paradigms the idea of an origin figures not as original plenitude but as the moment of the fall from grace, with the result that the origin seems always in the process of being displaced: having finished and discarded one detective story we disguise our disappointment by picking up another; having uncovered the Wolf Man's primal scene Freud allows that it may be no more than the phantasy evocation "of a possible infinite regress in the unconscious of the race" (Brooks 1985, 276). I have chosen to avoid discussing the question of origins in *Bleak House* in psychoanalytical terms, though I have benefited from both Brooks and Carroll. Hirsch is pertinent but unconvincing.

4. Henry Fielding defined Nobody as "all the people in Great Britain, except 1200," (*Covent Garden Journal* 14 January 1752) quoted by Gallagher. Calmann provides a full account of the tradition.

5. Brooks says, "the very premise of a Balzacian or a Baudelairian cityscape is the effort to move through and beyond a phenomenology to a total moral significance, to a vision of the landscape as an ethical framework and context for human life" (1974–75, 20), and this seems the essential point to be made of Dickens' cityscapes too. Of course the mystery at the heart of *Bleak House*, broadly conceived, has had previous attention, most notably in J. Hillis Miller's "Introduction" to the Penguin edition.

6. I have in mind not Dickens' personal religious beliefs but the condition epitomized by the image of Jo estranged from "the great Cross on the summit of St Paul's" (19.326). The novel abounds with orphans and victims of perverted filiation, and many of its most commonly discussed features reinforce the sense of an originary lack. Chancery is an apt synecdoche for the way in which social institutions have become destructive, in large part because its civil wardship of such matters as paternity and inheritance has devolved into a sterile and formalistic pursuit of origins which squanders the bounty it was meant to protect: the first step in Gridley's case is an absurd ritual of establishing that he is indeed his "father's son" (15.267).

7. Is it possible that "Nimrod, the Hunter" is an obscure intimation that the disease which contaminates Jo, Esther, and possibly even Lady Dedlock herself, emanates in some way from Nemo?

8. The phrase, deleted from the finally revised "Charles Dickens Edition" of 1868, is included in the Penguin text in square brackets.

9. For a very vigorous discussion of the significance of Esther's return to her origins which does just that, see White, an essay I came across after I had completed my own.

10. This is not to gainsay the fact that the metaphors of social health and remedy tend to work against awareness that what might be needed is radical structural change—even in the form of the surgeon's knife. Starting off in a new domestic abode is perhaps the furthest the bourgeois imagination can easily go towards conceiving a radical change in way of life.

11. The fullest account of Esther in these terms is perhaps Van Boheemen's. For a recent discussion see Rignall.

12. For a recent assertion of this kind regarding Esther see Peltason.

WORKS CITED

Auden, W.H. "New Year Letter." *Collected Longer Poems*. Faber: 1968.

Barthes, Roland. *The Empire of Signs*. London: J. Cape, 1982.

Bernstein, Carol S. "Nineteenth-Century Urban Sketches: Thresholds to Fiction." *The Celebration of Scandal: Towards the Sublime in Victorian Urban Fiction.* University Park, PA.: Pennsylvania State UP, 1991.

Brooks, Peter. "Romantic Antipastoral and Urban Allegories." *Yale Review* 64 (1974–75): 11–26.

————. *Reading for the Plot: Design and Intention in Narrative.* New York: Vintage, 1985.

Calmann, Greta. "The Picture of Nobody: An Iconographical Study." *Journal of the Warburg and Courtauld Institute* 23 (1960): 60–104.

Carey, John. *The Violent Effigy: A Study of Dickens's Imagination* (Second revised edition). London: Faber, 1991.

Carroll, David. "Freud and the Myth of Origin." *New Literary History* 6 (975): 513–28.

Collins, Philip, ed. *Dickens: The Critical Heritage.* London: Routledge and Kegan Paul, 1971.

Derrida, Jacques. *Dissemination.* London: Athlone P, 1981.

Dickens, Charles. *Bleak House.* Ed. Norman Page. Harmondsworth: Penguin, 1971.

————. *Oliver Twist.* Ed. Angus Wilson. Harmondsworth: Penguin, 1966.

————. *Our Mutual Friend.* Ed. Stephen Gill. Harmondsworth: Penguin Books, 1971.

————. *Sketches by Boz.* London: Oxford UP, 1957.

————. *A Tale of Two Cities.* Ed. George Woodcock. Harmondsworth: Penguin, 1988.

Foucault, Michel. *The Order of Things: An Archaeology of the Human Sciences.* New York: Vintage, 1973.

Gallagher, Catherine. "Nobody's Story: Gender, Property, and the Rise of the Novel." *Modern Languages Quarterly* 53 (992): 263–78.

Habermas, J. "Modernity versus Postmodernity." Quoted by David Couzens Hoy. "Introduction." *Foucault: A Critical Reader* Oxford: Blackwell, 1984.

Herbert, Christopher. "The Occult in *Bleak House.*" *Novel* 17 (1984): 101–15.

Hirsch, Gordon D. "The Mysteries in *Bleak House*: A Psychoanalytical Study." *Dickens Studies Annual* 4 (1975): 132–52.

Humpherys, Anne. "Generic Strands and Urban Twists: The Victorian Mysteries Novel." *Victorian Studies* 34 (1990–91): 455–72.

Klancher, Jon P. *The Making of English Reading Audiences 1790–1832.* Madison: UP of Wisconsin, 1987.

Marcus, Steven. "Homelessness and Dickens." *Social Research* 58 (1991): 93–106.

Maxwell, Robert. *The Mysteries of Paris and London.* Charlottesville: UP of Virginia, 1992.

Miller, David. *The Novel and the Police.* Berkeley: U of California P, 1988.

Nietzsche, Friedrich. *Human, All-Too-Human: A Book for Free Spirits.* Edinburgh and London: T.N.Foulis, 1909.

Peltason, Timothy. "Esther's Will." *English Literary History* 59 (1992): 671–91.

Pritchard, Allan. "The Urban Gothic of *Bleak House.*" *Nineteenth Century Literature* 45 (1990–91): 432–52.

Rignall, John. "*Bleak House*: the flâneur's perspective and the discovery of the body." *Realist Fiction and the Strolling Spectator.* London: Routledge and Kegan Paul, 1992.

Ruskin, John. "Fiction—Fair and Foul." *The Works of John Ruskin.* Ed. E.T.Cook and Alexander Wedderburn, Volume 34. London: George Allen, 1908.

Tanner, Tony. *Adultery in the Novel.* Baltimore: Johns Hopkins UP, 1979)

Van Boheemen, Christine. *The Novel as Family Romance: Language, Gender and Authority from Fielding to Joyce.* Ithaca: Cornell UP, 1987.

White, Allon. "Language and Location in *Bleak House.*" *Carnival, Hysteria, and Writing: collected essays and autobiography* Oxford: Clarendon P, 1993.

Williams, Raymond. "The Reader in *Hard Times.*" *Writing and Society.* London: Verso, 1984.

Nicholas Nickleby's Problem of Doux Commerce

Joseph W. Childers

From the outset I want to posit *Nicholas Nickleby* as a novel fundamentally shaped by the activity of commerce; it is a novel about doing business. Further, it is a novel about all the responsibilities involved in doing business: the responsibilities to one's self, one's heirs, one's employers and employees, and perhaps most importantly the responsibility of acquiring property, maintaining it, and ultimately using it to acquire more. Honor and duty—what in a different era was known as virtue—are intimately tied to making one's way. All relationships are, at bottom, contracts. They may not overtly require the exchange of capital for services, but whether articulated in terms of vegetables thrown over a garden wall or sado-masochistic homoerotic desire, they are linked to the demonstrable power of property; especially the power of those who have much over those who have less. For *Nicholas Nickleby*, as for Tennyson's "new style" northern farmer, it is "proputty, proputty" that sticks and "proputty, proputty" that grows. The good or ill that can come from the exercise of the power connected to property is always a consideration, often informing a moral dilemma as to the essential nature of this power. As I will argue in the following pages, characters may openly choose whether their money will underwrite benevolent or malevolent social activity, but their allegiance to good or bad is less important than their devotion to the capital they have gathered—or are striving to. And while the novel makes a number of nostalgic moves, attempting to recuperate the eighteenth-century concept of money making as a civilizing, "gentle," vocation, the text remains ambivalent about its efforts to present "business" as potentially meliorative and benevolent.

Property as an ambiguous moral imperative asserts itself early in *Nicholas Nickleby*, and even the very young are bound to take stock of what exactly is meant by doing good with one's wealth. This function of wealth and its

49

power is especially important to one half of a pair of Devonshire lads ten years or so before the turn of the nineteenth century:

> [They] had often heard, from their mother's lips, long accounts of their father's suffering in his days of poverty, and of their deceased uncle's importance in his days of affluence, which recitals produced a very different impression on the two: for while the younger, who was of a timid and retiring disposition, gleaned from thence nothing but the forewarning to shun the great world and attach himself to the quiet routine of a country life; Ralph, the elder, deduced from the often-repeated tale the two great morals that riches are the only true source of happiness and power, and that it is lawful and just to compass their acquisition by all means short of felony. "And," reasoned Ralph with himself, "if no good came of my uncle's money when he was alive, a great deal of good came of it after he was dead, inasmuch as my father has got it now, and is saving it up for me, which is a highly virtuous purpose; and going back to the old gentleman, good *did* come to him too, for he had the pleasure of thinking of it all his life long, and of being envied and courted by all his family besides." And Ralph always wound up these mental soliloquies by arriving at the conclusion, that there was nothing like money.   (*Nicholas Nickleby* 61)

Ralph Nickleby, Dickens' inimitable miser, was an exemplary student of this particular course of study, and except for a few, and usually momentary, lapses—after all, everyone is entitled to some weakness of character—he manages to construct all of his relationships in terms of money and the making of more money. Interestingly, however, even as a child learning that there is "nothing like money," Ralph's sophistic soliloquies depend upon linking lucre to the good it can do. In a parody of utilitarian economic theory, Ralph solipsistically argues for his own happiness. That, for him, is the greatest good. His father's "highly virtuous purpose" of saving his £3,000 legacy redeems his uncle's close-fistedness—creating a good where none before existed. Then in his reasonable way, Ralph realizes that the good that came of the money during his uncle's lifetime was not one that extended to his father or to others but rather a reflexive and reflective benefit to the man who possessed the wealth. According to Ralph's theory of trickle up economics, money may circulate but not endlessly, and it should, properly, always circulate in essentially one direction—his. The primary reason for spending money is to make more money. For Ralph every expenditure is an investment, designed to return a dividend. As a character he is completely defined by principles of getting and spending, of business, of commerce.

Steven Marcus has argued that the "aggressive force of intellect in the novel is directed against prudence—the conception which holds that life should be lived close to the vest, that incessant work, cautious good sense, deliberate action, and sobriety are the principal indications of virtue and the principal assurances of success" (95). In characterizing *Nicholas Nickleby* in this way Marcus suggests what others, like Raymond Williams, would later affirm, that the energy of Dickens' social criticism is essentially negative (Williams 48–52). A master at highlighting the shortcomings of Victorian mores, practices, and manners, the novelist often countermands his own critiques when attempting to put forth solutions to the social problems of his age. Marcus's discussion of the novel bears this out, for even as *Nicholas Nickleby* attacks a puritanical philosophy of prudence and many of its characters are ruined in their attempts to live a middle-class existence, it allows those characters who hold the *correct* attitudes toward property and its acquisition to rise to prominence and authority. *Nicholas Nickleby* is not so much an attack on the middle classes as it is a critical examination of those activities that helped to produce it and make it the dominant class of the Victorian period.

This is particularly important to recognize, for it underscores one of the central ironies of this novel. In lampooning and censuring the prudence, and thus the avarice and self-interestedness of the middle classes, *Nicholas Nickleby* criticizes the traits that emphasize competition and individualism. In a sense it criticizes society for not being "social" enough. Those who succeed—whether emotionally or materially—are those who are most cooperatively engaged with society, those who perceive their greatest duty to be to others. The ultimately prosperous Nicholas, Kate, Cheerybles, Tim Linkinwater, Miss La Creevy, Newman Noggs are motivated out of a desire to do for others rather than for themselves. The irony of this distinguishing between the deserving and the damned is that the problem of selfishness and individualism is represented as a *social* one that runs the gamut, from Peg Sliderskew to Sir Mulberry Hawk.

Nickleby's solution to this problem, however, is not to offer some sort of programmatic change to be implemented across society, making people more cooperative and strengthening their bonds of compassion. The change this novel advocates can not be legislated and administered from above but must be taken on by individuals, like the Cheerybles. Not surprisingly, but perhaps *imprudently*, Dickens' means of stopping and reversing social dissolution and alienation depends, in *Nicholas Nickleby*, on the very epistemology that created the problem to begin with: that foundation of Enlightenment bourgeois subjectivity—individualism. Nor should we dismiss this strategy out of hand from our poststructuralist, post-Marxian perspective. For Dickens as well as for many of his contemporaries, the social ills that resulted from the "rise" of the bourgeois subject also seemed best solved by perpetuating that construct, but with an emphasis on similarity and social unity rather than difference and competition. Building on the living legacy of Enlightenment thinking, the bourgeois subject, though potentially destructive both politically and socially, could also be enabling.

The strategy of creating a kinder, gentler world based on the blueprints that made renovation necessary in the first place means that those plans must be poured over to find what went wrong in their original execution. For *Nicholas Nickleby* the venue for such a search is the institution of business, of profits and corporations, of German trade and joint stock ventures, of speculation and usury, of exchange rather than production. Early on in the novel we are introduced to this institution and the roughness with which it can handle the naïve. The Nicklebys' destitution, and arguably the entire plot of the novel, turns upon Nicholas's father's attempt to imitate Ralph's success. But as Dickens points out: "Speculation is a round game; the players see little or nothing of their cards at first starting; gains *may* be great—and so may losses. The run of luck went against Mr. Nickleby; a mania prevailed, a bubble burst, four stockbrokers took villa residences at Florence, four hundred nobodies were ruined, and among them Mr. Nickleby" (63). Mr. Nickleby's response to his ruin is utter despondence: unable to score in "the round game" he loses everything, takes to his bed, and turns his face to the wall.

Such a harsh result is hardly what one might expect from the domain of *doux commerce* or gentle trade. Certainly the risk of loss is always present, as even the inexperienced Mr. Nickleby knows. But when he mildly balks at his wife's suggestion that he speculate, saying "but if we *should* lose it. . . . we shall no longer be able to live my dear" (63), it is doubtful that the good Mrs. Nickleby understood him to mean that a financial loss would literally take his life. After all, the realm of the middle classes, even for many of those who had retired to the quiet regularity of country life, had become defined by financial loss and gain. Mrs. Nickleby is no different, and her reasons for urging her husband to speculate and "repair their capital" are forward looking: putting Nicholas in the "way of doing something for himself" and providing a legacy (a dowry) for Kate. The chance she is willing to take, and which kills her husband, is a risk that must be run in order assure the Nicklebys a secure middle-class standing and to save them from shabby gentility—the fate of people like the Kenwigs.

Decisions to become a player in the speculative games that comprise the business world, and especially the business world of this novel, were supported in the late years of the eighteenth and the early part of the nineteenth centuries by social, economic, and moral theories which argued that engaging in commerce was a civilizing endeavor, necessary for bringing a free and ordered society into existence. Montesquieu is generally credited for popularizing the phrase "*doux commerce*" and for articulating and advocating this concept in his *L'Esprit des lois* (1748) (see Hirschman, *Passions* 60; "Rival" 1464). There he writes, "it is almost a general rule that wherever we find agreeable manners (*moeurs douces*) commerce flourishes; and wherever there is commerce, there we meet with agreeable manners" (vol. 2, 8). The near circularity of this statement and the presentation of the mutual constitutiveness of gentility and business is made clearer when Montesquieu, several pages later, focuses on the causal: "Commerce . . . polishes and softens (*adoucit*) barbaric ways as we can see every day" (81). This understanding of the effects of commerce on the social was widely accepted and promulgated by thinkers as divergent as William Robertson (*View of the Progress of Society in Europe* [1769]) and Condorcet (*Esquisse d'un tableau historique du progrés de l'esprit humain* [1793–94]). This conception of commerce became the predominant one, in the eighteenth century especially in England and France, entering all kinds of political discourse, reactionary and revolutionary alike. For instance, perhaps one of the most often read statements on *doux commerce* is in Thomas Paine's *The Rights of Man* (1792), where he writes of commerce as "a pacific system, operating to cordialise mankind, by rendering Nations, as well as individuals, useful to each other. . . . The invention of commerce. . . . is the greatest approach towards universal civilization that has yet been made by any means not immediately flowing from moral principles" (215).

Such a theory of commerce worked to defend the activities of the middle class as vital to the progress and development of civil society. As the wealth and power of the commercial class grows in a "free" state, the state as well as the members of the "commercial" class reap the profits. According to the concept of *doux commerce,* increased trade yields increased wealth, leading in turn to increased luxury—one type of which is leisure. But humans are active by nature, argue thinkers like David Hume, and it is activity and industry that contribute most significantly to our happiness. Thus in our increased leisure we acquire and perfect new, more specialized occupations, or as Hume puts it: the mind . . . enlarges its powers and faculties, and by an assiduity in honest industry, both satisfies its natural appetites, and prevents the growth of unnatural ones" (270).

Modern readers who are well informed on how important it is to keep one's unnatural appetites in check can see how easily such a theory was swallowed by the middle classes of the late eighteenth and early nineteenth centuries and how it then managed to lay in their stomachs—rather heavy and only partially digested—well into the Victorian period: the moral imperatives built into the concepts of *doux commerce* were affirmed by the secular gospel of work as well as by the heavily Calvinist religious movements of the early Victorian period. Thus whether in Carlyle and his acolytes or the evangelicism of the low Church movement and dissenting sects such as the Primitive Methodists or the Baptists, the residue of *doux commerce* remained to inform both moral and fiduciary activities.

If we go a bit farther with Hume's syllogism, we see that the effects of commerce extend a good deal beyond merely checking our unnatural desires. In his essay, "Of Refinement in the Arts," the Scottish philosopher argues that the results of expanding the "powers and faculties" of the mind, while leading to improvements in industry and the mechanical arts, also "commonly produce refinements in the liberal [arts]. . . . Profound ignorance is totally banished, and men enjoy the privilege of rational creatures, to think as well as to act, to cultivate the pleasures of the mind as well as those of the body" (270–71). In effect, we become humans, distinct from animals, and from there the ultimate benefits of commerce begin to flow liberally: as "refined arts advance" humans become more sociable; they flock to the cities; they "love to receive and communicate knowledge"; men and women meet in "an easy and sociable manner and the tempers of men, as well as their behavior, refine apace" (271). Thus, concludes Hume, "*industry, knowledge,* and *humanity,* are linked together by an indissoluble chain" (271), and luxury and leisure—the results of commerce—rather than contributing to a general immorality instead cause profligacy of all kinds to be scorned. As Hume writes, "the more men refine upon pleasure, the less will they indulge in excess of any kind, because nothing is more destructive to true pleasure than such excesses" (271).

The essay from which I am quoting was published in 1741, nearly one hundred years before the installments of *Nickleby* began to appear. And, while there is no evidence to suggest that Dickens was an avid reader of Hume, he was a keen observer of the class to which he belonged and upon which he relied for his own prosperity. He could see that the material success which had transformed the middle classes in the years since Hume had not led to greater leisure through which one could pursue specialized, "refining," activities, but to more work; that mammonism had replaced the Humean version of Enlightenment cosmopolitan humanism, and that instead of an increasingly civilized and refined—and thus moral class—the middle classes had become what conservative thinkers like Burke, Coleridge, Carlyle, and Disraeli most feared: they had become philistines. The uncivilized, uncultured of past ages, who as J. G. A. Pocock insists "had existed before the growth of commerce had made culture possible had been replaced by a bourgeoisie that existed after the relation between commerce and culture had become possible, but denied that [this relation] was a necessary one" (281). The increased consciousness of human collectivity that was to have resulted from trade was instead realized as a human aggregate, an assortment of individuals who based relationships on property, money, and labor rather than on the profound understanding that the philosophers of *doux commerce* had envisioned. Progress had made a wrong turn somewhere, and though material and political change continued almost unabated through the years of what Asa Briggs has labelled the "age of improvement," it was becoming ever more difficult to reconcile positive change with the opprobrium that "progress" seemed to produce. Thus Marx, in looking back over the violence and suffering produced during the commercial expansion of the eighteenth and early nineteenth centuries could write with ridicule, "Das ist der *doux commerce*" (*Das Kapital*, Vol. 1, Ch. 24, Sect. 6).

Notions of *doux commerce* that had advocated trade and business activity as the distinguishing characteristic of civilized nations had been replaced by Utilitarian and Manchester school economic theory in which morality and manners play a significantly less central role. Though Bentham's thought absorbed a good deal of the ideas of some of the most prominent of English and Scottish Enlightenment thinkers, the Shaftsburian ethos of humaneness that informed, in a less specifically religious way, so many of Hume's arguments was fairly lacking in Utilitarianism. The "virtue" associated with *doux commerce:* generosity, benevolence, self-sacrifice, and human understanding was superseded by the virtue of self satisfaction and "happiness" that Ralph understands to be linked to having and keeping money. Whatever "good" comes from Ralph's activities is not measured against some transcendental, transhistorical ideal, but relative to the pleasure it provides him. The eighteenth-century moral argument that justifies individual engagement in business as a means of contributing to the greater good of the social whole, no longer functions for him, since it requires that the ends of his commercial efforts be realized in a way that includes others' interests as well as his own. To work with another's welfare in mind is, of course, anathema to Ralph, and he refuses to justify or consider his activities in these terms. That refusal also removes him from civil society, where individuality retains an important status, but is subsumed by a privileging of the social whole. Ralph chooses instead to adhere to the novel's representation of utilitarianism, which so highly emphasized the role of the individual that the *needs* of large portions of society, which may very well be antithetical to the *pleasure* of the greatest number, at least theoretically go unmet.

I say at least theoretically, because a great deal of philanthropy continued to be carried on in the nineteenth century. And though we can easily identify Manchester school and utilitarian economic theories as predominate during the early years of the Victorian era, applications of their purest forms existed on relatively restricted scales. Further, as I have already pointed out, the residual morality of an early age softened some of the austerity of Benthamism and *laissez faire* economics, even as it often made political bedfellows of evangelicals and philosophic radicals on such issues as factory reform. Despite their partially shared genealogies and their occasional, uneasy alliance, however, *doux commerce* and political economy remained divergent and distinct ways of understanding one's place in early Victorian society, and they function as opposite and mutually exclusive *moral* paradigms for the decisions facing the characters in *Nicholas Nickleby*.

The fabric stretched between those two moral poles is a crazy quilt of public and private concerns, from the family to Parliament, and the thread that bastes each part of the patchwork into place is an institution that had attained a sort of hybrid existence, resembling the domestic in many respects, but also carried on in the most public of arenas. Of course I am talking about business itself. By the early 1840s industrialization had transformed Lancashire and much of the rest of Northern England and Southern Scotland. Industrial novels like Fanny Trollope's *Michael Armstrong, Factory Boy* and works like Friedrich Engels's *The Condition of the Working Class in England* make it clear that the business of production, of manufacture, took place outside the home in a specialized, Foucault would say disciplined, place: the factory. The home exists apart from that world. Readers of *Mary Barton* will recall, for instance, the incongruity of George Wilson's presence in the sumptuous Carson home, when he goes there to request relief for the Davenports.

But London was not so much an industrial city as a center of trade and commerce; and unlike *Great Expectation*'s Wemmick who escapes to his little castle and his aged P at the end of each working day, many of the characters of *Nicholas Nickleby* live in and work out of the same building. The dress making Mantalinis, Ralph the money lender, the German-merchant Cheerybles, clerk extraordinaire Tim Linkinwater, the usurer Arthur Gride, and even profiteering school-master Squeers in far-flung Yorkshire keep business a mostly private affair. The result is that with the notable exception of Edwin and Charles Cheeryble—whom I will be discussing at some length—these characters are suffused with the concerns and care of business in all aspects of their private lives. The Mantalini's domestic quarrels are forever linked to the profitability of the establishment. Tim Linkinwater's sole concern is with the orderly keeping of the house of Cheeryble. Even at the end of the novel, when he proposes to Miss La Creevy, it is not as though he is contemplating momentous change: "Come," [says Tim to the painter of miniatures], "let's be a comfortable couple. We shall live in the old house here, where I have been for four-and-forty year" (916). The best compliment he can possibly give to Miss La Creevy is that the time he has spent with her "has been the happiest time in all [his] life—at least, away from the counting-house and Cheeryble Brothers" (916).

Although the arrangement of living and working out of the same space, so that business and domestic concerns come to be intertwined in such a way that it is difficult to distinguish between them—for example Ralph seems to have no home life—even his dinner party is "business"—while the Cheerybles seem to have nothing but home life and the counting house is described as though it were a tidy little cottage—*Nicholas Nickleby*'s portrayals of these situations are really descriptions of the end of an era. True, since the 1720 South Sea Bubble incident and the passage of the Bubble Act, and with the South American and Mexican mining investment fiascoes of 1825 there had been a predominance of public prejudice against the formation of joint-stock companies. As the *Times* wrote in 1826, "trade is of a nature more likely to flourish in the hands of private houses than of corporate bodies, which last can never successfully resist the vigilance or skill of their more active rivals" (September 14). The implication of this attitude is somewhat paradoxical. The effects of trade, of commerce, were social: they helped to smooth the connections between people; they contributed to the formation of a "gentrified" public space. Yet, forming public corporations, drawing capital together in support of an intangible, though operative, entity defied a logic of representation that depended on correspondence. This was the "round game" of speculation that underwrote the activity of commerce, which was necessary to dulcify society. Again we see, however, that this process *doux* associated with commerce cannot come from an aggregate but from the privately held company. The social reaps the benefits even as the private flourishes in trade.

For a time in the 1830s, *all* large associations were stamped by the public as "bubbles and delusions" ("Law of Partnership" 62). Despite these obstacles of public perception, however, the capital demands of doing business on a large, and often international scale, made it increasingly necessary for companies to form themselves into extended partnerships and corporations. And with the passage of legislation aimed at making it easier to incorporate, private houses—many of which did do business out of structures that doubled as residences—became less viable as commercial entities. Thus while cottage industries, especially millinery and sweating, thrived well into the Victorian period, large companies like the United Metropolitan Improved Hot Muffin and Crumpet Baking and Punctual Delivery Company were soon the rule rather than the exception. At the end of *Nicholas Nickleby*, even the House of Cheeryble undergoes an expansion, taking on Tim Linkinwater and Nicholas as partners (note that Nicholas must purchase his partnership). And though the business remains "all in the family," as it were, it obviously changes with the times and the practices of the next generation.

The effects of running one's business out of one's home are double edged and contingent upon one's philosophy of property and commerce. For The Cheerybles, transactions are apparently based on exactly the sort of humaneness, civility, and responsibility that Hume and other advocates of *doux commerce* saw as arising out of trade. The Cheeryble Brothers enterprise is a family in which Charles and Edwin are the benevolent patriarchs, or uncles. From their right-hand man Tim Linkinwater to the well-meaning but inarticulate warehouse workers, everyone benefits from a kind of domestic tranquility that permeates the place of business. They harken back to an earlier time, and Dickens' representation of them is redolent with nostalgia for an era in which competition was not valued over community.[1]

When the Cheerybles are on the narrative stage the reader is in danger of a fate similar to the man who was killed on the East India docks—"smashed," as Tim Linkinwater tells us, under a cask of sugar—for the unblemished goodness of Charles and Edwin is often difficult to bear. As the novel progresses they only get more sweetly benevolent and their commercial concerns tend almost exclusively to philanthropy. Yet through it all they remain men of commerce and the beneficiaries of what Nicholas observes to be "a thriving business." One critic has argued that Dickens "has not the slightest interest" in the Cheeryble's money-making company (Marcus 112). This is no doubt true—certainly we see more of the particulars of Ralph's Gride's, and Squeers' professional habits—and indeed Dickens may not have been fluent enough in the discourse of *doux commerce* to depict how trade could amass a fortune without simultaneously devouring rivals. Nevertheless, the fact that the Cheerybles are businessmen is essential to the novel. As good-hearted as they may be, it is the profits of their enterprise that allow them to be generous. Nor do they ever forget that they are "self-made men." Robert Owen of Lanark Mills fame, perhaps the prototype of benevolent Victorian capitalism, has nothing on them; he at least began with £100. The Cheerybles, as they continually point out, were practically barefoot when they first began their commercial life. How they amassed their fortune is never discussed but one lesson seems not to have been lost on them. At one point, in the middle of a frenzy of munificence they recall themselves to their strong middle-class principles:

> "And I think, my dear brother," said Nicholas's first friend, "that if we were to let them that little cottage at Bow which is empty, at something under the usual rent, now—Eh, brother Ned?"
> "For nothing at all," said brother Ned. "We are rich, and should be ashamed to touch the rent under such circumstances as these. . . . —for nothing at all, my dear brother, for nothing at all."
> "Perhaps it would be better to say something, brother Ned," suggested the other, mildly; "*it would help to preserve habits of frugality, you know, and remove any painful sense of overwhelming obligations. We might say fifteen pound, or twenty pound, and if it was punctually paid, make it up to them in some other way*"
> (541; emphasis added).

And of course they do make it up to the Nickleby's but interestingly, the prudence which Dickens so stridently condemns in this novel is present enough in the mind of brother Charles to be blatantly articulated. Note also that Charles begins at £15 of rent, but immediately raises the "nominal" amount to £20. Something of the successful tradesman is left in him yet; and though it may seem that using that money to "make it up to them some other way," precludes any profit from their letting the Nicklebys the cottage at "something under the usual rent," the brothers are far-sighted enough to see that their "investment" in Nicholas will pay large dividends at a later date—returns that are incalculable on a balance sheet but which in human terms are invaluable.

Other aspects of the business life of the Cheerybles, though underplayed, move the plot of the novel. For instance, Frank Cheeryble returns from abroad, where he has been overseeing the brothers' continental interests, specifically to take a more active role in the home office's activities. His arrival sets in motion the Madeline-Nicholas and Frank-Kate marriage plots, thus further imbricating Cheeryble business activity and domesticity. The lines between the worlds of commercial and domestic economy become even more blurred when Newman comes to Nicholas with word of the impending marriage of Madeline to Gride. Nicholas is forced to act because the brothers are "both absent on urgent business," across the sea (presumably attending to their foreign interests) and incommunicado. By this time Nicholas has become a trusty agent of the House of Cheeryble, having been initiated into the mysteries of business, including "book-keeping and other forms of mercantile account" under the tutelage of Tim Linkinwater.

With the Cheerybles out of the country, Nicholas, as their appointed surrogate in the Bray affair, must consider not only his own feelings toward Madeline and Ralph, but also his obligations to the brothers, especially Charles. And although the brothers' connection to the Brays is not truly a commercial one, it does take on that aspect through the brothers' ruse of "buying" Madeline's embroidery. Further, the confrontation that ensues from Nicholas's intercession in the affair is informed by business interests and principles. Whatever warped desire Gride may have for Madeline herself, his primary lust is for her property. Ralph's involvement is purely monetary. His role, for which he trained in the Kate-Sir Mulberry Hawk-Lord Verisopht affair, is that of procurer, and his payment for playing the part will be handsome. Thus when Nicholas steps in to foil Gride and Ralph, the scene that follows, while obviously about true love and passion, is also about money, property, and power. In a sense Ralph and the Cheerybles' rivalry is defined in this scene, for when Ralph asks by what right Nicholas will prevent Gride from pressing his claim of Madeline's hand, Nicholas responds:

> By this right—that knowing what I do, you dare not tempt me further . . . and by *this better right, that those I serve, and with whom you would have done me base wrong and injury* are her nearest and dearest friends. *In their name I bear her hence.* Give way.   (818; emphasis added).

Nicholas's better right, as he points out, is not his own but the Cheerybles'. Unlike his rescue of Smike that was motivated entirely by insult and outrage, Nicholas's emancipation of Madeline is authorized by his attachment, both *filial* and *fiscal*, to the brothers. Their power, born of their virtue to be sure but effective because of their wealth, makes them imposing adversaries of Ralph. And as if calling upon the twin gods of morality and benevolence, Nicholas invokes their names as a sort of talisman of goodness with which to beat back the evil presence of Ralph and Gride.

Modern critics at least since Orwell have expressed difficulties with the Cheerybles as characters, arguing that they are, essentially, too good to be true. Because of their inflexible generosity and unfailing good nature they are, as Michael Slater has pointed out, the fairy godmothers of a novel that is far from being a fable. They are, he says, "an embarrassing failure" (29–30). I want to go a bit further and suggest first that not only are they too good to be true, but they are also too good to be good and, second, that not only do they fail as believable characters but as emblems of a more humane society that fashions itself from the nostalgic but by no means accurate remembrances of the ethos of a another era. Dickens himself never seems fully sold on the idea that commerce can refine humanity. Ralph, after all, has always been as he is. The tale of his father's early poverty and his uncle's wealth do not make him any more grasping, it merely supports his natural proclivities for avarice. By the same token, there is no indication that the Cheerybles actually *learned* their munificence from being successful tradesmen. If anyone is to be credited with their gentleness it would be, as the brothers themselves realize, their mother. Their success and their wealth have allowed them to exercise their good will far and wide, but even here the novel is not completely comfortable in its portrayal of these do-gooders.

For instance, at the end of *Nicholas Nickleby*, where so much is tied up in neat little matrimonial packages, we see Brother Charles and Brother Edwin exerting and enjoying their velvet-gloved influence. In a little charade intended to amuse the brothers and Tim and to expedite true love among the younger generation of characters, the brothers remind everyone who is really in charge. Before Charles explains the terms of the recovered Bray will to Frank and Nicholas he bids the young men shake hands and exhibit themselves before him as "fast and firm friends," an order they are willing enough to comply with, but which even if they were disinclined to follow they could hardly refuse. Once the friendly atmosphere has been established they begin to negotiate over Madeline—still fetishized as a commodity, despite being out of the clutches of Ralph and Gride—with Charles acting as mediator. Given what everyone save Nicholas knows, the scene smacks of kindness that borders on cruelty:

> "Now, Frank," said the old gentleman, "you were the immediate means of recovering this deed. The fortune is but a small one, but we love Madeline, and as such as it is, we would rather see you allied to her with that, than to any other girl we know who has three times the money. Will you become a suitor for her hand?"   (912)

Of course Frank declines the offer, for that is precisely what it is, saying that he assumed another had a greater claim upon her. In this he concludes, "Perhaps I judged too hastily."

This is all Charles needs to hear before he chastens his nephew: "How dare you think . . . " he says to Frank, "that we would have you marry for money, when youth, beauty, and every amiable virtue and excellence were to be had for love? How dared you, Frank, go and make love to Mr Nickleby's sister without telling us first and letting us speak for you?" As well meaning and good natured as this remonstrance may be, the effect is to authorize the power of property and wealth, to undercut Frank's agency in what, at least presumably, is his own affair, and to insist on the ultimately public performance of domestic institutions as well as private performance of public ones. "How dared you Frank," he essentially says, "attempt this on your own and thus wrest control of so many lives from us?" The gist of this scolding reaffirms the brothers' good intentions, perhaps, but it also reminds the young men that even though the brothers would have Nicholas and Frank make their own choices, the very granting of that license is a sort of *bourgeois oblige*. Charles is quite clear on this when he warm-heartedly says to Nicholas, "You acted nobly, not knowing our sentiments, but now you know them sir and *must do as you are bid*" (913; emphasis added). However willing Nicholas may be to follow this order, and however amiably is it issued, it is an order just the same.

Nicholas is bound to follow this command because he loves Madeline, but he must also obey because he now lives in the Cheerybles' world, and it is one they control rather closely. Nicholas is their salaried subordinate, their Newman Noggs. And though, like Newman, his connections to his employers go beyond mere payment for his services, he nonetheless is dependant on the brothers for his livelihood. The moral valences are different, but both Ralph and the Cheerybles link themselves to others monetarily. Every character in the novel who is closely connected to the Cheerybles is somehow obliged to them financially. In a way, the Cheerybles have entered the friends and family free-agent market and have put together the best set of acquaintances money can buy. Their cherished domestic space is run just as their business is. Indeed, there is no distinguishing between the two and the intersection between public and private is no intersection at all, but rather the shape of the Cheerybles' ontology. They, and because of their influence all those for whom they care, always exist both privately and public, domestically and commercially.

Notably, the agency Nicholas exhibits in the early part of the novel and which places him at odds with Ralph has been subsumed by the Cheerybles. In a sense, they have succeeded where Ralph has failed to control Nicholas, and as a result, Nicholas apparently has gained control of himself. Quite at odds with how the early portions of the novel have depicted Nicholas, the brothers read him as capable of self-governance in the face of the most trying circumstances. They select Nicholas as their representative in their attempts to help Madeline because in him, as brother Ned says, they can "repose the strictest of confidence." Frank might be "flighty and thoughtless," falling in love "before he well knew his own mind." And Tim, the brothers point out, "would never do, for he could never contain himself, but would go to loggerheads with the father before he had been in the place five minutes" (694). In Nicholas, however, they have observed the "domestic virtues and affections and delicacy of feeling which exactly qualify him for the job." (694). Nicholas has become the beneficiary *and* the product of the Cheerybles' peculiar brand of gentle business. As such he is more closely linked to them than ever, and thus more directly influenced by that connection. The brothers are in fact reproducing themselves in Nicholas and are overseeing each step of that process.

The control the Cheerybles exert over their world is not always articulated in terms of domestic virtues, and affections, and delicacy of feeling. For instance, when the brothers give Tim a gold snuff box stuffed with a large bank-note for his birthday, Charles warns the old clerk by "playfully" threatening his employee's cherished pet: "never say another word upon it or I'll kill the blackbird" (559). Charles, of course, would never do such a thing, but the threat carries a certain weight nevertheless. When one person tells another that she would never *think* of lying to him, rest assured that thought has just crossed her mind. Similarly, at the moment of his remark, Mr. Cheeryble entertained, however fleetingly, a vision of throttling that crow. As though shocked by his own remark and his ability to think such violence, he quickly repudiates the threat, saying that the animal "should have had a golden cage half-a-dozen years ago, if it would have made him or his master a bit the happier." Referring to beast and man alike in the third person seems intended more to convince himself than Tim that he really has nothing against the bird or his old bookkeeper.

Although I believe a strong case could be made for the Cheerybles as sinister characters, that is not a claim I want to make in this space. Rather, I want to remark on the incredible power that accrues to them through the effects of their philanthropic steamrolling as they gleefully force their good will on everyone who lies in their path, power that is always connected to the agency of other characters. Ostensibly, they try to preserve the choices and the dignity of those with whom they become involved, but they often come perilously close to insinuating their own will upon others, or, as in the case of Nicholas and Frank, they circumscribe the choices. Their presence and their influence cannot go unheeded: Tim Linkinwater, for example, when proposing to Miss La Creevy says that he could not have thought of such a thing without the brothers knowing it; even Ralph feels compelled to see Charles when he visits and to heed their summons to come to them.

Not in spite of, but rather because of their obnoxious goodness and their *deus ex machina* presence in the text, the Cheerybles cannot long stand at the novel's center. And while I am not prepared to make arguments regarding Dickens's intentions, his assurance in the Preface that the brothers were modelled upon real people can easily be read as a belated attempt to shore up the defects of their narrative functions. Although their machinations are the chief obstacle to evil having its way, Ralph emerges as the more interesting, engaging, and complex character. As emblems of a time gone by, the brothers do seem to evoke the sort of conservative nostalgia that critics like Marcus have identified as the essential political vision of this novel. But by portraying them in broad strokes and as the sources of a patronage so benevolent that it can seem cloying and unconsciously deleterious, Dickens undermines the possibility of the Cheerybles actually standing for a solution to the cash-nexus ethos that drives so many of the novel's characters. What Dickens portrays as true generosity and philanthropy themselves are never suspect in his novels, but the conventional symbolism associated with them, including the institutions that proclaim themselves philanthropic, is increasingly scrutinized in his later work. The Cheerybles in some ways, appear to be the last hurrah for a naive representation of an unsullied, middle-class goodness that was never without its darker side. In this reading of the novel, I want to point to the dirt on their hands, and suggest, after Derrida among others, that there is no gift that is *simply* a gift. One need only think of the grasping Casby of *Little Dorrit* or the controlling John Jarndyce of *Bleak House* to see what eventually becomes of Cheeryble-like figures. Similarly, the altruism that defines the brothers and their place in the narrative in the later works is associated less with the main stream of the middle-classes and more with socially marginal characters. Bastard children, circus children, transported convicts, golden dustmen and the like emerge as the unlikely moral and material benefactors of the later novels.

Although by the second quarter of the nineteenth-century a philosophy of "gentle trade" may have ceased to be a viable moral-economic theory, it is easy to see that the increased human community it advocated but which current business practices dissolved into the cash-nexus, attracted conservative, progressive, and radical thinkers alike: from Coleridge to Mill to Marx. The Cheerybles are by no means the answer to the problems that Dickens observed all around him, but their presence in the novel suggests the beginning of a perspective that sees the discourses and institutions of public and private life as inextricably intertwined. Such a perspective allows the novelist and his readers to engage in critique that can ask difficult questions and forego easy answers about the conditions of our existence. It clears a ground for literature as social commentary of the most vital and immediate sort. Ironically, it is the very *failure* of the Cheerybles as believable characters and as symbols of kinder, gentler business practices that can lead us to discussions of how property, wealth, benevolence, matrimony, patronage, etc. function across the boundaries of "private" and "public" which we see as informing the Victorian world, but which, in a novel like *Nicholas Nickleby*, have already become threadbare and incapable of maintaining the clear distinctions so often attributed to them.

NOTES

1. For a discussion of the links between sentiment and benevolence in the eighteenth-century see John Mullan, *Sentiment and Sociability : The Language of Feeling in the Eighteenth Century.*

WORKS CITED

Anon. *The Times of London*. September 14, 1826.

Anon. "Law of Partnership," *Westminster Review*, XX, (January, 1834): 58–71.

Briggs, Asa. *The Age of Improvement: 1783–1867*. London: Longman, 1979.

Condorcet, Marquis de. *Esquisse d'un tableau historique du progrés de l'esprit humain*. [1795]. Paris: J. Vrin, 1970.

Dickens, Charles. *Nicholas Nickleby*. [1839]. Harmondsworth, England: Penguin, 1978.

Hirschman, Albert O. "Rival Interpretations of Market Society: Civilizing, Destructive, or Feeble?" "*Journal of Economic Literature*. Dec. 1982. 20:1463–84.

Hirschman, Albert O. *The Passions and the Interests: Political Arguments for Capitalism before Its Triumph*. Princeton: Princeton UP, 1977.

Hume, David. "Of Refinement in the Arts." (1741). *Essays Moral, Political, and Literary*. Ed. Eugene F. Miller. Indianapolis: Liberty Classics Press, 1985.

Marcus, Steven. *Dickens from Pickwich to Dombey*. [1965]. New York: Norton, 1985.

Marx, Karl. *Das Kapital* Vol. 1. [1872]. Wien-Berlin: Verlag für Literatur und Politik, 1932.

Montesquieu, Charles Louis. *De l'esprit des lois*. [1748] Paris: Garnier, 1961.

Mullan, John. *Sentiment and Sociability : The Language of Feeling in the Eighteenth Century.* New York: Oxford UP, 1988.

Paine, Thomas. *The Rights of Man.* [1792]. New York: Dutton, 1951.

Pocock, J.G.A. *Virtue, Commerce, and History.* New York: Cambridge UP, 1985.

Robertson, William. *The Progress of Society in Europe.* [1769] Ed. Felix Gilbert. Chicago: Chicago UP, 1972.

Slater, Michael. "Introduction." *Nicholas Nickleby.* Charles Dickens. Harmondsworth, England: Penguin, 1978.

Williams, Raymond. *The English Novel: From Dickens to Lawrence.* London: Hogarth Press, 1984.

A Recipe for Perversion: The Feminine Narrative Challenge in *Bleak House*

LuAnn McCracken Fletcher

> The artist in his work must be like God in his creation—invisible and all-powerful: he must be everywhere felt, but never seen.
>
> *(Letters of Flaubert* I.230)
>
> Which is the right strategy—to engage in a radical critique of the dominant and thereby risk political annihilation (or at least permanent exclusion), or to legitimate oneself in its terms, with all the compromises (and all without a guarantee) which that entails? . . . . The most extreme threat to the true form of something comes not so much from its absolute opposite or its direct negation, but in the form of its perversion; somehow the perverse threat is inextricably rooted in the true and the authentic, while being, in spite of (or rather because of) that connection, also the utter contradiction of the true and authentic.
>
> (Dollimore 45, 121)

In a review of *Bleak House* printed in *The Spectator*, 24 September, 1853, George Brimley records his opinion of Esther Summerson, an opinion frequently quoted by more recent detractors of and apologists for her character:

> His [Dickens'] heroine in *Bleak House* is a model of unconscious goodness . . . her unconsciousness and sweet humility of disposition are so profound that scarcely a page of her autobiography is free from a record of these admirable qualities. . . . Such a girl would not write her own memoirs, and certainly would not bore one with her goodness till a wicked wish arises that she would either do something very "spicy," or confine herself to superintending the jam-pots at Bleak House. (924)

Brimley's comment on Esther is one of the wittier of the disparaging pronouncements made on her character since Dickens' novel first appeared.[1]

67

What interests me most about it, however, is the paradoxical assumption about the relationship between women and narrative which underlies its criticism. Brimley sarcastically calls attention to Esther's overly conscious unconsciousness of her goodness and suggests that if Esther were the "girl" her narrative makes her out to be, she would not be writing at all: "such a [good] girl would not write her own memoirs." The unstated implication is that Esther's narrative, by the mere fact of its existence, creates an Esther very different from the Esther it ostensibly describes. According to general cultural consensus, the "ideal Victorian girl" is to be unconscious of self. Indeed, she is to give up her self, as Sarah Stickney Ellis's description of woman's nature at its best implies:

> It is too much the custom with writers, to speak in . . . general terms of the *loveliness* of the female character; as if woman were some fragrant flower, created only to bloom and exhale in sweets . . . . How much more generous, just, and noble would it be to deal fairly by woman in these matters, and to tell her that to be *individually*, what she is praised for being *in general*, it is necessary for her to lay aside all her natural caprice, her love of self-indulgence, her vanity, her indolence—in short, her very *self*—and assuming a new nature, which nothing less than watchfulness and prayer can enable her constantly to maintain, to spend her mental and moral capabilities in devising means for promoting the happiness of others, while her own derives a remote and secondary existence from theirs. (40)

Ellis suggests that for a woman to be what her culture assumes she "is," she must "lay aside . . . her very *self*" and act a role different from what Ellis believes is her true nature. Ellis's description of the ideal woman is quite close to Esther's prescription for her own adherence to "duty," which perhaps explains Brimley's recognition of Esther as the ideal Victorian girl.

But such a "girl"—or woman, as the case may be—cannot write a life-narrative: how can one write an autobiography about a nonexistent self?[2] To do so is to attempt to narrate the unnarratable. And yet Brimley also assumes that Esther *has* done what he presumes can't be done: he calls her narrative an autobiography (a story of self) even as he acknowledges Esther's goodness, although he finds it boring, and hence identifies her with the Victorian ideal of womanhood (a story of non-self). In its criticism of Esther's character and Esther's autobiography, then, Brimley's comments allude to one of the major problematics of *Bleak House*: the connection between gender and narrative. As we shall see, in his creation of Esther's story, Dickens exposes the limitations of our assumptions about certain narrative conventions precisely because he creates a gendered narrative, a woman's narrative. In fact, Esther's voice forces us to realize, on the one hand, just how willing we are as readers to ascribe (consciously or unconsciously) "authority" and "objectivity" to "successful" narratives—narratives which turn out to be considered "masculine." And, on the other hand, how clearly we value (consciously or unconsciously) so-called objectivity and masculinity, at the expense of the personal and the feminine.

That Esther's narrative is written in a stereotypically feminine style seems to be a tacit assumption by most modern commentators on the novel, George Brimley aside.[3] Those critics who more overtly consider how Esther's style is feminine point to her indirection and doubt as characteristic of a woman's voice.[4] Such an assumption about Esther's narrative technique appears plausible—the narrator is, after all, a woman. But many of the commentators who take Esther's feminine style for granted also label the style of the third-person narrator as masculine, an assumption that is perhaps not as obvious as these commentators believe. Senf, for example, calls the third-person narrator's voice masculine because "his cool and analytical narrative, which reveals that he is usually ruled by the head, focuses on issues outside the home such as Chancery, politics, and social relationships"(22). Senf uses social stereotypes of masculinity to describe narrative style. Virginia Blain, on the other hand, points to narrative conventions to assign a masculine identity to what we generally call the omniscient narrator: according to the "assumptions we have been used to making about Victorian literature. . . . an omniscient narrator was masculine almost by definition" (32). Neither of these critics considers how the classification of the narrator as masculine correlates with specific narrative techniques: how, for instance, does the third-person narrator conduct his reputed analysis or display his reputed omniscience?

When a few commentators consider more closely questions of narrative style, they reach the conclusion that the two narratives of *Bleak House* are products of the same observer (which, of course, is literally true, as Dickens created both). Robert Newsom adheres to the masculine-feminine distinction between the third-person narrator's voice and Esther's voice but suggests that "it is nevertheless sometimes difficult to tell them apart. Esther, in particular, often falls into the voice of the other narrator, and this suggests that we may read them as alter egos" (87). Newsom's speculation suggests a kind of narrative relationship between the voices even as it separates them into masculine and feminine modes, a relationship which I believe is crucial to our understanding of how Esther's feminine voice contributes to the form of *Bleak House*. Like Newsom, Judith Wilt has suggested that the third-person voice and Esther's voice are two sides of the same narrator. Further, by calling attention to Esther's "confusion" as a more authentic narrative response to the hopelessly complex world of *Bleak House* than the definiteness of the omniscient narrator, Wilt inverts the usual critical valuation of the two narrators.[5] Together, Newson's and Wilt's willingness to see Esther's voice as at least as significant to the construction of *Bleak House* as the third-person narrator's provides an important corrective to the earlier critical tendency to privilege the omniscient, "public" voice of the third-person narrator and to see Esther's voice as merely an annoying distraction.

W. J. Harvey's discussion of the two narrative voices in *Bleak House* is typical of such early narrative studies. Harvey notes the general view of Esther as "insipid" (91) and suggests that, when Esther's narrative does provide us with an occasional unusual image or apt judgment, such moments demonstrate "Dickens chafing at his self-imposed discipline. . . . Even when, at moments of emotional stress, her prose strays into the purple patch, one feels that this is the rhetoric of an amateur, not to be compared, for instance, with the controlled crescendo of Jo's death" (92). The reference to "controlled crescendo" betrays Harvey's impression that the third-person narrator is a "better" narrator, and the implication that Dickens is "on the side of" the omniscient narrator is solidified in Harvey's culminating distinction between the two narrators: "despite the retrospective nature of her story, Esther must *seem* to be living in a dramatic present, ignorant of the plot's ramifications. Dickens [note, not the narrator himself, which would be the more logical comparison] is *really* omniscient in the other narrative; god-like he surveys time as though it were an eternal present and Esther must seem to belong to that present"(93). Harvey's discussion of the novel is typical of much criticism in its seemingly implicit association of the omniscient narrator with Dickens himself, or if not with Dickens specifically, at least with the social voice of the novel.[6]

Why do so many readers, with the exception of Wilt, reach the conclusion that the third-person narrator is masculine? Who do some critics sense a connection between the two voices, though the connection remains unexplained? Who do so many readers feel uncomfortable with Esther's narration and more satisfied with the third-person narrator's? The answer to the first question is, as I hope to demonstrate, that the third-person narrator *is* masculine, with the same kind of assumed control and authority over his narrative that we find in male first-person texts such as Dickens' *David Copperfield* or Charlotte Brontë's *The Professor*. The answer to the second question, as I also hope to show, is that in terms of actual narrative practice, the third-person portion of *Bleak House* does not differ substantially in technique—the way a story gets told—from Esther's portion. The difference lies primarily in the way Esther calls attention to the procedure of storytelling. In particular, she calls *our* attention to the way a story gets told and the tacit assumptions we make about narrative, the conventions we subscribe to when we read. In terms of the way her narrative violates our expectations, Esther Summerson's story is very much like Lucy Snowe's story in Charlotte Brontë's *Villette*, and it has a similar disturbing effect upon the reader[7]—hence, an answer to my third question. Esther's voice is open to disparagement because in her awareness of her reader in the shaping of her narrative, Esther exposes herself to that reader's interpretation and judgment of her narrative, much as Lucy Snowe invites the reader to participate in the construction of meaning in *Villette.* Unlike Lucy's narrative, however, Esther's narrative is juxtaposed with a narrative that purports to proceed along the lines of conventional expectations; thus, the reader who is made uncomfortable by Esther may turn to the third-person narrator in order to judge Esther unfavorably by the presumed contrast with the more "sophisticated" voice.

What bothers most readers of *Bleak House* is the way Esther continually calls attention to herself while denying her significance. And yet, in passages such as the following, Esther's profession of authorial modesty reveals her understanding of the obligations placed on her as narrator and the impossibility of fulfilling these obligations:

> I don't know how it is, I seem to be always writing about myself. I mean all the time to write about other people, and I try to think about myself as little as possible, and I am sure, when I find myself coming into the story again, I am really vexed and say, "Dear, dear, you tiresome little creature, I wish you wouldn't!" but it is all of no use. I hope any one who may read what I write, will understand that if these pages contain a great deal about me, I can only suppose it must be because I have really something to do with them; and can't be kept out.   (102–03)

The last sentence of this quotation might be seen as an apt rebuttal to George Brimley's criticism of Esther's narrative—and a challenge to his assumptions about women and narrative as well. Esther "can't be kept out" of her narrative: by the very process of writing her "portion of these pages" (17), she writes about—indeed, creates—herself. But her autobiography is not like the autobiographies of male characters; Esther writes for a different purpose, a purpose that assumes an audience, as their narratives do not.[8] Earlier in her account, Esther comments: "It seems so curious to me to be obliged to write all this about myself! As if this narrative were the narrative of *my* life!" (27). Who obliges Esther to write a portion of the novel's pages? Whoever it is, Esther is clearly aware that she is writing for an audience—"the unknown friend to whom I write" (767)—that expects her to tell her life-story, for whatever reason; further, *she* is aware of the third-person narrator, the writer of the other "portion" of the pages.[9] Consequently, Esther knows she is telling a story she is expected to tell—and to tell it in a particular way: note that she denies that this narrative is the narrative of *her* life, implying that if it were, it would be a different narrative. And yet she also realizes that, even if she is to tell the story of others, she will inevitably tell the story of herself. Try as she might to be "transparent"—to keep herself and her point of view out of the story—she finds that she *can't* be kept out. Esther's realization that

she "seem[s] to be always writing about [her]self" calls attention to the fact
that there *is* no such thing as a transparent narrator; narratives will always
contain the participation and interpretation of their creators.

Were we to be given the story of *Bleak House* solely by the third-person
narrator, we would, perhaps, be less inclined to question his seeming transparency.[10] Because Esther reflects on this question, however, we are more likely
to notice the hidden control of interpretation by the third-person narrator.
Those readers who would call the third-person narrator "omniscient" are
sensing something about his authority that his own claims of uncertainty
would contradict. When, for example, the third-person narrator considers
whether Tulkinghorn knows that Sir Leicester takes his lawyer's air of prescription and dress as a kind of tribute to the Dedlocks, he leaves the question
ostensibly unanswered:

> Has Mr. Tulkinghorn any idea of this himself? It may be so, or it may not; but
> there is this remarkable circumstance to be noted in everything associated with
> my Lady Dedlock as one of a class—as one of the leaders and representatives
> of her little world. She supposes herself to be an inscrutable Being, quite out
> of the reach and ken of ordinary mortals—seeing herself in her glass, where
> indeed she looks so. Yet, every dim little star revolving about her, from her
> maid to the manager of the Italian Opera, knows her weaknesses, prejudices,
> follies, haughtinesses, and caprices; and lives upon as accurate a calculation
> and as nice a measure of her moral nature, as her dressmaker takes of her
> physical proportions. . . .
> Therefore, while Mr. Tulkinghorn may not know what is passing in the
> Dedlock mind at present, it is very possible that he may.   (14–15)

While the third-person narrator claims not to know what is passing in the
Tulkinghorn mind, it is more than possible—indeed, it is certain—that he
does know. The servants of Lady Dedlock can read her "impermeable"
mind, and the third-person narrator can read the servants' minds—particularly
Tulkinghorn's—while taking a stance of doubt. What we have here is a knowl-
edgable narrator who maintains a fiction about uncertainty; this fiction is
reinforced by his use of the present tense, a tense which, in effect, suggests
that the narrator learns about events when we do, as they unfold. Clearly,
however, this assumed ignorance is a stance which ends up reinforcing the
narrator's power of interpretation: it allows the narrator to hide his control
over our perception of events under a pretence of disinterestedness. Perhaps
I can make this point more clearly by comparing the effect of the third-person
narrator's present-tense narration to the effect of a camera lens, which records
events as they happen. We assume that what is seen through a camera, which
"pans" a scene and records what occurs as it occurs, provides an objective
record of that scene and its events. We should keep in mind, however, that
the events are still being seen through the perspective of the camera lens: our

vision of the events is thus mediated by the lens and controlled by the lens, just as the third-person narrator controls the "truth" about Tulkinghorn that he wants us to believe.[11]

Audrey Jaffe has made some perceptive observations about omniscience which I want to focus on briefly:

> Omniscience, fundamentally the narrator's demonstration of his ability to move among and within the individual consciousnesses of characters in the novel, depends upon the narrator's marking the difference between those characters and himself—on his establishing the boundaries of character. As a pretense of unlimitedness, omniscience also depends upon the narrator's establishing characters' and sometimes readers' limitations: the boundaries of character are the limitations of character. Rather than being, as is often assumed, a stable body of knowledge, the sum total of a novel's individual consciousnesses, or the "voice of society," omniscience is a fantasy about knowlege [sic], an effect of narrative strategies by means of which a narrator demonstrates his knowledge.
>
> ("Omniscience in *Our Mutual Friend*" 91)

For Jaffe, omniscience is not an essential state of all-knowingness, though the term "omniscience" literally implies such a state.[12] It is, rather, "an active force that makes characters and readers aware of its presence" ("Omniscience" 91); it is a set of strategies by which narrators—or, in some cases, characters themselves—demonstrate their superior knowledge and in this way obtain power. The third-person narrator in *Bleak House* establishes his knowledge by establishing characters' limitations—Sir Leicester's ignorance of the tension between Lady Dedlock and Tulkinghorn, for instance—but more particularly by establishing readers' limitations: he demonstrates his knowledge by reminding us of our own ignorance while simultaneously supplying us with the interpretation he wants us to have. When he describes the carefully concealed hostilities between Lady Dedlock and Tulkinghorn, the third-person narrator couches the certainty of Tulkinghorn's aggressiveness in the language of doubt:

> Mr. Tulkinghorn comes and goes pretty often; there being estate business to do, leases to be renewed, and so on. He sees my Lady pretty often, too; and he and she are as composed, and as indifferent, and take as little heed of one another, as ever. Yet *it may be* that my Lady fears this Mr. Tulkinghorn, and that he knows it. *It may be* that he pursues her doggedly and steadily, with no touch of compunction, remorse, or pity. *It may be* that her beauty, and all the state and brilliancy surrounding her, only give him the greater zest for what he is set upon, and make him the more inflexible in it. *Whether he be* cold and cruel, *whether* immovable in what he has made his duty, *whether* absorbed in love of power, *whether* determined to have nothing hidden from him in ground where he has burrowed among secrets all his life, *whether* he in his heart despises the splendour of which he is a distant beam, *whether* he is always

treasuring up slights and offences in the affability of his gorgeous clients—*whether* he be any of this, or all of this, *it may be* that my Lady had better have five thousand pairs of fashionable eyes upon her, in distrustful vigilance, than the two eyes of this rusty lawyer, with his wisp of neckcloth and his dull black breeches tied with ribbons at the knees.

(357–58; my emphasis)

Contained within the "may be's" and "whether's" is the narrator's insistence on the legitimacy of Lady Dedlock's fear and on "all of this" as an accurate description of Tulkinghorn's motives. Though the narrator's proliferating possibilities are supposedly hypothetical, we are forced by their sheer number both to acknowledge the narrator's ability to "read" Tulkinghorn and, in turn, to grant authority to his interpretation of the tension between Tulkinghorn and Lady Dedlock. "Omniscient" this narrator is; "transparent" he is not. The third-person narrator's presentation of the hypothetical case to give him power over the reader is paralleled by Tulkinghorn's presentation of Lady Dedlock's history to the gentry at Chesney Wold in the form of a fiction about a great lady (505–06), a story which gives him power over Lady Dedlock. We might compare the effect of the third-person narrator's technique of professing uncertainty to the effect of Tulkinghorn's technique of withholding his opinions: "It is a part of Mr. Tulkinghorn's policy *and mastery* to have no political opinions; indeed, *no* opinions" (503; initial emphasis mine). Omniscience may be a fantasy about knowledge, but it is even more so a means of demonstrating power, as in *Bleak House* one gains control by conveying to the reader that one is *not* telling what one knows or believes.[13]

To make the assertion immediately above brings us back to the question of Esther, who has traditionally been faulted for her coyness, for not telling us what she knows or believes although she alerts us to her withholding of information. Even those readers sympathetic to Esther criticize her indirections about Woodcourt, for example; Michael S. Kearns calls her coyness a violation of "the principle of narrative decorum" (124). If Esther is conventionally assumed to be, in Joseph Sawicki's words, "a simple-minded truthteller, an autobiographical reporter" (216), we will find her withholding of truth, her refusal to tell us about her feelings, disturbing. We are not disturbed when the third-person narrator engages in the same sort of coyness,[14] because our expectations for third-person narration are different. But should they be? Jerome Meckier comments: "The allegedly objective third-person narrator animates fog and primeval slime, hallucinates about a waddling Megalosaurus, and describes spontaneous combustion. His satiric comments, despite being cast in the third person, are still only one man's opinions"(18–19). Meckier's clause "despite being cast in the third person" is explicable only if we realize that the convention of a third-person narrator's impersonality is merely a convention. Indeed, there is no such thing as third-person narration;

it is always first-person. Mieke Bal, following Gérard Genette, observes: "By definition, a 'third-person' narrator does not exist: any time there is narrating, there is a narrating subject, one that to all intents and purposes is always in the 'first person' " (237). Once we are aware that the comments of the third-person narrator are only "one man's opinion," in Meckier's words—they provide a single perspective on the events narrated which does not necessarily coincide with the perspectives of the characters involved—we begin to see how our unquestioned acceptance of the third-person narrator's transparency in *Bleak House* can lead us to ignore how we are, in fact, manipulated by this narrator. Even as the third-person narrator moves in and out of the consciousnesses of the characters with seeming invisibility, he still selects *which* consciousness will be represented at any given time and how much of it will be given. And yet how easy it is to accept the third-person narrator's voice as "objective" and to ignore the monolithic quality of his voice. Esther's narrative, however, exposes the fallacy of expecting objective "truth" from *any* narrative, whether we distinguish it as first- or third-person.

Like the third-person narrator, Esther projects hypothetical possibilities, but unlike this "omniscient" narrator, Esther suggests that these possibilities have their source in her own imagination, not in some external reality. When she meets Mrs. Pardiggle and her family, having met the Jellybys previously and commented on the neglect endured by the Jellyby children and Mr. Jellyby, Esther suggests:

> Suppose Mr. Pardiggle were to dine with Mr. Jellyby, and suppose Mr. Jellyby were to relieve his mind after dinner to Mr. Pardiggle, would Mr. Pardiggle, in return, make any confidential communication to Mr. Jellyby? I was quite confused to find myself thinking this, but it came into my head.   (95)

Esther's confusion here is generally attributed to her reticence about criticizing others, but our understanding of her supposition suggests that she, like the third-person narrator, uses a hypothetical case to convey an interpretation—with this crucial difference: Esther goes on to take responsibility for the interpretation, saying that she finds *herself* thinking this. Unlike Tulkinghorn—and the third-person narrator—who profess no opinions, Esther professes that what she says is *her* opinion and no one else's; this profession prevents her from attaining the kind of "mastery" that Tulkinghorn—and the third-person narrator—have. But lest we read Esther's lack of authority as making her an inferior narrator, we should consider the other implications of her "confusion." Esther generally finds herself confused when she senses alternate interpretations to her own personal opinions about who others are. She is particularly confused about Skimpole: while she mistrusts his "child" status, she realizes that Jarndyce and others find his claims refreshing; thus she hesitates to interpret Skimpole's actions as mercenary. Certainly Esther's evaluation of Skimpole is correct, but her endorsement of confusion allows other opinions of Skimpole to exist as valid, at least theoretically.[15] Esther's confusion thus includes a realization and acceptance of other viewpoints. In this respect, Esther's narrative demonstrates the same awareness of subjectivity as Lucy Snowe's in *Villette*: both narratives suggest, in Lucy's words, that "contradictory attributes of character . . . [are] ascribed to us, according to the eye with which we are viewed" (432). Much as *Villette* deals with the question of constructed "realities" both by making Lucy the victim of the interpretations of others and by exposing her as the inventor of interpretations—consider her drug-induced observations during her night in the park, for example—*Bleak House* places Esther in the position of discovering and commenting on her own interpretations.

In telling the reader that she has withheld the real identity of Dr. John, Lucy Snowe calls attention to her unreliability and so demonstrates her self-awareness as a narrator; similarly, Esther insists on the limitations of her narrative's authority. She distinguishes between her opinions and facts, making it clear that what she writes is her own vision, not an objective "true" vision: "I write down these opinions [of Richard's inability to discipline himself], not because I believe that this or any other thing was so, because I thought so; but only because I did think so, and I want to be quite candid about all I thought and did" (204).[16] By expressly limiting the authority of her narrative to its recording of her own opinion, Esther's comment calls our attention to an assumption which would otherwise be taken for granted—that a first-person narrative provides only the narrator's interpretation of events, not necessarily their literal truth—and leads us to question whether the same assumption should be made for a third-person narrative as well. Esther's narrative exposes its seams more than once: in foreshadowing Richard's disintegration, Esther remarks, "Ah me! what Richard would have been without that blight [of the suit], I never shall know now!" (461). Since Richard is dead when Esther writes her account, no one else will know, of course, what he would have been either, but Esther's phrase "I never shall know now" has the effect of calling attention specifically to Esther's limited knowledge of alternate possibilities, not to the more "objective" truth that there *are* no other possibilities. Similarly, when she looks ahead in her narrative to consider whether Ada remains loyal in her love for Richard, Esther again limits that consideration to her own vision:

> And she [Ada] kept her word?
> I look along the road before me, where the distance already shortens and the journey's end is growing visible; and, true and good above the dead sea of the Chancery suit, and all the ashey fruit it casts ashore, *I think* I see my darling.
> (472; my emphasis)

Not only does Esther's narrative highlight the limits of narrative objectivity, it also highlights the likelihood of narrative deception. Those who criticize Esther's coyness about her love for Woodcourt presumably wouldn't be bothered if Esther were to avoid all reference to her withholding of information, as for example if she were to disclose her love unconsciously. But to hint at her feelings and say that they don't matter is for Esther to reveal herself as self-aware, as able to take a perspective on her narrative process, again, as able to uncover her narrative's seams. When Esther begins to speculate on her ambivalent feelings towards Woodcourt's mother, her decision to postpone an explanation of them suggest her realization that, for the purposes of story, *now* is not the proper narrative moment to reveal the future: "These were perplexities and contradictions that I could not account for. At least, if I could—but I shall come to all that by and by, and it is mere idleness to go on about it now" (368). Such intentional emphasis on her strategy of narrative construction—she will choose what to tell when—contrasts with the third-person narrator's silence on this matter. The third-person narrator engages in the same process of withholding information as Esther, but unlike her, does not call attention to it.[17] The most obvious example of the third-person narrator's repression of information is his silence about the real murderer of Tulkinghorn.

Of course, this strategic silence along with a presentation of misleading evidence incriminating Lady Dedlock is a conventional part of fiction, most notably detective fiction, but to acknowledge the convention is not to do away with the fact of the narrator's deception; indeed, why *do* we accept this convention? I suggest that one of the reasons why we accept the convention of silent control has to do with our corresponding belief in a third-person narrator's apparent transparency and transparency's related quality, disinterested objectivity. There is a moment in the third-person narrator's presentation when we might become aware that the narrator has been strategically silent for the purposes of his story; this moment occurs when the narrator details Mrs. Bagnet's realization that Mrs. Rouncewell is the trooper George's mother. In explaining to Mrs. Rouncewell how she arrived at the connection between the Dedlocks' housekeeper and George, Mrs. Bagnet recalls that she made the discovery during one of George's visits to the Bagnets. The conversation between George and Mrs. Bagnet which led to her enlightenment about George's mother is given to us only at the moment when Mrs. Bagnet brings Mrs. Rouncewell to visit her son in prison (655–56): at the moment when the conversation actually occurred the narrative is silent, though it is otherwise detailed about George's visit (430–31). If we are surprised at the sudden disclosure of a conversation that we had no idea had taken place, we may reflect on how useful the withholding of information is for the purposes of telling a story without telling too much of it and so losing the reader's interest in the story's plot; this withholding in order to lengthen desire is characteristic of virtually all narrative. Yet even though the third-person narrator shows his hand at this moment, he does not make the kind of self-conscious comment on his technique that Esther does—which is not to say that he should, but merely to suggest that, without Esther's narrative, we might not consider reflecting on his technique.

The effect of surprising the reader with what one knows but hasn't told is that it makes one seem authoritative; surprise helps us to realize the control which so-called omniscience affords. Esther tells us that she is aware of Richard and Ada's love from its start but withholds her knowledge from the young cousins until Ada confides in her. When Esther discloses to Ada that she has known the secret all along, they sit by the fire, and Esther has "all the talking to [her]self for a little while" (160). Revealing to Ada her knowledge of the moment of falling in love *after* the event has taken place gives to Esther the power of omniscience and the control of the talking—the narrative—between the two women. When Esther lets the reader in on her (secret) knowledge *as* the event takes place—calling attention to but not telling her love for Woodcourt—she puts us in almost the same position she occupies in relation to Ada and her (secret) love. Almost. For while Ada reveals her love to Esther unknowingly, Esther reveals and conceals her love consciously. In terms of power, this narrative action makes Esther vulnerable: she lets us know as much about her feelings as she knows herself and so precludes the possibility of surprise.

Why should Esther want to expose herself in this way when she is clearly conscious that she *is* exposing herself? The answer to this question brings us back to the issue of what Esther's narrative can and cannot, should and should not contain. Esther's practice of revealing her feelings while not revealing them suggests that she finds it difficult to fulfill the writing task she feels she has been assigned, to produce a narrative which tells the stories of others through her own experience without creating a narrative of herself. In fact, Esther produces two narratives; one is the narrative of events she is "obliged" to tell: the narrative of others. By telling this narrative, Esther associates herself with the ideal Englishwoman who is, in Mrs. Ellis's words, a "relative creature" (123), a being who is to lose her own identity by the feeling of "disinterested love" for others, showing sympathy "until she becomes identified as it were with their very being, *blends her own existence with theirs*, and makes her society essential to their highest earthly enjoyment" (160; my emphasis). Ellis's last clause reveals the paradox which occurs when a woman accomplishes the loss of her individual identity through the act of sympathy: she ends up emphasizing that identity by making her society essential to others. The Victorian woman is in a double bind—told to lose her identity, she is also told how to make it omnipresent. The narrative required of Esther is the first of Ellis's prescriptions: the result of telling the story of others through her own life should be the blending of Esther's existence with theirs. Thus, when she comes to record her own emotions, she claims that she doesn't understand them and that they do not matter anyway:

> I was so little inclined to sleep, myself, that night, that I sat up working. It would not be worth mentioning for its own sake, but I was wakeful and rather low-spirited. I don't know why. At least, I don't think I know why. At least, perhaps I do, but I don't think it matters.   (211)

Esther's low-spirits as character, we detect, are due to her pain over the impending separation from Woodcourt, who is sailing the next day. Esther as narrator hesitates to identify the cause of her depression, however, because to do so is to focus on herself, and her personal feelings are to be forgotten, because they don't "matter" to the narrative she is obliged to tell. So, too, when she mentions that Woodcourt is seven years older than she is, she comments, "Not that I need mention it, for it hardly seems to belong to anything" (214). Indeed, as she remembers the events of the past, the narrating Esther sees that her past focus on Woodcourt's eligibility for marriage is important only to herself, and the story of herself does not belong in her narrative. When she comments on her past fear of betraying her mother through her mere existence, Esther claims that her emotions "matter little" that she "can relate little of [her]self which is not a story of goodness and generosity in others" (521). Once again, the narrative of herself is to be a story of others; her self and her emotions—past and present—matter little.

And yet, as Esther discovers, she "can't be kept out" of her narrative even though she "mean[s] all the time to write about other people." Esther's discovery highlights the paradox which Ellis's description of the true Englishwoman wets up: simply by writing about her experience of others and her sympathy with their feelings, Esther asserts her own identity. This assertion, we realize, is Esther's second narrative, the narrative George Brimley claims would not be told if Esther were the ideal woman. Mrs. Ellis suggests that if women "are endowed only with such faculties, as render them striking and distinguished in themselves, without the faculty of instrumentality, they are only as dead letters in the volume of human life, filling what would otherwise be a blank space, but doing nothing more" (123). Esther's narrative suggests, on the other hand, that in writing about her existence, she makes herself more than a dead letter in a blank space. Whether he knew it or not, Dickens in his creation of Esther holds up for inspection one of the nineteenth-century paradoxes about woman's identity. Even if he did not consciously consider that Esther's narrative explodes her culture's attempt to define the ideal woman, he portrays his understanding of Esther's paradoxical position.

Dickens reveals Esther's ''terror of [her]self'' stemming from the fact of her existence even though she believes she was not meant to live: "I was so confused and shaken, as to be possessed by a belief that it was right, and had been intended, that I should die in my birth; and that it was wrong, and not intended, that I should be then alive" (453). In Esther's awareness of her existence and of the impact which her existence has had on the lives of others, she finds her significance. In imagining Esther as a bastard child who is never publicly acknowledged by her parents and who nevertheless makes her presence oppressively felt in her mother's life at least,[18] Dickens captures the sense of a woman's position in Victorian England: expected to be a nonself, the ideal woman according to the definition nevertheless finds her identity in the pursuit of selflessness.

In highlighting the conflicting demands made upon Esther as a woman writer to disappear from her story and to tell her story, Esther's narrative also calls attention to the participation of the narrator in the construction of a story's meaning; that is, it calls attention to the assumed possibility of narratorial transparency as only a fiction. When we turn to the third-person narrative with Esther's discoveries about the impossibility of transparency in mind, we find that the third-person narrator conveys an assumption about his disinterestedness while he in actuality shapes our interpretation of the events he presents through his narrative choices. Esther is frequently aware herself of the effect of her narrative practices and her reader's response to them; the third-person narrator is seemingly oblivious of both. In this respect, the third-person narrator resembles David Copperfield as narrator: both present their accounts with a sense of assurance that comes from an unawareness of or a refusal to acknowledge any other interpretation of events than those they endorse, and both use particular strategies of silence and suppression, without calling attention to them, to maintain their control over interpretation.[19] For this reason, those commentators who feel that the third-person narrative represents a masculine voice are indeed sensing something about the narrative which finds its correspondence in masculine first-person narratives such as *David Copperfield* and Charlotte Brontë's *The Professor.*[20] The difference between masculine and feminine narratives, at least in Dickens, is epitomized, interestingly enough, by a reference Esther makes to another life-narrative contained in *Bleak House*, though only by allusion. She concludes her narrative of Harold Skimpole by telling us of Skimpole's posthumous autobiography:

> He . . . left a diary behind him, with letters and other materials towards his Life; which was published, and which showed him to have been the victim of a combination on the part of mankind against an amiable child. It was considered very pleasant reading, but I never read more of it myself than the sentence on which I chanced to light on opening the book. It was this. "Jarndyce, in common with most other men I have known, is the Incarnation of Selfishness." (729)

Skimpole's autobiography appears to have many of the components of other masculine autobiographies like *David Copperfield, The Professor,* and even *The Prelude*: Skimpole as the center of a world which conspires to victimize him embodies the egotistical perspective of David Copperfield, William Crimsworth, and Wordsworth's persona; and his insistence on monolithic interpretation—"Jarndyce . . . *is* the Incarnation of Selfishness"—parallels the inability or unwillingness to see alternate interpretations that characterizes the narratives of David and Crimsworth.[21] Skimpole's text can be seen as a parody, or at least a monstrous exaggeration, of an autobiographical narrative; seen in this light, it suggests that Dickens consciously or unconsciously realizes the tendency of autobiographies—his own autobiographical fragment included—to distort what they represent and perhaps explains why Dickens would be interested in experimenting with perspective and authority in *Bleak House.*[22]

Skimpole's story of his Life could be Esther's as well: she, too, might lay claim to the identity of a powerless child victimized by her world. In fact, Esther does allude to a conspiracy against her, but calls it " 'the general conspiracy to keep [her] in a good humour' " (290). But while Skimpole's interpretation of his life might be Esther's, his narrative methods are very different. Skimpole's apparent technique is to close down the process of interpretation by excluding perspectives other than his own; Esther's highlighted technique is to insist on the possibility of other interpretations, calling attention to her narrative as containing her opinions only, and not incontrovertible facts. Ironically, in the fictional world of *Bleak House*, Skimpole's Life is considered "very pleasant reading" while in the "real world" of *Bleak House* criticism, Esther's narrative has been denigrated and misunderstood. In fact, it is *un*pleasant reading for those who do not like their assumptions about narrative disturbed.

Disturbing and unsettling us seems, however, to be what Dickens had in mind in his creation of *Bleak House* as a whole. And the readings of Esther's narrative and its "coyness" reveal more, perhaps, about critical assumptions than about Esther herself. The last, frequently-cited example of Esther's violation of narrative decorum is her unwillingness to complete her final sentence:

> I know that my dearest little pets are very pretty, and that my darling is very beautiful, and that my husband is very handsome, and that my guardian has the brightest and most benevolent face that ever was seen; and that they can very well do without much beauty in me—even supposing—   (770)

It is interesting that, for the first time, Esther is noticibly assertive about her "interpretation"—she says she *knows* that those she loves are good-looking. But her final clause returns her narrative to the ambiguity which is characteristic of it: she asserts by non-assertion her own beauty and thus remains true to her double narrative of other and self. The effect of this final open-end-edness, for many critics, is that it unsatisfactorily resolves the problems that the novel as a whole raises. Marianna Torgovnick's comments are represen-tative:

> To end with Esther as narrator need not have been a fault in the novel, had Dickens allowed her to speak with the authority gained by her in the text after the death of her mother. Readers could excuse Esther's early sentimentality and coyness as a convention of retrospective first-person narration: such narratives often record things as they seemed to the narrator *at the time*, and reflect the narrator's growth during the novel. But such a narrative perspective demands that Esther tell the end of the novel with the maturity and depth shown during the Lady Dedlock sequence. . . . In not allowing Esther to continue her growth into a narrator capable of effectively summing-up the novel, Dickens settles for an ending that simply does not match the book's most successful passages.
>
> (55–56)[23]

Torgovnick and others make two implicit assumptions, first, that there must *be* a solution to the problems *Bleak House* raises and that it is the duty of the last chapter to provide an answer, if an answer has not been provided ear-lier—this is an assumption of closure—and second, that Esther's narrative should take on authority as she writes—this is an assumption, perhaps con-fined to the *Bildungsroman*, about narrative progress.[24] To take the second of these assumptions first, the criticism of Dickens' choice of concluding with Esther is that she should be allowed to speak with more authority. But as I have been trying to demonstrate, Esther's narrative as constructed by Dickens works to reveal the limitations of narrative authority—an authority tacitly assumed by the convention of omniscient narration—by emphasizing that, despite the assumption of authority, the process of interpretation is ambiguous and self-generated. This discovery contained in Esther's narrative is paralleled by the legal progress of Jarndyce and Jarndyce: when this particular law-suit is discussed, "no two Chancery lawyers can talk about it for five minutes, without coming to a total disagreement as to all the premises" (8). Esther's narrative and conclusion avoid assuming the fiction of definitive meaning. To return to the first assumption about Esther's duty as narrator, it might be helpful to ponder something which D. A. Miller notes in his discussion of the ideology of closure in *Mansfield Park*:

> Essentially, the ideology is one of settlement. Socially, it assumes that marriage is the permanent and proper means of recognition, the defining compact. Cogni-tively, it assumes that character can be known in all its essentials, and morally, that it can be pinned down on such knowledge. Linguistically, it assumes that adequate formulations are available to settle whatever needs to be formulated. It is evident that novelistic closure confirms each of these assumptions, institut-ing what is virtually an ideological paradise.
>
> (*Narrative and Its Discontents* 50)

If we look at Esther's conclusion in the light of Miller's comments, we note immediately that her final sentences work to undo any movement toward closure and its associations. Esther might seem to have achieved a defined identity in her marriage to Woodcourt—she is called "the doctor's wife" (769)—but her last sentence suggests that she declines to recognize herself definitively: told that she is pretty, Esther counters, "I did not know that; I am not certain that I know it now" (770). Her uncertainty and open-endedness suggests that her character at least cannot be known in all its essentials, nor morally pinned down. She cannot find an adequate linguistic formulation to settle things and, indeed, leaves her final sentence incomplete. The effect of her unconventional ending is to subvert the ideology of closure typical of the traditional novel as described by Miller along the lines of the "ambiguity" he discusses in George Eliot's *Middlemarch* or even along the lines of the "counterfinality" he claims is characteristic of Stendhal.[25] Esther's ambiguous conclusion refuses to participate in the nineteenth-century fiction of authoritative interpretation; like a "faulty" camera lens, it refuses to focus the events of the novel for us and, indeed, implicitly reminds us that our wish for such a focusing suggests our own complicity in the maintenance of a kind of Tulkinghornesque social authority.

When Dickens chose to write a portion of his novel in the voice of a woman, he discovered a narrative voice that would allow him to explore and expose narrative conventions. The feminine narrator, because of the paradoxical identities given to her as a woman in Victorian culture, may be given a narrative which is able to suggest the fictitiousness of social definition, of essential identity, of authoritative interpretation. In his decision to write as a woman, Dickens was enabled to consider the complex relationship among narrative, authority, and uncertainty. Here in *Bleak House* is Dickens's engagement—conscious or unconscious—with the limitations of what Henry James will later call "the mere muffled majesty of irresponsible 'authorship' " (20). When we read Esther's narrative, we, too, are enabled to reconsider the conventions we use to read omniscient narratives, such as the way we accord their narrators transparency, objectivity and, consequently, power. We are also forced to confront our frequently unacknowledged conflation of such "powerful" objectivity with a masculine writing style. In her refusal, thus, to assume the authority of an omniscient narrator, Esther as imagined by Dickens ends up doing something "spicy" after all.

NOTES

1. Merritt Moseley provides a useful survey of critical opinions on Dickens' creation of Esther since the first appearance of *Bleak House* (37). See also Slater, 255–56, 431.

2. Other reviewers of *Bleak House* when it first appeared also commented on the unreality of Esther Summerson, implying that such a angelic woman as she is reputed to be is inconceivable as a narrator: see Henry Fothergill Chorley's review in the *Athenaeum*, 17 September 1853, 1087–88, and an unsigned review in *Bentley's Miscellany*, October 1853, xxxiv, 372–74. Excerpts from both reviews may be found in Collins, 277 and 289.

3. For considerations of the way Dickens's creation of Esther and her narration reflects conventional Victorian social codes for women, see Senf, Kennedy, and Killian.

4. See Graver. Graver concedes that, "while Dickens had the genius to perceive that indirection is a strategy characteristic of women's writing, . . . [he] ultimately uses Esther's obliqueness not to subvert Victorian womanly ideals but to celebrate a dutifully willed acceptance of them'' (4). I do not deny that Dickens ends up reinscribing his culture's conventional view of women in Esther's narrative; however, as I hope to demonstrate, he does subvert conventional assumptions about narrative through his creation of a woman's voice.

5. Wilt hypothesizes that the third-person narrator is a "sister voice'' in the Cassandra vein to Esther's feminine voice (285). Wilt doesn't do more than allude to this hypothesis without developing an argument to support it. For reasons that will become clear as this essay proceeds, I disagree with Wilt's contention that the third-person narrator is feminine—and, more specifically, with her contention that the third-person narrator is a Cassandra figure—though I feel that she, like Newsom, is right to sense that there is a similarity between the two narrators beyond the matter of thematic concerns, and I acknowledge my indebtedness to her study.

6. E. M. Forster directly identifies the omniscient narrator with Dickens himself (79); later critics, like Harvey, are more subtle in making such an identification. Edgar Johnson complains about Esther's coyness and hypocrisy (766) but, in discussing the passage where the omniscient narrator describes the death of Krook, claims that "it is Dickens speaking with the voice of prophecy'' (782). See also Engel; Engel discusses Dickens' social voice in *Bleak House* with reference primarily to the omniscient narrator's descriptions (117–26). When he mentions Esther's narrative, he does so only to dismiss its significance *as* narrative: "Esther has a schematic place in the novel by being responsible'' (125). In other words, Esther's narrative is subsumed under the larger "social vision'' of the novel. More recently, Richard T. Gaughan has reinscribed this critical tendency to undermine Esther's personal vision, even though purportedly offering a defense of it: while he acknowledges the role that Esther's narrative plays as "the missing center of the third-person narrator's story'' (80), he also suggests that Esther "needs the third-person narrator's narrative as ballast'' (92).

7. Specifically, I have in mind the moment in *Villette* when Lucy informs the reader that she has been withholding information about the real identity of Dr. John. This kind of withholding leads some readers of *Villette* to criticize Lucy for her "coyness''; their irritation is, I would suggest, due to a kind of discomfort at being made aware of a reader's normally unconscious expectations for narrative.

8. Though the context of her discussion is here different from mine, Wilt makes an apt observation on masculine narratives: "David's and Pip's purpose in the writing, according to Dickens' narrative conceit, is first and last self-reflexive; they write to confess, to discover, to exorcise, apparently, but above all to rekindle emotions and to experience again their lives, the process by which they came to be" (303–04).

9. Newsom insightfully points out Esther's awareness of the third-person narrator and the difficulties this awareness causes for considerations of point-of-view (14–15).

10. For simplicity of reference and because I hope to demonstrate that the third-person narrator is, indeed, masculine, I will use the masculine pronoun in connection with this narrator.

11. That we are meant to see the third-person narrator's pretense of ignorance about the future *as* a pretense can be seen in the implicit distinction the narrator draws between his sphere of knowledge and the sphere belonging to the characters he describes. On the one hand, he comments ironically, perhaps condescendingly, on "the fashionable intelligence—which, like the fiend, is omniscient of the past and present, but not the future" (12). On the other hand, the third-person narrator himself possesses, as Jonathan Arac notes, the vision of "Ranke's God," to whom "all is immediate" (122). Arac compares the portion of *Bleak House* narrated by the omniscient narrator to Carlyle's *French Revolution*: in both works, the writers "combined the linear aspects of narrative with the solidity of completed significance" (122). The third-person narrator, thus, "knows" only the present, but it is a present more properly described as an eternal present, in which the temporal future is included.

12. Jaffe alludes to J. Hillis Miller's notion of the omniscient narrator as "a collective mind" (J. H. Miller 63). Jaffe's reference to an understanding of omniscience as "a stable body of knowledge" is reflected in Miller's argument that most Victorian novelists "place themselves within the mind of the community, or at least within the mind of that part of the community which most interests them. This means for most of the Victorian novelists the mind of the middle and upper classes. . . . The reader of a Victorian novel in his turn is invited by the words of the narrator to enter into complicity with a collective mind which pre-exists the first words of the novel and will continue when they end, though without the novel it might remain invisible" (67). In Miller's argument, the assumption is that, for Victorian novelists, the community mind always has held and always will hold the same concepts of what is important or what is "real." Miller doesn't demonstrate *how* the reader is made to acknowledge the collective knowledge (limited by class) which a Victorian narrator/author presumably displays; Jaffe, however, does attempt to analyze this narrative procedure in her article. Following the publication of this article—and after I had written the original version of this study of narrative voice in *Bleak House*—Jaffe published an extended study of omniscience in Dickens in which she quite correctly argues that "omniscience is not so much evidence for the possession of knowledge as an emphatic display of knowledge, a display, precisely, of what is not being taken for granted" (*Vanishing Points* 6). Jaffe's book also contains a chapter on *Bleak House* which,

while concerned with similar issues, takes a different directions from my own work, as I hope to make clear below.

13. The "invisible" control achieved by Tulkinghorn's silence anticipates, on the one hand, Michel Foucault's understanding of the way in which Benthamite disciplinary institutions work and provides an example, on the other, of D. A. Miller's understanding of the narrator in the nineteenth-century novel in *The Novel and the Police*, 24. I realize that my discussion of narrative and authority intersects with recent work on these topics, such as Miller's and Jaffe's. I am less concerned, however, with the way in which nineteenth-century narrative was a means to support specific social practice(s) than I am with the way in which particular narrative strategies both inscribe gender difference and reinforce assumptions of power and powerlessness associated *with* such difference. Further, I am concerned to show how the position of the feminine narrator serves to expose the fiction which upheld (and, in some cases, still maintains) a connection between critical "objectivity" or disinterestedness, on the one hand, and authority, on the other.

14. For other examples of the third-person narrator's coyness—which, however, are not usually registered as "coy"—note his propensity for leading questions which inform us that he knows the answer to the question but chooses momentarily to withhold the information from the reader; as for example in his speculating on what the connection may be between "the place in Lincolnshire, the house in town, the Mercury in powder, and the whereabout of Jo the outlaw with the broom" (197) or in his rhetorical question about the existence of Dandyism at Chesney Wold (144). A more obvious example of the way in which the third-person narrator tantalizes us with what he knows but won't tell is his comment, both to the reader and, indirectly, to Tulkinghorn, on the night of Tulkinghorn's murder. Tulkinghorn consults a clock to verify his watch's time: "If it said now, 'don't go home!' What a famous clock, hereafter, if it said to-night of all the nights that it has counted off, to this old man of all the young and old men who have ever stood before it, 'don't go home!' " (582).

15. Compare also Esther's confusion about Mr. Turveydrop. She finds it difficult to reconcile her distaste for his posturing to the respect in which Caddy and Prince hold him and so decides to keep her opinion to herself and to let the matter remain in confusion (293–94).

16. Sawicki also calls attention to this statement and advances a similar interpretation of it (213).

17. This is not to say that Esther *always* calls attention to her withholding of information. As with all first-person narrators, there are many places in which we as readers are aware of a textual suggestion that Esther is unconsciously suppressing her feelings—for example, her feelings of anger toward her mother.

18. Zwerdling provides an interpretation of Esther as psychologically damaged by her experiences in order to justify her so-called "coyness" as narrator.

19. It has become a truism in *David Copperfield* criticism that David shapes his autobiography so as to demonstrate that he is "the hero of [his] life," while consciously or unconsciously exonerating himself from blame in the seduction of little Emily and the death of Dora, to note two conspicuous examples. David as narrator is complacent in his interpretation of himself as hero—it is we the readers

who may find David as character to be less a hero than, in retrospect, he wants us to believe.

20. Because of the parallels between the strategies of control used by the masculine first-person narrators and the strategies used by the third-person narrator of *Bleak House* and because of the cultural narratives about masculinity and its authority, to which these fictional narratives may be compared, Wilt's suggestion that the third-person narrator is a Cassandra figure, a "sister voice" to Esther as narrator, can only be seen as a bit of wishful twentieth-century feminist projection onto a nineteenth-century text. To the culture in which it was produced, a narrator who voices, in Wilt's terms, "the *certainties* of the Victorian Prophetic Sublime" (285; my emphasis) could only be seen as masculine. Only a masculine narrator would be seen as possessing the social power to address "your Majesty," "my lords and gentlemen," and "Right Reverends and Wrong Reverends of every order," as the third-person narrator of *Bleak House* does (572).

21. Thus, it should be clear that when I call David Copperfield and William Crimsworth "masculine autobiographers," I refer to their attitudes and practices as narrators, not to their experiences as characters. It is certainly possible to read David and Crimsworth as feminine characters, as do several interpreters of the novels in which each appears.

22. Dickens' fascination with the issue of narrative authority, prior to his writing of *Bleak House*, is also evident in his correspondence with John Forster in October 1849, when he began sketching out plans for what was to become *Household Words*. As he considered the kind of narrative voice which would bind together the periodical's discussion of various subjects, he imagined "a certain SHADOW, which may go into any place, by sunlight, moonlight, starlight, firelight, candlelight . . . and be supposed to be cognizant of everything. . . . I want him to loom as a fanciful thing all over London." Edgar Johnson cites Dickens' correspondence in his biography of Dickens; he also notes that "Forster robustly poohpoohed this insubstantial Shadow, and Dickens gave it up in the end" (701). Clearly Dickens did *not* give up the idea: he transformed his "Shadow" into the third-person narrator in *Bleak House*.

23. See also Hardy, 13, cited by Torgovnick.

24. This notion informs Ian Ousby's discussion of *Bleak House* and leads him to miss entirely the uncertainty of Esther's ending: "At the end of the book . . . Esther . . . has become a testament to the power of the individual to achieve a clear-sightedness which is at once literal and metaphorical" (389).

25. See Miller's chapters on George Eliot and Stendhal, in particular pages 195, 201, and 267–68.

Works Cited

Arac, Jonathan. *Comissioned Spirits: The Shaping of Social Motion in Dickens, Carlyle, Melville, and Hawthorne.* New Brunswick, NJ: Rutgers UP, 1979.

Bal, Mieke. "The Narrating and the Focalizing: A Theory of the Agents in Narrative." *Style* 17 (1983): 234–69.

Blain, Virginia. "Double Vision and the Double Standard in *Bleak House*: A Feminist Perspective." *Literature and History* 11 (1985): 31–46.

[Brimley George]. Review of *Bleak House*. *The Spectator*, 24 September 1853, xxvi, 923–25.

Brontë, Charlotte. *Villette*. Oxford: Clarendon Press, 1984.

[Chorley, Henry Fothergill]. Review of *Bleak House*. *Athenaeum*, 17 September 1853, 1087–88.

Collins, Philip, ed. *Dickens: The Critical Heritage*. New York: Barnes & Noble, 1971.

Dickens, Charles. *Bleak House*. New York & London: W. W. Norton & Co., 1977.

Dollimore, Jonathan. *Sexual Dissidence: Augustine to Wilde, Freud to Foucault*. Oxford: Oxford UP, 1991.

Ellis, Sarah Stickney. *The Women of England, Their Social Duties and Domestic Habits*. New York: D. Appleton, 1839.

Engel, Monroe. *The Maturity of Dickens*. Cambridge: Harvard UP, 1959.

Flaubert, Gustave. *The Letters of Gustave Flaubert, 1830–1857*. Ed. and trans. Francis Steegmuller. 2 vols. Cambridge: Harvard UP, 1980–82.

Forster, E. M. *Aspects of the Novel*. New York & London: HBJ, 1955; orig. publ. 1927.

Foucault, Michel. *Discipline and Punish*. Trans. Alan Sheridan. New York: Vintage, 1979.

Gaughan, Richard T. " 'Their Places are a Blank': The Two Narrators in *Bleak House*." *Dickens Studies Annual* 21 (1992): 79–96.

Graver, Suzanne. "Writing in a 'Womanly' Way and the Double Vision of *Bleak House*." *Dickens Quarterly* 4, 1 (March 1987): 3–15.

Hardy, Barbara. *The Moral Art of Dickens*. New York: Oxford UP, 1970.

Harvey, W. J. *Character in the Novel*. London: Chatto & Windus, 1965.

Jaffe, Audrey. "Omniscience in *Our Mutual Friend*: On Taking the Reader by Surprise." *Journal of Narrative Technique* 17 (1987): 91–101.

———. *Vanishing Points: Dickens, Narrative, and the Subject of Omniscience*. Berkeley & Los Angeles: U of California P, 1991.

James, Henry. Preface to *The Golden Bowl*. New York: Penguin Books, 1985.

Johnson, Edgar. *Charles Dickens: His Tragedy and Triumph.* New York: Simon & Schuster, 1952.

Kearns, Michael S. " 'But I cried very much': Esther Summerson as Narrator." *Dickens Quarterly* 1 (1984): 121–29.

Kennedy, Valerie. *"Bleak House*: More Trouble with Esther?" *Journal of Women's Studies in Literature* 1 (1979): 330–47.

Killian, Crawford. "In Defense of Esther Summerson." *Dalhousie Review* 54 (1974): 318–28.

Meckier, Jerome. "Double Vision Versus Double Logic, Part One." *Dickens Studies Newsletter* 14 (1983): 14–21.

Miller, D. A. *Narrative and Its Discontents: Problems of Closure in the Traditional Novel.* Princeton: Princeton UP, 1981.

———. *The Novel and the Police.* Berkeley and Los Angeles: U of California P, 1987.

Miller, J. Hillis. *The Form of Victorian Fiction: Thackeray, Dickens, Trollope, George Eliot, Meredith, and Hardy.* Notre Dame & London: U of Notre Dame P, 1968.

Moseley, Merritt. "The Ontology of Esther's Narrative in *Bleak House*." *South Atlantic Review* 50, 2 (1985): 35–46.

Newsom, Robert. *Dickens on the Romantic Side of Familiar Things: Bleak House and the Novel Tradition.* New York: Columbia UP, 1977.

Ousby, Ian. "The Broken Glass: Vision and Comprehension in *Bleak House*." *Nineteenth-Century Fiction* 29 (1975): 381–92.

Review of *Bleak House. Bentley's Miscellany*, October 1853, xxxiv, 372–74.

Sawicki, Joseph. " 'The Mere Truth Won't Do': Esther as Narrator in *Bleak House.*" *Journal of Narrative Technique* 17 (1987): 209–24.

Senf, Carol A. *"Bleak House*: Dickens, Esther, and the A[n]drogynous Mind." *Victorian Newsletter* 44 (1983): 21–27.

Slater, Michael. *Dickens and Women.* London: J.M. Dent, 1983.

Torgovnick, Marianna. *Closure in the Novel.* Princeton: Princeton UP, 1981.

Wilt, Judith. "Confusion and Consciousness in Dickens's Esther." *Nineteenth-Century Fiction* 32 (1977): 285–309.

Zwerdling, Alex. "Esther Summerson Rehabilitated." *PMLA* 88 (1973): 429–39.

The Hat, the Hook, the Eyes, the Teeth: Captain Cuttle, Mr. Carker, and Literacy

Gillian Gane

Literacy is, if nothing else, the condition of postindustrialism.
—J. Elspeth Stuckey, *The Violence of Literacy* (19)

It is a typical critical move to find in Dickens' *Dombey and Son* oppositions between the House of Dombey and the little community of the Wooden Midshipman. Glossing over distinctions of detail, a broad view is that at one pole stand the House of Dombey and Son, the railway, mechanical clock time, unfeeling coldness, and the new age of mercantile capitalism (or, in a variation, the rigid masculinist values of the Firm); arrayed against this constellation of values stand the Wooden Midshipman, the ocean, natural rhythms, human warmth, and old-fashioned values (or, variously, the more feminine values of a wet and melting world).[1]

I explore here another opposition that similarly sets a new world against an old and the powerful against the powerless. Mr. Dombey himself figures only peripherally in my analysis, which focuses instead on Mr. Carker, the manager of Dombey and Son, and Captain Cuttle, who holds a similar position at the Wooden Midshipman, managing the store on Sol Gills's behalf during his long absence. The opposition at issue is the contrast between the modes of literacy of these two men. They stand in radically different relations to the world: Mr. Carker is a New Man exercising new modes of power that prefigure our own age, while Captain Cuttle is the relic of a bygone age of innocence—and literacy, broadly defined, is central to the difference between them. The Captain retains many of the habits of mind of an oral culture and is constrained rather than empowered by his limited literacy; he reads the world as ineptly as he reads the printed word, but he himself is a text easily read by others. Mr. Carker, by contrast, is a consummate reader of both texts and people; his readings of others are a source of power and his own speech is a means of manipulation, while he himself remains apparently impenetrable.

I examine, in turn, the two men's dealings with actual texts; their models of knowledge; the bodily correlates of their literacy; their speech; their modes of reading the world—and their own readability; finally, in analysing the novel's ending I find that Mr. Carker's downfall reveals him to be a man ahead of his times, a prophet of postmodernism.

READING TEXTS

Captain Cuttle reads with difficulty. He struggles even to decode in his prayer book what must be the familiar words of "forms of prayer appointed to be used at sea . . . . the good Captain being a mighty slow, gruff reader, and frequently stopping at a hard word to give himself such encouragement as 'Now, my lad! With a will!' or, 'Steady, Ed'ard Cuttle, steady!' which had a great effect in helping him out of any difficulty" (49:780).[2] When he turns to an unfamiliar text, his difficulties are compounded. He has struggled for years with a "prodigious volume . . . , five lines of which utterly confounded him at any time, insomuch that he had not yet ascertained of what subject it treated" (50:802).

Against these glimpses of Captain Cuttle reading we may set a picture of Mr. Carker reading business correspondence in the offices of Dombey and Son. He reads letters in various languages with assurance: "If there had been anything in the offices of Dombey and Son that he could *not* read, there would have been a card wanting in the pack." He reads "almost at a glance," except for one letter that he sets aside for close attention. As he reads he makes notes ("memoranda and references") and organizes the letters into piles— "dealing, and sorting, and pondering by turns." He resembles "a player at cards," "master of all the strong and weak points of the game," one "who was crafty to find out what the other players held, and who never betrayed his own hand"(22:372–73).

This is the only time we see Mr. Carker engaged with texts, unless we count his studying the company's accounts in Chapter 46. It is, however, enough to demonstrate that his position and practice as a reader are radically different from Captain Cuttle's. Where Captain Cuttle struggles to decode texts and sometimes loses the battle, Carker is master of what he reads: he is the one in authority over the text, focusing selectively on what is most important to him, and organizing the information he reads so that he can make use of it for his own purposes. If there is a sense of combat here, it is a combat Mr. Carker takes pleasure in, a game. In pedagogical terms, he is what teachers urge students to be, a strong reader, an active maker of meaning.

We do learn that "there is no want of books" (33:553) in Mr. Carker's home, although it is suggested that his books, like the pictures on his walls, are of questionable moral value ("Is it that the prints and pictures . . . are of one voluptuous cast—mere shows of form and colour—and no more? Is it that the books have all their gold outside, and that the titles of the greater part qualify them to be companions of the prints and pictures?" [33:554]).[3] He presumably reads for pleasure as well as for utilitarian business purposes, even if he does not do so in our presence.

We learn much more about Captain Cuttle's reading, partly because it is so intermeshed with his speech. Walter Ong reminds us that until well into the nineteenth century literacy was still closely associated with oratory, as attested by the enormous popularity of Dickens' own public readings of his works on both sides of the Atlantic. People read aloud; they memorized texts for public recitation in elocution contests; much of schooling consisted of reciting lessons memorized verbatim from books. For many, "reading" meant reading *aloud*, converting written words into spoken ones. When Captain Cuttle reads, he typically reads aloud, and he has indeed committed to memory a considerable portion of what he has read. He has Rob the Grinder read aloud to him for an hour every evening (39:629), and before he attends the wedding of Mr. Dombey and Edith Granger he calls on Rob to read him the marriage service (31:519). Every Sunday night the Captain himself reads aloud to the yawning Rob "a certain Divine Sermon once delivered on a Mount," although he knows it by heart, for "he was accustomed to quote the text, without book, after his own manner" (39:629). He also memorizes the entire text of the letter Sol Gills left for him, as he demonstrates in Chapter 56 (894).

Captain Cuttle's world is one in which books play a significant part, but it is simultaneously an intensely oral world. For the Captain, words read in texts are destined to be uttered aloud—and at times the text-to-speech circuit seems to bypass understanding: the utterance of texts is more important than their comprehension. His speech is full of nautical terms and memorized quotations, formulas, and set expressions typical of what Ong has called primary oral cultures. Yet in Captain Cuttle's world it is the written word rather than oral tradition that is the source of authority—and of his cherished quotations, as he himself takes pains to remind us; he tags these quotations with attributions to their putative sources and refers repeatedly to their physical locations in books: "Overhaul your catechism till you find that passage, and when found turn the leaf down" is a typical adjuration (4:97).

The highly literate Mr. Carker is only once observed reading and never refers to texts he has read, while the semiliterate Captain reads frequently and even more frequently invokes the authority of texts. Unlike Mr. Carker, Captain Cuttle has a profound faith in the truth and authority of the written word:

"as the Captain implicitly believed that all books were true, he accumulated . . . many remarkable facts''(36:629). He has no doubt of the accuracy of the newspaper report of the loss of the *Son and Heir* with Walter aboard, declaring that ''this here fatal news is too correct. They don't romance, you see, on such pints. It's entered on the ship's log, and that's the truest book as a man can write''(32:546). Explaining his responsibility for the Wooden Midshipman, he invokes the authority of the written word: Sol Gills ''has left me in charge by a piece of writing,'' he explains to Toots (32:541).

This faith in texts is connected to the Captain's sense of their physical properties. The ''prodigious volume'' he likes to read on Sundays was bought purely on the basis of its size, ''for he made it a point of duty to read none but very large books on a Sunday, as having a more staid appearance'' (50:802). His fetishistic belief in the written word extends beyond actual texts: he perceives speech as made up of letters, telling Bunsby that the ''opinion'' he gave ''has come true, every *letter* on it'' (39:638; emphasis added). And when Rob has difficulty in understanding the instruction to ''stand off and on,'' the Captain sees this as a deficiency in literacy: '' 'Here's a smart lad for you!' cried the Captain, eyeing him sternly, 'as don't know his own native alphabet!' '' (32:535). The written alphabet here stands for language in general—and Captain Cuttle seems to believe that the alphabet is uniquely English.

As will become clear in examining Captain Cuttle's quotations, he remains essentially untouched by most of what he reads; his understanding is often so garbled that the original text is barely recognizable. A few texts, however, do shape his worldview strongly. Folklore and song offer him models for young Walter's future, models specifically of upward mobility by means of marriage to the master's daughter. The legend of Dick Whittington is frequently invoked at the Wooden Midshipman, and the Captain buys a ballad which tells of ''the nuptials of a promising young coal-whipper with a certain 'lovely Peg,' the accomplished daughter of the master and part-owner of a Newcastle colliery,'' in which he ''descried a profound metaphysical bearing on the case of Walter and Florence'' (9:172). Both Sol and Walter himself indulge in the pleasant fantasy that Walter is destined to marry Florence Dombey, but they realize that it is highly unrealistic; the Captain, however, comes increasingly to see the marriage as a done deal.

Later, at his lowest point, abandoned even by Rob the Grinder on the heels of Walter and Sol, the Captain's perceptions of his isolation are shaped by images from *Robinson Crusoe*. Having ''felt almost as kindly towards the boy [Rob] as if they had been shipwrecked and cast upon a desert place together,'' he is now ''feeling as lonely as Robinson Crusoe'' (39:636). He dons his glazed hat every morning ''with the solitary air of Crusoe finishing his toilet with his goat-skin cap,'' and ''the savage tribe, MacStinger'' figures in his mind as equivalent to Crusoe's ''cannibals''(637).

Robinson Crusoe was "by far the most common shipwreck narrative" of the day, available in many cheap retellings, as William Palmer tells us, "a sort of universal furnishing of the Victorian consciousness, like ornamental table legs and lace antimacassars" (50); the legend of Dick Whittington must have been at least as well known among Londoners, and fairy tales of marriage into the ruling class are ubiquitous. It is likely that even people who couldn't read at all were familiar with these stories, so their influence on the Captain's thinking is no great tribute to his literacy.

MODELS OF KNOWLEDGE: CARGO AND CAPITAL

Captain Cuttle reifies words: "I never wanted two or three words in my life that I didn't know where to lay my hands upon 'em," he boasts to Sol Gills, explaining, "It comes of not wasting language as some do," and goes on immediately to reflect that he should "increase his store" (4:97). He sees himself as accumulating a *store* of words, *laying hands* on them, not *wasting* them. His thinking is a parody of the capitalist ethic of acquisition; in the context of literacy and learning, it evokes the banking model of education that Paulo Freire has criticized, in which students are seen as empty receptacles to be filled with deposits of static knowledge.

In fact the Captain sees all knowledge as property to be acquired and stored. Sol Gills, he declares, "waving his hook toward the stock-in-trade" of his friend's shop, is "chockful of science"(4:98), an encomium repeated several times later in the book (10:196; 23:410; twice on 56:892). "Science" is represented in the Captain's mind by the nautical instruments in the store: like the store, Sol is "chockful" of this materialized knowledge, and the full store *is* the very definition of knowledge. "Captain Cuttle's reverence for the stock of instruments was profound," we are told, and "his philosophy knew little or no distinction between trading in it and inventing it" (98); he has essentially no concept of invention—of scientific instruments, of knowledge, or of discourse: all exist as prefabricated objects: possession is all.

"Trading," furthermore, is beside the point: nothing is ever sold at the Wooden Midshipman over the entire course of the book. The stock is so snugly stored that moving it sounds difficult: "Everything was jammed into the tightest cases, fitted into the narrowest corners, fenced up behind the most impertinent cushions, and screwed into the acutest angles, to prevent its philosophical composure from being disturbed by the rolling of the sea" (4:88). Citing a passage that includes this sentence, David Musselwhite remarks on the "commodification and fetishization" at work: "the objects have lost all use value and assumed no more than a mere curio value for would-be collectors. There is a strong sense that the whole collection of instruments has become insulated and cocooned, muffled and displaced by their packaging, cases and wrappings'' (173). Musselwhite compares this passage unfavorably with a description of a marine-broker's store in *Sketches by Boz*, where we learn that much of the stock has been pawned or sold by impoverished sailors; however, not only does the Wooden Midshipman's merchandise have no history of use value, but it is never sold (a point Musselwhite does not make) that is, it has neither use value nor even exchange value as a commodity. Only Sol and the Captain value even its "curio value."

Sol Gills owns the shop, but Captain Cuttle in a sense *is* the Wooden Midshipman, "an animated version of the Wooden Midshipman over the shop he so often inhabits," as Northrop Frye puts it (79). The connection extends beyond his wooden appearance: as the stock sits unused on the shelves of the shop, so Captain Cuttle hoards words which are used for display rather than communication. If the emphasis on accumulation and possession is a symptom of capitalist society, this is an oddly baulked and perverted capitalism, without the crucial element of exchange.

David Trotter has pointed to the centrality of the concept of *circulation* in the eighteenth and nineteenth centuries, and to its influence on Dickens after he encountered the discourse of sanitary reform in the 1840s. Dickens favored the circulation of sewage, of air and water, and of knowledge (through the postal service and the circulating library, among other channels). "It would not reduce Dickens's politics absurdly to say that he was for circulation and against stoppage," Trotter maintains (103), and he argues that *"Dombey and Son* is the first novel in which the economy of trade and the vocabulary of Medical Police announce themselves to any purpose," citing in particular the metaphor of circulation in the famous description of the railway terminus and the vision of disease and moral contagion spreading from the slums (Trotter 126, 128, citing *Dombey* 15:290 and 47:737–38).

Trotter tells us that *Household Words* advocated strenuously for free trade and the flow of money, but Dickens' novels offer little evidence of an *economy* of circulation and exchange; the businesses in Dickens' fiction tend almost invariably to be "stoppages." Trotter himself cites several examples,[4] including a description of the offices of Dombey and Son. Yet for all the language of stasis and decay in this passage—"black sediment . . . gloom . . . mouldy . . . cavern . . . mysteries of the deep" (13:237)—Dombey and Son *is* involved in trade. Dickens' attitude towards business may be more complex than his attitude toward other circulatory systems; there are indications that he associated businesses *successfully* engaged in trade with filth.[5] The Wooden Midshipman, unlike Dombey and Son, is clean and orderly—it is "a snug, sea-going, ship-shape concern" (4:88)—but it is made quite clear that not a single transaction takes place there over a period of at least twelve years. The store and the Captain's mind are both circulatory dead ends, stoppages in the system where goods and words pile up to no purpose, cargo going nowhere.

Captain Cuttle's model of knowledge as cargo emerges at several points in the book. When he has to assimilate new information at odds with his existing ideas, for instance, he finds it "difficult to *unload* his old ideas upon the subject, and to *take a perfectly new cargo on board*" (15:283), and elsewhere he feels "bound to impart a morsel from his *store* of wisdom to an inexperienced youth" (50:792). Words in particular are reified as items in the mental cargo, as when he tells Mr. Carker, "there's a many words I could wish to say to you, but I don't rightly know where they're *stowed* just at present" (32:550), or when he responds to Rob the Grinder, "Don't you *pay out* no more of them words," as if words were either currency or rope (39:645; emphasis added in all cases).

Mr. Carker, on the other hand, claims that his memory is his *capital*: "It's the only capital of a man like *me*," he tells Mr Dombey (13:240). Both the Captain and the Manager use the language of business for matters of the mind, assigning them a commercial value, but there are significant differences: it is the objects of knowledge (words, ideas, "science") that the Captain sees as commodities, and he sees accumulating these objects as an end in itself; for the Manager, on the other hand, it is a human faculty, memory, that is the resource, and this resource is something to be *used* productively. The Captain's image is static, the Manager's dynamic. The Captain wants to own words as Mr. Dombey owns property; Mr. Carker uses his intelligence in furtherance of other goals.

This is one of several occasions when Mr. Carker juxtaposes Mr. Dombey's inherited wealth with the mental resources on which he himself must rely. On the subject of proficiency at games, he says of Dombey, "*He* has never had occasion to acquire such little arts. To men like me, they are sometimes useful" (26:456); and, shortly before the comment on memory quoted above, he remarks, "It's men like myself, who are low down and are not superior in circumstances, and who inherit new masters in the course of Time, that have cause to look about us" (13:240). Positioned as he is, the Manager must depend on his powers of observation; while Mr. Dombey can be sublimely indifferent to the world around him, Mr. Carker needs to "look about," to read his surroundings, with a perceptive eye.

The salaried servant of capital, hiring out his mental powers to serve the interests of Dombey and Son, Mr. Carker is a manager in exactly the sense in which we use the word today (although, as Raymond Williams tells us, this sense was a recent one in Dickens' day). He is a man ahead of his time, in the advance guard of both the managerial revolution (in terms of which salaried managers are said to have wrested control of businesses from the capitalist owners)[6] and the postindustrial age, in that it is essentially *information* that he manages: his ability to acquire, organize, and use information is the source of his power. As an information manager, he effectively controls the firm of Dombey and Son, and it is the information he possesses that gives him power over others.

Another necessary part of Mr.Carker's "capital" that makes him very much a modern man is his self-concealment, the gap between his public face and his hidden self. C. Wright Mills has written eloquently of the plight of white-collar workers in the twentieth century: they "sell not only their time and energy but their personalities as well"; they are "the new little Machiavellians, practicing their personable crafts for hire and for the profit of others" (xvii). Like any good manager, Mr. Carker has learned the art of manipulating others while suppressing his own feelings. He is kin to several other deviously ambitious underlings in Dickens' work, most obviously Uriah Heep, the scheming clerk who takes over Wickfield's business in *David Copperfield* and who, like Carker, affects humility and uses blackmail in his quest for power. Dickens himself evidently recognized that these were the men of the future: Ned Lukacher writes that not only did Dickens have "an extraordinary insight into the kind of fawning, obsequious villain he most despised," but that (at least by the time he wrote *Our Mutual Friend*) he had a "horrified recognition . . . that the future of England is in the hands of such men" (312).

THE VIOLENCE OF LITERACY

One component of Captain Cuttle's theory of knowledge that has no counterpart in anything Mr Carker says is his linkage of knowledge with pain and violence. Observing the nautical instruments which embody "science" for him, he reflects, "It's so comfortable to sit here and feel that you might be weighed, measured, magnified, electrified, polarized, played the very devil with: and never know how" (4:98). Not only is "science" or knowledge a profound mystery to the Captain; he knows it has the power to subject him to painful processes beyond his comprehension, and he marvels at this. Later we learn that his deep reverence for the intellectual powers of his friend Bunsby is based on the violence Bunsby has suffered, in particular the blows to the head: "There you sit," he addresses Bunsby, "a man as has had his head broke from infancy up'ards, and has got a new opinion into it at every seam as has been opened" (39:640). Bunsby's vaunted "opinions" in turn are seen by the Captain as having the power to strike others with the power of a blow to the head: Bunsby, he promises, will give Sol such an opinion "as'll stun him . . . as much as if he'd gone and knocked his head again a door!" (23:407). In lauding Bunsby's intellectual powers, moreover, the Captain claims, "There ain't a man that walks—certainly not on *two* legs—that can come near him" (15:283). The only person who might outshine Bunsby, that is, would be a *one*-legged man: for the Captain, mutilation is a sign of wisdom.

Perhaps the young Ned Cuttle suffered the ungentle ministrations of a Squeers, Creakle, or M'Choakumchild at one of the brutal schools that figure so prominently in Dickens' work; a regime of blows to the head accompanied by injunctions along the lines of "Get that into your thick skull!" would explain his belief that the getting of wisdom entails the violent breaching of the cranium. Yet the link the Captain sees between learning and violence is more than a naïve and idiosyncratic association on his part; though his notions of causality are confused, he offers genuine insight into the damage that learning and literacy can inflict.[7]

There is ample evidence for this in the two schools we see in *Dombey and Son*. Young Rob Toodles's enrollment at the Charitable Grinders school brings direct physical violence upon him, both inside the school and out: "I was chivied through the streets . . . when I went there, and pounded when I got there. . . . and that began it," he later laments, excusing his misspent life since (22:379). He is a walking parable of the hazards of education to working-class children, who risk ending up as aliens in two worlds, belonging nowhere.

While there is no obvious physical violence at Doctor Blimber's academy, this intellectual hothouse subjects the sons of the bourgeoisie to a "forcing apparatus" that makes them "blow before their time," a process that may not mark their bodies but destroys their spirits and damages their minds. Toots, the head boy, is a case in point; the forcing in his case has been "overdone" (11:206) and his brains are permanently addled. His thoughts now are trapped in "that leaden casket, his cranium" (2:234), and he can only chuckle and burble inanely; significantly, although he can read and write, he writes only letters addressed to himself (12:218)—his literacy, that is, generates only a closed communicative circuit returning to himself. David Musselwhite suggests that, with his ironic status as *head* boy, his "damaged head,"[8] and his self-referentiality (evidenced by his near-palindromic name as well as his letters to himself), Toots is close to a "mental block" (148).[9] Like Captain Cuttle, he is a communicative dead end, and he provides a compelling illustration of the damaging effects of education.

EMBODYING LITERACY: CAPTAIN CUTTLE'S HOOK AND HAT

Linguistic and intellectual stoppage and disability are inscribed on the Captain's very body. The hook and the hat are the physical features that most define him; both are associated with his relationship to literacy, and both signify pain and incapacitation. In the case of other seafaring amputees like Captain Hook in J. M. Barrie's 1904 *Peter Pan*, the prosthetic hook is a threat, a weapon made part of the body, but (except to children) Captain Cuttle's hook is never anything but funny. He uses it to arrange his hair and gesticulate, kisses it in homage to the ladies (10:198, for one example of several), bites it when he has the urge to bite his nails (15:283). The hook is replaceable with other tools that screw into its socket, a knife (9:180) and a fork (49:773); significantly, however, no writing implement ever attaches to the Captain's right wrist, and when he writes he uses his left hand (39:641). The loss of his right hand thus limits the Captain's ability to write; in the light of twentieth-century knowledge of hemispherical dominance in the brain, we might be tempted to see it as figuring some larger linguistic incapacitation.

Besides the handicap of injury, there is the Captain's hat, "such a hard glazed hat as a sympathetic person's head might ache at the sight of, and which left a red rim round his own forehead as if he had been wearing a tight basin" (4:97). The Captain goes nowhere without his hat: when his landlady, Mrs. MacStinger, vindictively appropriates it, the Captain remains trapped in his room; "she stopped my liberty," he explains (23:407). And yet this cherished hat is profoundly uncomfortable: tight-fitting and hard, it marks his body with a "red rim" (the phrase is repeated on 32:549, 39:637, and 49:775; it appears as a "red equator" on 10:194 and a "scarlet circle" on 17:306). This painful inscription is a link to the other "damaged heads" Musselwhite has pointed to, Bunsby's much-battered skull and the "leaden casket" of Toots's cranium: in all three cases, the damaged head entails a blockage of thought and language. The ill-fitting hat stands in the same relationship to Captain Cuttle as does his book-learning: both are alien, unyielding objects which uncomfortably constrain him, but he values both so highly as to consider them indispensable parts of his identity. While the hook represents a mutilation of his body by external forces, the hat is something the Captain has chosen to wear, a form of self-constriction.

The spectacles the Captain takes to wearing function similarly; "his eyes were like a hawk's," yet he considered wearing spectacles "appropriate" to his position in "the Instrument Trade" (32:553). Spectacles are classically the sign (or stigma) of the highly literate; others beside the Captain have worn them to appear educated, with the ironic consequence of impairing their otherwise clear vision.

EMBODYING LITERACY: MR. CARKER'S TEETH AND EYES

Mr. Carker's most salient features are his teeth, which are characteristically exposed in the semblance of a smile. They are presented in the first sentence introducing him (13:239); the next sentence tells us that "It was impossible to escape the observation of them. . . . " The preternatural teeth seem to observe us, like eyes; we cannot escape their surveillance. As the sentence continues, however, "for he showed them whenever he spoke," observer and observed change places, and we revert to the comfortable position of the observers rather than the observed. And yet the ambiguity is not fully resolved, and it is an appropriate introduction both to Mr. Carker's own double nature and to the extraordinary properties of his teeth.

Consider the way in which Mr. Carker reads a letter from Mr. Dombey, "slowly; weighing the words as he went, and bringing every tooth in his head to bear upon them"; one passage in particular "attracted his attention and his teeth" (22:375). Consider his observation of the Captain "with an eye in every tooth and gum" (17:304); his scrutiny of the company's accounts, "with the patient progress of a man who was dissecting the minutest nerves and fibres of his subject" (46:722); Rob the Grinder's fear of "every one of the teeth finding him out," his certainty that "Mr Carker read his secret thoughts" (42:676–77). Mr. Carker sees, and, in particular, *reads* with his teeth. His teeth and his eyes, the features that most define him and his relationship to knowledge and discourse, are conflated. Unlike Captain Cuttle's hook and hat, which are external appendages signifying mutilation and constraint, Mr. Carker's eyes and teeth are organs that actively penetrate the world. The Manager reads and sees with a penetrating sharpness that is almost an assault. He is a visual vampire.

We are reminded repeatedly of the dangerous power of Mr. Carker's eyes and teeth. Predictably, his teeth evoke the animals with which he is so often associated: for instance, to cite only two instances of many, he "grinned like a shark" (22:377), and "A cat, or a monkey, or a hyena, or a death's-head, could not have shown . . . more teeth at one time" (17:306). When, "with his white teeth glistening," he offers Edith a congratulatory kiss at her wedding, it is "more as if he meant to bite her" (31:525). Vampire-like, the teeth suck forth secrets; Rob the Grinder is particularly vulnerable to their magnetic power and confesses his sins, "just as if the teeth of Mr Carker drew it out of him, and he had no power of concealing anything with that battery of attraction in full play" (22:379). The Manager's "sharp glance" is linked with his "sharp smile" (42:680); his "devilish look" strikes "like a flash of lightning" (42:683).

Ironically, if Captain Cuttle can be labeled *oral* (as opposed to *literate*), Mr. Carker's teeth earn him the designation *oral* in a different sense. Ian Watt in "Oral Dickens," following Freudian theories of character development, finds him an example of "the oral sadistic character"—in fact, the "purest manifestation" in Dickens' work of "the fully developed pathology of the sadistic biter"—and suggests that he seems destined "to sink his ever-bared teeth into Edith's white breasts" (Watt 178). Even if his teeth are surrogates for his eyes and his power is above all visual, there is no doubt of Carker's sadism—and his *tongue* is incidentally suggestive, "the hot tongue revealing itself" in his "wolf's face" when he relays Florence's "dear love" to her father (26:442).[10]

If Captain Cuttle demonstrates the violence of literacy from the perspective of the victim, in Mr. Carker we see a perpetrator—a man whose acts of perception are violations of the Other he reads.

CAPTAIN CUTTLE QUOTES

The contrast between the two men extends to their very different modes of producing discourse. Captain Cuttle's speech is often obscure. His nautical exhortations—"Lay your head well to the wind," "Stand by," "Clap on," and the like—are baffling, and the signals he makes with his hook are cryptic: "like those Chinese sages who are said in their conferences to write certain learned words in the air that are wholly impossible of pronunciation, the Captain made such waves and flourishes as nobody without a previous knowledge of his mystery, would have been at all likely to understand" (17:299). His words sometimes have no discernible relationship to his intended meaning, as when "he growled, as if a choice and delicate compliment were included in the words, 'Stand by! Stand by!' " (23:406), and we are frequently reminded of his inability to express himself, his "mute, unutterable meaning" (15:280).

What most marks the Captain's speech, however, is his habit of quoting, which testifies to his reverence for the printed word; repeatedly we see him suffused with satisfaction after uttering what he considers a particularly apt quotation. His quotations also by implication reveal his low opinion of anything he could spontaneously say himself: in quoting, he *authorizes* his speech by appropriating the words of others. "Captain Cuttle shows an almost medieval fondness for supporting his opinions by an appeal to authority," says G. L. Brook in *The Language of Dickens* (194).[11] He is a walking intertext. Among the texts he invokes, the Book of Common Prayer and the Bible figure prominently; he quotes nautical ballads, patriotic songs, and other popular verse; he makes a single garbled allusion to *Macbeth*; he is familiar, as we have seen, with such popular legends as the tale of Dick Whittington and *Robinson Crusoe*; and he uses a range of clichés and sayings that must have been common currency in his time.

Yet the Captain's invocation of textual authority founders: he misquotes, he jumbles texts together, and he uses quotations in wildly inappropriate ways. He misreads the biblical *land* of milk and honey as "*lad* of milk and honey," which strikes him as just the epithet for Walter: " 'If there is a lad of promise—one flowing,' added the Captain, in one of his happy quotations, 'with milk and honey—it's [Sol's] nevy' " (10:196). He comically, and revealingly, mangles the wording of the marriage banns: "prowiding as there is any just cause or impediment why two persons should not be jined together in the house of bondage . . . '' (50:794). He interprets metaphors literally: the cate-chism's "keep God's holy will and commandments and walk in the same all the days of my life" becomes an admonition to "Walk fast, Wal'r, my lad, . . . and walk the same all the days of your life" (9:182). Spiritual qualities are concretized when the Catechism's definition of the sacraments as "an outward and visible sign of an inward and spiritual grace" is applied to Walter, who, according to the Captain, "is what you may call a out'ard and visible sign of an in'ard and spirited grasp" (23:406). When he speaks of "science, which is the mother of invention, and knows no law" (23:410), the Captain conflates two aphorisms and erases "necessity." And a fig tree, possibly from some other biblical source, becomes entwined with his recollec-tion of Proverbs XXII, 6, "Train up a child in the way he should go: and when he is old he will not depart from it," which, in the Captain's version, becomes a rather more self-interested maxim, "Train up a fig-tree in the way it should go, and when you are old sit under the shade on it" (19:340).[12]

What prompts a quotation is often random free association. For instance, when he greets Bunsby as "a man as can give an opinion as is brighter than di'monds," the diamonds remind the Captain of an Essex folksong, which he hastens to quote, "—and give me the lad with the tarry trousers as shines to me like di'monds bright" (39:638).[13] On the return of Sol Gills, the Captain exults in the sound of "[h]is wery woice. . . . your own formilior woice"and is promptly moved to utter a quotation containing the word "voice": " 'Tis *the* woice,' said the Captain impressively, and announcing a quotation with his hook, 'of the sluggard, I heerd him complain, you have woke me too soon, I must slumber again' '' (56:892).[14]

The Captain frequently identifies the sources of his quotations, as if he were labeling the inventory in his verbal warehouse and authenticating its worth. Yet his attributions are most often mistaken.[15] "Inaccuracy of quotation is matched by inaccuracy of attribution," says Brooks, who finds the "vagueness and inaccuracy of his attribution" as medieval as his habit of appealing to the authority of texts (194). The Captain's preferred source is holy writ: introducing himself to Toots with the doggerel verse "Cap'en Cuttle is my name, and England is my nation, this here is my dwelling place, and blessed be creation,"[16] he cites the Book of Job "as an index to his authority" (32:541). Similarly, he asserts confidently that "in the Proverbs of Solomon you will find the following words, 'May we never want a friend in need, nor a bottle to give him!' '' (15:281); the line (minus the words "in need") is actually the opening of a popular song by one John Davy.[17] When the Captain asserts his loyalty to Sol Gills, "who I'll stand by, and not desert until death do us part, and when the stormy winds do blow, do blow, do blow," he invokes his most popular religious source, "—overhaul the Cate-chism . . . and there you'll find them expressions" (23:407), although readers in Dickens' day would surely recognize the marriage service and Thomas Campbell's poem "Ye Mariners of England."

The Captain's quotations have an air of finality—beyond dialogue, response, or difference. He may alter the words of his source, but it never seems that there is any real interpenetration of his own thinking and the received discourse. He invokes the authority of the discourses he has appropriated, but at the same time these discourses are incorporated into his own language, reduced to its level of concreteness, functioning at most as ornamental gestures in the direction of some higher authority. The discourses Captain Cuttle quotes have for him the status of Bakhtin's *authoritative discourse* that is, "privileged language that approaches us from without; it is distanced, taboo, and permits no play with its framing context (Sacred Writ, for example)" (Glossary, Holquist 424). The source of the Captain's quotations often *is* Sacred Writ, of course, and he recites his quotations precisely because he conceives of them as having power. And yet of course he does change the "framing context" of the authoritative discourses he cites: he wrenches passages out of context, quite frequently desacralizing the sacred and often garbling the actual wording of his sacred writ. Because he does this unwittingly, by mistake, it does not change the status of his authoritative discourses in his own mind—though it does reveal the limitations of a mind that so readily grants authority to such heterogeneous discourses, and discourses that he has so little understanding of. For us, the readers, the Captain's mangled quotations effectively strip authority from the sources he cites.

MR. CARKER COMMUNICATES

Only once is quotation associated with Mr. Carker—in a context that has nothing to do with conventional texts. His dress is said to imitate to an extent that of "the great man whom he served," but to be less stiff: "Some people quoted him indeed, in this respect, as a pointed commentary, and not a flattering one, on his icy patron—but the world is prone to misconstruction, and Mr Carker was not accountable for its bad propensity"(27:457–58). Mr. Carker is here seen as a text, a commentary on the text that is Mr. Dombey—a text that subtly criticizes the source it "quotes"; the text-quoting-a-text that is Carker is in turn quoted and interpreted by readers, and subject to "misconstruction" on their part. The concepts of text and of reading here are far more complex than anything associated with Captain Cuttle—and what is real recedes into the distance behind layers of quotation and construction.

The "textuality" of Mr. Carker's presentation of himself is seen in the first paragraph introducing him:

His manner towards Mr Dombey was deeply conceived and perfectly expressed. He was familiar with him, in the very extremity of his sense of the distance between them. "Mr Dombey, to a man in your position from a man in mine, there is no show of subservience compatible with the transaction of business between us, that I should think sufficient. I frankly tell you, Sir, I give it up altogether. I feel that I could not satisfy my own mind; and Heaven knows, Mr Dombey, you can afford to dispense with the endeavour." *If he had carried these words about with him printed on a placard, and had constantly offered it to Mr Dombey's perusal on the breast of his coat, he could not have been more explicit than he was.*   (13:239; emphasis added)

Such is Mr. Carker's skill that he communicates a complex message as explicitly as if it were printed on a placard on his breast, but does so without uttering a word of the message itself. To complicate matters further, the message itself is that Mr. Carker is incapable of communicating the message he supposedly would like to: "there is no show of subservience . . . that I would think sufficient."[18]

The invisible placard with its "explicit" printed message is emblematic: in quoting, Captain Cuttle transmutes texts into oral utterances, but Mr. Carker mysteriously projects textual messages even when face to face with his audience, the Captain "oralizes" texts, the Manager textualizes speech—or even, as in this case, nonverbal communication. While the Captain's messages are often impenetrable, the Manager's message here has the precision and fixity of a text; his *intended* message, that is, is plainly legible—the complex self-referentiality of the message itself and its falsity are another matter.

Carker conveys a similarly complex and self-referential message, again by nonverbal means, in Chapter 26, where, after insinuating to Mr. Dombey that there is an undesirable relationship between Florence and Walter, he turns to the business papers in front of him and pretends to be examining the figures there:

He showed that he affected this, as if from great delicacy, and with a design to spare Mr Dombey's feelings; and the latter, as he looked at him, was cognizant of his intended consideration, and felt that but for it, this confidential Carker would have said a great deal more, which he, Mr Dombey, was too proud to ask for.   (26:443)

Mr. Carker *shows* that he *affects* to look at the figures—that is, he *pretends to pretend* to look at them. When he is dealing with an interlocutor whose intelligence he respects, Carker layers false impression upon false impression so that the other will have the task of peeling away one mask to find another beneath it, which he will believe to be the truth. As with the placard, Carker convincingly sends the message that he cannot convey the message he wishes to convey, in this case for reasons of delicacy—and the layered meta-messages effectively conceal the falsity of the main message itself.

In a number of other encounters Mr. Carker communicates by silent and mysterious means. He has a habit of mouthing words soundlessly, "not articulating the words, but . . . forming them with his lips and tongue" (17:307); when he tells Florence that there is no news of the ship on which Walter Gay is sailing to Barbados, for instance, she is "not even sure that he had said those words, for he seemed to have shown them to her in some extraordinary manner through his smile, instead of uttering them" (24:429). Even when his words are audible, he communicates by insinuation and indirection; his messages is as often in the gaps between the words as in the words themselves. To arouse Mr. Dombey's suspicions about the relationship between Florence and Walter, for instance, he does no more than segue conversationally from Walter to Florence—"Did I mention that there was something like a little confidence between Miss Dombey and myself?"—then leave an "impressive pause" (26:442–43). The message resides in the pause, the gap he leaves for Mr. Dombey to fill in.

Mr. Carker's discursive strategies are too various to analyze fully here. His interview with Captain Cuttle is a prescient paradigm of the psychotherapist's art ("What do you think now, Captain Cuttle?" [17:305]); his conspiratorial whisperings to Florence draw her into his power, asserting "a confidence between himself and her—a right on his part to be mysterious and stealthy . . . a kind of mildly restrained power and authority over her" (28:476–77); when he taunts Edith by speaking repeatedly as if she and Mr. Dombey "love each other with disinterested devotion," his sarcasm, intelligible only to her, reenacts the falsity of her own marital vow—"tendering her false oath at the altar again and again for her acceptance . . . like the dregs of a sickening cup she could not own her loathing of" (37:608, 609). He is a Great Communicator, a master of the arts of innuendo and subliminal suggestion, a paradigmatic modern man who exercises control by discursive means. An enumeration of the Manager's discursive repertoire would surely yield strong insights into the discursive practices that manipulate, deceive, and control us today.

Besides scrutinizing Mr. Carker's words, and his significant silences, we can also look at his structural role in the dissemination of meaning in the novel. Much of Captain Cuttle's movement through the novel takes the form of unsuccessful errands to transmit messages (compare his several futile attempts to bestow his worldly wealth on others)—or evasive maneuvers to avoid his imagined pursuer, Mrs. MacStinger. Mr. Carker, by contrast, is a kind of traveling dealer in meanings. His métier is intelligence, in both senses of the word (the first chapter in which he appears is called "Shipping Intelligence and Office Business"); besides being a manager, or a manipulator of people, he is a "confidential agent"(42:683; illustration on 685), one charged with secrets and conceivably involved in espionage; he is also simply an *agent*, one who acts. He garners secrets and travels around trafficking in them—dispensing a whisper here, a measured hint there—always alert to ferret out new secrets and put them in circulation; he prowls the streets, or picks his dainty way through the countryside, weaving chains, spinning webs—building networks of secret meaning, constructing plots, always compulsively making and circulating meaning. Mr. Dombey eventually appoints him as his messenger to Edith—but declares that "no message to Mrs Dombey with which you are or may be charged, admits of reply" (42:689); Edith, in turn, refuses to accept any messages he has for her from Dombey (43:715). As a conduit between two people who refuse to receive messages from each other, two communicative blocks, he assimilates information from each which he will use to destroy them both; the messenger, the channel of communication, is the victor.

Besides being readers of texts and producers of discourse, the Captain and the Manager also "read" and interpret the people and situations they encounter—they practice their literacy on the world, in terms of current definitions of literacy.[19] Dickens indeed anticipates such a definition by the frequency with which he speaks of characters *reading* one another. He alerts us, too, to a corollary of this mode of thinking: a person not only *reads*, but can *be read*.

CAPTAIN CUTTLE AS READER AND TEXT IN THE WORLD

It is surely emblematic that the five letters Sol Gills sends Captain Cuttle from the West Indies never reach him: part of what defines the Captain is his inability to receive communications. Even when he holds a text in his hands, or is face to face with an interlocutor, the Captain all too frequently misreads the message.

His perceptions of the world are shaped by an ideology that he has apparently absorbed along with his literacy: he has faith in his country, in the benevolence of his social superiors, and in fairytale endings for those he loves. Repeatedly he ignores signs that are obvious to others and reads in terms of his own wishful thinking. Convinced that Mr. Dombey has singled Walter out for special preferment, he believes that he himself is on terms of friendly complicity with the great man; he "never could forget how well he and Mr Dombey had got on at Brighton" (17:299). Setting out to consult Mr. Carker, he plans to "sound [him] carefully, and say much or little, just as he read that gentleman's character" (17:302); but his "reading" does not penetrate beyond Mr. Carker's teeth: "The Captain liked his answering with a smile; it looked pleasant" (304)—and he leaves the office "strongly confirmed in his opinion that he was one of the most agreeable men he had ever met" (308).

At the same time, Captain Cuttle is consistently and sublimely unaware of the impression *he* makes on others. It is not surprising that he is "unconscious"of Mr. Carker's well-concealed reaction to him (17:308). Mr. Dombey's contempt, however, is undisguised: he regards the "phenomenon" of the bowing and gesticulating Captain "with amazement and indignation," but the complacent Captain is immune to a look that "he ought to have been withered by"(10:194)—and there is high comedy in the play between the two men's radically divergent perceptions.

Captain Cuttle's words, we have seen, are often unintelligible. Yet he himself is a man of "transparent simplicity" (17:298), and others see through him with ease. The messages he intends to communicate are unreadable, but what he wants to hide is clearly exposed: he is an open book, a sign that anyone can readily read. His emotions are written on his face: on his discovery of Carker's perfidy, "Every knob on the Captain's face turned white with astonishment and indignation" (32:549); by the end, he "beams with joy" and "shines . . . with speechless gratification" (62:970). His eyes in particular are likely to reveal his state of mind: his "gaze, or rather glare" at Rob the Grinder, "full of vague suspicions, threatenings, and denunciations"(25:431), speaks as clearly as words; similarly, the eye he cocks at Mr. Carker is full of "significance," as telling "as if he had expressed his sentiments with the utmost elaboration"(17:305); elsewhere, meaning radiates outward ("such a beaming expression in his eyes" [17:309]) or builds up such pressure that he must wink "as a vent for his superfluous sagacity" (17:298).

MR. CARKER AS READER AND TEXT IN THE WORLD

Misreading the world, but easily read himself, Captain Cuttle is doubly victimized by literacy. For Mr. Carker, however, literacy, understood in the broadest terms, is the source of his power. He has neither rank nor material resources (the sources of Mr. Dombey's power), and he makes minimal use of physical force; his is instead a distinctively modern form of power based on knowledge, knowledge which itself is derived from observation or surveillance—from the gaze, in Michel Foucault's terms. Foucault is concerned mainly with the institutional uses of surveillance, with panoptical surveillance of large populations or with investigation of individuals as "cases," but Carker's "reading" is surely continuous with the disciplinary techniques Foucault describes as "acts of cunning, . . . of the attentive 'malevolence' that turns everything to account" (139); Carker illustrates Foucault's "meticulous observation of detail, and at the same time a political awareness of these small things, for the control and use of men": "from such trifles, no doubt," Foucault concludes, "the man of modern humanism was born" (141).

Where Captain Cuttle's eyes are windows revealing his inner self, Mr. Carker's are instruments probing the world, or even weapons. His gaze can be palpably injurious: Rob the Grinder is "fixed by Mr Carker's eye," like a specimen transfixed by a pin, "fruitlessly endeavouring to unfix himself" (42:678); the "something" that makes the hypersensitive Florence "recoil as if she had been stung" (24:427) when she first meets him is surely his gaze. Females in particular droop or shrink under his gaze: Edith does both at her wedding (31:525), and he enjoys "a secret sense of power in [Florence's] shrinking from him" (37:607). When he contemplates others in his own mind, Mr. Carker sees himself as "busy, winding webs round good faces, and obscuring them with meshes" (22:387)—as if his gaze were a sticky and noxious thread that clung to its objects.

Mr. Carker himself is virtually unreadable. He controls and manipulates others' perceptions of him—"He had his face so perfectly under control, that few could say more . . . than that it smiled or that it pondered" (27:457)—and artfully contrives the messages he wants to convey, as we have seen. When Mr. Carker looks at someone else, the relationship is typically asymmetrical: Mr. Carker *reads* the other, but the other does not see beyond the Manager's false surface and is furthermore unaware that he or she is being read. Carker is the reader who penetrates, interprets, and draws forth secrets; the other is the insentient and unreciprocating text.

The signal exception to this insentience is Edith. Her relationship with Carker is the most complex in the book, and the most resonant in associations with literacy. Edith is painfully aware from the start that Carker is reading her; after their first encounter, she tells her mother that it is he "who already knows us thoroughly and reads us right, and before whom I have even less of self-respect or confidence than before my own inward self; being so much degraded by his knowledge of me" (27:474). Her perception is reiterated on her wedding day: "Edith feel[s] still . . . that Carker knows her thoroughly, and reads her right, and that she is more degraded by his knowledge of her, than by aught else" (31:525)

When Carker observes Edith without her knowledge in the grove at Leamington, he sees her without the mask she habitually wears—and recognizes her kinship to him. They are both hirelings who must forfeit their pride to serve the same hated master; both must conceal their rage at this humiliation. Mr. Carker sells not only his skills and his time to Mr. Dombey, but also his personhood: his job requires a false front of servility and obsequiousness, beneath which he seethes with resentment and contempt for his master. Edith similarly is selling herself to Dombey in a loveless marriage, as she is only too bitterly aware. She speaks forcefully to her mother that night of how she has been marketed—"There is no slave in a market: there is no horse in a fair, so shown and offered and examined and paraded, Mother, as I have been''—and of the ''bargain'' that is about to be struck with Dombey: ''He sees me at the auction, and he thinks it well to buy me'' (27:473). Both Dickens and the critics have made much of the obvious parallel between Alice Marwood, who has been sold by her mother for sexual purposes, and Edith, who marries for gain, not love—but surely the parallel between Edith and Carker is at least as striking. The two of them wear different masks—his of fawning servility, hers of icy indifference—but their functions are the same, all the more so as Dombey himself makes so little distinction between the firm and his family life: they serve the greater glory of Dombey.

But there is another dimension to Carker's reading: not only does he read Edith's likeness to himself, he also reads her difference from himself across the divide of gender. ''In a world ordered by sexual imbalance, pleasure in looking has been split between active/male and passive/female,'' writes Laura Mulvey in a section of her essay ''Visual Pleasures and Narrative Cinema'' headed ''Woman as Image, Man as Bearer of the Look'': ''The determining male gaze projects its fantasy onto the female figure'' (19). The male gaze directed at the female body is likely to be sexualized, the gaze itself an assertion of power quite independent of any information it may gather. For some, moreover, there is a particular pleasure in the ''surreptitious observation of an unknowing and unwilling victim'' (17). All this is surely there when Carker looks at Edith, and contributes to making his gaze a weapon directed against her. When Edith rails against the ''license of look and touch'' (27:473) to which she has been subjected, we see her own awareness of the nature of the male gaze. If she feels humiliated by the public gaze of the suitors to whom she has been marketed, how much more is she mortified by Carker's secret observation of her unguarded private self?

When Edith and Mr. Carker are formally introduced, shortly after he has come upon her in the grove, we see the complex visual circuit between the two of them. Verbally, they exchange only polite formalities, each referring to the other in the third person; the significant communication is all in the movement of their eyes:

> As her eye rested on him for an instant, and then lighted on the ground, he saw in its bright and searching glance a suspicion that he had not come up at the moment of his interference, but had secretly observed her sooner. As he saw that, she saw in *his* eye that her distrust was not without foundation.
>
> (27:461)

Edith's ''searching glance'' reads Carker (it sees what he has earlier seen); he reads her reading him; she reads him reading her reading him. They are caught up in a recursive perceptual loop. And this is not the only time perceptions circle to and fro between them in this way: ''He saw it; and . . . she knew that he saw it'' (37:611); ''She watched him still attentively. But he watched her too'' (45:718). The external world recedes, and what is fore-grounded is perception of perception. We glimpse here the changing aware-ness of vision and visuality in the nineteenth century and move decisively towards the self-reflexive consciousness of modernism.[20]

Edith's intelligent awareness that she is being read by Carker, however, serves only to deepen her shame. She perceives his reading as a violation, as we see most vividly when he first calls on her after her marriage—the third direct reference to his *reading* her:

> Entrenched in her pride and power, and with all the obduracy of her spirit summoned about her, still her old conviction that she and her mother had been known by this man in their worst colours, from their first acquaintance; that every degradation she had suffered in her own eyes was as plain to him as to herself; that he read her life as though it were a vile book, and fluttered the leaves before her in slight looks and tones of voice which no one else could detect; weakened and undermined her. Proudly as she opposed herself to him, . . . and submissively as he stood before her, . . . she knew, in her own soul, that the cases were reversed, and that the triumph and superiority were his, and that he knew it full well.   (37:607)

Here again, knowledge and perceptions cycle back and forth between them. Edith feels that her secret shame lies exposed to Carker; she is ''weakened and undermined'' by his subtle reminders of his reading of her, as if his vampire reading drains her selfhood. She knows that she is known by him, knows that this knowledge reverses their social positions and puts her in his power, knows finally that he knows this, too. To be a text suffering a hostile reading is painful; to know that even this pain is itself read is the ultimate in-dignity.

''Triumph and superiority'' are Carker's: his malevolent literacy and the modern techniques of control and manipulation it makes possible enmesh his enemies in their insidious web. Mr. Carker will successfully coerce Edith into running off with him, and he will trigger the downfall of the firm of Dombey and Son. And yet in the end triumph will elude him, the ''new man'' will be undone, and—against all probability—his sinister schemes will be superseded by Captain Cuttle's fairytale vision.

CAPTAIN CUTTLE AND THE HAPPY ENDING

The ending of *Dombey and Son* is a fulfillment of Captain Cuttle's naïve fantasy: not only does Walter marry Florence Dombey, but Mr. Dombey is reformed and humanized (as if confirming Captain Cuttle's perception of his amiability), while the irredeemable villain Carker is eradicated. The Captain exerts no effective agency to bring about his desired ends; his obtuseness at best blocks communications, and at worst has disastrous consequences for those he loves. His intervention (the "little Business" he does "for the Young People" of Chapter 17) is in fact counterproductive, handing Mr Carker. valuable information that will be essential to his machinations; the Captain's vaunted simplicity and innocence make him a dupe for the powerful and an unwitting collaborator with those who should be his enemies. Yet the Captain gets his selfless wishes in the end, like the simpleton youngest son in fairy tales who achieves impossible ends against all odds. Romance prevails over realism, innocence over intelligence, the semiliterate Captain over the hyper-literate Manager.

There is ample testimony to readers' love of Captain Cuttle. A. N. Ward in 1882 found that "A romantic charm of a peculiar kind clings to honest Captain Cuttle and the quaint home over which he mounts guard"(46). Edgar Johnson seventy years later saw his thrusting his life savings on Florence as "heart-warming," "an illustration of the ludicrous forms goodness of heart can take without ceasing to be real goodness," and considered the Captain and Toots to be "among the great portraits of the book, both irresistibly ridiculous and both at the same time possessed of a true dignity shining through all their absurdity" (2:633). Words like *lovable, heartwarming, romantic, delightful,* and *quaint* recur in praise of Captain Cuttle; he evokes warm feelings in readers, yet always from a comfortable and condescending distance. We laugh at him because we know what he does not; our seemingly affectionate laughter is gratifying to our own self-esteem.

G. K. Chesterton was not amused by Captain Cuttle (he does not elaborate, conceding that this "may be a personal idiosyncrasy" [57]), but his remarks on Toots could just as easily apply to the Captain—and may reveal the concealed subtext of other encomiums:

> even if one calls him a half-wit, it still makes a difference that he keeps the right half of his wits. . . . the soul rises in real homage to Dickens for showing how much simple gratitude and happiness can remain in the lopped roots of the most simplified intelligence. If scientists must treat a man as a dog, it need not be always as a mad dog. They might grant him, like Toots, a little of the dog's loyalty and the dog's reward.   (60–61)

The intellectual arrogance here is chilling—and all the more so when Chesterton lauds the virtue of humility and quiescence in the poor and "imbecile." Dickens' "main contention," Chesterton suggests, is that

> to be good and idiotic is not a poor fate, but, on the contrary, an experience of primeval innocence. . . . the particular thing that [Dickens] had to preach was this: That humility is the only possible basis of enjoyment; that if one has no

other way of being humble except being poor, then it is better to be poor, and
to enjoy; that if one has no other way of being humble except being imbecile,
then it is better to be imbecile, and to enjoy. (60)

Half-wit, idiot, imbecile, truncated (''lopped''), simplified, doglike—Chesterton hammers home in the crudest terms his sense of intellectual limitation.
The virtues he praises in this intellectual underclass—gratitude, loyalty, con-
tentment (as manifested in the capacity for ''happiness'' or ''enjoyment''),
and, above all, humility—are not only themselves limited, but such as would
ensure the perpetuation of the status quo and the hegemony of the intellectually superior.

Chesterton's ''primeval innocence'' is echoed in the ''sacred simplicity''
George Gissing sees in Captain Cuttle (100): the Captain is a primitive, radically other and *lesser*, whose otherness demands our reverence. If Dickens,
as Philip Collins charges, participated in ''the Romantic primitivism which
finds virtue in the simple life and mind, and suspects vice in educated and
urban man'' (193), this primitivism finds a ready response in readers: the
homage Dickens and his readers alike render Captain Cuttle's goodness and
innocence is the guilty product of our own sense of literate superiority.

George Gissing explicitly connects the appeal of Captain Cuttle to the
fairytale elements in the novel. He rhapsodizes over Chapter 49, where Florence and Captain Cuttle live together like ''A wandering princess and a good
monster in a story-book'' (*Dombey* 776), a chapter he considers ''one of the
most delightful in English fiction'': ''With what infinite charm of fancy is
this picture set before us! With what command of happy illusion are we
reconciled to so many improbabilities! . . . our novel is become a sort of fairy-
tale'' (99–100). He sees the novel's charm as lying in its very implausibility,
in ''fancy,'' ''illusion,'' and ''fairy-tale,'' and proceeds to defend its anti-
realistic ending:

> The ''realist'' in fiction says to himself: Given such and such circumstances,
> what would be the probable issue? Dickens, on the other hand, was wont to
> ask: What would be the pleasant issue? . . . his view of Art involved compliance
> with ideals of ordinary simple folk. . . . An instinctive sympathy with the moral
> (and therefore the artistic) prejudices of the everyday man guided Dickens. . . .
>   The aim of fiction, as Dickens saw it, was to amuse, to elevate, and finally
> to calm. (101)

This picture is a troubling one: Dickens catering to consumer prejudice, yet
at the same time manipulating his readers, elevating and calming them through
the pie-in-the-sky of unrealistic happy endings where passive virtue and innocence are magically rewarded.

There is in fact some truth to this scenario. Dickens' original intentions for
Dombey and Son were considerably less fairytalish than the shape the novel

ultimately assumed. He foresaw the victory of vice over virtue in two separate ways: on one hand he intended Walter to go astray,[21] which would obviously eliminate the possibility of his marriage to Florence Dombey; on the other, he intended Carker to succeed in his sexual designs on Edith, which would drive Edith to suicide.[22] Had both these intentions been fulfilled, the novel's vision would have been markedly darker: no classic happy marriage between poor young hero and poor little rich girl—Captain Cuttle's *idée fixe* shown up as a ludicrously deluded fantasy—Edith violated, defeated, ultimately taking her own life—leaving Dombey and Daughter alone, incestuously cosy, as the only happy couple at the end. And consumer demand did indeed influence the changes Dickens made, although it was evidently Forster himself who persuaded him that Walter should not go bad and Lord Jeffries who vetoed the prospect of sex between Edith and Carker[23]—hardly Gissing's "ordinary simple folk."

MR. CARKER'S UNDOING

The means by which Mr. Carker is undone are worth exploring. At the novel's end the good, passive people—including Florence, Walter, the Captain, and Sol Gills—are set to live happily ever after, but not because of any action they have taken. It is a series of lesser players, characters of questionable moral stature within the frame of the novel, who restore the moral order, although this accomplishment goes unrecognized within the novel itself: Carker, having disempowered Dombey, is in his turn defeated by those whom *he* has abused.

Most surprising is the agency of three women in his destruction. Within the novel, females figure more often as texts read by others than as active readers themselves. Old Mrs. Brown cannot read at all (34:568), and Miss Tox is spied on by Major Bagstock with his double-barreled opera glass. Carker's surveillance, his malevolent reading, is above all directed at Edith and Florence. Women are hardly ever seen reading or writing texts; no woman is ever ever said to read people. We are told at one point that "Florence could not read . . . " (47:754); in fact her schoolroom literacy is not at issue (it is she, after all, who coaches her brother Paul at Dr. Blimber's)—the problem is that her emotions make it impossible for her to read (it is the night of Edith's flight). In general, Florence's literacy—her ability to read the world—is surely compromised by her powerlessness and emotional neediness, as shown above all by her consistent misreadings of her father's coldness.[24]

But Alice Marwood, whom Carker long ago seduced and abandoned, and her mother, Mrs. Brown, have nursed their hatred of Carker over the years. Through the long period of Alice's transportation her mother systematically spies on him and on the family of his employer. Mrs. Brown's encounter with Florence Dombey as a child was accidental, but in Leamington she is spying; while Carker is surreptitiously observing Edith, the witchlike old woman is spying on *him*. Mrs. Brown may be illiterate, but she reads human nature with acuity; she accurately predicts the course of Edith's marriage to Mr Dombey: ''. . . no love at all, and much pride and hate. . . . confusion and strife among 'em, proud as they are, and . . . danger''(34:574). Later, in London, just at the point when Carker is most intensely involved in scheming to bring about the downfall of the House of Dombey, he is ''unconscious of the observation of two pairs of women's eyes'' (46:723) and unaware of *their* scheming against *him*; the inscrutable Mr. Carker turns out to be readable after all. In a further irony, Alice and her mother's prime source of information is Rob the Grinder, whom Carker employed as a spy at the Wooden Midshipman, now unwillingly subverted into acting as a double agent.

These enemies of Carker's use his own tactics: literacy, spying, and blackmail. Rob himself, well trained by Carker, is acute enough to retrieve a scrap of the paper Edith has ripped up and to memorize the word on it, even though he cannot pronounce it. The rudimentary literacy he acquired at such cost at the Charitable Grinders School is central to his betrayal: the name of Edith and Carker's destination, Dijon, is never uttered but written out letter by letter in chalk. Rob's secret can be ''wormed out—screwed and twisted from him'' (52:820) because Mrs Brown knows the secrets of his past and can threaten to set his companions in crime onto him—can blackmail him, as Mr. Carker has blackmailed others. Even the proud Mr. Dombey is reduced to spying in this chapter, where he eavesdrops on Rob's interrogation from behind a door.

And finally there is Edith Dombey's transformation: the text that Carker once read resists his reading and demonstrates that *she* has read *him*. He arrives in Dijon expecting to find her sexually available,[25] ready to enjoy with him their shared revenge on Mr Dombey, their ''compensation for old slavery'' (54:854). But in running off with him, Edith has sacrificed her reputation; once this is gone, Carker no longer has power over her—the secret that was the source of his power is no longer a secret. She refuses his communications, returning the letters he has sent her with their seals unbroken (54:859), and he discovers that he has misread her after all. She is armed against all the means by which he would penetrate her, willing to turn her concealed weapon on herself if necessary: the text has risen against its reader.

So the master reader who himself seemed an impenetrable text turns out to be vulnerable after all; the spy has been spied on, the traitor betrayed. And *his* readings of others turn out to be fallible, too.

It may be necessary to underline this last point. It is easy to believe that while others (notably Captain Cuttle) may misread, Mr. Carker's incisive eye consistently penetrates through appearances to the truth. But consider the

Manager's implausible reading of Captain Cuttle himself: "You are deep, Captain Cuttle," he charges; "You hatch nice little plots, and hold nice little councils. . . . You conspirators, and hiders, and runners-away, should know better . . . " (37:550). Or consider the way he accuses his brother of hypocrisy and everyone who works at Dombey and Son of secretly hating and resenting Mr. Dombey, of being "pusillanimous, abject, cringing dogs! All making the same show, all canting the same story, all whining the same professions, all harboring the same transparent secret"(46:734). Mr. Carker is predisposed to descry hidden depths beneath the surface of others and to find perfidy lurking in those depths. He practices a hermeneutic of suspicion, seeing evil and deception everywhere—reading others, in short, as like himself.

Two constellations of images are associate with Mr. Carker's cognitive and discursive practices: images of *penetration* are frequently invoked, as we have seen, but there are also images of *fabrication* (the textile/textual associations of the term are apt)—weaving, web-spinning, meshes, coils, chains. The Manager's readings are fabrications, as constructed and situated as anyone else's; indeed, in the two examples cited above, the very notions of a false surface that must be penetrated and of hidden depths beneath it seem to be fabrications; where Mr. Carker sees "transparent secrets" there may instead be opaque openness.

We have seen that as a manager, Mr. Carker is a "new man" and that his techniques of surveillance and use of knowledge as a source of power link him to the forms of discipline Foucault sees at work in modern carceral society. We have seen his very modern use of discourse to manipulate and control. As hermeneut, moreover, Mr. Carker participates in the practices of many modern professions: the scientist, who dissects appearances to reveal hidden structures; the detective, who reads clues to uncover the workings of crime; the spy, who must observe unobserved; the psychoanalyst, who must see through the client's defenses to read the messages of the unconscious mind; and—not least—the literary critic, whose business is to unravel the secret meanings of texts. Practitioners of all these professions see themselves as penetrating beyond the surfaces of things to find truths invisible to the uninitiated, but we realize increasingly that all of them also fabricate the meanings they claim to read in the world. We realize now that reality is always constructed, that there are no foundational truths, that even the self is a fiction. And Mr. Carker, I will argue, shares at least imcipiently in this awareness; not only is he a new or modern man, but he participates in the postmodern disintegration of the self—he is, in short, in many ways our brother. In the end, no human agency is ultimately responsible for his death, nor is the deus ex machina of the train: Mr. Carker self-destructs—and he is never more our contemporary than in the process of his dissolution.

He have one earlier clue to the fragility of Mr. Carker's selfhood: his vision of himself in the mirror at the end of Chapter 26. This is described in prose that is extraordinary in its convolution and in its distancing, quite aside from the sadistic vision it presents:

> There was a faint blur on the surface of the mirror in Mr Carker's chamber, and its reflection was, perhaps, a false one. But it showed, that night, the image of a man, who saw, in his fancy, a crowd of people slumbering on the ground at his feet, like the poor Native at his master's door: who picked his way among them: looking down, maliciously enough: but trod upon no upturned face—as yet.   (456–47)

What is above all clear in this blurred vision that this is a man enmeshed in his own fabrications. If he *sees* anything in the mirror it is not James Carker in his bedchamber but a projective wish-fulfillment (or, indeed, a dreamlike version of his actual relationship to the world)—slumbering, unconscious victims (the comparison to the colonized Native's slavelike servitude is significant)[26] spread out at the mercy of ''a man'' who anticipates treading on their faces. As significant as the content of the image is the way in which it is perceived: through the *blur* on the mirror's *surface* Mr. Carker sees a *reflection* which *shows* an *image*; the image is of a man who *sees* himself in *fancy, looking* at slumbering others, and who, by implication, *anticipates* treading on their faces. This is self-reflection through a series of distorting mirrors or faulty speculative instruments, perceptions of perceptions and images of images, where what is seen becomes indistinguishable from what is fancied. Carker's sharp eyes, turned on himself, penetrating the blurred surface of the mirror as he has penetrated so many other surfaces, see only a fancied, a fabricated self. He sees a man who sees himself looking at others (whose own eyes are closed in sleep); ultimately, he sees little but the process of seeing itself, as if his toothlike eyes have eaten up his own identity. The unconscious objects of his gaze, the crowd lying at his feet, are more substantial than the man who perceives them: perhaps he exists only by virtue of their subjection to his look.

The tenuousness and contingency of Carker's own identity makes his final collapse more intelligible. After Edith has left, he panics quite atypically; what most alarms him is the prospect of encountering Dombey ''with his mask plucked off his face'' (54:862), ''his fox's hide stripped off'' (55:863): the prospect of exposing the nothingness beneath his fabricated public self terrifies him. He is now trapped in the readings of others just as he once trapped them—''the springing of his mine upon himself, seemed to have rent and shivered all his hardihood and self-reliance''—and the experience shatters him into fragments. Edith has subjected him to his own strategies; he is ''Spurned liked any reptile; entrapped and mocked; turned upon and trodden down[27] . . . ; undeceived in his deceit,'' and this sense of everything turning back on him (''some sympathy of action with the turning back of all his schemes'') is part of what motivates his irrational return to England (55:863).

From the first, Carker has been purposefully focused on furthering various interconnected schemes; his abduction of Edith and his ruinous undermining of Dombey and Son represent his culminating master plot. Planning a "voluptuous retirement" in Sicily, he has severed all ties to his former life; now that this plan has been foiled, he is left without a purpose. His questions as he sets out on his last journey—"Whither did it flow? What was the end of it?" (864)—have a cosmic resonance. Carker's identity has been determined by the scheming webs he has spun, and without them he is lost. Thus, too, his sense of the strangeness of his surroundings: he feels not only "The dread of being hunted in a strange remote place," but "the novelty of the feeling that it *was* strange and remote" (863). One senses that anywhere would now seem strange to him; his alienation is not from the environment he is in, but from himself.

The account of Carker's final journey is justly famous; its impressionistic style captures perfectly the fragmentation of Carker's consciousness. The man who has always been remarkable for his perfect self-control and for the sharpness of his perceptions is now bombarded with a thousand disconnected sensations and images: "The clatter and commotion echoed to the hurry and discordance of the fugitive's ideas. Nothing clear without, and nothing clear within. Objects flitting past, merging into one another, dimly descried, confusedly lost sight of, gone!" (865). Memories and hallucinations blend with sights glimpsed from the carriage windows, and Carker loses all sense of time and place. He cannot think clearly, but cannot escape his "fevered, ineffectual thinking" (866); he cannot sleep, but is trapped in his own "wearisome exhausting consciousness" (869). The reality of the external world recedes; the journey is "like a vision, in which nothing was quite real but his own torment" (868). He feels "paralysed," "impotent" (866), and self-divided: he has "a deadly quarrel with the whole world, but chiefly with himself" (868). Arriving at the railway inn, he is completely estranged from himself, yet still a prisoner of his own confused consciousness: "his drowsy senses would not lose their consciousness. He had no more influence with them . . . than if they had been another man's" (871). He senses that he is progressively losing "mastery of himself." The man who once used his penetrating gaze as a weapon can no longer focus: "the past, present, and future all floated confusedly before him, and he had lost all power of looking steadily at any one of them" (873).

At the end, eyes draw him magnetically to his doom. He is "irresistibly attracted" to the railroad during the night and observes as if mesmerized the "two red eyes" of approaching trains (872: the "two red eyes" are repeated on 873). Leaving the inn at dawn, he notices "the signal-lights burning feebly in the morning, and bereft of their significance" (874): signs no longer have significance for the man who used to be a compulsive meaning-maker—and two sentences later his own "faded eyes" echo the enfeeblement of the signal-lights in the light of the rising sun. Already, as he makes his way to the railway station, "Death was on him. He was marked off from the living world, and going down into his grave" (874). Dombey appears; "their eyes met" (874); Carker staggers onto the railway tracks, and his last perception is of the train's "red eyes, bleared and dim in the daylight, close upon him" (875). The man who once used his own eyes as weapons dies fleeing from Dombey's eyes into the eyes of the train.

Carker's physical fragmentation is heavily prefigured in the fragmentation of his consciousness. He loses his ability to make sense of the world, and with it his identity. It does not seem too outrageous to suggest that we witness here the dissolution of the subject.

CAPTAIN CUTTLE, MR. CARKER, MR. DICKENS—AND US

Several commentators have noted Dickens' hostility to the highly literate. Philip Collins, in *Dickens and Education*, identifies him as "a significant figure in the covert alliance between Romantic anti-rationalism and Victorian Philistine anti-intellectualism" (193). In *Dombey and Son* Dickens evidently intended to construct on the one hand, a lovable, semiliterate innocent and, on the other, a hyperliterate villain who uses his reading skills to manipulate others. I hope I have shown here that in many ways he subverted his own intentions. We may love Captain Cuttle and honor his decency, but we must in honesty admit that, painfully circumscribed by his limited cargo-model literacy, he is destined to be the dupe of the powerful and literate. Mr. Carker is a more complicated case.

Steven Marcus suggests that Dombey and Carker represent two sides of Dickens, as well as "two sides of modern humanity." Carker, he points out, "is almost the only person in the novel to whom art means anything, yet Dickens finds something sinister in the very quality of his relation to art" (349); he concludes that "it is part of the complex and divided nature of *Dombey and Son* that the voice which speaks so much of the truth and pronounces so much of Dickens's own judgment upon Dombey should belong to its villain—and should almost by the very fact of its intelligence be condemned" (351). David Musselwhite, who sees this novel as marking Dickens' "commodification" as a novelist and his abandonment of the more radical, "rhizomic," and "multi-perspectival" approach characteristic of *Sketches by Boz*, finds that "It is . . . Carker that is the real sacrifice that is made in *Dombey and Son*, for if there is anything left in the novel of Boz's particular gift for migratory wandering about the metropolis or of his ubiquitous vision and dispersed presence, it is embodied in Carker" (2039).

Mr. Carker of course is Dickens: planning, plotting, constructing and with-holding secrets, reading us reading him and calculating our reactions, artfully deceiving us, manipulating our emotions. And we too are Carkers, reading Dickens reading us. Carker is moreover such a "new man"—a self-made man whose self is fabricated from his readings of the world, a man who in the end self-de(con)structs—that he speaks clearly to us in the postmodern era of social constructionism. He smiles out at us from the text, an eye in every tooth, greeting us like Baudelaire: *Hypocrite lecteur, mon semblable, mon frère.*

NOTES

1. To identify only some of the sources invoking such polarities, Steven Marcus discusses the railway-ocean opposition and that between clock-time and natural time; Edgar Johnson opposes coldness and warmth, Julian Moynahan rigidity and fluidity, Nina Auerbach masculine and feminine qualities. Susan Horton offers an illuminating and to some extent skeptical overview of these oppositional struc-tures.

2. In references to *Dombey and Son*, the first number in parentheses designates the chapter; the second, after the colon, indicates the page number in the Penguin edition edited by Peter Fairclough.

3. Our observer (one of theose "supernumeraries" on whose presence David Trotter has commented) is in something of a quandary here: he cannot admit to personal knowledge of these despised volumes and so must resort to judging them on the basis of their titles alone. In so judging books by their covers he is not too far removed from Captain Cuttle's worldview, though the Captain might well have been deceived by the gilt lettering.

4. Two that he does not cite, both (like the Wooden Midshipman) shops where nothing is sold, are Krook's rag-and-bone business in *Bleak House* and the old curiosity shop. Krook reputedly "can't bear to part with anything I once lay hold of" (5:82), which makes his store like Chancery; "edax rerum," *devourer of things,* is "the motto of both," Forster tells us (2:115). The stock in trade of the old curiosity shop is even more antiquated than the outdated nautical instruments sold at the Wooden Midshipman; Northrop Frye comments that the shop "plays little part in the story, but is a kind of threshold symbol of the entrance into the grotesque world, like the rabbit-hole and mirror in the Alice books." He notes, too, that Florence Dombey's sojourn with Captain Cuttle at the Wooden Midship-man repeats *The Old Curiosity Shop*'s theme of the "girl-child among gro-tesques" (85).

5. The indications are most compelling in *Our Mutual Friend*, which features two separate enterprises engaged in recyling dead bodies (Gaffer Hexam's and Mr Venus's) and dustheaps that hold untold wealth. Humphry House points out that " 'dust' was often a euphemism for decaying human excrement" (167).

6. I wrote this before discovering that Kathleen Tillotson made the same observation, speaking of "Carker the 'new man,' the 'forerunner of the managerial revolution,' " and adding in a note that she could not trace the source of the quotation (177).

7. In our own times as in Captain Cuttle's: the subtitle of this section is the same as the title of J. Elspeth Stuckey's 1990 book.

8. Dickens complained of his own "damaged head" at the time he was writing *Dombey and Son*; the phrase is used in his letter of 20 October 1846 (*Letters* 4:638), and there are many other references to headaches in his letters from this period.

9. Musselwhite's concern is not with cognitive functioning; he connects the "damaged head" of Toots to Dickens' own headaches and mental distress, which Dickens himself attributed to the lack of crowded streets in Geneva, where he started the novel. Toots gave Dickens the opportunity to "relieve himself by comic sublimation of some of the distress he felt in his swollen head," Musselwhite suggests, and he argues ingeniously that the head-streets relationship finds a parallel in the marriage of Toots to Susan Nipper, "the 'yoking forcibly together' of the polar forces of the novel, of a head become numb by the pressures within it and an energy and volubility . . . that are potentially anarchic" (149).

10. The only tongue associated with Captain Cuttle is the "very smoky tongue" he brings in his pocket to Walter's farewell breakfast (19:340)—a poignant contrast that we can read in either sexual or linguistic terms.

11. Brook also informs us that the Captain is the Dickensian character "most fond of quotations" and suggests that "The characters who are most fond of quotations are not as a rule those who are intellectually outstanding" (192).

12. The Captain cites the second half of the Proverbs verse earlier, combining it with the famous message of the bells to Dick Whittington: "Turn again Whittington, Lord Mayor of London, and when you are old you will never depart from it" (4:99).

13. The folksong is identified in Bentley, Slater, and Burgis's *Dickens Index*, which is a goldmine of information on Captain Cuttle's sources.

14. This is Dr. Isaac Watts's "Sluggard," best-known in the twentieth century in the form of Lewis Carroll's parody, " 'Tis the voice of the Lobster; I heard him declare,/'you have baked me too brown, I must sugar my hair.' " Dickens and Carroll share the same sense of what is memorable and mockable in Watts's work: three pages later the Captain identifies himself as "Ed'ard Cuttle, Mariner, of England, as lives at home at ease, and doth improve each shining hour" (56:895), cheerfully combining nautical verses with Watt's encomium to the busy bee, which Carroll would later transmogrify into a crocodile. (Note, incidentally, that the Captain completely distorts the spirit of Martyn Parker's "Song," which is addressed to "Ye *gentlemen* of England / That live at home at ease" and laments these landsmen's inattention to "the dangers of the seas"; "Ye *Mariners* of England" are glorified in the title and the opening apostrophe of a different poem, by Thomas Campbell.) The Captain's vision of Mrs. MacStinger "when her angry passions rise" on the following page (896) is a third quotation from Watts ("But, children, you should never let / Such angry passions rise; / Your

little hands were never meant / To tear each other's eyes''). None of these three passages in Chapter 56 is attributed to Watts.

15. On the one occasion when the Captain does attribute a quotation to Dr. Watts, he is characteristically in error—though he manages to lead scholars of our own day astray. In Chapter 32 he instructs Toots to ''overhaul your Doctor Watts'' for the quotation ''when night comes on a hurricane and seas is mountains rowling'' (32:552), and both the Penguin edition's Notes and *The Dickens Index* suggest that the source is Watts's ''Ode on the Day of Judgement,'' the first verse of which runs:

When the fierce Northwind with his airy Forces
Rears up the Baltic to a foaming Fury
And the red Lightning with a Storn of Hail comes,
        Rushing amain down;

If so, the Captain's recollection of the verse would indeed be ''confused,'' as the *Index* suggests. Bartlett's *Familiar Quotations* (1955 edition) reveals the actual source of the quotation in a work considerably less edifying than Dr. Watts's didactic verse, ''The Sailor's Consolation,'' by William Pitt (d. 1840), the first verse of which runs:

One night came on a hurricane,
The sea was mountains rolling,
When Barney Buntline turned his quid,
And said to Billy Bowling:
''A strong nor-wester's blowing, Bill;
Hark! don't you hear it roar, now?
Lord help 'em, how I pities all
Unhappy folks on shore now!''

The Captain quotes the same verse again in Chapter 49, citing ''waves rowling'' and, a few sentences later, the whole of the last four lines, with only trivial changes (781).

16. I recall writing a version of this on the flyleaves of books in my schooldays in South Africa; variants appear in James Joyce's *Portrait of the Artist as a Young Man* and Thornton Wilder's *Heaven's My Destination* (for which it provided the title). G. L. Brook cites another version appearing in *Edwin Drood*.

17. I owe the identification of John Davy's song to Bentley, Slater, and Burgis's *Index*. Captain Cuttle's version of the Davy quotation, incidentally, is now enshrined in *Bartlett's Familiar Quotations*, where it is attributed to Dickens.

18. There are layers within layers here. The ''true,'' underlying Carker (supposing he exists)—say Carker$_1$—constructs a false Mr Carker who toadies to Mr Dombey, Carker$_2$; the false Carker$_2$ transmits a message that implies the existence of a perfectly obsequious Carker$_3$, a construction of a construction. Although this message is transmitted by indirect means, Mr. Dombey reads clearly this ''explicit'' message offered for his ''perusal,'' that is, he reads between the lines of

Carker₂ to see Carker₃ The process depends on Mr. Dombey reading just well enough to see Carker₃ without suspecting the true nature of Carker₁ and on Mr. Carker gauging exactly what Mr Dombey will and will not be able to read. Yet at the same time the process in which we as readers are involved depends on our knowing that Mr. Dombey is being deceived, that Carker₃ does not exist and that Carker₂ is false. We read Mr. Dombey's misreading and think we know the truth.

19. A representative definition comes from Patrick Courts's *Literacy and Empowerment*: "The word *literacy* . . . suggests a state of being and a set of capabilities through which the literate individual is able to utilize the *interior world of self to act upon and interact with the exterior structures of the world* around him in order to make sense of self and other" (4; emphasis in the original). (Courts goes on to characterize "print literacy," "oral literacy," and "media literacy" in turn.)

20. Jonathan Crary, exploring the changing construction of vision and visuality in the nineteenth century in a chapter titled "Modernity and the Problem of the Observer," argues that "the imperatives of capitalist modernization . . . generated . . . disciplinary techniques that required a notion of visual experience as instrumental, modifiable, and essentially abstract, and that never allowed a real world to acquire solidity or permanence" (24).

21. He explains his intention to show Walter "trailing away . . . into negligence, idleness, dissipation, dishonestly, and ruin" in a letter to Forster dated July 25–26,1946 (*Letters* 4:593; Forster 2:21).

22. He referred to her death in a letter to Forster dated 19 November 1947 (Forster 2:32).

23. "I see it will be best as you advise, to give that idea up," Dickens wrote to Forster about Walter on 22–23 November 1847 (*Letters* 4:658); on 21 December he wrote, "Note from Jeffrey this morning, who won't believe (positively refuses) that Edith is Carker's mistress" (Forster 2:34).

24. Quoting the passage where the Captain and Florence are seen as "nearly on a level" in their "simple innocence of the world's ways" (49:776), Nina Auerbach argues that Captain Cuttle is feminized: "Gills and Cuttle exchange loss of power for female selfhood" (120–21). Surely a more plausible explanation is that their apparent equality comes about because Florence's literacy is incapacitated.

25. It's not that Mr Carker expects to find Edith compliantly seducible. When he earlier envisaged their union, it was emphasized that "He saw her in his mind, exactly as she was. . . . with nothing plainer to him than her hatred of him." Given the sadism that Ian Watt has noted in his character, it seems likely that he takes particular pleasure in imagining forcing himself on her, deliberately humiliating her: "He saw her sometimes haughty and repellent at his side, and sometimes *down among his horse's feet, fallen and in the dust*" (46:735; emphasis added). It is rape that he has in mind; the prospect of overcoming Edith's resistance and humbling her pride arouses him.

His sadism is further underlined by the matter of Edith's hand: Edith has lacerated the hand he kissed "until it was bruised, and bled" (42:692); the next day, she is wearing a glove, and we are told that "He even suspected the mystery of the gloved hand, and held it all the longer in his own for that suspicion" (46:736)—that is, he realizes the extent to which Edith feels defiled by his touch, and the violence this impels her to do to herself, and the knowledge gives him pleasure.

26. Edward Said, in *Culture and Imperialism*, makes us aware of the significant presence of the colonies at the fringes of nineteenth-century British literature even well before the "age of imperialism." He quotes "the earth was made for Dombey and Son to trade in . . . " from the opening chapter of *Dombey and Son* (1:50) and comments: "The way in which Dickens expresses Dombey's egoism recalls, mocks, yet ultimately depends on the tried and true discourses of imperial free trade, the British mercantile ethos, its sense of all but unlimited opportunities for commercial advancement abroad" (14). "[A]ll the major English novelists of the mid-nineteenth century," he claims, "accepted a globalized world-view and indeed could not . . . ignore the vast overseas reach of British power. As we saw in the little example cited earlier from *Dombey and Son*, the domestic order was tied to, located in, even illuminated by a specifically *English* order abroad" (76). In addition to Dombey and Son's interests in the West Indies, Major Bagstock and his voiceless Indian servant provide another trace of empire in the novel. We might also note the imperialistic resonances of many of Captain Cuttle's favorite allusions; he speaks of "the constitution as laid down in Rule Britannia" (39:632) and frequently invokes Mariners of England, hearts of oak, and the like.

27. We recall his own fantasies of trampling others—in the mirror image above, and in his earlier vision of Edith herself "down among his horse's feet" (46:735).

WORKS CITED

Auerbach, Nina. "Dickens and Dombey: A Daughter After All." *Romantic Imprisonment: Women and Other Glorified Outcasts*. New York: Columbia UP, 1985. 107–29

Bartlett, John. *Familiar Quotations*. 13th ed. Boston: Little Brown, 1955.

Bentley, Nicolas, Michael Slater, and Nina Burgis. *The Dickens Index*. New York: Oxford UP, 1990.

Bloom, Harold, ed. *Modern Critical Views: Charles Dickens*. New York: Chelsea House, 1987.

Brook, G. L. *The Language of Dickens*. London: Andre Deutsch, 1970.

Chesterton, G. K. Introduction to the Everyman edition of *Dombey and Son*. London, 1907. Rpt. Ward 55–61.

Collins, Philip. *Dickens and Education*. New York: Macmillan, 1963.

Courts, Patrick L. *Literacy and Empowerment*. New York: Bergin & Garvey, 1991.

Crary, Jonathan. *Techniques of the Observer: On Vision and Modernity in the Nineteenth Century.* Cambridge: MIT P, 1990.

Dickens, Charles. *Dombey and Son.* 1848. Ed. Peter Fairclough. New York: Penguin, 1970.

————. *The Letters of Charles Dickens.* Ed. Kathleen Tillotson. Vol. 4:1844–1846. Oxford: Oxford UP, 1977.

Forster, John. *The Life of Charles Dickens.* 1872–1874. Ed. A. J. Hoppé. 2 vols. London: J. M. Dent, 1966.

Foucault, Michel. *Discipline and Punish.* Trans. Alan Sheridan. New York: Pantheon, 1977.

Freire, Paulo. *Pedagogy of the Oppressed.* New York: Seabury, 1968.

Frye, Northrop. "Dickens and the Comedy of Humors." *Experience in the Novel: Selected Papers from the English Institute.* Ed. Roy Harvey Pearce. New York: Columbia, 1968. Rpt. Bloom 71–91.

Gissing, George. "Dombey and Son." Originally an introduction to the 1900 Rochester edition. *Critical Studies of the Works of Charles Dickens.* 1924. New York: Haskell House, 1965. 89–102.

Holquist, Michael, ed. *The Dialogic Imagination: Four Essays by M. M. Bakhtin.* Trans. Caryl Emerson and Michael Holquist. Austin: U of Texas P, 1981.

Horton, Susan R. *Interpreting Interpreting: Interpreting Dickens's Dombey.* Baltimore: Johns Hopkins UP, 1979.

House, Humphry. *The Dickens World.* 2d ed. 1942. London: Oxford UP, 1960.

Johnson, Edgar. *Charles Johnson: His Tragedy and Triumph.* 2 vols. New York: Simon & Schuster, 1972.

Lukacher,Ned. "The Dickensian 'No Thoroughfare.' " Originally "Dialectical Images: Benjamin/Dickens/Freud." *Primal Scenes: Literature, Philosophy, Psychoanalysis.* By Ned Lukacher. Ithaca: Cornell UP, 986. Rpt. Bloom 281–315.

Marcus, Steven. *Dickens: from Pickwick to Dombey.* New York: Basic, 1965.

Mills, C. Wright. *White Collar.* New York: Oxford UP, 1951.

Moynahan, Julian. "Dealings with the Firm of *Dombey and Son*: Firmness versus Wetness." *Dickens and the Twentieth Century.* Ed. John Gross and Gabriel Pearson. 1962. London: Routledge, 1966.

Mulvey, Laura. *Visual and Other Pleasures.* Bloomington: Indiana UP, 1989.

Musselwhite, David. *Partings Welded Together.* London: Methuen, 1987.

Ong, Walter. *Orality and Literacy: The Technologizing of the Word.* 1982. New York: Routledge, 1988.

Palmer, William. "Dickens and Shipwreck." *Dickens Studies Annual* 18 (1989): 39–92.

Said, Edward. *Culture and Imperialism.* New York: Knopf, 1993.

Shelston, Alan, Ed. *Charles Dickens:* Dombey and Son *and* Little Dorrit: *A Casebook.* London: Macmillan, 1985.

Stuckey, J. Elspeth. *The Violence of Literacy.* Portsmouth, NH: Boynton/Cook-Heinemann, 1990.

Tillotson, Kathleen. *Novels of the Eighteen-Forties.* 1954. Oxford: Oxford UP, 1983.

Trotter, David. *Circulation: Defoe, Dickens, and the Economy of the Novel.* New York: St. Martin's P, 1988.

Ward, A. N. "One of its author's most ambitious endeavours." *Charles Dickens.* English Men of Letters Series. London, 1882. Rpt. Shelston 43–47.

Watt, Ian. "Oral Dickens." *Dickens Studies Annual* 3 (1974): 165–81.

Williams, Raymond. *Keywords: A Vocabulary of Culture and Society.* Rev. ed. New York: Oxford UP, 1983.

The Rhetoric of Reticence in John Forster's *Life of Charles Dickens*

Elisabeth G. Gitter

In the concluding pages of her *Life of Charlotte Brontë*, Mrs. Gaskell firmly asserts the responsibility of the biographer to respect the privacy of her subject's domestic life: once Miss Brontë has become Mrs. Nicholls, "Henceforward the sacred doors of home are closed upon her married life" (2:260). Invoking the Victorian biographical convention of avoiding public exposure of domestic life, Gaskell draws a clear line between the permissibly narratable life of the unmarried artist and the private realm of the home (Gittings 35; Shelston 49–50; Mendelson 16). "Standing outside" the closed doors of private, married life, sympathetic biographers like Mrs. Gaskell may catch glimpses and overhear murmurs, "telling of the gladness within," but even the most intimate biographer should not pry open the doors or peer through keyholes.

Mrs. Gaskell's position outside those discreetly closed doors was made much easier, of course, by the brevity of Brontë's married life: within nine months—and a few pages—of the wedding the bride was dead. As subsequent critics have suggested, Brontë's tragic demise solved potentially awkward narrative problems for her biographer, who would otherwise have had to invent a way to tell and yet conceal the life of a married female writer (Shelson 52; A. N. Wilson 98). Gaskell's solitary, suffering, literary Charlotte Brontë could not simply be transformed into a middle-aged new mother contentedly wed to an unliterary curate; her death in childbirth preserved both her married privacy and the narrative logic of her blighted life. The "happy eventuality," of her survival, as A. N. Wilson observes in the new *Eminent Victorians*, "would have ruined Mrs. Gaskell's biography" (98).

If Mrs. Gaskell was fortunate in being able to position herself comfortably—because briefly—outside the closed doors of her subject's home, John Forster, the friend and biographer of Charles Dickens, did not have such good luck. Forster's narrative, structured around the parallels he draws between Dickens and David Copperfield, required that Dickens' wife, like Copperfield's, die. But unlike Dora Spenlow Copperfield, who could not outlive her own narrative closure, Catherine Dickens survived to spoil the story of her husband's life. While Dickens could, as he put it, "kill" the Copperfield Dora (*Letters* 6:153), Forster was obliged to contend with the middle-aged Mrs. Dickens, whose embarrassing erasure from Dickens' life exposed their marriage to public scrutiny and created an awkward situation for his biographer-friend. Dickens could create in his Dora a failed wife who would grow lighter in her husband's arms, who would remain delicately and girlishly childless, and who would die young. Forster, on the other hand, had the nearly impossible task of representing a wife who grew literally and figuratively heavier until she was discarded, who exhibited a relentless fecundity, and who lived long enough to be cast off by the most famous and beloved Victorian celebrant of domestic happiness.

Unable either simply to suppress all of the details of the Dickenses' domestic situation, many of which had already been discussed in the press, or to reveal too much without further damaging Dickens' reputation, Forster developed a strategy of partial disclosure, a rhetoric of reticence that would at once tell and conceal the story of the Dickens marriage. Writing not only as an experienced "professional" biographer,[1] but also as an intimate of Dickens' family, godfather to one of Dickens' daughters, literary advisor and life-long confidant of Dickens himself, and co-executor of Dickens' estate,[2] Forster, in the biography, positions himself protectively in the doorway of Dickens' home. A sort of Victorian Janus, he can with one face see all that is within; with another face turned outward, however, he guards the home against intrusion. Proud of his close connection to the family and dependent upon that connection for the authority of his biography, Forster lets his readers know that he has been part of the family circle and is privy to its secrets. At the same time, however, he employs a variety of strategies—sleights of hand, as it were—that conceal or obscure information that might damage his subject's dignity.

The difficulty of Forster's position as protective friend and serious biographer was exacerbated by the publicity surrounding Dickens' 1858 separation from his wife. Writing in the early 1870s, Forster might protest, along the lines of Mrs. Gaskell, that "no decent person" would violate the "strictly private nature" of Dickens' domestic situation (2:206), but Dickens himself, in his earlier efforts to silence gossip about the separation, had already opened the doors of his married life. To defend himself against rumors of adultery with an actress or incest with his sister-in-law, Georgina Hogart, Dickens had waged a campaign, first of private and semi-private letter-writing and then of public denial and self-justification, eventually publishing a statement about his "domestic troubles" in the *Times*, the *Manchester Guardian*, and other newspapers, and on the front page of *Household Words* (Kaplan 393–96; Ackroyd 818).

Despite all this publicity, it was possible for Forster to suppress some of the secrets surrounding Dickens' "domestic troubles"—most notably the role of the "invisible" Other Woman, the actress, Ellen Ternan[3]—but he could not completely close doors that had been ajar for more than a decade. At the same time, he was also constrained in a number of ways from throwing them too widely open. As Dickens' executor and loyal friend, and as the friend of Dickens' children, he would not of course wish to invite too close a public scrutiny of the casting off of Mrs. Dickens. Moreover, as an established Victorian biographer, known for his lives of great men, he would need to protect his subject's virtuous reputation. Dickens' value as the subject of Victorian biography depended not only on his professional career, but also on the intersection of that career with a "track of godliness" (Epstein 115, 145–47). If Dickens was to be constructed as a Victorian hero—a worthy subject of late nineteenth-century biography in the tradition of Boswell and Carlyle—he would have to exhibit, in his life story, both literary genius and a noble nature (Houghton 316–18). Since Dickens' well-publicized straying from the path of nobility could not be hidden by his biographer, it would have to be excused, mitigated, or disguised.

Blaming Mrs. Dickens—alluding, as Dickens had done in his letters and conversation, to her mental instability, her lassitude, her indifference to her children, her satisfaction at the separation—might have made Forster's justification of Dickens much easier. But that strategy, too, was impracticable, in part because of the continued survival of Catherine Dickens, who tactlessly lived on until 1879. Indeed, (according, at any rate, to some unidentified newspaper cuttings in the Forster Collection), it was rumored that if Forster had not done her justice, Dickens' son Charley was prepared to defend his mother by publishing his own story of the separation (*Letters* 1: xvii). Even without that threat, however, it seems unlikely that Forster would have been so ungentlemanly as to have protected Dickens at his wife's expense. For as important, in biography, as the value of the subject, are the value and authority of the biographer. The biographer's worth, as Boswell himself understood, is established through conspicuous diligence, labor, and attention, and through a display of "scrupulous authenticity" (Epstein, 94, 115). That Forster understood this is evident from his strenuous efforts throughout *The Life of Charles Dickens* to establish his authority and reliability as a Boswell who observed and was told much, and who noted and could "perfectly recollect" all (1:4).[4] The undeniable, public, awkward facts of Dickens' family history—the birth of ten children in sixteen years, twenty-two years of marriage, the testimony of many people who knew Catherine Dickens and who had seen her happily together with her husband, Forster's own long and friendly relationship with Mrs. Dickens—would have made it difficult, if not impossible, for Forster, even had he wished to do so, to have blamed her without sacrificing his own authority, credibility, and, in William Epstein's phrase, "biographical power" (91).

Forster's attempts to reconcile the conflicting demands made upon him as Dickens' biographer—protector of the family's privacy, guardian of Dickens' reputation, credible memorialist—have earned him little praise from later critics. He has been accused of "pious camouflage" and of lacking "the hallmark of artistic genius, the dramatic instinct, 'the touch that imparts life'" (Gittings 35; Dunn 184). Edmund Wilson dismissed *The Life of Charles Dickens* as "an elaborate memoir," not a "real biography" (2). Edward Mendelson is more forgiving, attributing "the gap" that one senses in "the texture" of Forster's biography to the impossibility of reconciling two contradictory nineteenth-century biographical conventions: the earlier, Boswellian convention of memorializing the exemplary, admirable subject and the romantic, Rousseauian convention of analyzing personality through the revelation of origins, shameful secrets, and formative psychological crises (16–17).

Mendelson may be too generous in assuming that, in attempting to mold Dickens' life to the contours of *David Copperfield*, Forster was revealing the secret well-springs of Dickens' personality. He conveys accurately, however, the sense of cross purposes in Forster's biography, which is riddled with inconsistencies, gaps, obscurities, and nearly-incomprehensible compressions. While this unevenness of narrative texture may be dismissed simply as evidence of Forster's incompetence, it can also be understood, perhaps more usefully, as strategic. Forster's aims were contradictory and his position ambiguous, but he was not the unreflective memoirist Edmund Wilson describes. Rather, he was an experienced Victorian biographer, trying to construct Dickens' life story under the cloud of its spoiled ending. To deal with this central problem, Forster employed a variety of narrative and rhetorical strategies designed to show and conceal, to tell and then contradict, to obscure in the name of clarification.

Central to Forster's approach is the persona that he carefully constructs for himself in the first part of the biography, where he establishes his identity as Dickens' protector, confidant, and life-long friend, and as the chosen, authorized interpreter of Dickens' life. The book's dedication:

> To the Daughters of Charles Dickens
> My God-Daughter Mary
>   and
> Her Sister Kate
> This Book is Dedicated by their Friend
> And Their Father's Friend and Executor

asserts Forster's intention to serve as defender of the fatherless Dickens daughters and guardian of his subject's reputation. This announcement of his status as godfather and executor establishes Forster's position of family trust and intimacy: any conflicts between loyalty to Dickens and the biographer's need to tell a full story will, his dedication makes clear, be resolved on the side of Dickens.

Forster defines himself not only as a Dickens loyalist, but also as the anointed Dickens authority. Introducing himself on the second page of the biography with the phrase, repeated again and again in the biography, "He [Dickens] has often told me . . . ," Forster defines his own role as indirect object of Dickens' confidences and attention, as habitual, silent eye and ear (1:4). Dickens, he suggests, chose him for this role early in their friendship, both to lighten the "painful burthen" of memory "by sharing it with a friend" and to ensure, even "at this early time," that he would have his own Boswell. Although Dickens himself aided his biographer's work "by partially uplifting the veil in *David Copperfield*," he always confided in Forster "to the very eve of his death," with the understanding "strongly expressed" that Forster should tell his life (1:14).

Forster suggests that he was chosen by Dickens for reasons beyond friendship. The bond between them was forged in part by the practical help that the devoted Forster offered to Dickens: beginning in 1837, Forster not only acted as Dickens' literary negotiator and business advisor, but also corrected all of Dickens' work, either in proof or in manuscript, and Forster notes that gratitude for this labor prompted Dickens to dedicate his collected writings to Forster (1:71). But their connection, according to Forster, transcended the practical; they were also joined, as if by Kismet, by odd coincidences. The idea for Robert Seymour's first published drawing of Mr. Pickwick, for example, came from a description of a "fat old beau" from Richmond named John Foster. Equally astonishing to them both was the coincidence of Forster's birthday occurring on the same date as Dickens' wedding anniversary: "Here were the only two leading incidents of his own life before I knew him: his marriage and the first appearance of his Pickwick; and it turned out after all that I had some shadowy association with both" (1:59–60). These "shadowy associations" imply that, more than any ordinary friend, Forster is Dickens' destined true life-partner and helpmeet. Indeed, the declarations of affection from Dickens that Forster quotes echo marriage vows: ". . . it was your feeling for me and mine for you that first brought us together, and I hope will keep us so, till death do us part" (1:71). Suppressing their social estrangement during the last fifteen years of Dickens' life, Forster boasts that from the time of this declaration of attachment, for twenty successive years except when they were out of England, he, Dickens, and Catherine Dickens celebrated together their wedding and his birthday anniversary, almost as if he and

Catherine were both married to Dickens. Dickens' attachment to him, as Forster presents it in selections from Dickens' characteristically effusive letters, is "as strong as ever Nature forged." The ties between them, "never to be broken, weakened, changed in any way," will last, Dickens promises, even beyond the grave, "knotted tighter up, if that be possible" (1:357n).

The persona that Forster creates for himself—life-long companion, chosen biographer, family protector—allows him to control and contain the information about Dickens' life that he cannot suppress. Once Forster has established his own authority and value, he is able to interpose himself between Dickens and the messy historical realities that might spoil the nobility of Dickens' life story. Just as the Dickenses' wedding anniversary is elided with Forster's birthday, so that the observance of their many years of marriage becomes instead an annual celebration of Forster's mystical association with his subject, so the details of the marriage itself, indeed of Catherine's very existence, are overshadowed or screened by Forster's interpolation of himself into the narrative. In a variety of ways—through the inevitably "sly and manipulating" selection of quoted letters (Middlebrook 162), through compressions and distortions—he uses his authority to distance Dickens from embarrassing episodes in his own history; invoking his intimate knowledge of Dickens and his own trustworthiness, Forster constructs a picture of Dickens' domestic life that reduces his marriage to parenthetical phrases and almost entirely effaces his wife. At the same time, as if to fill the void left by Catherine's erasure or to distract the reader from domestic realities, he inserts himself into the story as Dickens' true companion and life-partner.

In Forster's biography, as J. W. T. Ley has pointed out, Catherine Dickens is seldom mentioned "save by way of record" (680); she is represented essentially as an absence. Her sisters are described and celebrated but she remains a cipher, the silent and invisible other in the occasional "we" of the letters from Dickens that Forster quotes. Forster, who knew Catherine Dickens intimately over many years, neither repeats any of her conversation nor gives any sense of her appearance or character: "not one picture has he given us of the wife and mother in her domestic circle" (Ley 680). When she is named, it is almost always through the screen of a letter in which Dickens either sends her regards to Forster or mentions her in passing. Forster does quote a letter crediting her with choosing from a list of possibilities the title for *David Copperfield*, although the letter goes on to note that Georgina also preferred it and that Forster himself, again at center stage, "hit upon it, on the first glance" (2:79).

Little else is revealed in the numerous Dickens letters quoted by Forster about what Catherine thinks or says, although Forster passes on, without comment, a few, presumably humorous, belittling references: "Kate wants to know whether you have any books to send her, so please to shoot here any literary rubbish on hand'' (1:107); ''We conveyed Kate up a rocky pass to go and see the island of the Lady of the Lake, but she gave in after the first five minutes, and we left her, very picturesque and uncomfortable, with Tom . . . holding an umbrella over her head, while we climbed on'' (1:154); ''I say nothing of Kate's troubles—but you recollect her propensity? She falls into, or out of, every coach or boat we enter; scrapes the skin off her legs, brings great sores and swellings on her feet; chips large fragments out of her ankle-bones; and makes herself blue with bruises'' (1:243).[5] Such jokes at Catherine's expense imply an attachment between Forster and Dickens that allows them both to laugh a bit behind her back; as one of the family, Forster is invited to patronize her also. These half-affectionate, mocking references are limited to the first half of Forster's biography; after 1851, as if in preparation for her ultimate removal, she fades almost entirely from the text, reappearing as a significant character in Dickens' life only in the 1857–58 chapter that tells of her dismissal.[6]

When Catherine Dickens is not presented through the screen of Dickens' affectionate letters to Forster, she is obliterated rhetorically. In the middle of a paragraph beginning and ending with the origins of the *Pickwick Papers*, Forster announces Dickens' marriage in language so convoluted as to be almost incomprehensible:

> At this time also, we are told in a letter before quoted, the editorship of the *Monthly Magazine* having come into Mr. James Grant's hands, this gentleman, applying to him through its previous editor to know if he would again contribute to it, learnt two things: the first that he was going to be married, and the second that, having entered into an arrangement to write a monthly serial, his duties in future would leave him small spare time. Both pieces of news were soon confirmed. *The Times* of 26 March, 1836, gave notice that on the 31st would be published the first shilling number of the *Posthumous Papers on the Pickwick Club, edited by Boz*; and the same journal of a few days later announced that on 2 April Mr. Charles Dickens had married Catherine, the eldest daughter of Mr. George Hogarth, whom already we have met as his fellow-worker on the *Chronicle*. (1:57)

This passage succeeds not only in effacing the bride, but also, in a manner characteristic of Forster, in obscuring the private by eliding it with the professional. Nothing is said about the courtship or the wedding itself: the marriage is distanced through its presentation as a newspaper announcement and subordinated to the central narrative of Dickens' career.

Forster effaces the fertile Mrs. Dickens even as the bearer of Dickens' children; she is never mentioned in Forster's announcements of their births (1:66, 85, 107, 146, 284, 378; 2:3, 77, 90, 123). Indeed, most of these announcements become the occasions for demonstrations of Dickens' deeper attachment to Forster, who seems to rush, after each of Catherine's confinements, to occupy the emotional center of Dickens' life:

Three days before a daughter had been born to him, who became a god-daughter to me; on which occasion (having closed his announcement with a postscript of ''I can do nothing this morning. What time will you ride? The sooner the better for a good long spell''), we rode out fifteen miles on the Great North Road, and, after dining at the Red Lion in Barnet on our way home, distinguished the already memorable day by bringing in both hacks dead lame.''

(1:85)

In Forster's narrative the births of the children are occasions above all for Dickens to draw closer to Forster and their world of shared male friendship; for Dickens even the christenings were significant not as religious or family rituals, but as opportunities ''to form a relationship with friends he most loved'' by naming his children after them or making them godfathers (1:146). Indeed, in describing the christening of Catherine Macready Dickens, Forster goes so far as omit her first name, observing not that she was named for her mother, but only that ''another daughter was born to him [Dickens], who bears the name of that dear friend of his and mine, Macready, whom he asked to be her god-father'' (1:107).

The virtual elimination of Mrs. Dickens as mother and wife frees Forster to offer an interpretation of Dickens' character that preserves his reputation without damaging hers. She becomes irrelevant to the story, as Forster molds it to the outlines of *David Copperfield*. Because he is Dickens' closest friend and chosen biographer, Forster says that he has been entrusted with the buried key to Dickens' personality and behavior: the trauma of his boyhood experience in the blacking warehouse. Forster argues that he and Dickens both understood that this painful and humiliating childhood experience, confided by Dickens only to his trusted Forster, has turned Charles Dickens into David Copperfield: ''the identity went deeper than any had supposed, and covered experiences not less startling in the reality than they appear to be in the fiction'' (1:7). Although Dickens disguised himself ''under the cover of his hero'' from his public's gaze, Forster is privy to the truth that *David Copperfield* had started out as autobiography, and that ''the poor little lad [Copperfield] . . . was indeed himself'' (1:20).

Like Copperfield, Forster's Dickens is morally unsoiled by his degrading early experiences, but they have left him permanently wounded in spirit and exquisitely susceptible to pain; he derived ''great good'' from these hardships, ''but not without alloy'':

The fixed and eager determination, the restless and resistless energy, which opened to him opportunities of escape from many mean environments, not by turning off from any path of duty, but by resolutely rising to such excellence or distinction as might be attainable in it, brought with it some disadvantage among many noble advantages. . . . A too great confidence in himself, a sense that everything was possible to the will that would make it so, laid occasionally

upon him self-imposed burdens greater than might be borne by anyone with safety. . . . when I have seen strangely present, at . . . chance intervals, a stern and even cold isolation of self-reliance side by side with a susceptivity almost feminine and the most eager craving for sympathy, it has seemed to me as though everything kind and gentle had sunk, for the time, under a sudden hard and inexorable sense of what Fate had dealt to him in those early years.
(1:34–35)

What Dickens self-pityingly describes in a letter quoted by Forster as "the never-to-be-forgotten misery" of "a certain ill-clad, ill-fed-child" is, Dickens and Forster agree, permanently stamped in his spirit; Dickens' adult experiences of domestic "never-to-be-forgotten misery" unavoidably reawaken the "shrinking sensitiveness" of his Copperfieldian childhood (1:35). Thus, Forster and Dickens are collaborators in constructing an interpretation of Dickens' character that is as much an apologia as it is a Rousseauian psychological analysis.

Establishing an identity between Dickens and Copperfield allows Forster to transform the unsavory story of a discarded wife into a narrative of Dickens' helpless suffering. Dickens' domestic discontents are simply Copperfield's:

David's contrasts in his earliest married life between his happiness enjoyed and his happiness once anticipated, the "vague unhappy loss or want of something" of which he so frequently complains, reflected also a personal experience which had not been supplied in fact so successfully as in fiction.   (2:109)

That "unhappy loss or want of something" to which, Forster notes, Dickens gave "pervading prominence" in *Copperfield* begins to take over Dickens himself, who complains in a letter quoted by Forster, "Why is it, that as with poor David, a sense comes always crushing on me now, when I fall into low spirits, as of one happiness I have missed in life, and one friend and companion I have never made?" (2:197). In the grip of this Copperfieldian restless discontent, Dickens is powerless to make the "considerate adjustment" or adopt "the moderate middle course" that a prudent but more ordinary man might choose (2:199). The very qualities and experiences that have made him great impel him to leave his wife:

Not his genius only, but his whole nature, was too exclusively made up of sympathy for, and with, the real in its most intense form to be sufficiently provided against failure in the realities around him. There was for him no "city of the mind" against outward ills, for inner consolation and shelter. It was in and from the actual he still stretched forward to find the freedom and satisfactions of an ideal, and by his very attempts to escape the world he was driven back into the thick of it. But what he would have sought there, it supplies to none; and to get the infinite out of anything so finite, has broken many a stout heart.
(2:200)

The tragic truth, Forster here implies, is that discarding his wife was, for Dickens, a necessary act; to remain with her, to accept the base metal of reality for the gold of the ideal, would have been to betray his sensibility, his greatness, and his own tragic past.

This apology, passionate and lengthy as it is, does not complete the difficult task of explaining Dickens' separation: Forster still had the awkward narrative problem of actually removing Mrs. Dickens from the scene. To do this, he once again elides the personal with the professional, folding the terms of the separation into a larger discussion of Dickens' public readings. Just as the announcement of Dicken's marriage is slipped into the middle of a paragraph about *Pickwick*, the news of the separation occurs in a paragraph lamenting Dickens' decision to appear on the stage for money. Again the domestic event is presented as a subordinate clause, and the private is overwhelmed by the professional:

> Exactly a fortnight after the reading for the children's hospital, on Thursday, 29 April, came the first public reading for his own benefit; and before the next month was over, this launch into a new life had been followed by a change in his old home. Thenceforward he and his wife lived apart.   (2:205)

At the same time, Forster again protects his subject by stepping forward to interpose himself between the curious or censorious reader and Dickens. He recalls that, at this difficult time in Dickens' life, he argued against any self-exposure, urging Dickens both to abandon the public role of actor and to refrain from public comment on his private troubles. "The course taken by the author of this book at the time of these occurrences, will not be departed from here," Forster insists. No decent person has any excuse for further speculation or curiosity, and Forster declares that he will remain silent on "strictly private" matters with which the "public have nothing to do" (2:206).

When Angela Burdett Coutts suggested to Dickens in 1863 that after five years' separation he meet his wife again, he replied that "a page in my life which once had writing on it, has become absolutely blank, and . . . it is not in my power to pretend that it has a solitary word upon it" (Kaplan 454). Forster, Dickens' chosen biographer, struggled in his *Life of Dickens* to make that annihilating wish come true. Using his own persona as a shield and screen, marginalizing references to Dickens' marriage, and effacing Mrs. Dickens as a character in the life of her husband and ten children, Forster contained and controlled—and almost erased—the narrative of Dickens' private domestic life. G. B. Shaw predicted that sentimental sympathy with Dickens would not survive far into the post-Ibsen twentieth century, and that posterity would take Catherine's side against a husband whose grievance against her only amounted to the fact "that she was not a female Charles Dickens" (*Letters* 1: xxii). Yet so effective was Forster's protection of his subject that it is only recent, feminist biographers like Phyllis Rose and Claire Tomalin who have whole-heartedly embraced the position, most succinctly expressed by Jane Carlyle, that "if one wanted to describe a man who had ill-used his wife, one could say he had played the dickens with her" (Rose 186).

Forster's success as Dickens' apologist took its toll, however, on the coherence of his biography. Like the hole remaining where a face has been snipped out of a family portrait, the empty space left by Forster's excision of Catherine Dickens mars his composition. Her representation in Forster's narrative as a "nobody" acts as a negation of the plot, a drain on its vitality and credibility (Kiely 61–62). Her absence even from her own childbed, for example, makes ridiculous Forster's assertion that all of Dickens' life, both before and after the "sorrowful period of 1857–58," took "the marvelously domestic home-loving shape in which also the strength of his genius is found." Forster evidently recognized this dissonance, for he appeals to the reader to overlook it: "the writer must not be charged with inconsistency who says that Dickens' childish sufferings, and the sense they burnt into him of the misery of loneliness and a craving for joys of home, though they led to what was weakest in him, led also to what was greatest" (2:394–95).

Appeals to the reader's sympathies notwithstanding, however, Forster's removal of Catherine from the *Life*, like Dickens' removal of her from his home, inevitably spoils the story. Forster's collaboration with Dickens in the erasure of his wife results in the creation of a lonely and suffering figure who, by her very absence from the text, draws sympathy away from the Copperfieldian Dickens that Forster has constructed. Indeed, Forster's invocation of Dickens' childhood misery and homesickness only highlights the absence of the faceless and voiceless wife and mother. Exiled from the page as well as from her home, the absent Catherine Dickens undermines the credibility of Forster's portrait of a suffering and haunted Dickens and drains it of pathos.

Forster does not reveal in his biography his own part in Dickens' domestic crisis. During the separation negotiations, he acted as Dickens' agent, meeting with Catherine, her mother, and her representative, Mark Lemon, to draw up a deed of separation that would spare them the publicity of going to court (Ackroyd 812; Kaplan 387). Forster's text thus reenacts the protective and collaborative role he played in Dickens' life: whether negotiating Catherine's actual dismissal or effacing her from the *Life*, Forster is complicitous as well as protective. More than simply an apologist for Dickens, Forster becomes, in his obliteration of Catherine Dickens, a participant in Dickens' own self-justifying fictions. Forster claims that he has "studied nothing so hard as to suppress . . . [his] own personality'' and that in presenting Dickens' character he has ''not shrunk'' from describing the ''grave defects'' that were revealed by Dickens' treatment of Catherine, but these claims are belied by Forster's complicity with Dickens in her extinction (2:377, 206). Far from suppressing his own personality, he has used it—indeed, augmented it—to protect his subject's dignity and to enhance thereby the value of his own narrative. While his strategies of reticence are self-serving and often clumsy, resulting in inconsistencies and unevenness, they are not naive: rather, they are sustained attempts to practice the nineteenth-century biographical art of concealing private life.

NOTES

1. More than any other biographer of his time, Forster made a business of biography (Dunn 183). He composed a number of the lives included in *Lives of Eminent British Statesmen* (1837–39), which he edited; he also wrote, in addition to his life of Dickens, biographies of Sir John Eliot (1864), Oliver Goldsmith (1848), Walter Savage Landor (1869), and Jonathan Swift (1875, unfinished).
2. Catherine Dickens' sister, Georgina Hogarth, was the other executor named in Dickens' will. As if to establish his own standing, Forster reprinted the will as an appendix to the biography. Since Dickens' relationship with his sister-in-law, who continued to live in his household after her sister was banished, was the subject of considerable rumor and speculation, appending the will may also have served to stir up old gossip. Of course the will also included a bequest to Ellen Ternan; appending it thus allowed Forster to avoid excluding her altogether.
3. In *The Invisible Woman*, Claire Tomalin demonstrates that Forster knew all about Dickens' relationship with Ellen Ternan and, in fact, at times cooperated as a go-between (179–80).
4. At times, Forster misrepresents or omits evidence in order to maintain his claims to authority and authenticity. For example, he conceals the cooling of his friendship with Dickens in the last fifteen years of Dickens' life by quoting letters to others as if they had been written to him (*Letters* 1: xv).
5. In the same letter, written during their trip to America, Dickens goes on to add some faint praise for his wife who, after travelling with him for a month over ''very rough country,'' has nevertheless managed to please him very much by not giving way to ''despondency and fatigue,'' and not screaming without justification: she has, he remarks, ''proved herself very game.''
6. Between 1851 and 1857 Catherine is mentioned a few times—as receiving a silver fruit basket (2:127), as participating in a conjuring trick (2:154), as being sent home from Boulogne with the children to escape an epidemic (2:158)—but there is almost no sense of her presence in Dickens' life.

WORKS CITED

Ackroyd, Peter. *Dickens*. New York: HarperCollins, 1990.

Dickens, Charles. *Letters*. Ed. Madeline House, Graham Storey, and Kathleen Tillotson. 5 vols. Oxford: Clarendon, 1965–81.

Dunn, Waldo. *English Biography*. New York: Dutton, 1916.

Epstein, William. *Recognizing Biography*. Philadelphia: U of Pennsylvania P, 1987.

Forster, John. *The Life of Charles Dickens*. 1872–74. 2 vols. New York: Dutton, 1966.

Gittings, Robert. *The Nature of Biography*. Seattle: U of Washington P, 1978.

Houghton, Walter. *The Victorian Frame of Mind*. New Haven: Yale UP, 1957.

Kaplan, Fred. *Dickens: A Biography*. New York: Morrow, 1988.

Kiely, Robert. "Charles Dickens: the lives of some important nobodies." *Nineteenth Century Lives*. Ed. Laurence S. Lockridge, John Maynard, and Donald D. Staines. New York: Cambridge UP, 1989. 59–81.

Ley, J. W. T., ed. *The Life of Charles Dickens*. By John Forster. 1872–74. New York: Doubleday, Doran, 1928.

Mendelson, Edward. "Authorized Biography and Its Discontents." *Studies in Biography*. Ed. Daniel Aaron. Cambridge: Harvard UP, 1978. 9–26.

Middlebrook, Diane Wood. "Postmodernism and the Biographer." *Revealing Lives: Autobiography, Biography, and Gender*. Ed. Susan Groag Bell and Marilyn Yalom. Albany: SUNY Press, 1990. 155–65.

Rose, Phyllis. *Parallel Lives: Five Victorian Marriages*. New York: Knopf, 1983.

Shelston, Alan. *Biography*. London: Methuen, 1977.

Tomalin, Claire. *The Invisible Woman*. New York: Knopf, 1990.

Wilson, A. N. *Eminent Victorians*. New York: Norton, 1990.

Wilson, Edmund. *The Wound and the Bow*. New York: Oxford UP, 1947.

Charles Reade's *Hard Cash*: Lunacy Reform Through Sensationalism

Ann Grigsby

> The tenacity of a private lunatic asylum is unique. A little push behind your back and you slide into one; but to get out again is to scale a precipice with crumbling sides.
> —Charles Reade, *Hard Cash*

Once popular and renowned as a literary artist, Charles Reade is now primarily resurrected as a foil to Charles Dickens and other more enduring Victorian novelists in occasional critical essays and doctoral dissertations. In his 1976 *Charles Reade* Elton Smith suggested that "Reade is placed just below the giants and just above the second rank of merely popular writers of the day. He remains in a distinguished but perhaps lonely limbo of his own" (157). Today, that distinction has diminished even more and Reade's fiction is further from critical revival than ever.

In the mid-nineteenth century, Reade achieved his greatest success in documentary novels advocating social reform. Even today Reade is recognized as the Victorian novelist who best utilized the insanity motif as a device in British sensational fiction. His realistic depiction of the abuses within the system controlling the insane asylums, especially in *Hard Cash* (1863), gained him fame and prestige. The political aim of exposing such abuses was important to Reade in *Hard Cash*; more significant critically was that beneath that reform agenda, the novel revealed the personal engagement of Reade the artist with those, like the insane, marginalized by Victorian society, and it developed through the metaphor of insanity, a revealing critique of Victorian materialism.

Despite his success as a novelist, Reade longed for recognition as a melodramatic playwright. He assumed that what worked on the stage would work in the novel as well; and evidently, he was not completely mistaken. Borrowing from melodrama, Reade used stock characters, rampant coincidence, and highly exaggerated incidents in his novels; in fact, in several scenes of *Hard Cash* Reade presented the dialogue in script form, even to the point of including stage directions. Like sensation novels, stage melodrama was noted for its similar reliance on the prominent themes of love, crime, and intrigue—all in excessive detail. Within melodrama, "credibility both of character and plot is sacrificed for violent effect and emotional opportunism" (Abrams 99), thus the author need not bother with detailed character development or intricate plotting devices, and as was Reade's desire, can move directly into his emotionally-charged reform issues and social critique. Emerson Sutcliffe confirms Reade's obligation to the stage in noting that "the constant succession of climaxes, of 'ups and downs,' which is an obvious feature of Reade's plotting, is essentially melodramatic—an effect of the contemporary theatre on his plot technique" ("Plotting" 851).

As in Reade's numerous melodramatic plays, the characters in *Hard Cash* are simple—several having "traveled" from Reade's preceding novel *Love Me Little, Love Me Long* (1859). With this economy in mind, Reade presented the Dodds—Lucy and David and their young-adult children Julia and Edward—who become financially and romantically entangled with the Hardies—the corrupt Richard and his more upstanding offspring, Alfred and Jane. Alfred and Edward meet at Oxford and become fast friends. Julia soon falls in love with the handsome Alfred, while Edward becomes involved with Jane.

Sea captain David Dodd is returning to his family on the last voyage of his ship the *Agra* carrying his life's savings of £14,000 with him. Within the novel's first volume, Captain Dodd defends the money from shipwrecks, pirates, mutiny, and tempests. In the second volume, Dodd's money, the "hard cash" of the title, triggers a series of events which cause several characters to be incarcerated in insane asylums. When he arrives back in England, Captain Dodd, obviously intelligent only on the high seas, naively entrusts his fortune to Richard Hardie just when the banker has experienced near financial ruin because of his unwise investments. The unscrupulous Hardie embezzles the money and throws Dodd into such an excited mental state that the sea captain loses his senses completely. Consequently, he is placed in a private asylum at the recommendation of the family doctor and friend, Dr. Sampson. When Alfred Hardie discovers his father's role in Dodd's illness and threatens to expose the crime, Richard Hardie has his son falsely incarcerated in a private asylum.

Despite insuperable odds, the characters end the novel enjoying Victorian domestic bliss: Alfred escapes from the asylum, takes first-class honors at Oxford, legally defends himself, and wins Julia as his wife; David regains his life, his sanity, and his fortune; and "as often happens after a long separation, Heaven bestowed on Captain and Mrs. Dodd another infant" (328 III xxii)[1] to mark a new generation of happiness.

Sutcliffe suggests, "In Reade's novels, the reader is kept in as high excitement and deep curiosity as possible through the characteristically melodramatic device of crowding together as many swift moving incidents as possible" ("Plotting" 851). The primary events of *Hard Cash* are highly dramatic and appear in rapid sequence in the narrative, allowing the reader the excitement of the theater while sustaining Reade's political message throughout.

In writing *Hard Cash*, Reade set out to find factual evidence with which to expose the problems of the institutions, administrators, and public agencies responsible for the treatment of the insane. He routinely turned to *The Times* which "provided Reade with a humanitarian theme directly expressive of his own thoughts and feelings" (Burns 203).

Reade scientifically devised a "great system" for gathering facts and research to amass sufficient evidence for this project. In an 1853 diary entry, Reade explained: "I propose never to guess where I can know" (qtd. in Bankson viii). Analyzing Reade's elaborate procedure, Winifred Hughes notes: "torn between mendacity and truth, alternately defensive and suspicious of his own creations, Charles Reade consistently takes refuge in documentary evidence to absolve himself of any blame" (76). Burns agrees with this assessment of Reade's writing method, and calls attention to Reade's "practice, in the novel itself, of inserting factual parentheses, and even footnotes, at every opportunity—a practice that gave the novel a more documented air" (213). Reade admittedly attempted to make his novel as factual as possible and subtitled it "a matter-of-fact romance." With a tone of uncertain timidity, Reade insisted that "If I can work the above great system, there is enough of me to make one of the writers of the day: without it, NO, NO" (qtd. in Bankson viii).

Reade "had been collecting data on 'Asyla' since perhaps as early as 1851" (Burns 202–03). He hired several secretaries to maintain the voluminous notebooks in which he recorded and pasted newspaper clippings, book extracts, and personal narratives about insanity. Sutcliffe notes that the books are "bulky, somewhat haphazard in arrangements, extremely miscellaneous, a medley in which significance is often snowed under drifts of inconsequential clippings" ("Notebooks" 64). In his unpublished dissertation, "Charles Reade's Manuscript Notecards for *Hard Cash*," Douglas Bankson details Reade's practice of extracting pertinent information from the various notebooks and transferring the documents on to large 18- by 24-inch notecards.

"The cards may have restrained Reade in some of his more critical attitudes toward religion and morality which would have offended his readers or taken him beyond the limits of simple fact" (Bankson 2). Like the fact-collecting habit of his fictional character Edward Dodd in *Hard Cash*, who "has been all these years quietly cutting up the *Morning Advertiser*, and arranging the slips with wonderful skill and method" (152 II xxv), Reade devoted much time and energy to the task of collecting and ordering the news of the day. Attempting to place himself beyond the often derogatory label of sensation novelist, Reade explained in the Preface to *Hard Cash*:

> These truths have been gathered by long, severe, systematic labor, from a multitude of volumes, pamphlets, journals, reports, blue-books, manuscript narratives, letters, and living people, whom I have sought out, examined, and cross-examined, to get at the truth on each main topic I have striven to handle. (3)

Despite his best efforts at this massive organizational project, Reade "simply could not maintain the desired focus in any but the Notecards devoted to clippings (Burns 211). He even admitted in his diary, "I have the desire for method, but not the gift" (qtd. in Bankson vi). According to Burns, "because the Notecards were so ill arranged and so unwieldly . . . he actually lost sight of an article . . . and did not rediscover it until later, when he wrote 'Forgot to use this—like an ass' " (212). This omission is hardly surprising considering the cryptic notations and random order of the notecard entries even when the information is neatly transcribed as Bankson has done. Reade indiscriminately mixed subjects including bibliographies, Lunacy Commission reports, snatches of dialogue, and personal memoranda together on the same cards. The author confused the issue even further by writing reminders of himself on the notecards, such as: "Hunt journals for details. . . . Much of this used in No. 20. . . . [and] Good for Preface" (Bankson, 34, 53, 55). In addition, many entries are elaborately cross-referenced to other cards and notebooks.

One of the most difficult obstacles facing the novelist was that the seemingly harsh treatments Reade dramatized were legal and practiced by respected medical professionals as viable alternatives for curing their insane patients. Burns illuminates the dilemma, noting:

> Although the asylum keepers may have been "soul-murderers," as Reade charged, few if any of them had, . . . committed atrocities in clear defiance of the letter and spirit of the Lunacy Laws. Their most reprehensible atrocities were those that they committed with full medical and legal sanction, often in the belief that they were helping their patients. (217)

Social historians agree that during the nineteenth century eccentric "cures" were tested on defenseless patients in the name of medical progress; however, authentic reform was occurring within the burgeoning psychological field. That this needed reform was slow and delayed by ignorance, prejudice, and economic pressures is evidenced by successive Lunacy Commission reports. His letters and other writings about the abuses within the asylums show that Reade was genuinely appalled by the state of affairs just after mid-century. Nonetheless, Reade's preoccupation with this topic may also indicate the author's more personal and symbolic interpretation of himself and of society as well.

Knowing from his own research that the newspapers were filled with articles on insanity and asylums, Reade took for granted that his readers were aware of the insanity problem. He was obviously frustrated that many Victorians seemed to condone a system in which abuses were rampant.

Roy Porter indicates that from the eighteenth century on, the two most common complaints about insane asylums were "illegal or improper confinement," usually at family instigation, and "gross brutality" (*Faber* 350). Reade eagerly tackled both of these issues in his novel, but this is only the beginning of his list of wrongs which he thought needed to be redressed. In addition to cruelty, brutality, and false incarceration, Reade attacked the indiscriminate distribution of opiates to subdue patients, and the sexual harassment and abuse suffered by patients within the asylums. Assuming that the public's apathy stemmed from ignorance, Reade set out first to document and then to dramatize some of the worst of the abuses. Sheila Smith notes:

> Reade chose specific incidents which aroused his indignation because of their injustice or inhumanity, transferred them thinly disguised into his novel, and relied upon melodramatic climaxes and occasional direct harangues to the reader to get his indignation across.   (147)

Through this method, Reade was able to convince readers of abuses within private insane asylums and of the ineffectuality of the regulations imposed by the Lunacy Commission. The passages depicting the different asylums offered anything but comfortable pictures as Reade realistically detailed abysmal living conditions and "cures" that seem more like tortures than medical treatments. Throughout the novel, patients are routinely forced to endure water dunkings, brutal beatings, painful physical restraint, loud noises, and sleep deprivation. Reports of decreased sales of Dickens' *All the Year Round* while Reade's novel was serialized there implies that Victorians recoiled from the realistic images of the mysterious insane asylums. At the same time they hungered for the exposé—both Elwin and Burns suggest that Reade "could look forward to realizing more than £5000 on the novel" (Burns 206), which means the author earned nearly £4000 from the publication of the three volume edition after a less-than-triumphant serialization.

Reade's frank realism in his portrait of asylum conditions became a heated political issue during the serialization of the novel; however, the political nature of *Hard Cash* had its origins even before the first installment was written. Reade's decision to publish with Dickens represented a tacit agreement that Reade would enjoy a certain degree of artistic freedom to criticize Victorian society at his own discretion. Whereas Dickens may have experienced an awkward embarrassment with other colleagues over the nature of the resulting novel, he was sincerely interested in securing Reade for his publication and was fully aware of Reade's reputation for social criticism. Dickens wrote to Reade about presenting a story for his periodical insisting, "It would give me the highest gratification to grace these pages with your name, and to have you for a fellow-labourer" (Rolfe 132–33). According to John Sutherland, Dickens paid Reade £800 for the serial rights with Reade retaining the copyright; however, while Reade and Dickens were in preliminary negotiations for *Hard Cash*, rival editor George Smith made Reade a far more generous offer of £2000 for an unwritten novel, with an additional £1000 if it were serialized in *The Cornhill*. Despite the obviously higher remuneration available, the question of possible editorial interference at *The Cornhill* decided the issue; Reade would work with Dickens on what was serially entitled *Very Hard Cash* running in forty weekly installments from 28 March to 26 December 1863.

Reade's rejection of a considerably larger *Cornhill* profit emphasizes his dedication to the asylum reform movement as well as his determination to assess honestly what he considered a hypocritical and judgmental society. An editor with less respect than Dickens for another artist's professional integrity might have sacrificed art for sales. As Sutherland claims, "Dickens comes out rather well as an editor . . . high-minded in withholding his editorial prerogative" (11) even though, Sutherland adds, "that part of the story which has the hero incarcerated in a lunatic asylum by his father shocked, alarmed and eventually turned away readers" (10).

Elton Smith confirms Sutherland's assertion, noting that "Despite Dickens's personal admiration, the serial was none too successful and was rumored to have lowered the circulation of the magazine by three thousand copies" while *Very Hard Cash* ran (108). If this figure is accurate, and Reade acknowledged it himself in a letter to Laura Seymour noting, "the story has done them no good, in fact they print 3000 copies less than at the outset" (qtd. in Elwin 173), the loss of sales represented only three per cent of *All the Year Round*'s circulation which consistently sold 100,000 copies; nonetheless, offending the paying public was not Dickens' usual procedure. Dickens was able to encourage Reade in drawing "his narrative to an end in a frantic gallop of events'' (Sutherland 10). The drop in sales may be attributable not only to Reade's stark realism in portraying the horrible asylum conditions, but also to his unwelcome account of the indifferent and materialistic society which allowed the real atrocities of the insane asylums to occur.

Instilling his lines with subtle meaning, Reade made sharp critical attacks within seemingly innocuous passages. For example, Reade criticized the prejudice against public insane asylums when David's astonished wife Lucy refuses her son's suggestion of moving David to a public asylum to save money. Like Reade, Edward's argument rests with the newspaper statistics, but ''In vain [he] cited the *'Tiser* that public asylums are patterns of comfort, and cure twice as many patients as the private ones do'' (54 III vi). Her common sense informs Lucy that her money and expensive presents would have less influence in a public institution. Harboring a commonly held fear, she also recoils from placing ''my husband, your father, in a public asylum, where anybody can go and stare at my darling!'' (54 III vi).

The connection between insanity and materialism Reade insisted upon is evident in many of his asylum descriptions. Personifying Reade's attack on the over-priced fees demanded by private asylum keepers, Lucy endures personal poverty to afford the institution's annual fee of £250, and can only hope her husband is well attended. Whether or not David is treated well, Lucy is at least appeased and catered to as an important client during her occasional visits to her husband.

Reade next focused on the tacit understanding by families that extra money will insure human treatment. Naive Julia fears the attendants may be angry when Lucy ''bribed them with money to use him kindly: I thought they would be offended and refuse it: but they took it'' (146 II xxv). Despite her good intentions, the gullible Lucy is paying for a comforting illusion. In return for her money, Lucy receives a practiced performance; when she visits, the asylum is set in order. The troublesome maniacs and the same prisoners like Alfred are taken safely out of sight and David is made to appear comfortable. When the paying family members retreat, however, the scene reverts to a less-than-ideal reality. Attendants become brusque and patients are again locked within their rooms in lonely isolation. Reade condemned the bribery and the hypocritical staging of proper and humane treatment.

Similar hypocrisy ensues when the Lunacy Commission inspectors arrive. When this occurs in *Hard Cash* at Silverton Grove House,

> The whole house was in a furious bustle. All the hobbles and chains and instruments of restraint were hastily collected and bundled out of sight, and clean sheets were being put on many a filthy bed whose occupant had never slept in sheets since he came there. (247 II xxxi)

Reade, the reformer, insisted, ''Inspectors who visit a temple of darkness, lies, cunning, and hypocrisy, four times a year, know mighty little of what goes on there the odd three hundred and sixty-one days'' (99 III viii). According to Reade, the suffering inmates never complain about their miserable conditions and brutal treatment because experience has taught them that

> The justices could not at once remedy their discomforts, whereas the keepers, the very moment the justices left the house, would knock them down, beat them, shake them, strait-jacket them, and starve them.   (251 II xxxi)

To reiterate his contention that no sane man could endure the daily routine in the asylums, Reade engaged Alfred in dramatic struggles. Within his first moments at Silverton Grove House, his first asylum, Alfred attempts a daring and painful escape: "He broke the glass with his shoulder, and tore and kicked the woodwork, and squeezed through on to a stone ledge outside, and stood there bleeding and panting" (225 II xxx). He landed in a water tank, floated to avoid drowning, feigned death to reach safety, and still energetically bounded across the lawn of the asylum dealing blows to any attendant near him. Once captured and back inside the institution, Alfred loses no chance to strike out and injure his keepers. After this initial display of force, he is considered "dangerous" and treated accordingly: "They took him to the strong-room, and manacled his ankles together with an iron hobble, and then strapped them to the bedposts, and fastened his body down" (230 II xxx). The details of this punishment are taken directly from Reade's notecards, one of which describes a "gentleman handcuffed & hobbled, and strapped on the bed of cruelty" (Bankson 73).

Alfred's athletic feats and action-packed beginning at the asylum contrast with the helpless condition to which he is later reduced. When the sane Alfred becomes unruly, he is calmed by "a powerful opiate" (243 II xxxi) even though the drug makes him violently ill. Reade explained that this practice is used often and that "the tranquilizing influences employed were morphia, croton-oil, or a blister" (246 II xxxi). Alfred is subjected to repeated beatings and rough handling, forced restraint, and the sexual advances of the head mistress. Reade described how the cowardly attendants attack helplessly bound patients and display "the art of breaking a man's ribs, or breastbone, or both, without bruising him externally" (264 II xxxii). Alfred would also have been a victim of this abuse had not the smitten Mrs. Archbold interfered to stop his tormentor. Reade addressed the reader in questioning the extent of this behavior: "And how many more, God only knows; we can't count the stones at the bottom of a dark well" (264 II xxxii).

Alfred's laments are ignored as the ravings of a violent maniac. On the evening that would have been his wedding night, Alfred is forced to substitute frustration for ecstasy. In a passage in which Reade clearly depicted the transference of the young bridegroom's thwarted sexual energy, Alfred wrestles and screams to no avail. In his desperation, Alfred "struggled, he writhed, he bounded: he made the very room shake. . . . The perspiration rolled down his steaming body. . . . [then] He lay still exhausted" (232 II xxx). Reade summarized the condition of all insane within the current asylum system in noting Alfred's realization: "No answer. No motion. No help. No hope" (232 II xxx).

Alfred suffers the humiliations of dressing before the crude attendants, the irritation of biting insects as he attempts to sleep, and the false hope that his correspondence is actually sent from the asylum. After he spurns the amorous intentions of the aggressive head mistress, Mrs. Archbold, his life becomes even more miserable as his few privileges are revoked and he is left to drive himself insane waiting for a justice system which is unresponsive: "He was to have no occupation now, except to brood and brood and brood" (125 III ix).

As often as the narrative allows, Reade reminded readers that even as an innocent Englishman, Alfred must struggle against the social injustice fraudulently placed upon him. Alfred eloquently tells the visiting magistrate, Mr. Vane.

> "You can do nothing for me but restore me to my dignity as a man, my liberty as a Briton, and the rights as a citizen I have been swindled out of."
>
> (256 II xxxii)

According to Reade, Alfred's predicament was a real threat to any citizen because the lunacy laws were vague and bureaucratic—drastically in need of reform. In a letter aimed at his critics, Reade contended:

> The fact would appear to be that under existing arrangements any English man or woman may without much difficulty be incarcerated in a private lunatic asylum when not deprived of reason.   (Preface 14)

Reade ominously ended the dramatic chapter detailing Alfred's false incarceration by warning readers: "Think of it for your own sakes; Alfred's turn today, it may be yours to-morrow" (232 II xxx).

Reade obviously intended to and did expose the dreadful conditions of asylums, but he also focused on aspects of the lunacy law which he saw as violating the civil liberties of British subjects. The laws Reade attacked were those actual guidelines from the Lunacy Commission regulating the incarceration and release of patients in asylums, laws which Reade satirically labeled "little trumpery statutes" (196 III xiii). From the early nineteenth century up to the time of the publication of *Hard Cash*, these laws were in a constant state of flux, passing through new legislation in 1828, 1845, 1850, 1853, 1858–1859, and 1862. These reforms cover numerous issues ranging from the property rights of the insane to the legal responsibilities of asylum keepers. Despite the apparent social concern over insanity, Reade complained that "the English Statutes of Lunacy are famous monuments of legislatorial incapacity" (196 III xiii).

The inevitable complaints against Reade surfaced before the serial run of the novel was even complete. Doctors and asylum keepers involved with the care of the insane claimed the sensational propaganda fiction Reade and others promoted as reform was actually a deterrent to the improvement of the system. In reply, Reade engaged in a virulent newspaper battle defending his accounts of the abuses within the asylums. One critic, Dr. J. S. Bushnan, proprietor of a private asylum at Salisbury, denounced Reade's fiction as "the terrible slander cast upon a body of professional men to which I am proud to belong" (Preface 6), and claimed Reade fabricated all of his information concerning the operation of private lunatic asylums. Similarly, a contemporary reviewer observed:

> The incautious reader is apt to imagine mad doctors to be scientific scoundrels, lunatic asylums to be a refined sort of Tophet, and the commissioners in lunacy and visiting justices to be a flock of sheep. This is the untruthful exaggeration of fact jumbled with fiction.   (qtd. in Parry-Jones 229–30)

Reade responded defiantly to such attacks, but especially to Dr. Bushnan's complaints, in a lengthy letter stating that in *Hard Cash* he offered only facts which came to him through the current newspapers, and he proceeded to relate the details of several recent cases of false incarceration.

The ensuing debate caused such controversy that Dickens added a disclaimer after the last installment of *Very Hard Cash*, declaring in large print that the opinions presented by Reade were not held by the management of *All the Year Round*. The diplomatic Dickens insisted:

> The statements and opinions of this journal generally, are, of course, to be received as the statements and opinions of its conductor. . . . [however], when one of my literary brothers does me the honour to undertake such a task, I hold that he executes it on his own personal responsibility, and for the sustainment of his own reputation.   (qtd. in Elwin 174)

In 1961, Richard Hunter and Ida Macalpine revealed through previously unpublished letters from Dickens to Dr. Harrington Tuke that Dickens personally knew the famous mental health reformer, Dr. John Conolly (534). Tuke evidently wrote to Dickens concerned by Reade's blatant ridicule of Conolly in the character of the inept asylum keeper Dr. Wycherley, whom Reade calls "a collector of mad people" (89 III vii). In response, Dickens wrote:

> I cannot imagine Mr. Reade has the least knowledge of what you tell me concerning Dr. Conolly. . . . Mr. Reade is enormously mistaken and damages a

good cause. But I cannot believe that he would wilfully be personal and cruel.
(qtd. in Hunter 534)

Caught between his friendly professional relationship with fellow artist Reade on the one hand, and an important social acquaintance with the noted physician Conolly on the other, Dickens attempted to distance himself from any disagreeable debates.

Twentieth-century historian Kathleen Jones criticizes Reade for being instrumental in agitating "the public preoccupation with the danger of illegal detention," (161) indicating that this abuse occurred far less frequently than Reade implied. While acknowledging Reade's thorough familiarity with the available literature on the asylums, Jones insists that "most of his information referred to isolated cases of abuse—not normal practice—discovered and rectified many years before *Hard Cash* was written" (163).

In spite of the attacks and the controversy, Reade did not moderate his strictures on insanity and thus on materialism. He insisted, "Once in a madhouse, the sanest man is mad however interested and barefaced the motive of the relative who has brought two of the most venal class upon earth to sign away his wits behind his back" (231 II xxx). This attack on overly compliant physicians, however, may have misrepresented the situation. Under the Lunacy Act of 1845, according to Andrew Scull in *The Most Solitary of Afflictions*, physicians were required to submit detailed first-hand reports of the patient's condition when admitting someone into an insane asylum; therefore, it is difficult to surmise exactly which lunacy laws Reade was criticizing. He addressed diverse topics, usually connected to monetary concerns, compiled from various time periods regardless of the recent legislation enacted to curb particular abuses within the system as he was writing *Hard Cash*. Reade implied that despite the written safeguards of regulations and laws to protect the insane, the operational reality of the asylum system was corrupt and easily abused. According to Reade, while reform was changing the condition of some asylums and their patients, most private asylums in England, even at mid-century, still administered inhumane treatment to the insane.

Reade particularly noted the injustice of the law which allowed any relative, no matter how distant, the right to sign the certificates which incarcerated a patient. In "Our Dark Places" Reade stated that any family member need only secure the opinion of two doctors, easily bought according to Reade, to establish the vaguely defined "satisfactory evidence of insanity" (156). In *Hard Cash*, Julia Dodd again speaks to the uninformed public when she notes in her diary: "It does seem strange that anyone but mamma should be able to send papa out of the house, and to such a place; but it is the law" (146 II xxv). David Dodd's sister Eve signs the papers committing him to the private asylum. In Alfred's case, his father, in order to distance himself from the act of incarceration, forces a feeble-minded uncle, "Soft Tommy," to authorize Alfred's detention.

Another point of contention Reade detailed concerned the limited rights of the insane under the lunacy regulations. Alfred discovers, soon after his escape from Drayton House,

> one of the galling iniquities of the system. . . . The prisoner whose wits and liberty have been signed away behind his back is not allowed to see the order and certificate on which he is confined—until *after* his release; that release he is to obtain by combatting the statements in the order and certificates.
>
> (184–85 III xii)

This absurd dilemma, Reade declared, is the basis of the injustice of the Lunacy Commission statutes which must be reformed to protect the insane. In the case of a sane man falsely incarcerated, the ill-logical operation of the law is amplified.

During his entire ordeal in the different asylums, Alfred continues to fight, "urged by that terror of a madhouse, which is natural to a sane man, and in England is fed by occasional disclosures, and the general suspicion they excite" (225 II xxx). Reade maintained his consistent public criticism by thus feeding the public more disclosures about false incarceration, brutal treatment, cruel punishment, and bureaucratic confusion surrounding patients' entrance to and exit from private insane asylums.

By making the asylum the villain in his melodramatic plot, and by presenting familiar melodramatic figures engaged in thrilling action in order to escape the horrors of the asylum, Reade hoped to convince readers of the danger in society's attempts to normalize all those whose actions placed them outside the rigid confines of socially-accepted behavior. Reade had a personal interest in this task of persuasion.

Reade's notecards and letters are filled with repeated defenses of his own sanity. Included in his collection of letters prefacing *Hard Cash* is a description of a woman he presented before the Lunacy Commission as falsely incarcerated. His justification of her mental stability is typical: "She was perfectly sane, as sane as I am" (9). In *Hard Cash* these words are echoed by an inmate assigned to feed Alfred who exclaims in astonishment, "Why, this man is sane; as sane as I am" (236 II xxxi). With slight variations, Alfred often exclaims: "I am as sane as any man in England" (253 II xxxi). And the ship's surgeon who proclaims David Dodd alive and well also acknowledges, "[he] is as sane as I am" (310 III xxi).

Beginning at Oxford, Reade himself was considered odd, eccentric, and even mad. Out of defiance to the demands for conformity placed upon him within the university setting, Reade began "wearing long curls, a bright green coat with brass buttons, and in general conducting himself so strangely—what with his fiddle playing and dancing the double shuffle" (Burns 31) that he made sure he would never fit it. Classmates maliciously nicknamed him "Mad Charles." In *Hard Cash*, Alfred suffers a similar rejection: "Alfred, finding the men of his own college suspected his sanity, and passed jokes behind his back, cut them all dead, and confined himself to his little Hall" (242 III xvii). Burns suggests that in Reade's "attempts at self vindication he was refuting without acknowledging the charges of madness that had been levelled at him since his undergraduate days—charges that he not only hated but feared" (201). Later in life, similar charges were brought against Reade as critics noted his eccentric behavior as proof of an unsound mind. W. B. Maxwell remembered visits to Reade's London home in which he encountered "a small antelope or gazelle" permitted to "wander freely from floor to floor and room to room indoors" (qtd. in Burns 324).

To counter charges of mental instability, Reade early turned to a dependence on logical organization based on Baconian principles which eventually led him to maintain his vast notebooks. This trait is also transferred to *Hard Cash*; when studying for his Oxford exams, Alfred withdraws into seclusion to study with Readian precision, using colored notecards and a rigid system of organization.

Unfortunately, Reade got carried away with his organizational technique, and even this practice invited negative comment. Hughes suggests, "Reade's passion for documentation . . . barely conceals his chronic doubt and ambivalence about both his own talent and the fictional process itself" (75). The more Reade strove to establish his stability, the more he engaged in erratic, suspect behavior. Critics like Bushnan complained that Reade was merely "a writer of sensation romances" (*Readiana* 6) and did not improve the condition of the insane through his interference. Burns indicates, "to all such attacks Reade invariably retorted in kind. No charge, no slight, however insignificant, was beneath his notice. He answered them all . . . as if his very life depended on it" (202). If not his life, perhaps Reade's precarious mental stability did depend on his continued reiteration of his own sanity. In his repeated claims of mental stability, Reade displayed his empathy with the insane, and others who feel the negative effects of being branded as "other."

Because of this empathy perhaps, Reade felt an obligation to expose the evils of the asylum system to the reading public. In 1858, Reade personally investigated the case of Fletcher, a supposedly sane man, incarcerated under false pretenses by his mercenary relatives. The author/reformer recounted this affair in the essay "Our Dark Places" reprinted in *Readiana*. Reade's description of the case echoed passages of his own novels, including *Hard Cash*, when he began:

On Friday last, a tale was brought to me that a sane prisoner had escaped from
a private madhouse, had just baffled an attempt to recapture him by violent
entry into a dwelling-house, and was now hiding in the suburbs.

(*Readiana* 151)

Reade investigated the case by examining the deceased father's will, and then
writing to the papers about the inequities of the system regulating the insane
asylums. As Reade noted in a letter to the *Daily News*, he also "hindered
[Fletcher's] recapture, showed him his legal remedy, fed, clothed, and kept
him for twelve months" (Preface 8). The author feverishly championed
Fletcher's cause, a man with a questionable hold on his mental stability even
by Reade's own account. Compton Reade in *Charles Reade: A Memoir* describes Fletcher as dangerous if not insane (82). As if determined to make a
personal statement regardless of the qualifications of the principal witness,
Reade supported Fletcher through months of hiding, delayed hearings, and
finally to the young man's victory in court legally establishing his sanity.

Fletcher informed Reade that "the keeper of the madhouse told him he
should never go out of it" (*Readiana* 154). This first-hand information was
enough to set Reade on a tirade against injustice. Reade determined that if
Fletcher, a "man, whose word I have no reason to doubt" was telling the
truth, then "he was a customer, not a patient: he was not in a hospital, but
in a gaol, condemned to imprisonment for life" (*Readiana* 154). From this
point on in the letters, Reade called for justice through publicity. Describing
the anxiety of the delayed trial on his protégé, Reade noted, "a lunatic is a
beast in the law's eye and society's; and an alleged lunatic is a lunatic until
a jury pronounces him sane" (*Readiana* 16–167). These words are repeated
verbatim in *Hard Cash* as Dr. Sampson defends Alfred against his accusers
(263 III xviii).

Throughout the collection of letters "To the Gentlemen of the Press"
which comprises "Our Dark Places," Reade established connections between
himself and the allegedly insane Fletcher. Reade described an elaborate game
he played to verify Fletcher's sanity, which established an official certification
of Reade's own mental stability as well. Reade took Fletcher to meet with
"medical men of real eminence, and not in league with madhouse doctors"
(*Readiana* 153). Consequently, Fletcher and Reade were ushered into a room
by Reade's friend and collaborator Dr. Dickson, who becomes Dr. Sampson
in *Hard Cash*. Another physician, Dr. Ruttledge, was told, " 'one of these is
insane, said to be. Which is it?' " (*Readiana* 151). The melodramatic scene
climaxes in both doctors having established not only the disputed sanity of
Fletcher, but more importantly, of Reade by twice proclaiming: " 'This one
is sane' " (*Readiana* 154). Reade reported that "the result of all this was a
certificate of sanity" for Fletcher (*Readiana* 154). The indirect result, of

course, was to give similar certification to Reade. Within the span of only a few paragraphs, Reade repeated his own claim to mental stability three times.

Possibly because of this personal involvement with the issues of insanity reform, Reade considered *Hard Cash* his masterpiece. Reade must have been pleased with the results of the novel. Not only was he able to exhibit his painstaking research and expose the actual atrocities of insane asylums, but also, most rewardingly, he was able to verbalize his criticisms about Victorian society in a dramatic and entertaining medium. Reade needed the liberty of storytelling or dramatic role-playing to facilitate his ambition to be a mediator of social progress. In this way Reade was able to explore and then present his personal engagement with the issues of insanity while maintaining his conviction of his own mental stability.

Possibly attempting the type of satirical attack indicting mid-Victorian England that Dickens had made famous in *Little Dorrit* (1855–57) using prisons and *Bleak House* (1852–53) using the legal system as metaphors of the stagnation of a declining society, in *Hard Cash* Reade condemned Victorian respectability based on materialism. Specifically, Reade emphasized the corruption possible when money becomes power. Dickens suggested an ironic alternative title for the serial, *As Safe as the Bank*, which would have equally indicated this element or Reade's social critique; the insane become merely money deposited into asylum banks to enrich corrupt proprietors. According to Reade, the entire private insane asylum system functioned on this improper and corrupt use of money. When cash became the dominant factor in decision-making, as it did often in the pages of *Hard Cash*, Reade contended, justice, morality, and common sense were forgotten. This disrupted state of affairs negatively affected every segment of society. Reade argued that the excessive attention paid to attaining, maintaining, and displaying material possessions caused society's intolerance toward those who did not conform to convention.

The characters in *Hard Cash* who actually suffer from insanity, do so because of a compulsive preoccupation with money. Richard Hardie, David Dodd, and James Maxley form fixations on cash and become unable to consider any other issue. Alfred, who is incarcerated while sane, is accused of a similar solitary delusion. While Reade, financially successful himself, did not directly equate wealth with insanity, he did censure the inordinate value placed on material wealth by society. One instance of Reade's critique of Victorian materialism is his in-depth characterization of Richard Hardie. Hardie is more than the melodramatic villain; he becomes Reade's symbol of Victorian society's false nature. In the initial scenes, Richard Hardie, the wealthy town banker, is respected as a model of the successful Victorian businessman. Society stood in awe of Richard Hardie because "at five and twenty. . . . He saved the bank'' (171 I v). He maintained his reputation for keen business because his youth ''was colder and wiser than other people's old age'' (172 I v). In actuality, as events unfold, he is corrupt, cruel, and immoral. Not only does he steal David Dodd's hard cash, but also he has disastrously speculated with his own children's inheritance—money to which he had no legal claim. He is unfeeling for the plight of the many loyal bank clients his embezzlement ruins, and remains callous to the end of the novel. Even at the deathbed of his daughter Jane, Richard schemes to conceal his illegal behavior and keeps Alfred from seeing his dying sister. To emphasize his critique, Reade doled out retributive justice to Richard, as the once powerful banker ends his days an idiot playing with coins. Although he has by now recovered his fortune, Richard regresses into an idiotic state because of the monomania which drove his professional life. In his delusion, Richard forced Alfred to take over his accounts, amounting to over £60,000, and ''entrapped Alfred into an agreement to board and lodge him, and pay him a guinea every Saturday at noon'' (333 III xxii). ''Richard Hardie died, his end being hastened by fear of poverty coming like an armed man'' (335 III xxii). Reade presented Richard Hardie as a sobering example of the moral ruin which results from excessive materialism.

Through his careful examination of individual characters, Reade presented his concern with the materialistic madness of society in general. Like many Victorians, Reade defined the manic, fast-paced, progress-at-any-price lifestyle of England in the 1860s as insanity. Eminent Victorian doctors like George Robinson ''had no qualms about linking what he took to be the increasing incidence of insanity with social progress'' (Rance 118). While historians generally concur that there was not an epidemic-scale increase in insanity during the nineteenth century as many Victorians feared, there was an increased awareness of mental illness as a serious condition capable of afflicting all levels of society. If Reade's criticism of Victorian respectability was not exactly that ''all the world is mad''—he certainly suggested that the false appearances and hypocrisy caused by the materialism of his society were a kind of madness. Society refused to see itself as related to the insane, so part of Reade's purpose became linking the materialistic obsession of Victorian society with the insane and their asylums.

As Reade attempted to show, both groups are easily corruptible, lie without remorse, are convinced that cruelty is necessary and acceptable, and that authority should loom over weaklings or those unable to resist the more powerful. Moreover, Reade was eager to portray the asylums in terms of great country homes, which they closely resemble. Silverton Grove House is ''a large square mansion of red brick. . . . It stood on its own grounds, and the entrance was through handsome iron gates'' (220 II xxx). In Dr. Wycherley's establishment, ''the linen was clean, and the food good'' (8 III i). In both of these asylums, the "first class" insane dine in formal evening dress and abide by the etiquette of respectable society. The gentlemen may read and smoke, and the ladies sew or paint just as their sane counterparts in respectable Victorian society do. Each of the similarities between the appearance in the asylums and respectable society strengthened Reade's contention that excessive Victorian materialism was itself a form of insanity. While Reade's contemporary readers may have resisted connecting themselves to the insane depicted in *Hard Cash*, the fact-related novel did reach an audience anxious to understand the asylum system if not completely prepared for Reade's realism in depicting that system.

In an 1863 notice appended to later editions of *Hard Cash*, Reade noted: "this great question did not begin with me in the pages of a novel, neither shall it end there" (21). George Orwell wrote of Reade, "He wrote of life as he saw it, and many Victorians saw it in the same way: that is, as a series of melodramas, with virtue triumphant every time" (36–37). In his greatest literary success, *Hard Cash*, with several public and private agendas in mind, Reade used the Victorian insane asylum system as a medium through which to establish his social criticism.

NOTES

1. The edition of *Hard Cash* used for reference throughout this essay is the DeLuxe Edition, The Grolier Society, Boston, 1912. I have included the page, volume, and chapter numbers for each quotation.

WORKS CITED

Abrams, M. H. *A Glossary of Literary Terms*. 5th ed. NY: Holt, 1988.

Bankson, Douglas Henneck. "Charles Reade: Manuscript Notecards for *Hard Cash*." Diss. U of Washington, 1954.

Burns, Wayne. *Charles Reade: A Study in Victorian Authorship*. NY: Bookman, 1961.

Clareson, Thomas D. "Charles Reade's Letter Book: From Shadows to Substance." *Princeton University Library Chronicle*. 47.2 (1986): 224–28.

Elwin, Malcolm. *Charles Reade: A Biography*. London: J. Cape, 1931.

Hughes, Winifred. *The Maniac in the Cellar: Sensation Novels of the 1860's*. Princeton, NJ: Princeton UP, 1980.

Hunter, R. A. and I. Macalpine. "Dickens and Conolly. An Embarrassed Editor's Disclaimer." *Times Literary Supplement*, 11 August 1961.

Jones, Kathleen. *Lunacy, Law, and Conscience, 1744–1845.* London: Routledge and Kegan Paul, 1955.

Orwell, George. *Collected Essays, Journalism and Letters of George Orwell.* Eds. Sonia Orwell and Ian Angus. Vol. 2. NY: HBJ, 1968. 2 vols.

Parry-Jones, William. *The Trade in Lunacy.* London: Routledge and Kegan Paul, 1972.

Phillips, Walter C. *Dickens, Reade, and Collins: Sensation Novelists: A Study in the Conditions and Theories of Novel Writing in Victorian England.* 1919. NY: Russell and Russell, 1962.

Porter, Roy, ed. *The Faber Book of Madness.* Boston: Faber and Faber, 1991.

Rance, Nicholas. *Wilkie Collins and Other Sensation Novelists: Walking the Moral Hospital.* Rutherford, NJ: Fairleigh Dickinson UP, 1991.

Reade, Charles. *Hard Cash.* Boston: The Grolier Society, [1863].

———. "Our Dark Places." *Readiana.* Boston: The Grolier Society, n.d.

Rolfe, F. P. "Additions to the Nonesuch Edition of Dickens Letters." *Huntington Library Quarterly* 5.1 (1991): 115–40.

Scull, Andrew, ed. *The Most Solitary of Afflictions: Madness and Society in Britain, 1700–1900.* New Haven: Yale UP, 1993.

Smith, Elton E. *Charles Reade.* Boston: Twayne, 1976.

Smith, Sheila M. "Propaganda and Hard Facts in Charles Reade's Didactic Novels: A Study of *It Is Never Too Late to Mend* and *Hard Cash.*" *Renaissance and Modern Studies* [University of Nottingham] 4 (1960): 135–49.

Sutcliffe, Emerson Grant. "Charles Reade's Notebooks." *Studies in Philology* 27.1 (1930): 64–87.

———. "Plotting in Reade's Novels." *PMLA* 47.3 (1932): 832–63.

Sutherland, John. "Dickens, Reade, and *Hard Cash.*" *Dickensian* 81.1 (1985): 5–12.

Mindless Millinery: Catherine Gore and the Silver Fork Heroine

Winifred Hughes

I.

For George Eliot, surveying the literary scene of the 1850s, the most prominent class of "silly novels by lady novelists" seemed to be what she termed the *"mind-and-millinery* species." In that typically Victorian hybrid, even the popular heroine was expected to function as "the ideal woman in feelings, faculties, and flounces," effortlessly combining the height of fashion with moral and critical acumen. If the emphasis on "mind" was new, the requisite "millinery" harkened back to the venerable prototypes of the 1820s and thirties, when the silver fork or fashionable novels reigned and the queen of the lady novelists was Mrs. Gore. These two generations of silly novels, as Eliot recognized, were historically linked: if mind-and-millinery fiction had displaced the silver fork, it was also a lineal descendent. Even when its heroine began to develop a case of seriousness or religious enthusiasm and took to "read[ing] the Bible in the original tongues," she still had to contend with the "intrigues of the vicious baronet" and the vagaries of Almack's, while her moral worth was inevitably validated by her social status. She was expected to make the most dazzling of matches and to wear "some family jewels or other as a sort of crown of righteousness at the end." The lady novelists themselves, Eliot imagined, must be writing their works "in elegant boudoirs, with violet-colored ink and a ruby pen," "inexperienced in every form of poverty except poverty of brains" and willfully ignorant of any class of people "who even manage to eat their dinner without a silver fork" (Eliot 301, 302, 304, 319).

In 1856, when Eliot published her observations on silly novels in the *Westminster Review*, Catherine Gore (1799–1861), the most prolific and durable of the silver folk novelists, was still actively spilling her violet-colored ink. She had begun her career in the 1820s, the silver fork heyday, making her mark with such trendy titles as *The Manners of the Day* (1830), *Pin Money* (1831), *The Hamiltons* (1834) and *The Diary of a Désennuyée* (1836). Under the aegis of Henry Colburn, the publishing mogul behind the silver fork vogue,[1] Gore had helped to originate its best-selling formula: scenes of aristocratic high life, set in the Regency or its prolonged aftermath, specifically tailored to exploit the fascination and anxieties of an emerging—and often social-climbing—middle-class audience. During the socially and politically volatile interim of the 1820s and thirties, while England debated the first Reform Bill, the silver fork novel, however self-consciously ephemeral, evidently touched a popular nerve in its open preoccupation with shifting class boundaries and insecurities. Its fixation on the elegantly scandalous mores of the Regency evoked both nostalgia and disapproval in its not quite Victorian readers. Its tone tended to combine, if not to confuse, adulation of the fashionable aristocracy with light-hearted satire of their foibles.

Gore herself, not unlike Thackeray after her, strikes an ambivalent, at times evasive, pose in relation to her own highly seasoned fictional materials. In private life, she was a card-carrying "exclusive," as members of fashionable Regency society liked to call themselves; her marriage to the otherwise feckless Captain Charles Gore supplied the indispensable family connections, while she maintained her position financially through the tireless labors of her ruby pen. Whatever her narrative guise, however biting her wit, Gore always wrote as a privileged insider, more amused and tolerant than indignant at the excesses of her rakes and coquettes. Although she never flinched from betraying the secrets or exposing the vices of the aristocracy and its fashionable satellites, she did so without any personal pretension to virtue. She identified with high society even as she satirized it. Thackeray, whose literary debt to her was profound and largely unacknowledged, found her attitude to be "utterly worldly," inseparable from the values and behavior of the heartless beau monde that she both inhabited and anatomized.

> Supposing that Pall-mall were the world, and human life finished with the season, and Heaven were truffled turkies and the Opera, and duty and ambition were bounded in dressing well and getting tickets to Lady Londonderry's dancing teas, Mrs. Gore's "Sketches of Character" might be a good guide book.
> (*Morning Chronicle* 142)

Gore's fashionably amoral stance was deeply troubling to Thackeray, as he indicated just at the time he began contemplating his own epitome of the silver fork novel in *Vanity Fair*: "A direct morality is not called for, perhaps, in works of fiction, but that a moral sentiment should pervade them, at least, is no disadvantage" (140). Thackeray himself has been criticized in much the same terms for his complicity with the vanities of the great world; the uneasiness that pervades his reviews and journal entries on Mrs. Gore stems from an unwilling recognition of their fundamental affinities.

Gore's social comedy, which evokes the nuances of behavior and attitude in circles both fashionable and would-be fashionable, is generated by the clash of two conflicting systems of value—Regency and proto-Victorian—neither of which she entirely rejects or endorses. The hero of her late novel *Self* (1845) describes the proponents of these value systems as "two bad things," classifying them according to the equally unflattering epithets of "humbug" and "humdrum" (374). Gore's "humbugs" espouse the worldly code of values associated with the Regency and the social elite. Their main occupation is the unabashed pursuit of pleasure—dressing and eating well, seeing and being seen at all the right balls and clubs and dinner parties during the London season. Their conduct is regulated by the fashionable notion of "*bon ton*"; they frankly prefer artifice to nature, elegant deception to awkward sincerity. Their gaiety, buoyancy, and wit make them irresistibly alluring to those outside their enchanted circle, the assorted parvenus, hangers-on, and social climbers who become their victims.

Gore's "humdrums," on the other hand, are her proto-Victorians, middle-class in attitude if not always in rank and devoted to domestic values. Their simplicity and artlessness seems hardly a match for the blandishments of aristocratic seduction or intrigue, while their capacity for feeling makes them vulnerable in ways that the humbugs fail even to comprehend. When humdrums and humbugs are rivals or marry each other, they provide Gore's typical plot, through which she traces an intricate process of conflict and adjustment that parallels and reflects the larger historical transition from Regency to Victorian, from aristocratic oligarchy to bourgeois democracy.

Although she is perhaps best remembered for her definitive dandy novels *Cecil; or, The Adventures of a Coxcomb* and its sequel *Cecil, a Peer* (both 1841) with their irrepressible male narrator, Gore saw herself primarily as a women's writer. She introduces *Pin Money*, for example, as "an attempt to transfer the familiar narrative of Miss Austen to a higher sphere of society, . . . a Novel of the simplest kind, addressed by a woman to readers of her own sex" (Preface). It is women's experience in high society that normally functions as the mainspring of her fiction. Writing in the expansive triple-decker form of the day, Gore likes to use multiple heroines, exploring alternative models of femininity along a continuum from humbug to humdrum. Gore clearly admires the power, resilience and charm of her aristocratic Regency heroines, although she is also aware that *The Woman of the World*, as she titled a novel in 1838, may harden into a dangerous sexual predator. She sympathizes with her gentler, more domestic heroines—forerunners of the Victorian angel of the hearth—but remains deeply apprehensive about the consequences of their submissiveness and their psychological vulnerability.

Gore's own ideal for her aristocratic heroines calls for a balance or accommodation between the values of fashion and domesticity. Withdrawal from the temptations of society, into an insulated and feminized domestic sphere, presents no workable or desirable solution in the silver fork milieu. As Lord Willersdale tells his repentant wife in *The Manners of the Day*, ''Pray do not persuade yourself that I object to your moderate enjoyment of all such amusements as become your situation in the world. . . . The virtue that takes refuge in a hermit's cell, evinces little confidence in the strength of its own principles'' (II, 24–25). In Gore's silver fork novels, the emerging middle-class domestic ideology, about to be embraced by the Victorians, is not yet fully formed and not yet privileged in relation to competing, here specifically aristocratic, constructions of gender. The world—in the specialized sense of the beau monde—is still seen as the proper sphere of operation for women in the upper classes.

II.

Gore's novels tend to open with marriage: if experience ends at the altar for the typical bourgeois heroine, for her silver fork counterpart it has only just begun. Aristocratic marriages are more likely to be arranged, often against the heroine's will, and she is more likely to be left on her own in an exposed and public position without much interference from her husband. Plunged into the vortex of fashionable society, no longer burdened or protected by a chaperone, she will suddenly become fair game for the machinations of rakes and ''detrimentals,'' or ineligible younger sons. Standards of conduct seem hard to come by; a little flirtation is clearly expected, while the proper sort of liaison may even be openly condoned. The ''quarantine laws of fashionable life,'' as Gore calls them, may be sufficiently rigorous, but they are generally applied ''to the shame, rather than to the sin—to offenders convicted of *mauvais ton*, as well as of moral irregularities'' (*Pin Money* I, 155). For the newly married silver fork heroine, increased, if undefined, danger is accompanied by a heady sense of freedom and a potential scope of action unknown to the middle-class Victorian angel.

In *Pin Money*, one of her most delightful comedies of manners, Gore focuses explicitly on the links between class values or expectations and the content of the feminine ideal. Gore's Frederica is presented as a decidedly ordinary heroine with ''no preternatural pretensions to perfection'' (I, 6), recently married to an amiably mediocre baronet, Sir Brooke Rawleigh. At her debut in the character of matron, she is confronted with a bewildering array of role models, running the gamut from her mother Lady Launceston, an inert invalid, to her aunt Lady Olivia Todcaster, a so-called ''managing woman'' who rushes into law suits and touts the equality of the sexes. At the pinnacle of fashion stands the almost legendary Lady Rochester, distant but symbolic, who has managed her love affairs not only with discretion but with unfailing class-consciousness. As one society gossip observes, "The errors of Lady Rochester are at least respectable. . . ; no one has more strictly preserved the dignity of her rank in life.—The first admirer for whom she forfeited her reputation was royal; and as to *all* the rest . . . I do not believe she has ever strayed out of the peerage" (I, 130). Although Lady Rochester herself remains unassailable, she offers a dangerous paradigm for social climbers like the pretty little Mrs. William Erskyne, a rattling, empty-headed flirt who finally elopes not with, but to, a reluctant Lord Calder. Even adultery is subject to rigid class distinctions: the middle-class Mrs. Erskyne, unlike the incorrigible Lady Rochester, suffers irretrievable ruin. Gore's aristocratic hero, Lord Launceston, draws the battle lines between classes when he decisively repudiates his supposed engagement to the "soap-boiler's" heiress Leonora Waddlestone. "I have no taste for such diminutive goddesses," he declares; "—I require, even in a woman, even in my wife, more decision of character and more nobility of aspect" (II, 192).

Leonora of course is middle-class, burdened with a grandfather in trade and a vulgar parvenue mother who wants to buy her daughter's way into the peerage. The daughter herself, in accordance with her elegant given name, is refined and lady-like, but humbly aware of the precarious social position implied in her cumbersome family name of Waddlestone. She is insistently and pointedly described as small, fragile and submissive, in marked contrast to the bold and dashing aristocratic women with whom she is placed in unequal rivalry. As Gore's novels make clear, the celebrated domestic angel or "proper lady" of the conduct books, to borrow Mary Poovey's term, is entirely a bourgeois creation.[2] She labors under all the familiar restrictions of propriety, not only because she must fulfill her function in the middle-class domestic economy but also because she can only be a lady by courtesy, earning the honorary title through her own manners and behavior rather than acquiring it through birth.

Leonora's passivity and dependence—even her physical diminutiveness—are seen as appropriate to her rank but as largely irrelevant to the situation of her acknowledged superiors. To Lord Calder, patrician connoisseur of art and women, she seems a "delicate exotic," while to Gore's heroine, "Leonora is a mild, intelligent, endearing creature; but no more to be compared in qualities and endowments with my high-minded cousin [her aristocratic rival], than in dignity of birth and station" (II, 166, 185). In silver fork society, mildness is no match for high-mindedness, and the bourgeois angel remains peripheral, here ultimately married off to an obscure younger son. In Gore's early novels, set in the pre-Victorian period, middle-class values and fortunes, far from posing any serious threat to the aristocratic ascendancy, are still simply there to be appropriated as necessary in order to reinforce it.

In direct opposition to the "diminutive goddess," Gore proposes the daring, unconventional figure of Lady Mary Trevelyan, the woman Lord Launceston will eventually marry. We first hear of Lady Mary as the heroine of a remarkable series of distant exploits, disapprovingly recounted by the middle-class widow Mrs. Woodington.

> I am far from wishing to cast any imputation on Lady Mary; —only it *was* considered to argue very unusual—*courage*—on the part of a young and beautiful woman, to defend her father, pistol in hand, when they were surrounded by banditti among the ruins of Paestum; and to command the manoeuvres of her yacht when they were chased by an Algerine at Lepanto.   (I, 63)

Brandishing pistols and navigating yachts, to say the least, are not among the usual conduct-book acquirements of middle-class young ladies.

Back home in England, Lady Mary further highlights the unavoidable connection between class roles and gender roles when she temporarily abdicates her social position to masquerade as a hired companion. Clearly her behavior cannot be fitted into any accepted middle-class mold, nor does it finally need to be. What looks "showy" and "forward" in a paid dependent can be taken for granted in a highbred heiress. Even her penchant for pistols and fast horses can be accommodated without difficulty. At the same time Gore's text confirms her unquestioned status as auxiliary heroine. Within a self-confidently aristocratic framework, there appears to be no pressure on the silver fork novelist to tie feminine virtue to fragility or helplessness, nor are such qualities considered in the least attractive to a practiced rake of Lord Launceston's caste. Lady Mary's sexual assertiveness—her active pursuit of Launceston and public flirtation with him—need not be perceived as threatening to a class that is typically less preoccupied with controlling appetites than with discreetly indulging them.

In Gore's depiction, a fashionable newlywed like Frederica Rawleigh is much more likely to face sneers and gibes at her excessive connubial bliss than any conduct-book restrictions on her activities outside the domestic sphere. The frantically modish Louisa Erskyne chides her for her "odious provincial habits," showing the degree of sarcasm that could be attached to notions of domesticity in Regency high society: "You positively deserve to be painted, framed, and glazed, and hung up in the parlour of the Rawleigh Arms, . . . pointing out the nest of two turtle-doves to a lady in yellow shoes and a blue veil,—ticketed with the pleasing title of Domestic Felicity" (I, 77). Although Frederica will find out her mistake in taking up with a Mrs. William Erskyne, literally outclassed in the aristocratic games of exclusivism and seduction, she acquires a more suitable companion in Lady Sophia Lee, whose "decided taste for brilliant crowds, and all the stir and excitement of the gay world" is not to be equated with a taste for vice. "I am passionately fond of riding,'' as she tells Frederica, ''but I have no pleasure in mounting a vicious horse'' (II, 88). For a woman in Frederica's position, ''born and educated in and for the great world'' (I, 35) there is no moral or social imperative to curb her natural enjoyment of life in the beau monde.

Within the insulated aristocratic context of the silver fork mode, Gore makes no suggestion of irreconcilable conflict between fashion and domestic duties. As Lord Launceston puts it, summing up Gore's own implicit ideal:

> There are still, thank heaven, women to be found in our own rank of life, who reconcile a cheerful indulgence in the pleasures of society with unsullied purity in their domestic character; and without making a recluse of my wife, I am satisfied that I can preserve her from the contact of the vicious and the degrad- ed,—the female flirt and the female gamester. (II, 57)

Domesticity is assigned no special priority here; it makes no excessive or exclusive demands on aristocratic wives as Gore depicts them. Neither Freder- ica nor Lady Mary has to choose between ''the life of a cauliflower,'' as Louisa calls it, on her husband's country estate and the reckless abandon of the gambler or the adulteress. It was only in the bourgeois Victorian novel that a radical split would begin to develop between the household angel and the increasingly negative figure of the woman of the world. The fictional idealization of the middle-class ''diminutive goddess''—problematic for Gore as for Thackeray after her—would become a primary signal of the ultimate Victorian rejection of the Regency and of the cluster of social and moral values it had come to represent. The physical tininess of Dickens' heroines, all the Little Nells and Little Dorrits, can be construed as specifically and deliberately anti-aristocratic. The diminutive middle-class heroine is meant to be not only more moral but in general more manageable than her aggressive and physically robust silver fork counterpart.

The central theme of *Pin Money*, the focal point for Gore's analysis of conflicting models of pre-Victorian womanhood, is rather baldly announced in her title. ''Money and its making,'' as Ellen Moers has trenchantly ob- served, ''were characteristically female rather than male subjects in English fiction'' (*Literary Women* 67). But they were also inherently middle-class subjects: Gore's aristocrats, both male and female, find themselves more im- mediately concerned with money and its spending, or money and its inheriting. From the silver fork perspective, the only valid—and unbridgeable—class distinction is ''that which exists between those who buy and those who sell'' (*Pin Money* I, 131). The selling of oneself in marriage, normally of paramount feminine concern, is here interestingly displaced onto the poignant figure of Mr. Waddlestone. Originally an impecunious gentleman by the name of Ed- ward Meredyth, Leonora's father has bartered away not only his class status but his patronymic and his very identity for the sake of his wife's ''soap- boiling'' riches. The issue for Frederica, unlike Mr. Waddlestone or Jane

Austen's heroines, is not how to get money in marriage but how to get control of her own inherited fortune. Her dowry of 10,000 pounds entitles Frederica to what was termed a "separate maintenance," consisting of jointure and spending money legally outside her husband's regulation. The nuptial contract typical of an aristocratic arranged marriage confers on her a degree of economic independence unfamiliar to the middle-class heroine.

But Gore shows herself equally reluctant to associate her aristocratic heroine with financial transactions, which bear too much of the taint of middle-class trade. The plot of *Pin Money*, in which Frederica promptly falls into extravagance and debt, reveals one powerful historical impulse behind the nineteenth-century idealization of women. As the ruling elite became increasingly discredited—here even Sir Brooke resorts to bribery in his election campaign for the corrupt borough of "Martwich"—certain essential elements of the old aristocratic ideal were more and more likely to be transposed onto the newer feminine ideal. Victorian women, like the traditional nobility, would at least in theory symbolize the endangered values of disinterestedness and detachment from the profit motive. Even middle-class women would not have to inquire into the sources of their own wealth, which had long remained invisible for the landowning class as they could not for "soap-boilers" and other manufacturers of tangible and vulgar products. In the emerging commercial and industrial society, the middle-class domestic angel would come to take over the function once reserved for the honorable and incorruptible aristocrat of popular myth.

Gore's heroine in *Pin Money*, both woman and aristocrat, is in the end doubly protected from "so mean a feeling as pecuniary anxiety" (II, 186). It is only briefly, during the crisis of the plot, that Gore exposes the darker, more sinister underpinnings of this kind of convenient social arrangement. When Frederica attempts to pay off a secret gambling debt to her would-be seducer Lord Calder, her footman steals the bank note, temporarily implicating her in crime. Under ordinary circumstances, as the narrator emphasizes, the upper classes are exempt even from any knowledge of the turbulent underworld of those who serve them and whose labor supports their luxuriously idle existence.

> The tissue of fashionable life is of so flimsy and artificial a texture,—so little of reality exists in the position, sentiments, and apprehensions of the lordly community, that crimes and punishments assume an ideal and visionary character in the eyes of its members. . . . Their hearts are too buoyant, their own destinies too unsubstantial, to impart a belief in the tangible existence of want, and crime, and judgment. (II, 143–44)

Real and unreal change places phantasmagorically, so that neither class can so much as believe in the everyday experience of the other.

Undoubtedly much of the popular appeal of the silver fork novels—best sellers, after all, in their day—can be traced to the sense of buoyancy and immunity that infuses the genre as a whole. For a newly expanded middle-class audience, the novels offered a potent fantasy of unlimited freedom of action, a fantasy of exemption from the customary restraints of moral duty as well as from the sordid requirements of money-getting. For middle-class women in particular, the not-so-proper titled lady represented a striking alternative to the conduct literature and a vicarious release from its strictures. Gore's married heroines lead remarkably independent lives, pursuing their own careers as socialites and matchmakers while their husbands take up hunting or politics. Their spheres may be separate, but both are public and primarily located outside the confines of home. Even home itself is compartmentalized into male and female territories. In the townhouses or country mansions of the aristocracy, husbands and wives generally manage to avoid the pressures of bourgeois domestic intimacy by occupying separate suites of bedrooms and thus preserving an inviolable psychological space by means of literal architectural barriers between them. Gore's ultimate in fashionable couples maintains a relationship in which the husband considers his own to be "the best of wives, because she is wise enough to let him pass his life at his club, well-bred enough to be civil to him in public, and judicious enough never to see him in private" (*Diary of a Désennuyée* 8).

The conventions of the Regency beau monde, in contrast to those of bourgeois propriety, did not allow for much protection of women, even by their husbands, from what Sir Brooke calls "the profanation of libertine approach, and the contagion of frivolous companionship." Horseback riding and opera boxes provided occasion for flirtation and familiarities that would have had to be resented "in the domestic privacy of home" (*Pin Money* I, 73). Silver fork scenes, in fact, rarely take place at home or in private drawing rooms, except at moments of crisis. Where Jane Austen, for example, has to remove her characters outdoors, to Box Hill or its equivalent, in order to obtain a clarifying explosion, Gore has to force them back inside, back home, in order to confront their accumulated marital misunderstandings. Her heroines are typically threatened not with the Gothic traumas of confinement or claustrophobia but with the opposite hazards of publicity and exposure. They are drawn through all the preliminary stages of seduction, only to be saved in the end while their less cautious alter egos plunge forward into elopement and divorce. Those reckless plunges of the anti-heroines may be said to embody the fear that accompanies the desire for freedom; feminine and middle-class anxieties are built into even the most aristocratic of Gore's plot lines. Perhaps because she shared her reader's fantasies and apprehensions, Gore knew precisely how to exploit the aura of glamour and the sense of immunity enveloping her aristocratic characters, while at the same time her satirical tone

furnished an outlet for any nagging remnants of disapproval that might otherwise have spoiled the reader's enjoyment. In *Pin Money*, as in her other early
novels, the heroine's independence, tested out imaginatively and purged of
its potential dangers, can still be essentially affirmed.

III.

Whether it ratifies an alliance of convenience or a runaway love match,
marriage in Gore's fiction is inherently problematic for women of all classes.
Gore substantially anticipated Thackeray in her pioneering fictional explorations of "the marriage country" from the woman's point of view. Thackeray
was only following her lead when he satirized the novelistic convention of
the happy ending in marriage in a famous passage from *Vanity Fair*:

> As his hero and heroine pass the matrimonial barrier, the novelist generally
> drops the curtain, as if the drama were over then: the doubts and struggles of
> life ended: as if, once landed in the marriage country, all were green and pleasant
> there; and wife and husband had nothing but to link each other's arms together,
> and wander gently downwards towards old age in happy and perfect fruition.
>
> (250)

Gore is even less likely than Thackeray to drop the curtain with "the fatal
ceremony of matrimony," as she routinely calls it (*Manners of the Day* III,
249), and even more likely to map out the byways of "the marriage country"
in graphic and harrowing detail. In novel after novel, Gore examines the
troubling implicit equation between the two conventional forms of novelistic
finality. As one of her characters puts it in *Mothers and Daughters*, "Death
and marriage!—Yes! You are quite right in reminding your friends that these
terms are synonymous" (331).

At the opening of *The Manners of the Day*, Gore's narrator contrasts the
merely "*bon mariage*," the practical goal of most fashionable ingenues and
matchmakers, with what she calls the "*mariage délicieux*," known primarily
for its extreme rarity of occurrence. In Gore's view, the latter variety represents an elusive medium between Regency worldliness and proto-Victorian
sentiment, a phenomenon scarcely to be met with under the prevailing conditions of modern life.

> While the worldly-minded assign to the qualifications of the good match an
> undue preponderance, the etherialized and sentimental discover an equally obsti-
> nate prejudice in favor of blue eyes or brown,—of the aërial perspective of a
> damp cottage covered with honeysuckles. . . . But between these fierce extremes,
> the happy medium of fair and firm and honest affection is rarely achieved; and
> the Paradise of domestic happiness . . . would appear to be seated in some re-
> mote region, still undefined by Admiralty charts; or guarded by the sword of

angry cherubim from human approach. (I, 2–3)

Gore typically has little faith in the pastoral delights of "damp cottages" or in the prospects for marital happiness, whether in high life or low. Her own domestic paradise is situated not at home by a Dickensian hearth, not indoors, not even in England, but more indefinitely "in some remote region," across unknown seas and inaccessible to ordinary humanity. It is emphatically not the prerogative of any particular social class, not even the middle one. Domesticity, like the world of fashion, is something to be taken in moderation; it is never considered enough in itself for either heroes or heroines.

Gore sounds the cautionary note most explicitly when she attempts to imagine the fate of the proto-angel trapped within the worldly conventions of a fashionable aristocratic marriage. In *The Hamiltons; or, Official Life in 1830*, set against the political backdrop of reformist agitation and Tory resistance, Gore works out her own deepest apprehensions about the underlying fragility of the idealized "diminutive goddess." Her heroine, Susan Hamilton, epitomizes the conduct-book virtues of sweetness, dependence, docility; but Gore's plot is calculated to expose her inherent vulnerability, revealing those very virtues as potentially self-destructive and incapacitating. Susan, we are told from the outset, "was a mild graceful creature, incapable of inflicting or enduring pain. . . . But she was inert, timid, and endowed with limited capacities of mind" (21). When she fixes her innocent affections on the heartless dandy Augustus Hamilton—just as Thackeray's Amelia Sedley will later idolize George Osborne—Susan receives a warning from her more strong-minded sister Marcia: "You are only too generous,—too confiding: It is because you are so slow to believe in the existence of wickedness that you would trust your happiness, your person, the purity of your mind, to the keeping of one who despises all things good and holy" (69).

To the fashionable Augustus, "accustomed to be loved" and to be forgotten, she seems attractive merely "as a beautiful bit of china,—a choice picture,—a rare exotic; and, perhaps, as affording a charming contrast to his last world-worn rouge-seared love" (72, 39). The persistence of her affection in spite of his neglect and the shock of her reported illness ultimately have the power to move him to a proposal of marriage, if not to domestic habits. The opposition of his domineering father Lord Laxington, a parvenu Tory placeman who has reposed "perfect confidence in the want of principle of his son," further goads him into what he sneeringly refers to as "the amendment of my morals. . . . For once, Sir, I am about to perform an honorable action" (39, 74). Gore, well before Thackeray's portrayal of the Osbornes, brilliantly dramatizes the bitter conflict between father and son: "It was a fearful moment. The father insulting his worthless son;—the son, secretly despising the scornful father" (73).

After their marriage, Augustus tyrannizes over his submissive wife, openly ridiculing her "*bourgeois* notions" of domesticity (160) and taking advantage of her ignorance in order to resume his previous affair with her girlhood friend Caroline Cadogan. To please him, Susan learns to control her unfashionably strong emotions, afraid that he will "despise her, even for loving him too tenderly," while she plays her part on the tawdry stage of fashion among people who seem to be, in anticipation of *Vanity Fair*, "mere puppets in a pageant" (174, 78). When she expresses her initial anxieties about the complicated arrangement of their separate bedrooms or their lack of privacy in Lord Laxington's house, she is reduced to silence by her husband's all-purpose maxim: "We must live both with, and like, the rest of the world" (89). Aristocratic society, as Susan painfully discovers, has no use for the domestic angel or her typically middle-class values. Sensibilities or feelings of any sort are automatically dismissed as exaggerated whenever they exceed "the barriers of ice erected by the Exclusives as a safeguard to their Arctic circle" (92). Susan's elegant sister-in-law Julia Tottenham, long trained in "the school of worldliness," has acquired the self-protective "art of loving nothing, and of nothing desiring to be loved" (233). She consoles herself for a disappointing marriage and disagreeable husband by party-going and by receiving callers every afternoon after breakfast. As the ingenuous Susan exclaims, "Being 'at home' in your sense is the very reverse of being 'at home' in mine! I fear we shall not agree in our notions of domesticity" (95).

The process of Susan's own disillusionment is gradual and genuinely poignant, traced with a degree of subtlety and restraint that sets Gore decisively apart from the ordinary run of silver fork novelists. The private tragedy of the Hamiltons' marriage is linked to a wider social and historical context: "[Susan] had discovered that the intense affection of wedded life, the mutual all-in-allness she had read of in story, and heard of in conversation, belonged neither to the position she occupied, nor to the age she lived in" (151). Gore could not have known in 1834 how pervasive that ideal of all-in-allness would very soon become in the Victorian popular consciousness, but she could—and did—remain skeptical about its realization outside of story and conversation, even as she later chronicled the increasing triumph of bourgeois attitudes and the downfall of aristocratic exclusivism.

Unlike the middle-class conduct writers, who were her predecessors and contemporaries, Gore regarded the angel figure with uneasiness and ambivalence. Her angel in *The Hamiltons* is by definition a victim, powerless to redeem a corrupt society, powerless to save her degenerate husband, although there are moments of tenderness between them and moments of compunction on his part. The angel's innate submissiveness suggests disturbing images—later to be fully elaborated in *Vanity Fair*—of oriental harems and sexual sadomasochism. "Women are apt to revere, as the pious are said to rejoice, *with trembling*. They dearly love the despot whose despotism they denounce. From the omnipotent Sultan, to the petty tyrants of May Fair, Blue Beard is sure of his Odalisques!'' (106). Although this particular passage explicitly refers to Susan's unquestioning reverence for the leaders of the Tory party by whom she is surrounded, its implications are reflected back over the feminine trembling and masculine despotism that typify her marriage. When Gore sent Thackeray a copy of *The Hamiltons* at the time of its reprinting in 1850, he appears to have recognized the fundamental kinship between Susan Hamilton and his own Amelia Sedley—and to have acknowledged as well his complicity in male fantasies of sexual domination. As he wrote in a letter to Gore: "Susan is a party after my own sort—mild and sweet charming but not inebriating I should like to have such a woman to bully. She would like it so too" (*Letters* II, 724).[3]

Like Thackeray's Amelia, Gore's angel is finally unable to rely on her passive, conduct-book virtue to protect her from marital sorrow or exploitation. She has not married a benevolent father figure but a violent, tyrannical Blue Beard, whose abuse during her pregnancy causes the premature birth of their sickly child and whose notorious philandering violates the "domestic sanctuary" (301) on which she has centered her whole life. Neither her harmlessness nor her timidity can prevent her from experiencing "the hollowness of human happiness" (152), as inevitable a disillusionment for Gore as it is for Thackeray. Unlike Amelia, however, Susan Hamilton is not rescued by an early widowhood but is forced to endure the everyday presence of an unfaithful husband. Here Gore goes Thackeray one better in charting the damaging psychic terrain of "the marriage country." Although Susan forbears to expose her husband as the actual father of Rodolph Cadogan's supposed heir, she continues to live with him only on terms of sexual estrangement and firmly refuses to have any further contact with his mistress.

On the eve of Augustus's fatal duel with Cadogan, when she thinks he is about to elope with her rival, Susan unexpectedly musters the courage to reject his tentative advances: "You have injured and insulted me by every means in your power. But my own self respect shall secure me from the pollution of your caresses. . . . I would sooner throw myself upon the stones below than receive from you the slightest token of tenderness'' (318–19). Hamilton assures her that he is "no enterprising Knight Templar," picking up her reference to Scott's *Ivanhoe*—in other words, no rapist—and that he has come to her "in kindness." The scene, which ends in "renewed enmity" and turns out to be their final parting, is pervaded with the bitterest irony: Augustus for once is in earnest, moved at least temporarily by the possible approach of death; Susan for once is unyielding, stirred to rebellion against "this hollow show of repentance," having "learned to mistrust, on his part, every pretence of courtesy or kindness, as the prelude, or screen, to some treacherous act.'' Augustus goes to his unrepentant death ''suspecting that she was, after all, little less heartless than the rest of her sex'' (320).

Freed from his living presence, Susan falls back, like Amelia, into a state of sentimental necrophilia, finally able to exercise her angelic devotion on behalf of an unchanging ideal as she could not on behalf of her inconstant husband. Like Thackeray after her, Gore recognizes that only the dead can be fully possessed.

> All restraint was at an end. There was nothing,—there was no one to interpose between herself and the dead.—Augustus was her own again. Who,—who would mourn for him with a tenderness and a constancy like hers! (339–40)

But the angel's faith in her own redemptive powers—as she says, ''I am sure Augustus would have one day learned to love me again. My patience would have won him back to me''—is not upheld by the narrative: the unidealized Augustus Hamilton remains ''callous to the last'' (343, 341). Gore makes clear that her heroine's self-sacrificing devotion is nothing more than a futile illusion, as vain as any of the other vanities in the world that Gore shares with Thackeray. At the end of the novel, the widowed Susan is pressed into remarriage only by a deathbed promise to her father-in-law, whom she has angelically cared for since the loss of his only son. Gore leaves us on the last page with the ambiguous, perhaps ominous, image of the new Lady Claneustace still wearing her mourning garments on her second wedding day.

It was Gore's unique perspective as a consummate woman of the Regency living on and writing novels well into the heart of the Victorian era that enabled her to look critically at the domestic heroine and to examine the darker and more troubling implications of this increasingly popular middle-class ideal. The typically unhappy fate of her fictional angels reflects her continuing doubts about their viability as models of femininity. Some of them are unable even to survive at all. In *Mrs. Armytage; or, Female Domination* (1836), the ''diminutive goddess'' is literally killed off by her mother's refusal to allow her marriage to the man she loves. Sophia Armytage cannot be saved by the conventional platitudes spouted by her patriarchal confessor: ''A spirit such as yours, my dear child, is pre-assured of domestic happiness'' (II, 244). Gore, no less than Thackeray, doubts that pre-assurance, calling into question both the social and psychological ramifications of feminine weakness and submissiveness. Society as Gore depicts it offers no place for the idealized angel. Sophia is a hothouse plant, too delicate to endure the inevitable compromises and disappointments of ordinary life in the human world. ''I find it difficult to live,'' she declares. ''The moral air I breathe is too cold and insufficient for my existence'' (III, 46). Like those of Thackeray and Dickens, Gore's angel is ultimately an angel of death.

IV.

Gore's fecundity as a popular novelist was legendary. While Thackeray was still struggling through his lengthy journalistic apprenticeship, he called her in print "the most productive of English writers," marvelling at "how Mrs. Gore can write so much, so often, and so well" (*Morning Chronicle* 139). Fifteen years and a score of novels later, the writer of her obituary in the *Times* observed that "the most remarkable point of all this fertility is that in the 200 volumes there is scarcely to be found one dull page. Mrs. Gore's wit was inexhaustible" (5). Over a period of more than three decades as a social satirist, Gore never really abandoned the silver fork genre that had made her famous, in spite of the shifting cultural climate and her own sagging profits. In her old age, she declined to refurbish her opinions in order to conform to the prevailing standard but remained fundamentally divided in her allegiance, casting a satirical eye on both Regency humbug and Victorian humdrum. What other writer of the 1840s would be capable of describing "the domestic affections" as "a chloride, by the operation of which all the noxious particles afloat are precipitated to the bottom" (*Dowager* II, 105)? While she acknowledges their "singularly purifying influence on the mind," her unconventional choice of metaphor reserves a measure of distaste and clinical detachment, as though she is trying chemical experiments of a not particularly agreeable kind on her hapless characters. Even in her last novel, Gore continued her protest against the idealization of the middle-class domestic angel, mocking what she now called "the Lambkin school" of Victorian ingenues (*Two Aristocracies* II, 258). As the Regency became increasingly discredited, so did Gore's favorite kind of heroine. To a large extent, Gore's silver fork fiction, informed by a declining aristocratic ideology, represents what the middle-class conduct writers like Sarah Lewis and Sarah Ellis were reacting against. The newly dominant ideology of domesticity, with its worship of "diminutive goddesses," completed the middle-class Victorian project of rejecting the Regency and the aristocratic ascendancy. Beneath the froth and the fashionable millinery of Gore's silver fork heroines, the Victorians found something deeply threatening to their class and cultural identity.

Thackeray, who died less than three years after her, never quite closed the books on Mrs. Gore or settled his complicated accounts with his immediate predecessor in chronicling "the vanity-fair of the day," as she regularly titled it, and in painting "all the booths and shows of the great fair of fashion . . . blazing in their fullest effulgence" (*Dowager* II, 197, 120). His parodies and reviews of her work could be merciless—especially so when her attitudes and values came closest to his own—but at the same time he had enormous fun with her absurdities and was not in the least above seriously borrowing and expanding on her themes and techniques. As Juliet McMaster notes of all the parodies in *Novels by Eminent Hands*, "the process as I see it . . . involves not only reaction but absorption and imitation" (310). In his prize novel "Lords and Liveries, by the Authoress of 'Dukes and Déjeuners,' 'Hearts and Diamonds,' 'Marchionesses and Milliners,' etc. etc.," Thackeray deftly captures not only the snobbish mannerisms and exuberant celebration of high life typical of the silver fork mode, but the tone of the satire as well, the routine sigh at the profligacy of the dandy hero, which in fact is the main source of his allure, and the lip service to "that Morality which is so superior to all the vain pomps of the world!" (174). Like Gore, Thackeray clutters his text with fashionable jargon, gossip, brand names, bets, newspaper clippings and accounts of duels. By the end, his newlywed hero and heroine "have not more than nine hundred thousand a year, but they live cheerfully, and manage to do good" (184). This is wonderful, but it is not Mrs. Gore. If it were, Thackeray would have to dramatize the details of the young couple's marriage, which would inevitably turn out as dreary and troubling an affair as Ivanhoe's successive matches in *Rebecca and Rowena*. He would have to write a novel that would be uncomfortably close to one of his own. For the object of his parody had preceded him in writing those "middle aged novels" he called for, in which "adventures, and pains, and pleasures, and taxes, and sunrises and settings, and the business and joys and griefs of life go on after as before the nuptial ceremony" (*Rebecca and Rowena* 74).

After the triumph of his own great silver fork novel, *Vanity Fair*, Thackeray himself gained access to fashionable society and made the personal acquaintance of his old adversary, towards whom he never entirely lost his feelings of ambivalence. Although he stayed at her house and took the walks and ate the dinners, he wrote to Jane Brookfield that he was "ashamed of them somehow" (*Letters* II, 699). In his last letter to Gore, he still felt the need to defend himself against reported charges, in the recent preface to a reissue of *The Banker's Wife* (1843), that he had stolen the idea for Colonel Newcome from one of her characters (*Letters* IV, 196). When he reread her *Sketches of English Character* (1846), he joked rather maliciously that "I also think I perceive likenesses of myself in the Standard Footman, in Sir Oswald Moody, in the Plausible Man, in Felix Flutter, and the Link-boy," before nervously admitting the force of her barbs: "Cruel woman! Why do you take off our likenesses in that way?" (*Letters* III, 74). When she sent him a copy of *The Hamiltons*, he responded with an uneasy—and self-revealing—recantation of his former strictures against silver forkery.

And I think some critics who carped at some writers for talking too much about fine company ought to hold their tongues. If you live with great folks, why should you not describe their manners? There is nothing in the least strained in these descriptions as I now think—and believe it was only a secret envy & black malignity of disposition which made me say in former times this author is talking too much about grand people, this author is of the silver fork school, this author uses too much French & c. (*Letters* II, 724)

It is eminently characteristic of Thackeray that this belated retraction should be part abject capitulation to the influence of "fine company," part generous acknowledgement of his earlier jealousy and payment of a just debt.

NOTES

This essay was researched and written with the support of a National Endowment for the Humanities Fellowship, for which I am extremely grateful.

1. For general background on the silver fork novel, see Rosa, Hart, Hughes, Adburgham, Sadleir, and Moers, *The Dandy*. The best contemporary account is Bulwer. The derisive term "silver fork" originated in Hazlitt (146). On Gore specifically, see Colby.

2. For extensive background on "proper ladies" and conduct books during the late eighteenth and early nineteenth centuries, see Poovey, who describes the conduct books as reproducing the system of values of bourgeois society (xiii).

3. Colby (83–84) notes the plot parallels, which she calls "coincidental but remarkable," between *The Hamiltons* and *Vanity Fair*, but concludes that Thackeray apparently did not read the novel until 1850. It seems to me, given the extensive and detailed knowledge of Gore revealed in his early reviews as well as in his parody "Lords and Liveries," that Thackeray may well have read it earlier, although he was in a much more benevolent frame of mind following the triumph of his own silver fork novel.

WORKS CITED

Adburgham, Alison. *Silver Fork Society*. London: Constable, 1983.

Bulwer, Edward Lytton. *England and the English*. Ed. Standish Meacham. Chicago and London: U of Chicago P, 1970.

Colby, Vineta. *Yesterday's Woman: Domestic Realism in the English Novel*. Princeton: Princeton UP, 1974.

Eliot, George. "Silly Novels by Lady Novelists." *The Essays of George Eliot*. Ed. Thomas Pinney. New York and London: Columbia UP and Routledge and Kegan Paul, 1963.

Gore, Catherine. *The Diary of a Désennuyée*. New York: Harper, 1836.

————. *The Dowager; or, The New School for Scandal*. London: Bentley, 1840.

————. *The Hamiltons; or, Official Life in 1830*. London: Bentley, 1850.

————. *The Manners of the Day*. London: Colburn and Bentley, 1830.

————. *Mrs. Armytage; or, Female Domination*. London: Colburn, 1837.

————. *Mothers and Daughters*. London: Bentley, 1834.

————. *Pin Money*. Philadelphia and Baltimore: Carey and Hart, 1834.

————. *Self*. Paris: Baudy, 1845.

————. *The Two Aristocracies*. London: Hurst and Blackett, 1857.

Hart, Francis Russell. "The Regency Novel of Fashion." *From Smollett to James*. Ed. Samuel I. Mintz et al. Charlottesville: UP of Virginia, 1981.

Hazlitt, William. "The Dandy School." *Examiner* (November 18, 1827). Rpt. in *Complete Works*. Ed. P. P. Howe. Vol. 20: *Miscellaneous Writings*. London and Toronto: Dent, 1934.

Hughes, Winifred. "Silver Fork Writers and Readers: Social Contexts of a Best Seller." *Novel* 25 (1992): 328–47.

McMaster, Juliet. "*Novels by Eminent Hands*: Sincerest Flattery from the Author of *Vanity Fair*." *Dickens Studies Annual* 18 (1989): 309–36. New York: AMS, 1989.

"Mrs. Gore." *London Times* (4 February 1861): 5.

Moers, Ellen. *The Dandy: Brummell to Beerbohm*. London: Secker and Warburg, 1960.

————. *Literary Women*. New York: Doubleday, 1976.

Poovey, Mary. *The Proper Lady and the Woman Writer*. Chicago: U of Chicago P, 1984.

Rosa, Matthew Whiting. *The Silver Fork School*. New York: Columbia UP, 1936.

Sadleir, Michael. *Edward and Rosina*. Boston: Little, Brown, 1931.

Thackeray, William Makepeace. *Contributions to the Morning Chronicle*. Ed. Gordon N. Ray. Urbana: Illinois UP, 1955.

————. *The Letters and Private Papers of William Makepeace Thackeray*. Ed. Gordon N. Ray. Cambridge: Harvard UP, 1945.

————. *Novels by Eminent Hands*. *Works*. Vol. 5. London: Macmillan, 1911.

————. *Rebecca and Rowena*. *Works*. Vol. 5. London: Macmillan, 1911.

————. *Vanity Fair*. Ed. Geoffrey and Kathleen Tillotson. Boston: Houghton Mifflin, 1963.

Louisa Gradgrind's Secret: Marriage and Divorce in *Hard Times*

Anne Humpherys

> "Is it possible, I wonder, that there was any analogy be-
> tween the case of the Coketown population and the case of
> the little Gradgrinds?" Charles Dickens, *Hard Times*

In Nathaniel Hawthorne's gothic story "Rappacini's Daughter" (1844), a
brilliant scientist "instruct[s his daughter] deeply in his science, [so] that, as
young and beautiful as fame reports her, she is already qualified to fill a
professor's chair" (1049) as her would-be lover Giovanni learns. But the
father has done more: in a diabolical experiment he has had his daughter tend
poisonous flowers through which she, Beatrice, becomes literally lethal: her
kiss, her very breath kills. Though he has also arranged to give her a lover
by infecting Giovanni with the poison, Beatrice, knowing that the antidote
will be fatal to her, both sacrifices herself for her unworthy lover and rejects
her father's gifts by killing herself.

The parallel between Hawthorne's gothic story and Dickens' most ungothic
novel of hard facts is close. Louisa Gradgrind, like Beatrice, is the victim of
a terrible fatherly experiment that the fathers justify in the same way: they
intend to make their daughters more powerful. The experiments, however,
are fatal both to the women and to others. Louisa's equally insufficient lover
Harthouse is humiliated by his contact with her and disappears into Egypt,
and though the sudden and untimely deaths of her husband and her brother
are not her doing directly, they are at least metaphorically the result of their
relationship with her. And in the most resonant connection, the innocent and
idealized working-class hero, Stephen Blackpool, dies painfully as a result of

Research for this paper was supported in part by a PSC-CUNY Faculty Grant. An
earlier version of this paper was delivered at the Dickens Universe in Santa Cruz,
California, in August 1994.

two brief encounters with her. In a further parallel, Louisa's failure to remarry after Bounderby's death is a kind of death; like Beatrice's suicidal rejection of her father's gifts, Louisa, though she had accepted the husband her father gave her, lives out her life in the shadow of other people's happiness and fulfillment.

The father-daughter plot in these two works is archetypal—present in Western culture from the Old Testament Jeptha, Lot, and Dinah to *Iphigenia in Aulis* to *King Lear* to Jane Smiley's *A Thousand Acres*.[1] There is a conflict in all these stories between social needs and private desires that usually surface—indeed usually generate narrative—at the point of the daughter's marriage. Daughters must move out of the family and make new alliances through marriage to keep the biological, political, and economic health of the community, but the dynamics, particularly the sexual dynamics, within the family itself resist the moving out of the daughter. Sometimes the desire to keep the daughter grows out of the father's romantic attachment to her as she supplants the woman he first loved, who has dwindled into a wife, a fictional pattern seen in *Oedipus at Colonus*, in *King Lear*, and in "Rappacini's Daughter" and *Hard Times* (Louisa is her father's "favorite child" [165] and "the pride of his heart" [163][1] The father of Western father-daughter narratives frequently tries to negotiate his desire to keep the daughter by selecting the man she marries (not uncommonly she is given to his relative or friend), thus giving an additional turn to Eve Sedgwick's thesis of homosocial desire.

But there is another reason the daughter needs to stay within the family in these narratives. She is also needed to serve, save, redeem, ultimately to sacrifice herself for the father, as does Iphigenia, Cordelia, Florence Dombey, or Louisa Gradgrind. To the degree that the Western narrative of the father-daughter concerns the redemption of the patriarch, the daughter's continued presence in the family is essential. So, as Fred Kaplan in his biography of Dickens states, Louisa's return to her father's house is the means of redeeming him even as the patriarchy in general in that novel is redeemed by sisterhood. (309)

This benign thesis[3] places the center of interest in *Hard Times*, as in most Western narrative, in the development of the father's story. But there is another story possible, that of the daughter. From her point of view, the sacrifice that might redeem the father can be fatal, as with Iphigenia or Cordelia. The daughter's story is not frequent in Western narrative, but "Rappacini's Daughter" suggests where we might find it, that is, in the gothic. For though Hawthorne's gothic story is centered on a representation of male abuse of knowledge and power, the daughter's story—the conflict between her desire for her father's love and her desire for self-fulfillment and autonomy—vies for center stage with the father's, particularly at closure, as it does in many gothic novels. In that most ungothic novel, *Hard Times*, Louisa's story is less visible and more problematic, but it is present intermittently, injected into the narrative not through the gothic but through the 1860s version of the gothic, the sensation novel and its interrogation of the institution of marriage.

The sensation novel in *Hard Times* is similar to the under-narrated sensation novel at the heart of *Bleak House* (the illicit affair of Honoria and Captain Hawden[4]) and the undeveloped sensation novel at the bottom of *Great Expectations* (the story of Estella's mother Molly) in that, like these other marginalized women's stories in Dickens' novels, Louisa's story of the explosive potential of a woman's repressed desires generates the narrative and powers its development. Even though the novel's overt interest is in the father's story and his need for redemption, Louisa's repressed feelings about her father, her marriage, her husband, and her lover, and the actions she takes as a result of these repressions cause the reversals of fortune for both Bounderby and Gradgrind that make up both the plot and the overt themes of *Hard Times*. That is, through her self-assertive action Stephen is suspected of robbing the bank which ultimately leads to the unmasking and humiliation of Bounderby, and also through her return to her father's house, Gradgrind experiences doubt about his life's work and is turned into a "wiser man, and a better man" (203). It is important to note that these changes in the fortunes of Bounderby and Gradgrind are not the result of the essentially passive ministering affections of a "good daughter" such as Florence Dombey or Little Dorrit. This version of the father's story in *Hard Times* is represented by Sissy, not only by her nursing presence in the Gradgrind house but also by her unquestioned forgiveness of her own father's abandonment of her. On the other hand, Bounderby and Gradgrind's fortunes change because of Louisa's subversive self-assertion—in other words, because of her similarity to a sensation novel heroine.

Louisa's repressed feelings and self-assertion not only cause havoc among the men in her life (not to mention her own life), but they cause a little havoc in the text as well. From the point of Louisa's marriage, there are a number of puzzling gaps in the story. One such gap, though a common one in Victorian fiction, is the configuration of the sexual nature of Louisa's marriage. There has been vigorous critical controversy over this subject.[5] Louisa's physical repugnance for Bounderby (as in the scene where she tells Tom she wouldn't mind if he cut out the place on her cheek where Bounderby kissed her) and the clear sexual desire that motivates him suggests there might be some sexual trouble between them from the start. But when we meet them months after the honeymoon, Louisa and her husband appear to live calmly together, which suggests to me that, however unsatisfactory, there has been conjugal sex.

Does it matter? We know that no Victorian novel could directly depict the sexual nature of human experience even in marriage. Why should we care whether or not Louisa and Bounderby have had sex? It matters because the uncertainty about Louisa's sexual knowledge is one of a number of puzzling elements about her marriage. Her sexual experience or lack of it certainly would help us understand her feelings for Harthouse, which are rather mystified in the text. Why do her feelings for Harthouse result in her leaving her husband and returning to her father? Further, what does she have in mind in that return, and what does her father intend when he asks Bounderby to permit her to stay in her father's house "on a visit"? Finally, why does Louisa not remarry after Bounderby's death, that is, why does Bounderby die if by that Louisa is not freed to find happiness and fulfillment?

Of course, there are explanations for these events in the father's story. Louisa has to return and stay in her father's house to save him through her self-sacrifice. But in order for that story to dominate, questions about what Louisa might want must be suppressed. However, Louisa's story is not totally absent because it is part of another concern in the novel—that of marriage and divorce.

Though the introduction of the issue of divorce into *Hard Times* is as much the result of personal and political forces as narrative ones, once in the novel, it takes on a life of its own, as it were, and begins to disrupt the coherence of the narrative. Through the issue of divorce, parts of Louisa's story enter the narrative and vie for center stage with her father's story.

It is a critical truism that Dickens expressed his own boredom with his wife and marriage through Stephen Blackpool's desire for a divorce. Kaplan says that in the portrayal of Stephen's wife, Dickens gives vent to his feelings about his wife Catherine's "incompetence, clumsiness, withdrawal from responsibility" (309). But there was also considerable contemporary interest in the subject, for the first divorce reform bill was being debated in Parliament at the same time that Dickens was writing *Hard Times*.[6] (The actual bill was not passed until three years later.)

The need for some reform was widely felt. As Bounderby makes clear to Stephen, divorce in 1854 was difficult, complicated, and costly. The only "cause" for divorce was adultery, which for women suing had to be "aggravated" by incest or bigamy, though, in fact, legal separations were granted women for abandonment and cruelty. (There were only four full divorces granted women prior to 1857.) Three separate legal actions, including a bill in the House of Lords, were necessary. Legal separation "from bed and board" was possible, but women in that position had no legal rights, nor a right to their own earnings, nor to custody of their children, nor could either party remarry.

But even though part of the stated motivation for reform was to protect women and increase access to divorce, the debates over the Matrimonial Causes Bill, as it was officially called, had a large element of bad faith in them.[7] For example, efforts to scuttle the Bill entirely were cynically based on arguments that it did nothing for the poor or to equalize the position of women. In the end, divorce law reform essentially continued the status of divorce as an instrument primarily for well-off men to assure that, as Lord Cranworth put it, women not be able to "palm spurious offspring upon their husbands" (3 Hansard, CXLV, 813).[8]

Nonetheless, given his personal situation and the current debates about divorce reform, there is nothing surprising in Dickens introducing the issue of divorce through Stephen. But once in the text, the issue of divorce, like the debates in Parliament, threatens to shift the discussion of a man's issue to women's issues. That is, in Parliament the desire to make it easier for men to get divorces opened the door to a vigorous campaign for changes in the Married Women's Property Law, while in *Hard Times* Stephen's desire to get out of a bad marriage invites us to look at all the marriages in the text and to see that, in fact, nearly all are abusive not to husbands but to wives.

Take Mrs. Sparsit, for example. The novel's plot would work as well, in fact better because more consistently, if she had been a social-climbing, money-grubbing husband hunter. Such bad behavior would justify Bounderby's humiliating treatment of her. But in fact, she was manipulated into a marriage with a boy fifteen years her junior by Lady Scadgers, probably because she thought he was a good match. In the event he is a very bad husband: he spent all his money and "when he died, at twenty-four . . . he did not leave his widow, from whom he had been separated after the honeymoon, in affluent circumstances" (37). If Mrs. Sparsit were not so much in Bounderby's camp and so hostile to Louisa, we might notice how badly she has been treated.

More troubling, however, is Mrs. Gradgrind. Though she is generally represented dismissively throughout the novel (the list of characters refers to her as "feeble-minded"), it takes very little to see that she is in a terrible marriage. Her imbecility in fact appears to be a product of her marriage.[9] Gradgrind chose her because "she was most satisfactory as a question of figures" and "she had 'no nonsense' about her" (19). Though she may have been weak-minded to start with, she was presumably not at the time of her marriage an "absolute idiot" (19). When we meet her later in her life with five children, she is close to being one. How did that happen? She herself describes the process by which she has been turned into an idiot as "never hearing the last of it", that is, when she ventures to say anything she is instantly and abruptly put down. So that "the simple circumstance of being left alone with her husband and Mr. Bounderby, was sufficient to stun this admirable lady . . . so, she once more died away, and nobody minded her" (19). The repeated use of the word "died" in connection with Mrs. Gradgrind's ceasing to talk throughout the novel indicates the brutality of her suppression. When she is literally dying she tells Louisa " 'You want to hear of me, my dear? That's something new, I am sure, when anybody wants to hear of me' '' and later " 'You must remember, my dear, that whenever I have said anything, on any subject, I have never heard the last of it; and consequently, that I have long left off saying anything'' (148–49).[10]

Mrs. Gradgrind is a particularly troubling character because her brutalization is articulated (if never actually represented), but her story, like Mrs. Sparsit's, is systematically undercut by laughter, and both are meted out punishment: Mrs. Sparsit has to go live with the woman who made her marriage, Mrs. Gradgrind dies without even a claim to her own pain. While for the most part we think Mrs. Sparsit more than deserves her blighted life, the discomfort in our responses to Mrs. Gradgrind is a sign of a disruption in the narrative that is the result, I would argue, of the interrogation of marriage introduced by the divorce plot.

But Mrs. Sparsit and Mrs. Gradgrind are minor figures. The most serious gaps in the narrative introduced by the issue of divorce concern Louisa. Most of Louisa's story is unnarrated, but one possible version is suggested, nonetheless, through the systematic analogy drawn between her and Stephen.[11] In the structure of the novel her story alternates and contrasts with Stephen's. Louisa's questions to Sissy about Sissy's parents and their marriage were answered not only by the young girl's description of their compatible and happy marriage but also both by contrast and repetition in the two following chapters in which Stephen tells Bounderby about his own miserable marriage and wish for a divorce and then fantasizes about an ideal marriage with Rachael. More metaphorically, Stephen's subsequent murderous thoughts about his wife are followed by Louisa's capitulation to Bounderby's "criminal" proposal. Another contrast represents the emotions that bring both Louisa and Stephen to the brink of disaster: Louisa's assertion of herself in intimate, dangerous, but under-represented conversations with Harthouse are followed by Stephen's equally dangerous self-assertions to Slackbridge and Bounderby. Louisa has two important scenes with her father; Stephen has two with his "father" Bounderby. Louisa's aborted "fall" from the bottom of Mrs. Sparsit's staircase into "a dark pit" is completed by Stephen's fall into the dark Old Hell Mine shaft. Finally, Louisa's leaving her husband and "dying" to the story is followed by Stephen's actual death.

Louisa and Stephen are further linked to Tom's betrayal of them both, while Tom's robbery of the bank acts out retribution on Bounderby for him, his sister, and Stephen (and also substitutes for Harthouse's intent to "rob" Bounderby of his wife). However, in a crucial scene in which the three are brought together by Louisa, Tom displaces his guilt and perhaps his sister's, too, onto Stephen. (Certainly both Stephen and Rachael initially think that Louisa is as guilty of using Stephen as Tom is.)

The most telling connection between Stephen and Louisa is in their equally dreadful if quite different marriages. Stephen and Louisa's responses to their bad marriages are similar: both turn to sympathetic others though they both resist acting on the needs and desires released in them by these others.[12] The four illustrations for the novel reflect this linking of Louisa and Stephen in their responses to their marriages: two are of Harthouse, Louisa's would be lover; a third is of Stephen and Rachael with Stephen's wife, who is reaching out from the bed curtains for the poison. The fourth is of Stephen rescued from the Old Hell Mine Shaft, Rachel's hand in his while he delivers his unlikely speech on class relations.[13] The first three point to Louisa's and Stephen's failed marriages; only the fourth relates to the industrial theme, though as we shall see, that theme is integrated with the marriage question as well.

But this parallelism between Louisa and Stephen is broken at a crucial point; Stephen's desire to end his marriage is sympathetically treated, but not achieved. On the other hand, Louisa's marital situation, while it is never narrated directly and poses a number of unanswered questions, actually ends in a permanent separation.

The steps leading to this outcome show the imbrication of the divorce plot with the father/daughter plot. Tom tells Harthouse that Louisa married Bounderby to do her brother a service, but Louisa also accepted Bounderby's proposal to please her father, whose heart was set upon it, as her mother tells her (148). Gradgrind for his part has given Louisa to a man "as near being [his] bosom friend" (16) as possible, an exchange that is in the process of being repeated by Tom "giving" Louisa to his bosom friend Harthouse.[14] But though the second exchange negates the first, it ultimately leads to the fulfillment of both Louisa's need for a "divorce" *and* the archtypal fatherly desire expressed in Gradgrind giving Louisa to Bounderby in the first place—to keep the daughter for himself.

Because the two narrative forces have the same drive—to separate Louisa from her marriage—they work together and climax in a single scene—that between Gradgrind and Bounderby that achieves the separation and makes Louisa's return to her father permanent. In that scene, Gradgrind tells Bounderby that he wants Louisa to remain with him "on a visit," a request he justifies by suggesting that Louisa, like Lady Audley, is mentally unbalanced, thus offering the strongest reason he can for the unorthodox arrangement he desires.[15] But Louisa has never behaved in a selfish or improper way—not to Stephen to whom she gave money, not to Tom who from the very beginning recognized that he did not "miss anything in [her]" (43), not to her father or mother, nor to her husband, and in fact she has been the soul of kindness and propriety to all (in this she resembles Oliver Twist or Florence Dombey more than Esther Summerson or Tom Gradgrind).[16] During her courtship by Harthouse, the narrator as much as admits that she has an incorruptible good heart: "in her mind—implanted there before her eminently practical father began to form it—a struggling disposition to believe in a wider and nobler humanity than she had ever heard of, *constantly* (my italics), strove with doubts and resentments" (125).

But in spite of all this, her father in his justification to Bounderby says she has qualities that are "harshly neglected, and—and a little perverted" (178).[17] Gradgrind has to assert Louisa's mental imbalance because the separation between her and Bounderby is entirely contrary to legal definitions of separation and the attitudes that underlay the law, as articulated in this *London Times* comment on the aborted 1854 Matrimonial Causes Act: "Beyond all doubt, it is for the general public interest that marriage should be practically considered an immutable condition of life, to the end that it should not be hastily contracted, and that those placed in it should be stimulated by the pressure of necessity to accommodate themselves to one another" (15 July 1854).

Bounderby, thus, is quite correct to refuse the separation. In fact, in his response he actually uses a key word from the divorce debates. "I gather from all this" he says to Gradgrind, "that you are of the opinion that there's what people call some incompatibility between Loo Bounderby and myself" (178–79), a sentiment frequently used derisively as in this *London Times* comment that "Society would be unhinged, and the next generation would be strangely educated if mere incompatibility of temper were a ground for divorce" (27 January 1857).[18]

Nonetheless the main effect of Bounderby's ultimatum that Louisa be home by noon the next day is that Gradgrind is saved from having to explain what he means by her "perverted" qualities or to expand on his "visiting proposition" as Bounderby puts it. Louisa returns permanently to her father. It is if she never left her father's house, a situation forshadowed by both Mrs. Sparsit and her husband Bounderby's insistence on continuing to call her Miss Gradgrind and Tom Gradgrind's daughter after she is married. She thereby fulfills the father's plot of redemption, even as she acts out Stephen's desire "to be ridded" (59) of his spouse—and perhaps Dickens' desire for the same thing as well.

But it is a hollow victory for *her*; she suffers a kind of narrative death, essentially disappearing from the narrative, dissolving into her father's story. What *her* feelings about her marriage and her husband and her return might be are unnarrated, though they have been vaguely suggested in the fire symbol and in her earlier conversation with her father about Bounderby's proposal (a chapter tellingly entitled "Father and Daughter"). Even in the climactic scene when she confronts her father and appears to speak her heart and mind, she still cannot name her own desire.[19] In this Louisa is perhaps closer to Dickens' inner turmoil about marriage and divorce than Stephen ever is.

Even so, in this climactic confrontation between father and daughter, the daughter's story, released by the divorce plot, is the closest it ever comes in the novel to breaking through the father's story and entering fully into the text. Though Louisa does not voice her feelings about Bounderby nor her thoughts about her marriage, she admits her strong feelings for Harthouse: "There seemed to be a near affinity between us. . . . If you ask me whether I have loved him, or do love him, I tell you plainly, father, that it may be so. I don't know!" (163) she says, but "I have not disgraced *you*" (my italics).

The confrontation between a forgiving father and a sinning daughter was a familiar trope in Victorian popular literature, particularly in melodrama. Dickens' use of it here, while it keeps the titillating possibility of the daughter's "fall," significantly revises the scene. Instead of the erring daughter begging for forgiveness from the father, the almost-erring daughter accuses the father of responsibility for her faults. By this revision, the daughter's story for a moment overpowers the father's story. The emergence of the daughter's story is further strengthened by the way in which the final tableau is aborted. Catherine Gallagher, who first pointed out the melodramatic reversals in this scene, says that the conventional melodramatic father/daughter scene ends in a tableau in which the father forgives the daughter with a full embrace between them, in other words a visualization of the dynamic of the father's plot in which the daughter returns to his arms. But as Gallagher also points out, in *Hard Times* this resolution is violently disrupted; rather than seeking a forgiving embrace, Louisa begins to fall to the floor; as her father "tightened his hold in time to prevent her sinking on the floor . . . she cried out in a terrible voice, 'I shall die if you hold me! Let me fall upon the ground!' " (163)[20] Like Beatrice Rappacini, Louisa rejects the conventional relationship and insists on controlling her own story.

Finally though, I differ from Gallagher's reading of this scene. She sees in the failure of the confrontation to end in the loving embrace a sign that Gradgrind saves Louisa by letting her go. That certainly would be the way the daughter's story should develop. But unfortunately it does not really happen that way in the novel. It is true that Gradgrind does not embrace Louisa; instead he passes her off to Sissy, who puts her to bed, and after a subdued exchange in which the daughter forgives her father, the two women act out the melodramatic trope precisely. Louisa "fell upon her knees" and cries "Forgive me, pity me, help me! Have compassion on my great need, and let me lay this head of mine upon a loving heart." Sissy acts for the father by reintegrating Louisa into the paternal sphere through *her* embrace: "O lay it here! . . . Lay it here, my dear" (168). Sissy then somewhat astonishingly continues to act for the father by sending Louisa's lover away. (Gradgrind is willing to play the father's role to the husband he has chosen for her, but not to the lover she has picked for herself, showing perhaps once again the power of Eve Sedgwick's model of homosocial desire.) One reason the scene between Sissy and Harthouse has struck most readers as unbelieva-ble—even ridiculous—is because this melodramatic confrontation is conven-tionally acted out by either the father or the brother. As the good daughter, Sissy's assumption of the father's role here cannot really work.

Daniel Deneau has argued that Louisa must have had no real feelings for Harthouse because he is never referred to again after Sissy sends him away. But Sissy's "second object" in her conversation with Harthouse suggests something different, for there seems little reason to make him leave immedi-ately and forever if Louisa, who has given Sissy "her confidence", is not still in some danger from her own heart and Harthouse's presence (172–73). The fact is, we have no idea *what* is on Louisa's mind; from the point she returns to her father's house, her story remains untold.[21] Not only is Louisa not "saved,"[22] her story essentially disappears from the text.

With the return of Louisa to her father and the disappearance of Stephen, the father's story emerges as the only story and the issue of marriage and divorce is also erased from the text. This narrative move is achieved more or less seamlessly because of the imbrication of Stephen and Louisa—he representing the industrial theme, she the education theme and the divorce theme moving between them. In fact, issues of class and gender frequently were substituted for issues of marriage and divorce in the divorce reform debates. The reason for making divorce more difficult for the poor and for wives, members of Parliament argued, was that "the poor and women [are] particularly susceptible to moral lapses," as Mary Lyndon Shanley says. "Parliament's fear of the disruptive potential of female sexuality was as great as its distrust of the unrestrained passions of the poor" (365–66).[23] However, the debates on divorce reform achieved precisely what Parliament feared; they inevitably opened the way for women's issues and working-class issues to enter the arena of public concern.

The sensation novel worked in a similar way, though the development is reversed. These novels examine women's desires and the inadequacy of mid-dle-class marriages to fulfill them, but in the conclusion they reinscribe the "heroine" into conventional roles. Lady Audley, who dared to make her own destiny, is declared even by herself to be "mad" and thrust out to die in a lunatic asylum; the self-reliant and adventurous Magdalen Vanstone in Col-lins's *No Name* falls into a death-like illness to be reborn as the passive wife of a sea captain.

The ending of *Hard Times* resembles in a general way these sensation novel's endings. Both Louisa and Stephen end badly, arguably Stephen worse than Louisa though her brother Tom's rejection of her compounds her lonely future. Louisa, even though she has not fully acted on her desires—she has not run away with Harthouse—lives unpartnered, a guest at the banquet of Sissy's domestic happiness, doing her father's work, atoning for his sins.[24] Stephen dies painfully by falling down a mine-shaft.

The gratuitousness of Stephen's death and the underexplained events that lead up to it suggest how difficult it is in the end to integrate the gender and class issues involved in the divorce plot into the conventional father's story which dominates the last pages of *Hard Times*. In his final words, Stephen seems to lay the blame for his death on the misunderstandings between capital and labor—fathers and children—but actually his death has come about because of his terrible marriage and frustrated relationship with Rachael. The focal point for both this relationship and his death is his promise to Rachael. As many critics have pointed out, this promise is inexplicable,[25] but even more puzzling is why Rachael does not release him from it when she sees what the result of his adhering to it is. And why does Stephen, whose refusal to join his fellow workers is based on this promise to Rachael to avoid trouble with the masters, then insist on justifying his colleagues to Bounderby, thereby essentially provoking his master into dismissing him, thus achieving precisely what Rachael made him promise to avoid? And most importantly, why are these actions followed by such a painful and gratuitous death?[26]

Stephen's death has been justified as Dickens' recognition that there is no way out of the class war. Nicholas Coles says "Stephen is killed off by the combined forces of both classes . . . and there is no manner of hope in either of them" (168).[27] However, if we think of Stephen's story as it connects to Louisa's through the marriage and divorce plot, we may see an additional reason for his death. Though overtly Stephen is the only one whose miserable marriage seems to call for divorce, the linking of Louisa and Stephen has opened a crack through which we see that for women much less dramatic situations than Stephen's make marriage a repressive institution. Though intermittently in evidence, this insight has been downplayed through laughter at Mrs. Sparsit and Mrs. Gradgrind and through narrative silence about Louisa. But in order to completely erase this story so the father's story can dominate the closure, the divorce issue must be killed *in* Stephen, who has been its overt spokesman.

This is Louisa Gradgrind's secret: she killed Stephen Blackpool, though unlike Lady Audley she did not personally push him down the well. Louisa's action of seeking Stephen out in his home, accompanied by her brother as an escort, has led to the suspicion of Stephen's robbing the bank, his hurried return, and ultimately his death. Further, Louisa also narratively necessitates Stephen's death. Though she is the embodiment of the sensation heroine's story of repression and lack of fulfillment in marriage, Stephen has carried the weight of her story. So even as she cannot remarry, though the healthy Bounderby dies five years after the separation, Stephen cannot live to marry Rachael. The sick Mrs. Blackpool survives, the healthy Stephen dies, thereby removing the last vestige of the divorce plot. The novel ends where it began—with the now-chastened father and sacrificed daughter together again, and for all time.

Dickens' letters emphasized what a strain the writing of *Hard Times* was for him, and when he finished he remarked "Why I found myself so 'used up' after Hard Times I scarcely know" (Norton *HT,* 275). Usually this is understood in terms of his struggle with the weekly number format. But I think that there are other tensions at work as well: the introduction of divorce into the novel (for whatever reasons Dickens did so) is a disintegrating force. Perhaps the struggle to contain and ultimately eliminate that force also contributed to Dickens' creative exhaustion. (Of course, Dickens had personal reasons for not wanting to concentrate on divorce from the woman's point of view.)

Kaplan remarks that the subject of divorce was still on the novelist's mind even after he finished *Hard Times* when he made an entry in his notebook about a proposed story of "a misplaced and mismarried man." While the "mismarried" is perfectly understandable to us in terms of Dickens' own situation, the "misplaced" is a more curious expression. It suggests a helplessness in the unfolding of one's life, a definition of life as one of accidental placement and lost possibilities rather than fatal choices or actions, a sense that life's miseries as well as its happinesses are the result of where one is placed and not of what one is. And even as the word "misplaced" perhaps gives poignant insight into Dickens' state of mind, it can also serve as a kind of coda to the glimpses of another "misplaced" person—Louisa. Thinking of himself perhaps but speaking for Louisa even as she has spoken for him,[30] Dickens says, as he develops the idea for his story of the "misplaced and mismarried man", that he—or she—is "Always, as it were, playing hide and seek with the world and never finding what Fortune seems to have hidden when he was born" (Kaplan 310).

NOTES

1. See Lynda E. Boose, "The Father's House and the Daughter in It: The Structures of Western Culture's Daughter-Father Relationship" in the seminal collection of essays on this subject edited by Lynda E. Boose and Betty S. Flowers, *Daughters and Fathers* (19–74).
2. Kristin Flieger Samuelian points out that Bounderby's insistence on being a self-made man is a rejection of the maternal. Though she does not link this to the father-daughter plot, clearly the "absence" of the mother in the Gradgrind family enables the father to substitute the daughter emotionally for his wife, even as Mr. Bennet does in *Pride and Prejudice* and with similarly negative results.
3. Rosemarie Bodenheimer has a similarly benign view of the father-daughter plot in *Hard Times*. "Out of the reconciliations with her father and Sissy, Louisa's end too is mitigated by a retrieval of childhood . . . Both Gradgrind and his daughter are tested for their loyalties to past connection, and both pass the test, Louisa

when she returns to the father who hurt her and Gradgrind when he defies Bitzer and the law of the land'' (205). Such readings, completely supportable within the father's plot, accept that the daughter's place is with the father and minimize the cost of this ''successful'' conclusion.

4. According to Phillip Collins, one stage version of *Bleak House* was entitled *Lady Dedlock's Secret* (173).

5. Robert Lougy says it is unconsummated (246), as does John D. Baird. Juliet McMaster, on the other hand, says ''I find no evidence for Robert Lougy's astonishing claim that the Bounderby marriage is unconsummated, nor does he provide any'' (423).

   But, to paraphrase Mrs. Gradgrind ''though there is some sex somewhere in the room, I can't absolutely say Bounderby has got it.'' Edgar Johnson says Louisa ''prostituted'' herself when she married Bounderby; Monroe Engel calls attention to the ''extraordinary sexual image'' by which Mrs. Sparsit imagines Louisa's capitulation to Harthouse (362). Daniel Deneau's analyzes the sexual way in which Louisa's feelings for Tom are articulated, in particular in the scene after the robbery when she comes into Tom's bedroom ''in a loose robe,'' barefoot, and with her hair down. (366–67). Robert Fabrizio has a long section analyzing Louisa's sexual feelings for Tom (75–78). Catherine Gallagher talks of the ''sexual exploitation'' of Louisa and argues that ''fancy and incest'' are inextricable in the text (164).

6. When the bill was first entered in 1854, there was little public interest, but there were several subsequent articles in *Household Words* on the subject written by Eliza Lynn and W. H. Wills. These articles are generally rather conservative; they recognize abuse of women particularly in terms of property but also argue women should not get upset over their husbands' infidelities. Dickens himself wrote a later article on the subject, entitled ''The Murdered Person'' (*HW* 14 [11 Oct. 1856]), which emphasized two targets: the high cost of divorce actions and the legal disabilities which placed a wife's resources in her husband's power even after the marriage had failed and the parties separated.

7. Poovey remarks that the debates ''raised the possibility that married women's anomalous position would be questioned and even changed. That this did not happen suggests how reluctant lawmakers were to examine their assumptions about women, the relationship between the sexes, and the gender bias of British law.'' She also believes the debates over the law were important because by ''acknowledging the fact of marital unhappiness, they inevitably exposed the limitations of the domestic ideal.'' (52) Poovey further remarks that ''The very fact that legislators explicitly addressed the issue of class inequity [how the expense kept the working class from having access to divorce] and not the sexual double standard suggests that, while the social and economic unrest of the 1840s had forced legislators to conceptualize class relations as a problem that needed attention, the social relation between the sexes was not yet open to the same kind of scrutiny'' (58).

8. Gail Savage argues, based on statistical analysis of the reports from the Divorce Court, that in fact many women and lower-class people were able to get divorces under the new law.

9. Jean Ferguson Carr discusses Mrs. Gradgrind and recognizes her suppression by the father's discourse. Though Carr points to a reference that equates Gradgrind to Bluebeard, she does not link the treatment of Mrs. Gradgrind to the marriage theme.

10. McMaster notes that "we are to understand that [Mrs. Gradgrind] has been so crushed and ground by Gradgrind facts that she is scarcely alive" (415), but she does not treat her as an abused wife.

11. Gallagher notes the parallel of Louisa and Stephen, seeing it as ultimately, after the opening chapters, "only" metaphoric. Her point about the connection concerns the ultimate failure in the novel of the parallel of the family and society (150–52). See also Stanley Friedman.

12. Baird analyzes how Dickens suggests that sexual promiscuity is part of Mrs. Blackpool's degeneration, which would give Stephen grounds for divorce. Louisa does not commit adultery, nor does Bounderby, so neither of them would have grounds for divorce under the law, either before or after the Matrimonial Causes Act (408).

13. The focus of the illustrations on the marriage theme is at odds with the different titles Dickens had in mind—"According to Cocker"; "Prove It"; "Hard Heads and Soft Hearts"; "A Mere Question of Figures." (Craig, 11). This split between title and illustration suggests a similar split in the narrative between the marriage, Louisa, Stephen story and the industrial-mathematical Louisa, Stephen story, though as I suggest later on, the two are linked toward the end of the novel. Craig in fact suggests a connection when he gives as one meaning of the phrase "hard times" "the more pervasive state in which people felt that the essential and permanent conditions of their lives hemmed them in inflexibly."

   The three divisions of the novel—Sowing, Reaping, Garnering—as fertility metaphors also suggest a marriage focus rather than an industrial one.

14. Robert Barnard interprets the scene where, speaking of Louisa to Harthouse, Tom rips the petals from a rose as a symbolic sacrifice of Louisa. (378–9)

15. In the popular play Fox Cooper made of *Hard Times* almost immediately after the final number was published in *Household Words*, Gradgrind makes no proposition to Bounderby at all; Bounderby simply gives his ultimatum. Nor does Gradgrind suggest Louisa is "perverse"; in fact he insists she is an "angel" and Bounderby a "scoundrel." I think Cooper is doing more than simplifying here. He is also trying to correct a place in the narrative that he senses rings false, either because incomplete, underdeveloped, or a locus, as we would say, of contesting discourses. I think many revisions that popular dramatists make when turning novels into plays indicate similar aporias in the texts.

16. An observation of Raymond Williams seems particularly apt here: "*Hard Times* is composed from two incompatible ideological positions, which are unevenly held both by Dickens and by many of his intended readers. Put broadly, these positions are: first, that environment influences and in some sense determines character; second, that some virtues and vices are original and both triumph over and in some cases can change any environment" (169) and further "that though 'circumstances' may affect, even radically affect, the *history* of a character, his or her true formation lies elsewhere, and the capacity for change, whether in an

individual or in the general 'circumstances', is similarly rooted in primary personal qualities, often of course related to some wider, usually religious, source" (170).

17. Deneau argues that the "perversity" is the incestuous feelings Louisa has toward Tom.

18. Bounderby also says "I am Josiah Bounderby, and I had my bringing-up; she's the daughter of Tom Gradgrind, and she had her bringing-up; and the two horses wouldn't pull together" (181), a metaphor than Lynn Shanley notes also marked the divorce reform debates. These echoes of the debates in Bounderby's speeches in this scene demonstrate that Dickens was following the parliamentary arguments as reported in the press.

19. Carr argues that "Louisa and her mother, and even Dickens, cannot find words for what is missing from their lives, words having been usurped as the tools of the Gradgrind system" (170).

20. In his dramatization, Fox Cooper insists on restoring the melodramatic trope to this scene, thus both recognizing the power of the melodramatic mode and also, again, sensing there is some confusion here about whose story this is. Louisa's words "I shall die if you hold me" are followed by her sinking to the ground, but in the play this is immediately followed by her father "raising her up and supporting her off" saying "My child! my child! . . . I would give worlds to annul this cursed fatal marriage."

21. David Lodge remarks that "we hardly ever get inside the girls' heads at all—they are primarily objects in the perceptual fields of other characters" (385).

22. In discussing an earlier version of this paper at the Dickens Universe, several people made compelling arguments that what happens in this and the closing paragraphs of the novel is that Louisa and Sissy form a sisterhood that substitutes for—and is superior to?—the conventional patriarchal model of human and family relationships. That is, while I see Sissy acting for patriarchy, they see her as the source of a woman's counter-community. What prevents my acceptance of this argument is the almost unbearable sadness of the conclusion, where all the positive possibilities for Louisa are deliberately raised by the author ("Herself again a wife—a mother—lovingly watchful of her children. . . . did Louisa see this?") only to be cruelly denied ("Such a thing was never to be." [219]) Louisa does not deserve this; in her feelings for Tom, for Sissy, for Stephen—for everyone—there is no evidence that she is emotionally unable to find happiness as a wife and mother. The inexplicable harshness of this conclusion indicates to me that there is some force in Louisa that must be suppressed, even punished. What could it be except her self-assertive actions as a sensation heroine made possible by the introduction of divorce into the plot?

23. Caroline Norton, who was one of the major forces behind the changes in the law regarding married women's property, also linked the two: our "legists and legislatures . . . never *will* satisfy, with measures that give one law for one sex and the rich, another law for the other sex and the poor." (Quoted in Shanley 359). Bishop Wilberforce, on the other side of the debate, also made the connection in opposing the re-introduction of the Divorce Bill in 1856. First he remarked (as though he had Louisa in mind) "How constantly it [has] happened that the evil

which [has] resulted in a direful tragedy [has] had its commencement in the lightest cause—some difference of temper, some little alienation of affection, exposing the wife to the arts and approaches of another. But if the woman were guarded by the sure conviction that no more happiness in married life was possible, the temptation might altogether fail." He then moved immediately to the lower classes, "who" he says give "no indication of any wish for relaxation of the law; it [is] perfectly well known that a legal divorce [is] an impossibility, and to that circumstance might be traced the sacredness of the marriage tie among the lower orders of the English people which [is] so remarkable." (Quoted in Poovey 58–59).

24. Based on the penultimate paragraph of the novel, Samuelian sees Louisa ministering to the working class for the rest of her life, thus fulfilling Stephen's final words. This makes a neat conclusion to my thesis of Stephen's substituting for Louisa at the end by making Louisa in turn substitute for him. There has been some critical confusion over whether this passage applies to Sissy or to Louisa. The passage reads "But, happy Sissy's happy children loving her; all children loving her; she, grown learned in childish lore; thinking no innocent and pretty fancy ever to be despised; trying hard to know her humber fellow-creatures, and to beautify their lives of machinery and reality with those imaginative graces and delights, without which the heart of infancy will wither up. . . ." (219). Philip Collins (191–2) and John Holloway (169) read these lines as referring to Sissy not Louisa. Though I think on close reading it is clear the passage refers to Louisa not Sissy, the confusion by such eminent Dickens authorities points to the uncertainty at the end of the novel about the nature of Louisa's final position.

25. Barnard says it is an "inexplicable promise which she didn't want him to make and apparently doesn't insist that he keep" (376). But see n. 70 in Coles's essay where he points out the survival of a fragment deleted by Dickens in which Stephen gives an "angry speech over the maiming of Rachael's little sister in a factory accident, followed by Rachael's rebuttal of his anger and Stephen's promise to avoid it in future." He continues "Dickens's reasons for deleting so vital and moving a passage are a matter for speculation." Craig in his introduction to the Penquin edition of the novel says the vagueness of the promise "makes us begin to think that Dickens is not even implying an adverse judgement of trade-unionism, but sliding out of dealing with it at all" (29). On the other hand, Joseph Butwin argues that "the inclusion of documentation of specific abuses in the novel would give too great a validity to the working-class activism of the union, thereby undercutting the role Dickens intended for its middle-class readers" (179). In this light it is interesting to note that Slackbridge's denunciation of Stephen short-circuits "the awkward (for a middle-class advocate for the poor) political issues involved in union organization" (Coles, 165) in the same way that Bounderby's ultimatum that Louisa be home by noon the next day short-circuits explanations of her separation from him as well as her father's judgment of her "perverted" qualities.

26. The final scene in the Fox Cooper drama again differs radically from that in the novel, and in its differences perhaps recognizes that the novel's assignment of rewards and punishments at closure is problematic. The play attempts to correct

this according to both theatrical and cultural norms. Thus, Tom confesses to the burglary but is saved by Louisa giving him the money to replace the theft. Gradgrind then says "it was no robbery, after all. The money was removed by Tom from one place to another, and is on the premises at this very minute." Nor does Stephen die. Equally important is Bounderby's response: "Blackpool, you have suffered a martyrdom through error and misconception. If you recover of your wounds, I'll make you some amends. First, I'll give Rachel to you for a wife. Secondly I'll give her the £150 as a marriage portion, and that's not all I'll do for the pair of you." So not only Gradgrind but Bounderby too is reformed, and Louisa can thus do the right thing: "Mr. Bounderby, I will now cheerfully accompany you back to the home you have provided for me, and must insist upon it that you allow your good mother to supply the place of Mrs. Sparsit." Bounderby "suspends work at the factory for seven days", pays "full wages during all the time" and gives "my wife Louisa" £200 to "distribute amongst you" to provide "you with a few necessities and comforts these 'Hard Times.' "

27. Humphry House says that Stephen "might have become the material of genuine tragedy, if Dickens had been prepared to accept his death from the beginning as inevitable and unanswerable . . . [but] Dickens did not want to admit that Stephen's bargaining power—whether against Bounderby, his marriage, of life itself—was negligible, but wrote as if there might be an unexpected solution at every turn" (206).

28. In her confrontation with her father, Louisa says her "old strife" was "made fiercer by all those causes of disparity which arise out of our [hers and Bounderby's] two individual natures" (162) perhaps reflecting Dickens's own sense of the power of "incompatibility" in marriage.

WORKS CITED

Baird, John D. "Divorce and Matrimonial Causes: An Aspect of 'Hard Times' " *Victorian Studies* 20 (1977): 401–12.

Barnard, Robert. "Imagery and Theme in *Hard Times*" in Norton Critical Edition of *Hard Times* 367–79.

Bodenheimer, Rosemarie. *The Politics of Story in Victorian Social Fiction.* Ithaca: Cornell UP, 1988.

Boose, Lynda and Betty S. Flowers. *Daughters and Fathers.* Baltimore: Johns Hopkins UP, 1989.

Butwin, Joseph. "*Hard Times*: The News and the Novel" *Nineteenth Century Fiction* 32 (1977): 166–87.

Carr, Jean Ferguson. "Writing as a Woman: Dickens, *Hard Times*, and Feminine Discourses" *Dickens Studies Annual* 18 (1990): 161–78.

Coles, Nicholas. "The Politics of *Hard Times*: Dickens the Novelist versus Dickens the Reformer" *Dickens Studies Annual* 15 (1986) 145–79.

Collins, Phillip. *Dickens and Education*. London: Macmillan, 1965.

Cooper, Fox. "Hard Times: A Domestic Drama in Three Acts." London: Dicks Standard Plays, [1854].

Craig, David. "Introduction." *Hard Times*. Harmondsworth: Penquin, 1969, 11–36.

Deneau, Daniel. "The Brother-Sister Relationship in *Hard Times*" in the Norton Critical Edition, 362–67.

Dickens, Charles. *Hard Times*. Norton Critical Edition, 2nd edition. ed. George Ford and Sylvère Monod. N.Y. Norton, 1990.

Engel, Monroe. *"Hard Times"* in Norton Critical Edition, 360–62.

Fabrizio, Robert. "Wonderful No-Meaning: Language and the Psychopathology of the Family in Dickens' *Hard Times*." *Dickens Studies Annual* 16 (1987): 61–94.

Friedman, Stanley. "Sad Stephen and Troubled Louisa: Paired Protagonists in *Hard Times*." *Dickens Quarterly* 7 (1990): 254–62.

Gallagher, Catherine. *The Industrial Reformation of English Fiction*. Chicago: U of Chicago P, 1985.

Hawthorne, Nathaniel. *The Novels and Tales*. New York: Random House, 1937.

Holloway, John. *"Hard Times*: A History and a Criticism" in *Dickens and the Twentieth Century* ed. John Gross and Gabriel Pearson. London: Routledge and Kegan Paul, 1962, 159–74.

House, Humphry. *The Dickens World*. London: Oxford UP, 1941.

Kaplan, Fred. *Dickens: A Biography*. New York: Morrow, 1988.

Lodge, David. "How Successful is *Hard Times*?" in Norton Critical Edition of *Hard Times*, 381–89.

Lougy, Robert. "Dickens' *Hard Times*: The Romance as Radical Literature" *Dickens Studies Annual* 2 (1972): 237–54.

McMaster, Juliet. *"Hard Times*: 'Black and White' " In Norton Critical Edition, 411–25.

Poovey, Mary. *Uneven Developments: The Ideological Work of Gender in Mid-Victorian England*. Chicago: U of Chicago P, 1988.

Samuelian, Kristin. "Being Rid of Women: Middle-Class Ideology in *Hard Times*. *Victorian Newsletter* 82 (Fall 1992): 58–61.

Savage, Gail L. " 'Intended Only for the Husband': Gender, Class, and the Provision for Divorce in England, 1858–1868" in Kristine Ottesen Garrigan, ed. *Victorian Scandals: Representations of Gender and Class*, Athens: Ohio UP, 1992, 11–42.

Shanley, Mary Lyndon. " 'One Must Ride Behind': Married Women's Rights and the Divorce Act of 1857" *Victorian Studies* 25 (1982): 355–76.

Stone, Lawrence. *The Road to Divorce*. London and New York: Oxford UP, 1990.

Williams, Raymond. "The Reader in *Hard Times*" in *Writing in Society*. London: Verso, n.d. 166–74.

The Genesis of the Last Novel: *The Mystery of Edwin Drood*

Wendy S. Jacobson

Scholars gathering to discuss *The Mystery of Edwin Drood* at Santa Cruz in August 1993 centered on essentially similar concepts in their readings. Robert Tracy discussed Dickens' borrowing "from himself" and journeying through earlier novels as he wrote his last (42), and Gerhard Joseph, relating the life to the fragment, saw Dickens' "career . . . as a series of repetitive acts that marks an aesthetic journey, of doing the same fanciful thing over and over again" (16). This paper argues that Dickens not so much revisits the past but does what he has always done: he re-writes his own life, his own fancies, and in so doing reconstructs myths. He also returns to sources that persistently haunt the novels. Two of these have a shaping influence on *The Mystery of Edwin Drood* and in this work relate to each other: the Genesis 4 story of Cain and Abel and Shakespeare's *Macbeth*.[1]

The Cain and Abel story, basic to our conception of the human condition, stands "out of the vast repertoire of Western myth . . . for the extraordinary longevity and variousness of its appeal" (Quinones 3). Ricardo Quinones points to Byron's *Cain* as an originatory work initiating the post-Romantic sense of the myth of Cain and Abel as different from that of the past, so that the Cain figure, no longer only a precursor of evil and a fratricide, becomes the intelligent and complex questor. "He is the only character in the drama whose intelligence is probing, who seems to be a character of consciousness as well as of conscience."[2] Elie Wiesel, in his re-telling of the story, reflects precisely this, that the Cain upon whom Byron and Dickens dwell is a post-Romantic figure, victor/victim, prey to God's whim yet creator of his own destiny. Commenting that "no other Biblical situation contains so many questions or arouses so many uncertainties" (53), Wiesel's most relevant point for the purpose of an assessment of the world of Cloisterham is, that the Genesis story is set in the fallen world, and has as its background the parents

197

of these sons who have a memory of paradise. "Called upon to share their parents' haunted kingdom, they quarreled over heavenly favors and finally confronted one another in every role that defines man's relationship to other men" (53).

Man's relationship to other men and the role of fratricidal sacrifice is gathered into the motif of the city. The sanctuary to which the Dean of Cloisterham refers so patronizingly has its source in the story of Cain, founder of the first city and associated with the cities of sanctuary established in order to provide refuge "for the children of Israel, and for the stranger, and for the sojourner among them that everyone that killeth any person unawares may flee thither" (Numbers 35:15).

Crisparkle's attempt to protect Neville is countered by the bland thinking of the Dean who reminds him that "The days of taking sanctuary are past." (Sanctuary as a legal recourse was abolished in England in 1623.) So, "Minor Canon Row knew Neville Landless no more; and he went withersoever he would, or could, with a blight upon his name and fame" (16, 146).[3] Not only is the cadence of this prose biblical, but the intent is evocative of Genesis: shunned by the world, Cain becomes a fugitive and a vagabond. Neville Landless is overtly described by Honeythunder as Cain (17.149). Other references occur: Neville is assaulted and insists that he " 'has no chance but to set his mark upon' " his attackers, alluding to the words: "And the Lord set his mark upon Cain, lest any finding him should kill him" (4:15); when Jasper asks where Edwin is, Neville replies " 'Where is your nephew? . . . Why do you ask me?' " (15.133) echoing: "Where is Abel thy brother? And he said, I know not: Am I my brother's keeper?" (4:9). Neville's departure from Cloisterham (the sacred city?) for London (the secular city?) is interesting: perhaps the sacred and the secular cities are inverted in that Cloisterham is associated with death and fear whereas London becomes the sanctuary to which Rosa and Neville and even Miss Twinkleton flee to the protection of Grewgious and Tartar.

In an article entitled "Cain: Or, the Metaphorical Construction of Cities," Gerald L. Bruns describes the city in terms evocative of Dickens' city, the polis inhabited by nameless transgressors:

> The building of cities is rooted in the idea of banishment from the soil . . . the destruction of the household, of being the outcast of the settlement, of being marked for life, that is, being the marked man or the fugitive. . . . Beneath the polis there is the labyrinth. (74)

Bruns reminds us of Augustine's thesis that "the City of God and the city of the world" are not separate, but that "as far as human history goes, the former lives like an alien inside the latter" (18.1.391) so "at the centre of the city is the pariah or the scapegoat" (Bruns 79). This ambiguity accords with the doubleness in *The Mystery of Edwin Drood*, with Jasper's life being conducted between the two cities; and this in turn accords with the same issue in the Cain and Abel story, of "an encounter with the lost brother, the sacrificed other," the struggle between good and evil with its "great purpose" being "to address a breach in existence, a fracture at the heart of things". Fraternity itself conjures up an image of "the dream of the human family, the pastoralism of the heart, a vision of unity and concord and co-operation . . . summarized" in the image of the siblings. But this idyll itself ushers in "difference, discord, and division" in that the "Cain/Abel story represents a shattering reminder of the fragility of the human compact" (Quinones 3).

The polarities of fraternity and death have an ironic complicity, and the violence endemic in the Bible story—a reminder that the opposite of brotherhood is murder—marks the Cain theme in literary history as one of "inwardness, emotional tension, and secret conflict" (Quinones 6). These words, so apt to the Cain and Abel story, are pointers to the central concerns of Dickens' novel, the tension between love and death, between a man and his kin. The power of the Cain and Abel story rests in large measure upon its "dualistic nature" so that it "presents rival principles in opposition."[4] Genesis and Dickens recognize a tragic basis to existence, a dark event at the heart of society, a sacrificial act which initiates a reciprocal violence to which mankind is ever in thrall. Of course, the sacrificial act, theologically, involves the laying down of the self in submission to a higher good while Cain's is not a significant act, perhaps, in as much as it is not for the good of the "tribe."[5] The dark event, the murder of Abel, is motivated by envy and the mysterious sense that the "other" is pleasing to God; this undermines the social desire for unity of whatever sort. Beginning with Byron's drama of *Cain* (although, Mary Shelley's *Frankenstein* (1818), in its presentation of the monster created by the self, ought perhaps to have this honor), this theme is intensified in post-Romantic literature whereafter the Doppelgänger, typified in the two brothers at variance, pervades nineteenth-century art.

Cain haunts man's conscience. Claudius knows that the murder of *his* brother, King Hamlet, "hath the primal eldest curse upon't" (3.3), recalling the story of man's second offence against God and the first murder. Envy, selfishness, and murder conjoin with that earlier defiance in Eden. And murder, the commentators teach us, is what has happened in *The Mystery of Edwin Drood*. Collins, impatient perhaps of arguments like mine, warns that "whenever Dickens thought about murder, echoes of *Macbeth* came into his mind" (*Charles Dickens: The Public Readings* 299). There are indeed "echoes of *Macbeth*" in this novel; moreover, useful comparisons can be made between the play, the novel, and the Genesis story: Macbeth's embittered kingship, the unfruitful tilling of Cain's soil, the wearying drudgery of loathsome duties in Cloisterham, are alike; Cain's alienation from the community is echoed by Jasper's and Macbeth's; all suffer the "wakeful misery of the night," for all are "girded by sordid realities" which torture their imaginations; the sense of a lost Paradise and of Hell pervades both Genesis and Shakespeare's play as it does this novel: " 'In the distasteful work of the day, in the wakeful misery of the night' " Jasper tells Rosa, he is " 'girded by sordid realities . . . wandering through Paradises and Hells of visions.' "

On Shakespeare and Dickens, Alfred Harbage has written movingly about Bill Sikes that "we see that he has done with his killer just what Shakespeare has done with his. He has effected a transplant, giving to a creature who lacked a conscience his own conscience and ours"; it is naive, he says, to assume that writers "so successful in portraying murder must have the capacity to commit it" when "what they had was the capacity to repent it"(*The Shakespeare Dickens Analogy* 61). Macready first made the comparison between Dickens and himself as ' "Two Macbeths!" ' after he attended a performance of the 'Sikes and Nancy' Reading. Echoes of *Macbeth* are undeniable:

> At times, he turned to beat this phantom off, though it should look him dead; but the hair rose on his head, and his blood stood still, for it had turned with him, and was behind him then. He leaned his back against a bank, and felt that it stood above him, visibly out against the cold night sky. He threw himself on his back upon the road. *At his head it stood, silent, erect, and still: a human gravestone with its epitaph in Blood!!*   ("Sikes and Nancy" 484)

Each image is apt, and each is found in Macbeth's horror of Banquo's ghost. "If Dickens had not known *Macbeth*," asks Harbage, "would the slaying of a gangster's moll have created in a London slum a sense of almost doomsday horror?" (*Aspects of Influence* 126). By the same token, if Shakespeare and Dickens had not known the story of the first murderer shunned by man and also by God so that his punishment was too great to bear, would either have re-written the myth? "And the Lord said unto him, therefore whosoever slayeth Cain, vengeance shall be taken on him sevenfold. And the Lord set a mark upon Cain, lest any finding him should kill him" (4:15).

The presence of the Cain and Abel myth is suggested by echoes that permeate *The Mystery of Edwin Drood* quite as frequently as do those from *Macbeth*, perhaps most strikingly in our recognition that Jasper, living "apart from human life," is as removed from fellowship as is Cain. What draws us to the novel is this insight into a man who lives in isolation, who knows, as does Macbeth, that he "must not look to have . . . troops of friends" (5.3.25). Macready's performance of Macbeth concentrated on his withdrawal from his companions (Downer 330) and we are told of Jasper that "it is curious to consider that the spirit of the man was in moral accordance or interchange with nothing around him" (23.203). He is trapped as much by his inner life as by the narrow limitations of the cathedral precincts. In the words of Lawrence Frank:

John Jasper, superficially beyond the pale of sympathy, reveals the extent to which human energy may be twisted and inverted. . . . [his] rebellion takes the form of perversity and self-absorption. . . . in a world whose values are . . . inadequate to man's psychological and moral predicament. In creating John Jasper, Dickens explores the ambiguities of human consciousness denied by a society no longer understanding itself or the human beings for whom it exists.

(194–95)

This notion is commensurate with that of Byron's *Cain* in which artistic creation is a rebellion against a stifling conformity: Byron's poet figure is courageously linked "against the forces of convention and tyranny" with other "figures of rebellion in the Christian and Classical traditions: Satan, Cain, and Prometheus" (Russell 184). Jasper does have elements of the Byronic hero particularly in his compulsion/revulsion effect on Rosa; there is that in his creation which is crucially dependent on his disturbing sexual power.

Jasper is often depicted as diabolic: he describes the Cathedral services as "devilish"—" 'Must I take to carving [demons] out of my heart?' " he asks miserably (2.11). In the Sun-Dial scene he sets "his black mark upon the very face of day," describes " 'Paradises and Hells of visions' ", and the "preservation of his easy attitude" is "diabolical" in its contrast with "his working features and his convulsive hands" (19.170–71).

Jasper's characterization, however, is not like that of Fagin, Quilp, or Compeyson at whose fates we are more horrified than compassionate.

The walls and ceiling of the room were perfectly black, with age and dirt. . . .
In a frying-pan which was on the fire . . . some sausages were cooking; and standing over them, with a toasting-fork in his hand, was a very old and shrivelled Jew, whose villainous-looking and repulsive face was obscured by a quantity of matted red hair.
(8.50)

The red-headed devil holds a fork at a cauldron, presides over the fire of hell, and runs the underground world of crime, but the funny touch of the pork sausage, together with fixed images of devilry, make Fagin's characterization, though splendid, a static portrayal. Another character with red hair and of mythically evil proportions is Monks, a sidekick of the devil's, a snivelling terrified tortured being, who falls into fits, has "a broad red mark, like a burn or a scald" (46.296) on his throat, is the bad brother of the pure hero, yet is protected from the end that comes to Sikes because, terrified of bloodshed, he shies away from murder. Shaped in the mode of a myth, or fairy-tale, he is larger-than-life. He is a grotesque, a parody of biblical Cain:

The man shook his fist, and gnashed his teeth. . . . He advanced towards Oliver, as if with the intention of aiming a blow at him, but fell violently on the ground, writhing and foaming, in a fit.
(33.207)

About Sikes, Dickens' "Preface" debates whether "every gentler human feeling is dead within such bosoms" (xxviii) in a way that he does not consider doing in connection with Fagin or Monks in whom there is clearly no gentle humanity, nor has there ever been. But in Sikes, and more subtly in Jasper, is explored the enigma of how it may be that a human being lives though "every gentler human feeling" dies within his bosom. The Cain-Abel myth "provides a perfect locus" for this preoccupation because it scrutinizes the ambiguities of the human condition balanced between the ethical and the evil, and dramatizes "the struggle on the part of a character offended by the conventional moral code" (Quinones 19–20). The fascination with Cain is like that with John Jasper—it is paradoxical and contradictory, and ultimately mysterious.

Generations have puzzled over why discord should arise when Cain's sacrifice is rejected. His offering is the first indication in the Bible of prayer, and is an assertion of Cain's identity as a "tiller of the ground" by which means he would find favor in the eyes of God. When Dickens makes Jasper a musician and choirmaster, and has his talents become a source of misery and oppression to him, there is a tenuous but interesting connection in the motif that recurs in accounts of Cain, whose descendants, "artificers in brass and iron" who also "handle the harp and organ" (Genesis 4:21–22), are the first artists (Mellinkoff 1, 103). God rejects Cain's offerings of the fruits of the earth, and accepts Abel's blood sacrifice: "If thou doest well, shant thou not be accepted? and if thou doest not well, sin lieth at the door" (4:7). There is a careless indifference in this, an "arbitrariness of preference" which invalidates Cain's offering. "All life," Quinones argues, "is an offering where one is being judged" (12). In the scene in which Jasper confesses disappointment and disillusion with his own life compared with that of his nephew, which promises to be exciting, creatively active, and loving, there is an echo of Cain's situation; he feels rejected, bound to suffer and toil hopelessly in the world while others prosper; perhaps, too, Edwin's circumstance has something of Abel's in it. The vulnerability and crushing sense of rejection experienced by the offerer "might explain the special appropriateness of the Cain-Abel story within a setting of artists" because the nature of artistic endeavour consists in "distinctive presentations of the self" wherein "the totality of one's being is defined and placed on the line" (Quinones 12–13). Jasper is an artist, and there is some deep sense of loss, pain, fear, trouble of some kind, associated with his work.

The dualistic nature of the Cain-Abel story is also vivid in Dickens' novel; Jasper has precisely the qualities that Quinones ascribes to Cain, a "questioning, dissatisfied, probing critical intelligence." He lives in a narrow meanspirited environment dominated by the smugness of the Dean and Mrs. Crisparkle; and Crisparkle, perhaps a type of Abel, "stands for the consolidation of the religious spirit with the social structure of the day." Jasper is impatient, even mocking, of the good Crisparkle's reverence for traditional values represented by the ancient English cathedral, the image of which dominates in such a bizarre way the opium fantasy that opens the novel. This "contest of values" (Quinones 13) inevitably leads to violence, shocking in the peaceful and sacred precincts; equally, violence may be an appropriate response to a society impervious to the misery inflicted on its choirmaster and disloyal to its actual ideals when it rejects the stranger, Neville Landless, on tenuous grounds on the morning of Christ's nativity. "Violence is crucial to the Cain-Abel story" in its concentration on the spread of sin; in other words, the first killing is another Fall, because man is made in God's image. The ideal of fraternity culminating paradoxically in murder, points to "a vortex of emotional fury" that has been a rich source for visual and literary artists (Quinones 13). Post-Romantic literature has grasped and reiterated this paradox of brothers and death, exploring persistently the Doppelgänger motif.

This Doppelgänger motif (Carol MacKay called it "our old friend" [12]) is present in Dickens' work from the beginning, in Oliver Twist, whose identity is lost and who struggles to withstand the dark other and regain his rightful heritage, until the enigmatic first lines of *The Mystery of Edwin Drood*: "An ancient English cathedral town? How can the ancient English Cathedral town be here!" We are taken into an hallucinatory mingling of Turkish robbers with English choirboys, to discover a "scattered consciousness . . . fantastically [piecing] itself together" (1.1). But it is not only Jasper's consciousness that is split for it soon transpires that the conscience of Cloisterham is also in trouble: it is a rigid society masking its cruelties in pious conventions. Likewise, Edwin Drood represents all that Jasper longs to be, and Neville Landless, dark, alien, with no prospects, also in love with Rosa Bud, is Jasper's dark self. In the cathedral gatehouse, when the unhappy musician intervenes between the two young men who represent, on the one hand, all his desires, and on the other all he represses, he encounters "the externalized manifestation of his own warring states of mind" (Frank 177).

So we come again to the Cain-Abel story wherein the sacrificed brother becomes "a lost portion of the self, a self that is abandoned, sundered, the twin, the double, the shadowy other . . . able to express all the dimensions of some lost portion of life that the foundation sacrifice in its fullest meaning acknowledges" (Quinones 11). The story presents an archetype that, in murdering his brother, Cain murders his own self.

Jasper, the last of Dickens' ambiguous villains, arose out of the same intriguing emotional and imaginative world that produced his first one, Bill Sikes. When Dickens returned to *Oliver Twist* for the purposes of the "Sikes and Nancy" reading, he returned to what Steven Marcus described as "his first and most intense representation of the crisis of his young boyhood" (375): an expression of another aspect of himself is revivified in the character of Sikes with whom Dickens sympathetically identifies. (Albert Hutter and others have noted that Dickens also identifies with John Jasper [36].)

In that reading, Sikes is goaded by Fagin and humiliated by Noah Claypole into pain and rage. Though careful to lock Nancy's door, and remembering Fagin's advice not to be " 'too—*violent*—for—for—safety' ", he strikes Nancy with the pistol, "twice upon the upturned face *that almost touched his own*" and then "*shutting out the sight with his hand seized a heavy club, and struck her down*!!" (482–83). Terrified, he cannot bear to turn his back upon the corpse, and leaves the room in which it lies, though Nancy's eyes, *ITS* eyes, pursue him until he is almost mad.

Reviewing the novel in 1844, R. H. Horne expressed horrified pity for the "detestable wretch" who is hunted down like "a wild beast . . . with tenfold more ferocity than ever was fox, or boar . . . our sympathies go with the hunted victim in this his last extremity" because he is "one worn and haggard man with all the world against him . . . we are not with the howling mass of demons outside" (199–200). Bill Sikes takes on that dimension shared with Headstone and Jasper—and Macbeth and Cain: we change our allegiance from "the howling mass of demons" to "this hunted-down human being."

Violence emanating from pain is followed by horror, terror, and flight "into the solitude and darkness of the country"; then Bill Sikes takes "the desperate resolution of going back to London" because "there's somebody to speak to there, at all events," but those who were "his fellow-thieves" shun him. "All three men shrank away. Not one of them spake" (484–85). Bill Sikes, like Cain, is cast out from the community and ejected from the sight of God.

One thesis has it that "the novelist had familiarised himself with violence and the need to act out violence" (Sanders 205), and although we are warned by Collins not to take too seriously the claims that Dickens was identifying with his villains when he wrote " 'I am . . . murdering Nancy' " or " 'I do not commit the murder again . . . until Tuesday' " (*Dickens and Crime* 267–68), violence is a recurrent preoccupation. The relevance in this for my argument lies in Jasper's murderous thoughts which, although not explicit in the novel, are, perhaps, part of a dark fantasy, a dark aspect of himself, to which we have been given no access. This image, of a hidden guilt, evokes the very ambiguity of "fallen man," the man who sins and repents, and invents God to explain and forgive the mystery of his sin—the man who kills the brother he loves. Sikes arouses the vengeful anger of the community, so that "It seemed as though the whole city had poured its population out to curse him" (50.327); it is perhaps this lynching against which God protected Cain. As the rabbis point out, "God's mercy to the guilty who repent of his sin is infinitely greater than that of man" (Hertz 15). Cain's agony, that "from Thy face shall I be hid," reveals him to be not wholly bad. Fagin is wholly bad, damned and without grace, but Sikes is not of the devil's party because he is not without remorse. That he should be brought to death by his own horror rather than by external forces of law and vengeance might leave the reader with a sense of justice done, but also with horrified compassion.

Collins, who demonstrates Dickens' conviction that murderers are always vile, concedes that "Sikes becomes, in a sense, a sympathetic character" (1962, 263), and in the case of Headstone, allows that though "very wicked" and "responsible for his actions," he is pitiful in the scene in which "Charlie Hexam, his one remaining object of affection, finally repudiates him and leaves him 'in unutterable misery' " (*Dickens and Crime* 263, 285). This distressing scene compares with that in which Grewgious looks down upon Jasper, grovelling, "a heap of torn and miry clothes upon the floor" (15.138). Jasper "undergoes a process of total disintegration," however, like Wrayburn and Riderhood in *Our Mutual Friend*, having descended into "the regions of the godlike river" after the Christmas Eve storm, he is "granted the opportunity to deny or to accept the potentiality for change" (Frank 185).

Such potential may suggest that the impulse of the novel is Resurrection.[6] The disconcerting first chapter ends with the intoning of evensong: "WHEN THE WICKED MAN—"; these words, capitalized in the text, come from Ezekiel, promising that "When the wicked man turneth away from his wickedness . . . he shall save his soul alive" (18:27). The phrase is noted in the Number Plans followed by "Touch and Key-note." "It is a key-note which was surely intended to stand for the novel as a whole," Sanders avers (208–09). Though the "wicked man" indulges in debauchery in the first lines of the opening chapter, he is nevertheless promised salvation by its end. There is the promised salvation because wickedness is the other side of salvation; there is a balance between life and death, so that in that last wonderful assertion, of the brilliant morning that shines on the old city, the sun penetrates the cathedral and preaches the Resurrection and the Life (Sanders 208–09; *MED* 23.215).

Will this cathedral in which the "cold stone tombs of centuries ago grow warm; and flecks of brightness dart into the sternest marble corners of the building, fluttering there like wings (*MED* 23.215) reject its choirmaster? On the next and last page of the novel, the choirmaster's enemies are ranged against him in the extraordinary and grotesque figures of the "astounded" Deputy and the fist-shaking Princess Puffer, and although Mr. Datchery "falls to with an appetite," having solved, perhaps, his mystery, it is *force majeur* up to us, in a sense, to decide.

In the case of Sikes and Headstone, man is less merciful than is God in the story of Cain: the demons are in the mob that yells for the murderer's blood and the hunted man destroys himself. Suicide and lynching are the punishments meted out by man; that which is meted out by God, according to Genesis, comes as a result of Cain's plea: "Behold thou hast driven me out this day from the face of the earth; and from thy face shall I be hid; and I shall be a fugitive and a vagabond in the earth; and it shall come to pass, that every one that findeth me shall slay me'' (4:14). Sikes flees because he has cut himself off from man and God and ''every one that findeth me shall slay me.'' The punishment, greater than mankind can bear, is mitigated in so far as Cain is protected from vendetta: ''Therefore whosoever slayeth Cain, vengeance shall be taken on him sevenfold. And the Lord set a mark upon Cain, lest any finding him should kill him'' (4:15). The history of this mark has shown how man persists in being less merciful than God (Mellinkoff 154–55).[7]

The redemption of Eugene Wrayburn demonstrates, on the other hand, God's mercy. He is saved from drowning by the woman who loves him, and although the last words of the novel indicate that Society rejects his marriage to her, clearly God (and Mr. Twemlow) do not—for the union is a religious and redemptive commitment to love and to grace. On the other hand, there is John Jasper, enigmatic and compelling, with a dark aspect of his personality purporting to violence and obsessionally directed towards murder, or so some commentators say, and yet his anguish can be recognized though his fate remains unknown.

The interest that this paper has in the characters of Sikes and Jasper goes beyond their being ''villains'' similarly compounded. Sikes's return to Dickens' creative life as the major attraction in the farewell season of public readings in 1869 and 1870 is fascinating. Six months after the private reading of ''Sikes and Nancy,'' and in May 1869, Dickens began to ''cast about for a new subject'' (Dolby 416–17). In September 1869 the title was settled and a celebratory dinner held: a month later the first number of *The Mystery of Edwin Drood* was read to Forster. Meanwhile the farewell reading program was being planned and rehearsed; Dickens wanted ''to leave behind . . . the recollection of something very passionate and dramatic'' and he fulfilled this promise. '' 'I shall tear myself to pieces' '' he whispered just before the last performance in March 1870 after which he would '' 'vanish from these garish lights . . . for evermore.' '' It is supposed that the excitement and intense exhaustion brought about by the forty-minute performance hastened Dickens' death three months later, but he was driven by an obsessional desire to repeat the reading ''over and over again.'' After each performance, an uncontrollable craving to go through it again would overtake him; he ''was, moreover, discovered in the grounds at Gad's Hill re-enacting the murder of Nancy a day or two before he died'' (Collins, *Public Readings* 465; Dolby 386–87, 449).

All this while he was creating John Jasper, who describes his own dreams as a journey that he needed to repeat obsessively, '' 'over and over again . . . hundreds of thousands of times' '' (23.206).[8] Jasper and Sikes are, on the face of it, very different, the one an elegant and artistic member of a sophisticated and respectable cathedral community, the other a brute raised in the violent slums of London's seamy underworld, a house-breaker and bully; but they are both wrought from the same source: from the figure of the man whose evil pursues and destroys him, the man who kills the thing he loves. This figure, widespread in an era concerned with ''the personality in which evil is always threatening from within'' (Welsh 130), finds its prototype in Cain who, having killed his good brother (his ''good self'' some analysts would have it) is pursued into the wilderness of sin and expulsion from the sight of God, and thereby into damnation.

That the ''shadow of Macbeth'' persists throughout the works ''implies that Dickens was drawn to the soul in torment.'' His ''vivid rendering of the tormented consciousness'' (Morgan) of Cain causes his readers to respond to Sikes and Jasper with pity and fear for the sinner. The fact that interpretations of the story of the first murderer shift between compassion for, and condemnation of, Cain generates tension in the portrayals: the first man to kill is also the first man to beg for forgiveness and mercy, to earn the protection of God. He thus represents a complex but very real possibility for moral regeneration.

NOTES

The Chairman's Fund Educational Trust of Anglo American Corporation and De Beers Consolidated, together with Rhodes University are gratefully acknowledged for their generous support during the preparation and presentation of this paper.

1. Gerhard Joseph pointed out in discussion that the myth of Abel and Cain is not only repeated throughout the Dickens canon but ''Genesis itself does the same thing in setting up fraternal conflict in generation after generation, as we move through the Patriarchs.''

2. Jeffrey Burton Russell's account of Mephistopheles argues for a change in the early nineteenth century of the vision of the devil: ''distaste for the church'' aroused the notion that the Romantic hero, in his ''rebellion against unjust and repressive authority,'' became a type of the devil:

   The Romantic idea of the hero . . . stands in contradiction to the classical epic notion of the hero. . . . The Romantic hero is individual, alone against the world, self-assertive, ambitious, powerful, and a liberator in rebellion against the society that blocks the way of progress towards liberty, beauty, and love; the Romantics read these qualities into Milton's Satan. Their admiration for Satan was not Satanism, however—not the worship of evil.

   (174–75)

3. References to *The Mystery of Edwin Drood* (*MED*) are to chapter and page numbers in the Clarendon edition on which the World's Classics edition is based. Chapters are short and references may be found readily in other editions.

4. That the Cain/Abel story recurs in Dickens' work as motif, allegory, emblem, and so on, has often been noted: John Cunningham, for instance, points to Magwitch's

Christian name, Abel, and that "we see Compeyson and Magwitch, linked like Cain and Abel, in a death-grip" (11). The use of the story is not always so imaginatively done, however, as in "Cain in the Fields," written with R. H. Horne for *Household Words*. Here the metaphor of Cain is merely convenient, repeated mechanically to enforce condemnation of "the red-handed descendants of Cain" murdering and robbing in the countryside (280).

5. A colleague, Jeanette Eve, recommended that I indicate that I am not arguing that Dickens is drawing exclusively on the Genesis myth; the presence of Crisparkle, notably in Chapter 10 in his reference to Christ, demonstrates that the larger context is Christian.

6. As do, for example, Thacker (111) and Sanders (206–17). That Edwin Drood's "resurrection" is concomitant with thematic concerns in other novels is the thesis of my own cautious proposals in *The Companion to The Mystery of Edwin Drood* (5–9).

7. Ruth Mellinkoff agrees with Quinones's thesis that there are shifts in the way Cain is perceived, and that he is represented in Jewish thought as either unregenerate and a marked beast, or as a sinner who sincerely repents, is marked with the horn, an honourable sign in the ancient world denoting strength and glory, thus singling him out as even heroic (5 and 60).

8. Fred Kaplan makes the connection between the characterization of John Jasper and the murder of Nancy Reading when describing the "kind of self-hypnosis" manifesting "the compulsiveness, self-destructiveness, and power over others . . . that he was to depict so brilliantly in the final year of his life in the character of John Jasper" (239). This is a footnote and Kaplan does not take this enticing point further.

WORKS CITED

St Augustine. *The City of God*. Trans. Gerald G. Walsh, et al. New York: Image Books, 1958.

Bruns, Gerald L. "Cain: or, The Metaphorical Construction of Cities." *Salmagundi* 74–75 (Spring/Summer 1987): 70–85.

Byron, George Gordon, Lord. *Byron*, Ed. Jerome J. McGann. Oxford: Oxford UP, 1986.

Collins, Philip. *Dickens and Crime*. London: Macmillan, 1962.

———. *Charles Dickens: The Public Readings*. Oxford: Clarendon P, 1975.

Cunningham, John. "Christian Allusion, Comedic Structure, and the Metaphor of Baptism in Great Expectations." To be published, South Atlantic Review.

Dickens, Charles. *The Mystery of Edwin Drood.* Ed. Margaret Cardwell. Oxford: Clarendon P, 1972.

———.*Oliver Twist* (1837–39). Ed. Kathleen Tillotson. Oxford: Oxford UP, 1982.

———. *Our Mutual Friend.* (1864–65). Ed. Michael Cotsell. Oxford: Oxford UP, 1989.

———. "Sikes and Nancy," in *Charles Dickens: The Public Readings.* Ed. Philip Collins. Oxford: Clarendon P, 1975. 465–86.

———. With R. H. Horne, "Cain in the Fields," *Household Words* 1 (10 May 1851).

Dolby, George. *Charles Dickens As I Knew Him.* 1885. New York: Haskell House, 1970.

Downer, A. S. *The Eminent Tragedian.* Cambridge: Cambridge UP, 1966.

Frank, Lawrence. "The Intelligibility of Madness in *Our Mutual Friend* and *The Mystery of Edwin Drood.*" *Dickens Studies Annual* 15 (1976): 150–95 and 207–09.

Harbage, Alfred H. *The Shakespeare Dickens Analogy.* Philadelphia: American Philosophical Society, 1975.

———. "Shakespeare and the Early Dickens," in *Shakespeare: Aspects of Influence.* Ed. G. B. Evans. Cambridge: Harvard UP, 1976. 109–34.

Hertz, J. H., ed. *The Pentateuch and Haftorahs.* London: Soncino P, 1965.

Horne, R. H. from *The New Spirit of the Age. Dickens: The Critical Heritage.* Ed. Philip Collins. London: Routledge & Kegan Paul, 1971.

Hutter, Albert D. "The Novelist as Resurrectionist: Dickens and the Dilemma of Death". *Dickens Studies Annual,* 12 (1983), 1–39.

Jacobson, Wendy S. *The Companion to "The Mystery of Edwin Drood."* London: Allen & Unwin, 1986.

Joseph, Gerhard. "Who Cares Who Killed Edwin Drood? Or, On the Whole I'd Rather Be in Philadelphia". Unpublished paper. Dickens Universe Conference. U of California at Santa Cruz, August 1993.

MacKay, Carol Hanbery. "Supraimagery in The Mystery of Edwin Drood". Unpublished paper. Dickens Universe Conference. U of California at Santa Cruz, August 1993.

Marcus, Steven. Dickens: *From "Pickwick" to "Dombey".* London: Chatto & Windus, 1965.

Mellinkoff, Ruth. *The Mark of Cain.* Berkeley: U of California P, 1981.

Miller, Joseph Hillis. "Introduction." *Oliver Twist*. By Charles Dickens (1962). Rptd. as "What the Lonely Child Saw: Charles Dickens's Oliver Twist," *Victorian Subjects*. Hemel Hempstead: Harvester Wheatsheaf, 1990.

Morgan, Arthur. private discussion, 24 July 1993.

Paroissien, David. *The Companion to "Oliver Twist"*. Edinburgh: Edinburgh UP, 1992.

Quinones, Ricardo. *The Changes of Cain: Violence and the Lost Brother in Cain and Abel Literature*. Princeton: Princeton UP, 1991.

Russell, Jeffrey Burton. *Mephistopheles: The Devil in the Modern World*. Ithaca: Cornell P, 1986.

Sanders, Andrew. *Charles Dickens: Resurrectionist*. New York: St. Martin's P, 1982.

Thacker, John. *Edwin Drood: Antichrist in the Cathedral*. London: Vision P, 1990.

Tracy, Robert. "Murder in the Cathedral: Dickens's Book of Common Prayer," Unpublished paper. Dickens Universe Conference, U of California at Santa Cruz, August 1993.

Welsh, Alexander. *The City of Dickens*. Oxford: Clarendon P, 1971.

Wiesel, Elie. "Cain and Abel: The First Genocide" in *Messengers of God: Biblical Portraits and Legends*. 1976. Trans. Marion Wiesel. New York: Random, 1976; 1977. 44–81.

Pip and Jane and Recovered Memories

James Kincaid

Great Expectations and *Jane Eyre* live for us only as shady memories—that is all we have, all we can lay claim to. The novels are not here with us except as we can remember them. To say, further, that these are novels about memory, that we are creatures of memory, that you are right this minute not really reading me but busy devising memories that you can live by and in and through: all that is indubitable—and important—but confusing. The reason it is confusing is twofold: we do not know whose memories we are talking about and we do not know whether what we mean by that word "memory" is what we publicly pretend to believe memory is or what we secretly know memory to be.

Let me begin by getting us into the same boat on these two points. First, whose memories are these anyhow? We *could* be talking about Jane's memory and Pip's memory, or Dickens and Brontë's memory or Victorian memory or archetypal memory—but I am not interested in any of that and neither are you. We are talking here about modern ideas of memory, our memories, and how we use them. That is all we care about anyhow, you and I. Second, what is a memory? We usually hear that memory operates like a computer, storing and retrieving things, using electronic forklift trucks to take things off brain-shelves; but down deep we all know that this is not so, that memory does not go fetch things. It makes things, constructs them, tells stories—the stories we need and demand. Memory is not an operation like mining but an art like making a pot or a plot. Memory is of no use in testing the accuracy of its narratives, telling us whether something happened—whatever that means. Memory *is* of use in helping us imagine the shape of our lives, giving us a way to get through those lives with a good or an ill grace. Memory does not tell us where we have been but where we wish we had been, or feel doomed to have been, or need to have been—all in order to convince ourselves that we are somewhere particular right now. Memories and memory plots parade a fake concern for the past; but they exist in the first place because they make

211

allowances for the future: bid us Godspeed and trace out maps, hand out permission slips for the field trips we are eager to take up ahead. Memory plots are in the hands of travel agents, not archaeologists; they give us the illusion of a past so we can build the reality of a future.

My thesis is, therefore, that both *Great Expectations* and *Jane Eyre* interest us so intensely because of what they grant to us, give us permission to do, as we read them in reference to ideas of memory now current. But there is more to my thesis than that—and I will not hide it: we read *Jane Eyre* as a recovered memory plot and *Great Expectations* as a Freudian repression plot. *Jane Eyre* is compelling because it constructs so movingly the great Western lie—that we can make our own plots—and also, paradoxically, tells us we can do that now because in the past someone else made our plot for us. That is, Jane is the self-made heroine who traces her origins back to a gothic story of victimization, where she was made by others. This is the drama of the modern recovery narrative, played out exactly as in today's pop-psych view of development: childhood trauma (usually sexual trauma), sickness, multiple personality disorder, and final healing by conquering the demons of the past and being born again as a wonder child. According to this plot, which certainly has its appeals, Jane can say she is solely responsible or somebody else is solely responsible—depending on what suits her. This is the Protestant plot of Robinson Crusoe or Horatio Alger superimposed on a Freddy Krueger tale of terror. It is a straight-line genetic plot, confident that there is a single self-sufficient being, an atomized self. Notice how blind Jane is to class, politics, race, nationalism—to any context beyond the personal and psychological. In terms of memory, Jane's is the plot of the very early Freud and of modern anti-Freudians like Bass and Davis[1] and the thousands of therapists and hypnotists working to recover beings based on hidden or repressed traumatic memories; that is, *Jane Eyre* sees repression as a mechanical device of nay-saying, hiding facts too painful to be endured except by such means as splitting into multiple personalities.

Now *Great Expectations* also employs repression, but a different version of it: repression here is not a shut-off valve or a blanket covering a single secret scene, but a fog or mist that lifts only onto other foggy and uncertain scenes. Memory for Pip never gives him back a clear beginning picture, much less one where someone else is at fault, much less one where who's at fault is important. Instead of a gothic story of innocents and monsters, Pip's memory, like Freud's later, writes an ironic story of being implicated, where everybody and nobody is at fault and where we had better find a plot more useful to us that one of blame and causality and victimization. Pip cannot isolate himself from the world of pain and he cannot isolate himself from all around him: the convict and the smear of the sin and sloth and greed and goodness in the world. That is my thesis.

I know you are hoping that I will restate this argument, which was good but went by pretty fast. You are saying that I should give it to you all over again for clarity's sake. And since I have, in fact, come up with another fine way to say exactly the same thing and hate to lose it, I am glad to oblige. *Jane Eyre* is the simple story Dickens tried to write in *David Copperfield* and found he could not—the linear self-pitying success story which turns memory into a self-gratifying machine. What happens in *David Copperfield* is that the book broadcasts its lack of success in trying to bury so much complex material, its inability to write a satisfying victim-success story, to be *Jane Eyre*; so Dickens' great revisionary novel, *Great Expectations*, simply gives up, releases *David Copperfield*'s buried material, and lets it play. *Jane Eyre* is brilliantly effective because brilliantly and blissfully ignorant of its denial of the repressed; *Great Expectations* does what it does by releasing us from genetic plots and showing us how behind one convincing plot or memory there is always another convincing plot or memory, every victim is a victimizer, every gothic story is also ironic, every assertion of purity is an admission of guilt; so that, finally, defenses collapse, paranoia melts away, and all plots flow into acceptance. There are no rewards, not even the reward of clarity. The final word is Cordelia's denial of plots—no cause, no cause. Cordelia's renunciation of causality is followed by her strangulation, we recall; but the release from the causal may also lead to bliss. Who can tell? In such a world, we may find saintliness but we will never find a plot.

I am interested, then, in the way these novels can be made to play out a current controversy about memory, as we work the books into our own memories and exploit them to make plots of our own. I have no interest in explicating these novels or providing interpretations, and I regard any questions about the accuracy or the validity of my comments as impertinent. I want to concentrate on the gulfs and empty spaces opening up between these two books as one constructs them in memory. Ignore any correlations you may be tempted in a weak moment to draw. These books play out deep and terrifying contradictions; dropping into the space between them is dropping into the Mindanao Deep. Some may want to build bridges between the books and then pretend that they have "found connections." Let them. We would sooner fry up our own hand and eat it. We are practitioners of irony, we are, those of us who aren't deconstructionists, which is even better, and we see no connections.

MEMORY

Much of the recent popular controversy about memory relates to the *Jane Eyre* plot, recovered memory, and the assignment of guilt and innocence in courtrooms. Can memory, repressed or not, yield accurate stories of fault, blame, criminal responsibility? What is accuracy? What is repression? How does the circuitry of the brain work? How is it affected by trauma? Is a child's brain like that of an adult? Are memories retrieved from storage or, as *Time* magazine put it, "nothing more than a few thousand brain cells firing."[2] Is memory, as Elizabeth Loftus says, like a glass of milk stirred into an ocean, dispersing and merging on different levels, so that retrieval is never possible because new combinations are always being formed?[3]

I will answer all these questions by talking about myself. Always the best plan. When I was six I was at my grandmother's and stole a very large cake she had baked. I ate the whole thing, though I was induced to do so by an older female cousin named Dorie, who had warts; my grandfather, who was a horrible man, barely human, caught me eating the cake and came at me with a switch. My female cousin, who had probably snitched on me, lurked nearby and laughed so hard her warts shook. But my grandmother rescued me, told me I could eat all the cakes I wanted, gave me another on the spot, yelled at my grandfather, and told him if he wanted to beat somebody he should take after that bewarted wretch Dorie. This is a firm memory, guaranteed by the assurance with which I see it and feel it. I can bring back detail after detail, precise and rich and sensuously full. I do not need confirmation by way of facts or others' testimony. Neither would you.

Which is lucky, since my mother and my brother and my cousin Dorie, who seems to have had the warts removed surgically or maybe she chewed them off—all these people say that not one part of that story is true or could be true. They say grandma never ever baked cakes, only pies, that it was actually an uncle who told stories of stealing a pie (not cake) when he was a boy, that we had not visited grandma's when I was six, and that we had never been there at the same time as Dorie. And Dorie never had warts. In other words, insofar as this happened at all, it happened to another, but most of it did not happen at all. Actually, very famous people have spoken of this same sort of false-memory experience, Piaget for one, usually in order to show that our assurance that something happened bears no relation to whether it did happen.

This is not my point at all. My point, which is a better one, is that memory is a sustaining story-telling agency that manages to pick up from various points of the brain, and our own past, and the stories available in our culture at the moment what we need in the way of a plot. It really is dipping into the ocean to work back to that glass of milk, which is no longer, if it ever was, a glass of milk but something far more complex and good to drink and alive with connections everywhere. Asking whether memories are accurate is tragically misguided since it is both the most trivial question we can ask and the one we can certainly never, ever answer.

Now, according to *Jane Eyre* and recovered memory people, memory works to retrieve eventually in pristine forms something like video tapes of original scenes. What it would mean to have an accurate view of an experience even as you were going through it escapes me—I do not have the slightest idea what is happening right now as I fiddle with this paper and look out the window and eat Doritos; so what would it mean to have accurate recall of it? But waive that. This *Jane Eyre* view of memory is clear: the adult memory and the child memory are continuous, and we can, maybe through hypnosis, re-establish a full linkage between these memories, especially the most painful ones, which are entirely responsible for making us what we are today. This is presumably the foundational view of memory Freud considered early on when he attributed virtually all psychic disorders to childhood seduction, to incest. Such a view generates a fantasy plot, as I have said, that is very popular, since it tells us that there is a single secret we can uncover, that this secret is dark indeed but imposed by somebody else, and that this secret, if massaged in the right way, can make us whole and well. This secret can, according to this model, reveal our essence, the inner child, and heal it, in the process killing off the multiple personalities we no longer need, and releasing the wonder child that is *US*. Let us call this the melodramatic view of memory.

But another view—we can call it the ironic view of memory, the view of scientists, false-memory people, and the later Freud—suggests that the secrets may be there but that they take different forms at different times and are never blunt and clear and single. The secrets are surrounding us, behind us, just around the corner; and they are, when we get past the shallows, right there inside us, involving us, working their way through us, and not merely external and demonic. Further, we know that the child's memory—eidetic and more or less photographic, unable to forget—yields around the time of puberty to a *different organism*, an adult memory that learns to forget, to channel and to direct things to gradually acquired scripts or master-plots by which we understand the world and speak of it, understand and formulate our own plots. That is, the adult and child memories are radically discontinuous, really different things; and when we hearken back to childhood memory, we are hearkening back to something which is no longer there. There is another vital point here, which even memory people do not always acknowledge—that memory is mainly formed by culture and history in the large sense, these agencies giving us the basic stories we blend into our own trifling personal narratives. In addition, and much more important (don't skip over this, now) our culture molds the forms these stories take, the genres, modes, and narrative conventions that give our memories shape and meaning. We see and tell as we are able, which means "as our culture directs us." Our culture right now yells at us a gothic and monstrous story of memory, which is why people are remembering that way. It's the frailer holdout model of memory I'm trying to stress here, the scientific, Freudian, mysterious, unknowable, ironic, opaque, plotless memory—and the sad muted plots of failure and acceptance that come from them.

JANE EYRE

Jane makes it clear enough what she is doing—"say whatever your memory says is true!"[4]—she has Miss Temple tell her in a pivotal scene of self-justification, and from that point Jane is off and running, using memory as she likes to create the story that has meant so much to so many. She says she is "only bound to invoke memory" where she knows it will be interesting, which means when it will cohere with her masterplot, which here has a fine and nearly unwavering simplicity. At one point, Rochester says to her that to have such an absolutely pure limpid memory, "without blot or contamination, must be an exquisite treasure," and maybe we hear some irony there. But probably not, since Jane's compelling presentation of her childhood admits of no irony, depends entirely on the naive and therefore powerful plot of fairy tales, the story of the child surrounded by monsters. It is remarkable that she never modifies that plot; it is even more remarkable that she uses it as the basis for her assertion of adult being. We begin in the world of the child—and we stay there. It's a world where the self is so secure that it has no need at all for self-awareness.

This is the textbook story of child abuse and recovered memory, of the effects of trauma, the splitting of personality into multiples, and the recovery: a triumphant fable of identity in the received mainstream modes and thus so in conformity with our usual movie-of-the-week stories as to be perhaps insipid. Maybe it will be necessary to wait for a new epoch, a cultural paradigm shift, before we can once again read *Jane Eyre* with pleasure, though of course it is not exactly the novel's fault it has become hackneyed. Jane tells us that the self is there from the beginning, integral and solid, like the soul, a computer hard-drive, or the energized plastic in the middle of a golf ball. Adrienne Rich speaks of Jane being "unalterably herself," Gilbert and Gubar of "her awakening to what she is."[5] And they are right: in the novel, it's just a question of finding the right plot to affirm what she's been all along, if only people had seen it.

The key is the Red Room, of course, the basic gothic scene and memory to be recovered and replayed into the myth of origins. Surrounded by monsters and injustice everywhere, Jane is absolutely pure and simple, entirely aloof from responsibility and from contamination. She is implicated in nothing, and even when she feels guilty it's simply because somebody else unjustly loaded that guilt on her. She asks us to regard her and her childhood in exactly the way she regards it: with indignation, measureless pity, and deep, deep admiration. Of course it is not Jane we respond to in this way these days but ourselves, reading through these recovered memory stories back to that little victim, so beaten upon and so courageous—me. Jane's fairy-tale origins are, as I say, with monsters, even more ghoulish than the ones David Copperfield evoked—specifically ghoulish. John Reed, for instance, is all soft flesh and drool and mouth, a kind of dribbling, slobbering maw, like the beast in "Alien." Jane says, "every morsel on my bones shrunk when he came near," because of course he is always about to start chewing on those morsels—gumming them like a carp.

Before I got sidetracked on mouths, I think I was writing about the Red Room as the primal scene in the recovered memory plot. Jane says that even after all these many years, "I can see it clearly." There it is! See it and use it to verify what she has been and is. Let us read that scene. She is put into a Masque-of-the-Red-Death room where all the secrets are, the room where all the plots will be let out. Inside this room, for instance, is the cabinet where Mrs. Reed keeps all the secret things, the keys to the buried plot, much like Long John Silver's map. Jane looks in a glass and reads her reflection as little, little, little and white—terrified—pitiable—shut in with a ghost—her reason howling even then, "Unjust, Unjust!" "Why was I always suffering, always browbeaten, always accused, always condemned?" She is pure victim and nothing but victim; "victim" consumes her. And how delicious this is, how pure the paranoia and the absolute self-justification. This is the self-indulgent glory that can come only when we feed our childlike egos until they swell as large as the moon.

From this point, she can invent scenes where she is in control and endowed with immense power. Having defined herself as the victim of injustice, she claims the right to dispense justice and gets away with it too. She makes even Mrs. Reed quake in her boots with her denunciations. Only in this sort of memory fantasy are things so delightful; only in fantasy do we get not only the last words but all the words; only in fantasy are we entangled in nothing but virtue, isolated like the martyr-hero, vindicated and applauded. Jane even takes curtain calls.

But there are other ways we might read even this scene. These alternate readings probably do not attract us much, but let's do them anyhow. Start with the denunciation-of-Mrs.-Reed scene, which Jane says leaves her "winner of the field." Winner of what exactly? What is the "field"? What is she fighting Mrs. Reed for? Control of the secret, right? But what secret? The secret battle is for control of Mr. Reed, the dead uncle/father/husband that this little Electra is wrestling the mother for. According to this reading, Jane *invades* the Red Room because her desires compel her to be there. There she enjoys the love of the father/uncle but cannot tolerate that victory or acknowledge her own power; so she defends against it by denying her triumph, saying the Devil made her do it, that it was really done *to* her. This shadowy parallel to, say, Hamlet, where the family romance is also displaced onto an uncle (you recall), produces intense guilt in Jane precisely because she does win: she wins the love of her uncle, the secret, that she has known all along—and has enacted in the red bedroom, ritualized, she says, "on the tabernacle of the massive bed," after a symbolic S/M scene where she is tied down with garters.[6]

You may not want me to go on with this, and I offer it really as an indication of how we do not read this scene. No, we do not. It is not a scene of ironic complicity for us, not a scene where one set of possibilities calls up contraries and spins off into new modes and new narratives. The very few complications we might notice, we do not. Bessie, for instance, tells Jane that if the kid goes about dreading people they are not going to like her, but that ties Jane into the general commonplace world in a way averse to Jane's gothic, to recovered memory victim plots, and to our own needs as readers. So we ignore such things.

From this point, I get bored with my own narrative, so I'll rush it. Remember, I'm tracing the standard construction of this novel as a heal-the-victim, recovered-memory story. Jane starts proliferating personalities, creating alters and multiples to express her fracture from this external Red Room trauma. These multiples, we can, if we like, think of as external and independent characters; but try not to do that: they are, in our plot, simply psychic functions, aspects of Jane's sickness and her temporary survival strategy. We have mentioned the monster-multiples, and they keep appearing, each without any real motive except to act the way monsters always act: to externalize and deny internal threats. Even Mrs. Reed is not motivated—"it was in her nature to wound me"—and Mr. Brocklehurst is simply the big, bag wolf—"what a face he had . . . what a great nose! and what a mouth! and what large prominent teeth!" These ogre or cannibal scenes have the intensity and hyperbole of nightmare, the arctic winds at Lowood, Jane says, threatening to flaw her skin right off, which is more than Jack London claimed for the Yukon. Time stands still in this scrumptious gothic world: Brocklehurst, after denouncing her, freezes everyone in dead silence for *ten minutes* to let his words sink in, surely the longest dramatic pause in history. But it is as fitting to this sublime memory, as is Brocklehurst's injunction that everyone look at her: "You must watch her, keep your eyes on her, weigh well her words." What a dream! Look, ma—no hands! Watch me, watch me! This is a megalomaniac book, and it is a dangerous, megalomaniac fantasy we are nursing in our culture with these recovered-memory plots.

Notice that Brocklehurst switches positions, becomes benign, when he is no longer needed as a monster. There is even a hint that Jane gets a testimonial from him later. As the success story starts to take over, the same characters and scenes are simply reupholstered. Lowood, a terrifying torture house, becomes the scene of her academic triumphs: "I became first girl of the first class," the once-rebellious Jane crows, now the complacent institutional product, a student-of-the-month. It's Heathcliff growing up to be Pat Buchanan, Allen Ginsberg as a realtor, Jane Fonda doing the tomahawk chop (which shows how nightmares come true).

Here are some other MPs/alters/splits, all of them used to move from one stage to another of this melodrama and then be cast off or killed as the dominant personality absorbs them or does not need them any longer. Helen Burns is a double figure who is pure guilt, sees only her *own* fault and no external injustice, who is otherworldly and virtuous. She exaggerates, safely contains, and thus drains away these dangerous possibilities. Jane can load all shame, responsibility, and inconvenient virtue onto this handy multiple, who hauls them away and entombs them for her. Then there are Mr. Lloyd and Miss Temple, fairy godparents who give Jane little testimonials from time to time and thus support and exonerate her memory: Jane says she imbibes a bit of Miss Temple, and then can kill her off.

But let us get to the interesting multiples, aspects of Jane that she is desperate to disown. Take Adele, who comes on the scene flouncing like Shirley Temple, singing of love and seduction "in very bad taste," Jane sniffs. Adele is a daughter of France, a Lolita, a slut, dressed up like a wee whore to make a point.[7] The child loves to loll about on mattresses and piled-up pillows before enormous fires, like Brooke Shields in *Pretty Baby*. She is introduced so that she can be repudiated, both Jane and Rochester sneering at her regularly and making a point of saying how repulsive they find her: Rochester says he would rather be kissed by a dog. Adele is the bad playmate personality, the one who does everything wrong. She is, specifically, the sexualized child, the one who has seduced Uncle Reed, the one complicit in the eroticism. Adele can have all that loaded on her, so that Jane can imagine herself pure, at the same time that she is playing out the eroticism through this double. When she no longer needs Adele, she simply re-makes her, deFrenchifies and desexualizes her by means of a sound English education. Before that, she has split Jane's childhood, draining off and fiercely denying all the desire and sexuality being vigorously expressed and exercised.

Rochester is not simply or even mainly the fairy prince but another bad-child multiple; this one is the naughty doll we beat, punish, and subdue, only to forgive and then merge with or at least master. Rochester plays out the bad memories, the bad past, and thus keeps Jane's pristine. After the aborted wedding, the old Rochester is killed off and a new one formed: "Now Mr. Rochester was not to me what he had been"—in fact is another character by the same name—a helpless wretch testifying to Jane's sanctity and, of course, absolute power and self-sufficiency. By this point, Jane is nothing if not self-made.

The Rivers alter is a later form of Helen Burns, representing threatening self-abnegation. Jane must combine in her self-image purity with self-glorification and self-indulgence, and Rivers gives her a chance to clear the way for this. Put another way, Jane's fable is one of complete and static childish self-gratification. Rivers embodies and drains away the notion of dynamic *change* or fluidity and allows Jane to fantasize a set world of luxuriant power fantasy. Rivers not only beckons to a new world and challenges, but to the future: he tells Jane to resist, firmly, any temptation ''to look back.'' In terms of Jane's fantasy that is the voice of Satan! Thus, this aspiring, moral, complex man, Rivers, is another useful multiple to contain issues and attitudes and, most of all, narratives, that need to be smothered.

The Bertha multiple has been discussed by all sorts of smart people with whom I do not want to compete, so I leave her to you, mentioning only that her laugh comes at first from Jane's pillow, as if from inside it. Bertha, you see, is a vampiric multiple, stealing like the Count on beds in the night. Vampires represent a very dangerous (for Jane) and ambiguous coalescence of attack and invitation, death and life. They suggest not only complexity but complicity, neither of which Jane will have any truck with; so she lives through Bertha's violence and rebelliousness for a bit and then slaughters her too when the fun is over.

So, at end, Jane settles in, justified and smug, having the best of all worlds there with her little maimed hubby in a kind of twittering soap opera reminiscent of ''Melrose Place,'' where she cultivates his jealousy in the approved sit-com manner and keeps him in line with her little womanly wiles, perhaps hiding his white cane when he gets feisty. This is what the recovered memory narrative comes to, the hot-fudge-sundae plot of victim restored to simple, plump, unthreatened selfhood.

GREAT EXPECTATIONS

You can read this section before I write it; your memory is now working in a déjà-vu mode, even if you have not absorbed lots of scholarly essays and learned how predictable they are. Let me try to evoke rather than argue the sense I have of Pip's memory and of our memory, the tragic memory of Freud and Sophocles. This memory empowers the stories that offer no way out at all, only a way in and back—not into the light of self-appropriation and self-laudation but into the very dim regions of Weir, misty mid-regions as Poe said, the unmappable interconnecting caves of fault and injustice, guilt and forgiveness, and blessed inconsequence. ''It just doesn't matter!'' Bill Murray says in a scene in *Meatballs*, psyching up a group of campers the night before a big athletic event. That's what Cordelia says and Joe Gargery. ''We don't know what you done, but we wouldn't have you starved to death for it, poor miserable, fellow-creature." We don't know what you done—we don't know—and here's food. That's one kind of noncausality working in this book. We don't know—here!

Another, of course, acknowledges that the innocent suffer. Terrible injustice is epidemic and not just everywhere generally either, but right here, coming through the roof and down so hard on those who have no chance against it. It attacks Mrs. Joe and Miss Havisham, who think for a while they are Jane Eyre and can live in a victim plot. The same is true even for Magwitch, who in his tortured way imagines for a time that he too is Jane: his own childhood amounts to an awareness that "someone had taken the fire away." Who, why, what to do about it? Those are Jane's questions and she builds a plot and self by insisting that they are the real and true questions. But Magwitch finally sees them melt away; they cannot give him a plot he can use for much.

Here is Pip: "I had known *from the time when I could speak*, that my sister, in her capricious and violent coercion, was unjust to me" (my emphasis). Unjust! Unjust!: those are the very words that echo in Jane's head and define her, the words she uses to recover her childhood memories and the motive for her courageous anger, his insistence on her victimization, her belief in a world and a plot that makes sense based on the working out of justice. But Pip never has to recover anything; he knows it all along, *from the time he can speak*; and he knows also the irrelevance of justice. In one way, this irrelevance is harrowing, since it suggests an absurd, empty universe: Pip, as a child, also knows from the time when he can speak that there is no help anywhere, no use in pleading injustice into the vast silence; just a few pages before his statement on Mrs. Joe's mistreatment he considers cosmic justice from the standpoint of a convict, a hunted thing alone and without any story: "And then I looked at the stars, and considered how awful it would be for a man to turn his face up to them as he froze to death, and see no help or pity in all the glittering multitude."

Of course, this does not keep him from entertaining from time to time the sense that he is ill-used, as he says, "by somebody or by everybody, I can't say which." It is as if the sense he has of being victimized is loose somewhere, flying around in the room and refusing to alight. He wants to find Jane's plot, but knows always how useless it is for him. All he can manage is a kind of parody of Jane's self-righteousness by blaming, of all people, Biddy. Pip, even as a snob, can never wash himself or his memory so clean as to be comfortable in gothic plots of self-justification. His plot is never linear and never clear: even the famous opening scene does not give us Pip's origins but the irrelevance of origins. Pip's plot does not begin, nor does it move from point to point, certainly not toward healing an original trauma. Instead, it slides toward absorbing that trauma and all traumas, not as violations from outside but as points of contact, small warm breaches even if they are violent, in the cold indifference of a cosmos that itself never offers any pity or help.

Pip's parody of the linear recovery plot means that his memory works exactly counter to Jane's, giving him, time and again, not luscious scenes of ego gratification and justification, but complexity, squirm-inducing embarrassment, acts of meanness and spite. His parody plot even includes some mock multiples, often taken seriously as psychic dream terrors but actually more like alternate images he must embrace. Jane kills off her multiples, while Pip takes them all home—often reluctantly and often with terrible embarrassment—but home they come into his heart. Compeyson and Orlick and Bentley Drummle *may*[8] be seen as aggressive multiples, carrying out a fantasy plot of vengeance for Pip, but notice how shadowy and internalized and unimportant they are, appearing magically behind and beside Pip as if from within him—as he more or less acknowledges with a shrug. None of these can make a plot—or an excuse.

There are also multiples who seem to be trying out or testing for Pip various extraordinary strategies for living in an unknowable or empty world: Jaggers's attempt to be pure aggression, to take hold of all secrets, all plots and to lash out at everyone, playing the part of attorney for the defense, prosecution, and judge all at once; Wemmick, too, with his famous and desperate schizophrenia. But most remarkable are all the witty self-mocking multiples: the toadies around Miss Havisham—Pumblechook, and Trabb's boy. There is certainly a Pumblechook somewhere behind Jane Eyre, though it would be unthinkable for her to conjure up a self-mimicking Trabb's girl. But Pip never musters much anger or even ridicule for these figures. *We* may laugh at them, but Pip sees in them too much pain, his pain, the pain he has caused, and everyone's unearned pain. He sees this pain even in the aspiring Wopsle, a St. John Rivers figure in a new key. Instead of displacing his *own* absurd ambition and vaingloriousness onto Wopsel and then draining them off and disavowing them, as Jane would, Pip sees in Wopsle the asinine and brightly human attempt to make our own plot, a soaring foolish plot that aims to lift even the whole of English drama with it. Pip's response: "I was so sorry for him." So sorry for the fool and so forgiving to the villain: "Oh Miss Havisham, I want forgiveness far too much myself to be bitter with you." "Remember reader, he were that good in his heart."

As he looks back in memory at his worst self, the prig ashamed of his home and turning his back on the man who loves him, Pip cannot come up with a formula, a plot that would explain things—at least not in terms of "fault":

> How much of my ungracious condition of mind may have been my own fault, how much Miss Havisham's, how much my sister's, is now of no moment to

me or to any one. The change was made in me; the thing was done. Well or ill done, excusably or inexcusably, it was done"   (14, pp. 134–35)

Now of no moment to me—or to any one. It is a clue planted kindly for us: don't look here for the plot; don't think in terms of blame or fault or causality. In case we miss that nudge, Pip later brings up pointedly the *possibility* of forming his life as a victim plot, brings it up and rejects it, this time with a new ripeness, what he calls a "softening." He is returning for his sister's funeral:

> It was fine summer weather again, and, as I walked along, the times when I was a little helpless creature, and my sister did not spare me, vividly returned. But they returned with a gentler tone upon them that softened even the edge of Tickler. For now, the very breath of the beans and clover whispered to my heart that the day must come when it would be well for my memory that others walking in the sunshine should be softened as they thought of me.

The passage starts with what looks like a vivid recovered memory that can define him, but immediately steers away from the past, from self-definition, from clarity; it moves from the particular child, isolated by the injustice plot, to a sweet confederation of being and beans and other people's memory in the future. The very breath of the beans and clover mixes with his memory, the memory drawn from that glass of milk spilled into the sea. The breath of the beans and clover and Pip's own being become part of the memories of others walking in the sunshine, trying not to be drawn into the hard plots of blame and hate and self-absorption. He only hopes that, in that beautiful word, he can help *soften* them as we in our reading might also be softened in the way we read memory and create plots from it.

For all memory reaches back and evokes the most helpless of us, those looking with least protection into the bitter and abandoned night, the children. Our current recovered memory plots may be healing adults or children within but they are murdering our actual children. We have developed so much pity for ourselves and are so bent on vindicating adults that we treat the children about us as excrescences—no better than Adele. Like Rochester, we'd rather hug a dog, and we'd much rather hug our own inner child.

Remember reader, he were that good in his heart. Pip comes not to forgive villains but to find the very idea vanish into the mist. His world is both so bleak and so blessed it can hold neither fault nor plots. It just does not matter. My cousin Dorie and my punishing grandfather, who never hit anybody. Someone had taken the fire away. We don't know what you done, but here's food. No help or pity in all that glittering multitude. Ill-used by somebody or by everybody, I cannot say which. I was so sorry for him. Dorie didn't have warts; she was lovely. How much may have been my fault, how much Miss Havisham's, how much my sister's, is now of no moment to me—or to any one. My sister was unjust to me. My dear grandmother would have given me all the cakes in the world. The very breath of the beans and clover whispered to my heart that the day must come when it would be well for my memory that others walking in the sunshine should be softened as they thought of me.

This is a memory we can construct, a memory in the future—not even our memory but the memories others will form in new worlds, kinder to the dear children and to all miserable fellow creatures, that good in their heart, in a time when perhaps we will be more willing to form our plots and mold our memories by heeding the soft, blameless songs of clover and beans.

NOTES

1. Ellen Bass and Laura Davis, authors of the massive best-seller, *The Courage to Heal: A Guide for Woman Survivors of Child Sexual Abuse* (New York: Harper and Row, 1988), with future editions, workbooks, and workshops galore.
2. *Time*, 17 July 1995, p. 47.
3. Elizabeth Loftus and Katherine Ketchum, *The Myth of Recovered Memory: False Memory and Allegations of Sexual Abuse* (New York: St. Martin's, 1994), p. 3.
4. Since there are so many editions of *Jane Eyre*, since I have so many quotes (mostly small), since all readers of this journal are scholars and will not only recognize all these quotes (from a canonical novel, after all) but will know themselves the extent of their accuracy (moderate), since lots of chapter and page references mess up the appearance of the page and are annoying, since I am not a pedant, and since I can't find any place where I wrote down the location of these quotes, I will rely on the reader's good sense and good will to provide the references. In other words, I won't tell you. The editors of this journal don't like this at all and regard the reasons given above as "twiddle." They are good editors, but they are editors, we remind ourselves, and are forced to act and think like editors. Some of them may be interesting people in their private lives, but here they are only editors. I once knew an IRS agent who played the oboe. I do wonder, between you and me, where these quotes came from exactly. I have every reason to suppose they came from the novel and that I used some system in copying them down, but maybe I just paged through the novel and copied out whatever I happened to hit on straight into my text. To tell the truth, I can't recall, which just goes to prove a lot of what I am saying in this essay about memory, or at least I think it does.
5. You'll find these in the Norton edition of the novel, ed. (and very well) by Richard J. Dunn. Of course I copied these quotes from the original, not the Norton, reprints. That is scholarly practice. But, then, you could not be expected to know or care about such things, which is why I suggest that the Norton is quite good enough for your purposes.
6. She's only *threatened* with being tied down by garters, close readers of the novel will be saying; but that's why we all so dislike close readers. They never really

get it. In this case, they may be right—I haven't checked—but if they are "right" (those quotation marks are significant), why then it just goes to show you, doesn't it?

7. Jane seems to hold the child accountable for her apparently sluttish clothes, as if Adele did her own shopping. Somebody is tarting her up this way, and for some purpose.

8. The italics here are meant to indicate heavy sarcasm, a device we all tell our students to avoid. But here they are not only justified but expressive as no other way of saying "May, if you cannot keep yourself from slogging once more down that dreary path" could be.

Domesticating History: Revolution and Moral Management in *A Tale of Two Cities*

John B. Lamb

In *A Tale of Two Cities*, as Charles Darnay awaits the judgment of the Revolutionary Tribunal, Dickens' narrator speculates on what has drawn Darnay and men like him to the "wild infection" that is, for Dickens like Carlyle before him,[1] the madness of the French Revolution: "In seasons of pestilence, some of us will have a secret attraction to the disease—a terrible passing inclination to die of it. And all of us have like wonders hidden in our breasts, only needing circumstances to evoke them" (310). Dickens' novel is a story of "profound secret[s] and myster[ies]," of "buried" desires enclosed in the "Darkly clustered houses" (44) and hearts of his characters. After more than six years of marriage to Lucie Manette, Darnay, once the aristocrat and now the prosperous bourgeois, grows "restless" (267) and leaves the bliss of his English home and the respectability of his wife to court the fierce, passionate, and raging female, La Revolution, who is embodied in Thérèse Defarge and her bloodthirsty sisterhood, the women of St. Antoine. For while the looks of the men of the Revolution are "dark, repressed, and revengeful," it is on the features of the women that the frightful insanity and signs of social violation that are the French Revolution are most clearly written:

> The men were terrible . . . but, the women were a sight to chill the boldest. From such household occupations as their bare poverty yielded, from their children, from their aged and their sick crouching on the bare ground famished and naked, they ran out with streaming hair, urging one another, and themselves, to madness with the wildest cries and actions. (252.

This is the "disease" that Darnay has "an inclination to die of," a transgressive and passionate energy that is both sexual and political. In *A Tale of*

227

Two Cities, female revolutionaries, like Madame Defarge, represent a nexus of Victorian anxieties relating to gender and class, particularly those related to sexual and political revolt. As Linda M. Shires suggests, in the 1830s and 1840s, "that which threatens the hegemonic status quo becomes linked to the female who sexually stimulates others into a fascination with horror or sublime exaltation" (148). The danger and power that those revolutionary women possess is not only that they will violate the rules and regulations of bourgeois society, particularly those inherent in Victorian domestic ideology, but that they also will spread the madness of their revolt to others, unleashing a carnal and civil carmagnole whose chaotic potential is both threatening and boundless.

Throughout the Victorian period there were long-standing anxieties about female sexuality and working-class political revolt, both of which were seen as a threat to middle-class life and property. Revolutionary desire posed as big a threat as sexual desire, and the French Revolution served as a convenient metaphor for social ruin as well as political upheaval. As Jeffrey Weeks points out, "sexual collapse seemed the necessary path of social revolution; sexual and family decorum a vital part of social stability" (27). To an anxious middle-class population continually threatened by political instability and economic uncertainty, the ideals and ideology of bourgeois domesticity were seen as central to moral discipline; domesticity was the only safe-haven from the horrors of a revolutionary world.[2] In fact, the middle-class institutions of family and home were thought to have immunized England against the very disease of Revolution like the one that had infected France in 1789, and during the Victorian period, the discourse of revolution "makes as its object, not the Bastille or the factory, but the home" (Shires 156). The revolutionary women immortalized in Carlyle's history and translated nearly wholesale into *A Tale of Two Cities*, symbolize those socially transgressive energies Victorian culture labeled as pathological. Insanity is one of the most powerful models of pathology,[3] and during the nineteenth century, it is coupled with sexual activity as signs of deviant behavior. Such were the signs Dickens' friend John Conolly, the physician to the Middlesex Lunatic Asylum at Hanwell, read in the histories of his working-class female patients:

> some of these were women of middle age, who had been handsome, and who possessed considerable acuteness of intellect, ingenuity and activity, but whose lives had been a sort of troubled romance. Profligate, intemperate, violent, regardless of domestic ties, their children abandoned to all the evils of homeless poverty, themselves by degrees given up to utter recklessness—they had been the cause of ruin and shame to their families and the history of their wild life had closed in madness.   (*Treatment* 127)

As Lynda Nead suggests, revolution itself was equated with "*deviant* femininity" (6) (Dickens' France is a place without mothers or with mothers who abandon their children), and it was defined in relation to the standards and practices of domestic life. Like the sexualized female, the revolutionary was seen as a source of disease and corruption as well as political dissent, and like her working-class counterparts at Hanwell, she was "both eroticized and condemned" as an immoral pollutant (Mort 47).

Against such moral contaminants and the pathology that is revolution, Victorian culture pitted the forces of various practices of "moral treatment," complex systems of intervention and social control aimed at restoring the self-discipline and individual responsibility perceived to be at the heart of bourgeois ideology and conspicuously absent in the pathological individual. Under the rubric of morals and moral management were "subsumed a terrifying catalogue of barbarous habits," particularly the "collapse of family life" and "political sedition" (Mort 47). In *A Tale of Two Cities*, revolution is perceived as a social phenomena whose moral etiology (revolution = madness = sexual and political transgression) is marked by an ensemble of signs—restlessness, rage, passion, vehemence, etc.—which allow the reader to designate such behavior as pathological. Revolutionary energy and activity in Dickens' novel stands out as that which is lacking relative to the standards of domesticity, and the characteristics that define revolution and the revolutionary female are purely negative. In *A Tale of Two Cities*, as well as in bourgeois culture at large, the revolutionary is not just retarded in her socialization; she is also in a profound state of anomic crisis. She has not yet interiorized, or has rejected, the values by which patriarchal society thrives and maintains its own self-control. Like the middle-class Victorian home or the Victorian asylum, *A Tale of Two Cities* performs its own therapy of interiorization as Dickens seeks to define and manage transgressive political and sexual energy and to erase history by inscribing onto both the novel's content and its form the Victorian psychiatric practice known as "moral management."

II

During the first half of the nineteenth century, there was a long struggle to reform the treatment of the mentally ill, and Victorian medical psychology sought to reclaim the insane as moral subjects, subjects lacking control and self-restraint, who for various and often unknown reasons had failed to internalize the moral standards of the middle class. The most significant development in nineteenth-century psychiatric reform was the domestication of insanity; the violent therapeutic practices still used to "tame" the wildly asocial in the early part of the century were replaced by the "invisible" discipline of a facsimile of the bourgeois family life. The cornerstones of this new discipline, as Elaine Showalter points out, were moral insanity, moral management, and moral architecture: [4]

"Moral insanity" redefined madness, not as a loss of reason, but as deviance from socially acceptable behavior. "Moral management" substituted close supervision and paternal concern for physical restraint and harsh treatment, in an attempt to re-educate the insane in habits of industry, self-control, moderation, and perseverance. "Moral architecture" constructed asylums planned as therapeutic environments in which lunatics could be controlled without the use of force.   (29)

Writing in 1833, James Cowles Pritchard, the ethnologist and senior physician to the Bristol Infirmary, noted in *A Treatise on Insanity* that in cases of moral insanity the "moral and active principles of the mind are strangely perverted and depraved," and that the "power of self-government is lost or impaired" (15). Hence, he defined moral insanity as "madness consisting in a morbid perversion of the natural feelings, affections, inclinations, temper, habits, moral dispositions, and natural impulses" (16). Furthermore, Pritchard maintained that moral insanity, or "moral perversion" as he also referred to it, was marked by an "unusual prevalence of angry and malicious feelings" (26).

In a similar manner, John Conolly, who along with Samuel Tuke and John Gardiner Hill was one of the most notable British psychiatric reformers, argued that in mental disorders the "social feeling is lost and sympathy with others seems extinct." Insanity tears "away the conventionalities of life." Yet, while many of the insane were, according to Conolly, depraved and given over to evil tendencies, for some, virtues and kind feelings existed, "buried and obscured, but not lost" (*On Some of the Forms of Insanity* 7).

The concept of moral insanity, therefore, was socially constructed. It was a generalization that denoted the absence of those "conventionalities" and "feelings" that were the staples of middle-class Victorian life. "Insanity" designated any behavior that deviated from the norms of bourgeois domesticity. As a working term in the rhetoric of social distinction, it was, in most cases, an exaggeration of the attributes the middle class ascribed to the laboring population. As Michael Donelly suggests, moral insanity and the signs of madness it called into play emerged during the Victorian period "ideologically charged" (133), and madness was defined by moral standards inherent in the relations between both the classes and the sexes.

Moral management was *the* central component in a Victorian psychiatric strategy that attempted to neutralize and manipulate mental illness through a complex system of social control, and it offered the promise of a "cure" by non-medical means. Corresponding to the moral explanation of insanity, moral therapy involved, as Elizabeth Fee notes, the "Close supervision of patients, the control of behavior and especially sexual behavior, and the inculcation of work discipline." Deficient in self-control and self-discipline, the insane had to undergo "a personal re-evolution, to be re-brought up." Psychic equilibrium could only be achieved through a return to childhood, and since "the experience of childhood was the locus of formation of moral (and sexual) identity, the adult in search of cure must recover, re-create, and relive childhood" (640).

At the heart of moral management was the notion that without moral discipline the passions "acquire greater power, and a character is formed subject to caprice and to violent emotions" (Pritchard 131). Moral management sought to instill and reassert powers of self-control, and like other forms of social repression, it was authorized by the very threat of social anarchy it was said to identify and cure. But moral treatment was not based on an organic or psychic etiology. It was based instead on a moral symptomatology drawn from a middle-class perspective on mental health that found is fullest expression in the domestic order. As Robert Castel convincingly argues, in moral management there existed "less a medical theory of illness than a *social perception of health*, against which the pathological stands out as that which is *lacking* in relation to (the) normality characterized by orderliness of conduct, equilibrium between affectivity and intelligence, the capacity to adopt social roles without fail." Since it lacked the requirements of scientific rationality, moral management was "*permeable to non-medical norms*, and ready to reinterpret within the framework of an extramedical synthesis representations which have no theoretical relation to medically founded knowledge" ("Moral Treatment" 253, 251). These representations are, as Castel rightly notes, simply the values of the dominant class, particularly order, discipline, the sanctity of the family, work, and respect for authority.

Moral architecture, the construction and maintenance of a morally disciplined environment, was, therefore, a direct outgrowth of the politico-moral ideology of moral management. The new asylum was necessitated by the need to re-instate in the pathological individual exactly the same norms that reigned in bourgeois society, particularly work, the strict organization of time, and due respect for and submission to patriarchal authority. Hence, institutions like the York Retreat and Hanwell were conceived and at least partly constructed on the model of a middle-class home complete with surrogate family, and the "domesticated" asylum provided the controlled atmosphere for a "regression to infantile existence combined with a new moral upbringing" (Fee 640). By reconstructing the social discipline and structure of the family, these asylums aimed at reproducing a fictional domesticity that would encourage the interiorization of domestic values and revive, as Michel Foucault points out, the "prestige of patriarchy" (*Civilization and Madness* 253). There madness was controlled through the arrangement of space and through daily activities and routines. The insane lived within a comfortable but highly controlled domestic regime, and female patients were encouraged to participate in the patterns of middle-class domestic life by engaging in the "customary" female pursuits of sewing, knitting, crochet, and fancy work. The external organization and internal domestic economy of the asylum was thought to provide a special environment which embodied the very values and the order whose interiorization was the condition for cure. In the morally managed asylum, Conolly asserted, "Those even who came in a state of dangerous violence seemed so acted upon by the character of the house" that they became "composed," "orderly in habits," "active" and "useful" (*Treatment* 121).

III

Madame Defarge is the epitome of the "frightful moral disorder" (376) and the monstrous abuse of "all laws, forms, and ceremonies" (344) signified in revolutionary passion. With her rich, "dark hair" and her "supple freedom" (391) of movement, she has, Dickens' narrator claims, "a kind of beauty" (390); and like the nineteenth-century working-class women on which she is partly modeled, she is both eroticized and condemned. But Thérèse Defarge clearly suffers from moral insanity; her affections, habits, and moral attitudes have been perverted, and she is full of anger and malice. Her "moral perversion" has transformed her into a "furious" woman "absolutely without pity" (391), and her shadow falls "threatening and dark" (297) on both Lucie and her child. Furthermore, Madame Defarge's "register," "Knitted, in her own stitches and her own symbols" (202), is a ghastly semiotic impenetrable to the eyes of the State, which symbolizes male anxieties about the unknowable and uncontrollable nature of female sexuality. In pursuing the "family annihilation" (381) of the Darnays, Thérèse Defarge threatens not the aristocracy, but the bourgeois domicile, and it is no surprise that her madness is finally incarcerated and, indeed, erased in Lucie's Paris home.

But it is Sidney Carton's interiorization of the norms of bourgeois domesticity—especially self-discipline, self-denial, and self-sacrifice—invisibly imposed upon him in the "anchorage" of Lucie Manette's home, that most clearly indicates the success of moral management. For while Lucie saves both her father and husband "from the edge of the grave" (160), restoring her father to sanity and rescuing Darnay from the "terrible attraction" of the French Revolution, it is her "weaving the service of her happy influence" (240) through the wasted tissue of Carton's life, that crowns her success and the success of domestic discipline. For Carton, who begins the novel as the "idlest and most unpromising of men" (117), ends it as a man "who had wandered and struggled and got lost, but who had at length struck into his road and saw its end" (342).

Lucie is the novel's chief resurrectionist, and her recalling of Carton to middle-class respectability parallels the recalling to life of her father and husband. For Sidney Carton is more than just Charles Darnay's physical double. He is, Dickens' novel suggests, a man previously drawn to the "Loadstone Rock" of some secret sexual passion, some "fall" in which, like the Revolution, the qualities within Carton "good by nature" had become "warped and perverted" (307). Like Darnay, Carton has "lost" himself in a Paris of revolutionary fever, a Paris in which he is an "old student" (341). For Dickens' depiction of revolution, like Carlyle's includes comparing it and the revolutionary mob to the elemental forces of a rising, "remorseless," and uncontrollable sea: "The beach was a desert of heaps of sea and stones tumbling wildly about, and the sea did what it liked, and what it liked was destruction. It thundered at the town, and thundered at the cliffs, and brought the coast down, madly" (51). With "deep wounds" (238) in his heart, Carton is already a victim of revolution's transgressive energies; there are "waste forces within him, and a desert all around" (121). Carton epitomizes the individual infected with moral insanity, the "man of good abilities and good emotions, incapable of their directed exercise, incapable of his own help and his own happiness" (122). He is the antithesis of *A Tale of Two Cities*'s conventionally "sane" person, the "orderly and methodical" Jarvis Lorry, whose face is "habitually suppressed and quiet," drilled "to the composed and reserved expression of Tellson's Bank" (49). Lorry's house, Tellson's Bank, is Lucie's house writ large, a place where you can "meditate on your misspent life" (83), and like the asylum, it "imposes its restraints and its silences" (113).[5]

It is Lucie who cures Carton, who transforms him as she transformed her father into a man with "great firmness of purpose, strength of resolution, and vigour of action" (161). She "binds" him, as she has bound her father and husband, with the invisible strands of domestic discipline: "Ever busily winding the golden thread which bound her husband, and her father, and herself, and her old directress and companion, in a life of quiet bliss" (239). And the "Home" which she establishes in England and transplants to France are identically arranged. In both, everything has "its appointed place and its appointed time" (304). It is a place of rest and repose, a quiet "harbour from the raging streets" (123), and it duplicates the "Perfect order, perfect cleanliness, and great tranquility" (Conoly, *Treatment* 54) prevailing in the well-managed asylum. It is a place "more abundant" (242) than the revolutionary waste, where everything turns and revolves around Lucie. There she reigns, the model of feminine respectability; there her "duty," "faithful service," "affection," and "thrift" merge with obedience and proper submissiveness. Like the morally managed asylum, it is not a home, but a caricature of a home, not a place of freedom but a place of moral discipline and social control, as Carton's confession to Lucie betrays:

I wish you to know that you have been the last dream of my soul. In my degradation I have not been so degraded but that the sight of you with your father, and of this house, made such a home by you, has stirred old shadows that I thought had died out of me. Since I knew you, I have been troubled by a remorse that I thought would never reproach me again, and have heard whispers from old voices impelling me upward, that I thought were silent forever.
                                                                                          (181)

That "remorse" is the beginning of Carton's cure; his sacrifice is the end. Because "sacrifice" is at the heart of domestic ideology; it is the law of Tellson's house and Lucie's home. Carton must be cured so that Lucie's home and Tellson's house can be preserved, so that the domestic idyll that ends *A Tale of Two Cities* and saves the State can resist the transgressive forces of history that threaten it.

IV

But "sacrifice" is the law of the Revolution as well and reminds us that the maenadic Therèse Defarge is Lucie's terrifying other. Sexual and political revolution or "restlessness," Dickens seems all too painfully aware, come not from without, but from within, perhaps even from skeletons hid in our own domestic closets.[6] We have all, like Dickens himself, "done and suffered" (29) what is depicted in the pages of the novel. In the history of every family lies a "buried" tale of transgression, and it is that history that *A Tale of Two Cities* first seeks to manage, but finally wishes to annul.

In this historical novel, then, Carton's restoration to the bourgeois fold, his interiorization of the norms of domestic ideology, signals, ironically, the death of history, for when Carton goes to the guillotine, "Memory" dies. The domestic realm in Dickens' novel is an atemporal space, a timeless utopia where Lucie follows Lucie in endless succession and where time is ordered, regulated, and finally erased in an endless series of occupations. As Louis Marin suggests, utopia knows nothing of time or change: "It is constituted by the representation of the identical, of the 'same' of repetitive indifference. . . . it is immobile representation and repetition compulsion" (xxiv). Such repetition works toward what Peter Brooks calls a "binding of textual energies that allows them to be mastered" (101); revolutionary desire is bound by the repetitive sameness of domesticity itself. The domestic is the space without history, particularly the history of a society's or an individual's madness. It is a lacuna of history that makes bourgeois culture possible, and hidden within domestic ideology is Victorian society's desire not to master memory, but to master forgetfulness, to make absent the political and sexual desires that threaten hegemony.

Domestic ideology defines subjectivity not only in terms of sexual identity, but, like moral management, in terms of rationality and morality as well. It rewrites the historical in terms of the psychological and reduces the collective nature of sexual and political revolutionary struggle to individual instances of moral pathology. As Nancy Armstrong suggests, domestic ideology and domestic fiction unfold "the operation of human desire as if they were independent of political history" in the creation of "a private domain of the individual outside and apart from social history" (9, 10). Domestic ideology turns history into case histories constitutive of personal identity and redirects political violence into the world of social relations where political rights are renounced in the pursuit of a model of mental health that encourages submission. But history, whether in the form of Chartist agitation, the Industrial Revolution, or the political disturbances on the Continent, constantly destabilizes existing gender and class relationships, reshaping and reorganizing subjectivity and the sexual division of labor on which domesticity thrives.

As Carlyle had taught Dickens, history *is* revolution, and in *A Tale of Two Cities* revolution is degradation and not the progressive fiction that the middle-class so wanted to believe. History as revolution is essentially transgressive and crosses not only the boundaries of established political and social practices, but also exposes the limits of those ideologies and discourses of social control (like moral management or domesticity) that define and delimit those practices. Moral insanity is inherently contradictory: buried beneath the surface of anti-social tendencies lie a host of bourgeois virtues. Hence, it is also revolutionary, always potentially "ruptural." Like moral management, domestic ideology must constantly reclassify the alterity it meets. It must dissolve the essentially contradictory nature of the revolutionary, "morally insane," individual and must control this rupture of transgressive energies by making a *tabula rasa* of the insane individual, erasing previous "historical" influences and rewriting the subject as morally consistent. Like all ideological practices, domesticity seeks to transform the individual "traversed and worked by social contradiction" into "a consistent subject in control of his [or her] own destiny." The power of the family as an institution of moral management, therefore, is its fusion of ideology and law. It not only "puts every individual in a place as a consistent [rational] subject," but "ensures that those who go wrong are judged in the name of this consistent [rational] subjectivity" (Coward and Ellis 75, 77). Because it is based on an imaginary etiology of insanity, moral management is, therefore, itself an imaginary resolution or "cure" of psychic contradictions, and domesticity "an ideological act in its own right with the function of inventing imaginary or formal 'solutions' to unresolvable social contradictions" (Jameson 79). But as the parallels to moral management should make clear, domestic ideology works, in fact, by a double invention: before it can "cure" the "wild infection" of revolution, it must first rewrite social contradiction in terms of a moral symptomatology and symbology of mental illness. It must create the very ensemble of signs which label social contradiction and revolutionary behavior as inherently pathological, as different from socially regulated modes of behavior. Such labelling authorizes domestic ideology itself; like moral management, it becomes the formal solution to a crisis only it is capable of perceiving.

The pathology of revolutionary change threatens the idea of progress central to the Victorians' conviction that their place in history was somehow unique, and the notion of progress was "imposed upon history to create the sense of order the Victorians craved" (Bowler 3). History in *A Tale of Two Cities* is not order but chaos; it is the carmagnole, that manifestation of collective insanity that blurs the boundaries of class and sexuality, the morally corrosive and deviant dance where "women danced together, men danced together, as hazard had brought them together" (307). History is the perversion of the once "innocent" past. Just as moral treatment must erase from the patient "all intrusions of history and spontaneity" (Castel, "Moral Treatment" 258), so, too, Dickens' novel must silence the "echoes" and wash away the "Headlong, mad, and dangerous footsteps" (243) that bring the threat of revolution into the Manette household and Victorian society. Domestic ideology is threatened by any suggestion that it is historical and subject to radical change, and written into the form and content of *A Tale of Two Cities*, it becomes the primary containment strategy by which Dickens attempts to morally manage and ultimately repudiate the forces of revolution.[7] While Lucie is a kind of domesticated Clio, whose golden thread unites her father "to a Past beyond his misery, and to a Present beyond his misery" (110), both past and present are incarcerated in the same domestic space. Here, as in the recurrent patterns of asylum life, domestic synchrony replaces the diachrony of history.

Despite the Victorians' glorification of history and historical process, then, *A Tale of Two Cities*, like other nineteenth-century novels permeated by domestic ideology, betrays a societal anxiety about history, and it suggests that the bourgeois myth of history as progress is the saving fiction that attempts to mask a notion of history as the pathological, as *difference*, as domesticity's terrifying other. In *Tale of Two Cities*, Clio is really Thérèse Defarge and her lesson is, "Judge you! Is it likely that the trouble of one wife and mother would be much to us now?" (298).

V

Thomas Carlyle's solution for the pathology of revolution is nomination or what he called "right-Naming": "History, and indeed all human Speech and Reason does yet, what Father Adam began like by doing: strive to *name* the new Things it sees of Nature's producing. . . . Any approximation to the right Name as value; were the right Name itself once here, the Thing is known henceforth; the Thing is then ours, and can be dealt with'' (333). As Michel de Certeau points out, historians, like doctors or exorcists, respond to social transgression "through a labor of naming" (246). Like the doctor, the novelist's task is also "one of nomination," which aims at categorizing the socially deviant and "confining them in a place circumscribed by [the novelist's] knowledge"; a knowledge that is "assumed to be capable of *naming*" (247). Following Certeau, we might also argue that the novelist of domestic fiction is opposed to the revolutionary female because through her "madness" she "betrays the very linguistic topography with which the social order can be organized" (247). Like the doctor of the insane, the novelist engages in defining who the revolutionary other is by placing him or her "in a topography of Proper names," (255) and that act of denomination is "intended to reclassify a protean uncanniness within an established language" (255–5). By labelling the revolutionary subject as morally insane, the novelist "assigns to [that] subject a locus in language and therefore 'secures' an order of sociolinguistic practice," (256) which is domestic ideology itself. Domestic fiction recodifies the "uncanniness" of gender and class by "designating a determinate name" (256) drawn from the nomenclature of bourgeois morality.

As D. A. Miller suggests, "the genre of the novel *belongs* to the disciplinary field it portrays" (21), which in the case of *A Tale of Two Cities* specifically, and nineteenth-century novels by middle-class writers generally, is moral management, because moral management as an ideological form of social control most clearly displays the linguistic practice indigenous to the bourgeois novel itself: the renomination of gender and class within the discourse of bourgeois value. Like discipline itself, the novel as a form of social control is both "a complex social function" and a "political tactic" which conceals the repressiveness and violence of the asylum behind a therapeutic model of family life (Foucault, *Discipline and Punish*); like moral management, it hides "the relationships of force under relationships of meaning" (Castel, *The Regulation of Madness* 170).

Moral management, as Robert Castel insists, is the "ideal model" and "paradigm of every authoritarian pedagogy," and as a metaphor for the novel's ideological process, it underscores the way in which the nineteenth-century novel, particularly domestic fiction, excludes the marginal, "morally insane" figure and preserves the social and ideological status quo:

> It is still a matter of deploying strategies for subjugation. It is the same armory of disciplinary techniques that is capable of both effecting the recovery of reason (i.e. a return to the predominant form of normality) and also of subduing the people (i.e. causing them to internalize the rules that ensure the reproduction of bourgeois order). (*The Regulation of Madness* 121)

The nineteenth-century novel becomes the site for the re-evolution and recovery not only of the characters, but of the reader as well. The novel is the locus for moral therapy, because like the asylum it provides an imaginary substitute for the social and familial environment. The novel as asylum seeks to re-educate its readers, to re-create correct patterns of thinking and to re-establish appropriate standards of behavior.

In *A Tale of Two Cities*, domestic space is no longer the opposite of the asylum, no longer the private home from which the insane individual is removed and to which he or she must return. It *is* the asylum, and as such, it is the specific location for the management of political and sexual transgression. It harbors the pathology that is history as its double, containing, controlling, and canceling it. And just as Lucie's home is the site for Carton's transformation, so too the nineteenth-century novel turns readers into what Foucault calls "docile bodies" that may be "subjected, used, transformed, and improved" (*Discipline and Punish* 131). In his engagement with the novel the reader is uprooted from his familiar historical environment—England in the late 1850s, the site of contemporary forces of sexual and political disruption—and relocated in a special environment whose internal economy, the triumph of domestic ideology over revolution, embodies the order whose repeated interiorization is the condition for his successful integration and "return" to the real world. Here, the reader is exposed to the fate of those like Madame Defarge who have failed to interiorize the values that order bourgeois society.

Novel reading, particularly the reading of serialized novels like *A Tale of Two Cities*, mimics the patterns of managed asylum life, redistributing time. It replaces the processive "history" of reading with a monthly exercise, with discrete and yet homogeneous experiences of the text's duration and its ideology. The privacy of novel reading isolates the reader from the outside world, from the uncontrollable and contradictory forces of history, which is the place where his disorder is produced, and transplants him into an imaginatively ordered space co-extensive with the domesticity itself. As Linda K. Hughes and Michael Lund suggest, "the virtues that sustain a home and the traits required of serial readers so often coincided" (16). In this ordered therapeutic space, the reader lives in the "lucidity of the law," a law he once more makes his own. In the world of the novel, as in the asylum, moral order is "reduced to its bare bones of law, obligations, and constraints," and the novel functions as the model of an ideal society, "in the sense of being ideally reduced to order" (Castel, *The Regulation of Madness* 75).

The imposition of ideal order by the novel is backed by the relationship of authority between the novelist and the reader. Similar to nineteenth-century psychiatric reformers, Dickens attacks the more violent forms of treatment of the insane, symbolized in Dr. Manette's incarceration in the Bastille, while instituting the "invisible" discipline of moral management and the managing function of the asylum in everyday life. *A Tale of Two Cities* is an elaborate case history of the diagnosis, treatment, and cure of the social body infected with the pathology of revolution. Dickens casts himself in the role of the attending physician or benevolent asylum head and his narrator evinces those qualities without which "no man can be personally successful in the moral treatment of the insane":

> A faculty of seeing that which is passing in the minds of men is the first requisite of moral power and discipline, whether in asylums, schools, parishes, or else-where. Add to this a firm will, the faculty of self-control, a sympathizing distress at moral pain, a strong desire to remove it, and that biologizing power is elicited, which enables men to domineer for good purposes over the minds of others.
>
> (Bucknill and Tuke 489)

The "power" which allows the novelist to "domineer" for moral purposes over the minds of his readers is clearly taxonomic, an ordering of signs. Like the expert in moral treatment, Dickens carefully nominates, codifies, and regulates the behavior of the characters in his novel in his attempt to "declare the truth" about revolution.[8] The novelist, like the asylum physician, is omnip-otent, if not completely omniscient: "innermost personality," Dickens admits, is ultimately "inscrutable" (44). His power lies, therefore, not in the knowl-edge of the sexual or political secrets at the heart of social disorder and individual pathology, but in his control over the signs which confirm that such secrets must and do exist. The novelist is a specialist in the symptomatology of social disorder, and Dickens "seeks the narratable in that which deviates most markedly from the normal, in the criminal, the outside-the-law, the unsocialized, and the ungoverned" (Brooks 153). Unable to fathom the root causes of social anomie, he directs attention instead to the signs or symptoms of social unrest, and those signs are simply those which "distinguish patholog-ical behavior from socially regulated modes of conduct" (Castel, *The Regula-tion of Madness* 97). Such symptoms—like Carton's lassitude or Madame Defarge's malice—signify a preponderance of moral causes, particularly polit-ical and sexual transgression, which in turn legitimize moral therapy (here, in the form of domestic ideology) as the only means of treatment capable of eradicating the moral causes of pathology and restoring the insane individual to rationality, to the regulated modes of conduct that constitute the bourgeois, domestic norm. The relationship of the novelist and his reader is, therefore, analogous to that between the doctor and the patient; it is a relationship of authority that binds the novelist to the reader "in the exercise of a power that [lacks] reciprocity" (Castel, *The Regulation of Madness* 75), since it is only the novelist who can order the signs that designate transgressive behavior. Such a relationship suggests that the reader suffers from the disorder of moral insanity, from those "buried" but no less transgressive energies that political events and social conflict, or history, generate. The novel interpellates the reader/subject as "free" and responsible for his own actions, as the point of origin of his own transgression and cure. Although readers may aspire to the ideal of characters like Lucie Manette or Jarvis Lorry, the determinate names the novel designates for them are "Thérèse Defarge" or "Sidney Carton." The novel as asylum is a "world constructed in the image of the rationality" (Castel, *The Regulation of Madness* 76) embodied by the novelist, and the novel multiplies his power, since the order of things that triumph in the novel—domesticity and rationality—come to life as a moral order backed by society itself. Thus, the diagnosis and judgment of pathology at the heart of the Victorian novel becomes for the reader a social reality. It is only when he has regained his rational autonomy, has interiorized domestic ideology, that the novel pronounces him cured. It is only when he puts down the novel that the novelist's power is ostensibly canceled.

That power, however, is never really canceled, since the novel and the world "outside" are constructed by the same ideology. The reader's return to the world of lived experience, therefore, merely attests to the "truth" of the novel and the novelist's disciplinary vision. For the discourse of the novel, like moral management, is constructed around a social perception of health, ordered by the same moral symptomatology and symbology, and permeated by the values of the middle class. Domestic ideology, moral management, and the nineteenth-century novel are all forms of authoritarian pedagogy, of a re-educational process that seeks to suppress the focuses of sexual and political revolt and to extinguish them at their source—the revolutionary, "morally insane," subject. But just as *A Tale of Two Cities* betrays a societal anxiety about the forces of history, it also betrays an anxiety about the doctor's or novelist's power to morally manage transgression and cure the pathological. For if revolution and madness are marked by "restlessness," so, too, is writing; and throughout the 1850s, a period of intense personal restlessness for Dickens, he equates that restlessness, and indeed madness, with novel production itself.[9] As Peter Brooks points out, "The plotted novel is a deviance from or transgression of the normal, a state of abnormality and error which alone in 'narratable' " (84–85). The "ferocious excitement" of writing that caused Dickens to run "wildly about and about" a new novel in his own creative carmagnole is a form of imbalance that Dickens appears powerless to cure and Dickens often appears in his letters to be as much writing's victim as its master.

Doctor Manette cannot save Madame Defarge's sister from her madness, from the "high fever of her brain," (331) a "frenzy" so great that he does not even unfasten the bandages that restrain her. Thus, Dickens' novel unconsciously draws a disturbing parallel between the State bonds that the brothers

Evremonde use to imprison Defarge's sister and the domestic bonds or "golden threads" that Lucie employs to save Carton and her husband from moral insanity and revolution. Lucie's threads, therefore, are the "invisible" ideological counterpart to the Evremondes' more brutal and arbitrary forms of incarceration and disguise the violence at the heart of domestic ideology. Rather than liberating the reader, rather than making him a "free" and autonomous subject, the novel as asylum places him "within a moral element where he will be in debate with himself and his surroundings: to constitute for him a milieu where, far from being protected, he will be kept in perpetual anxiety, ceaselessly threatened by Law and Transgression" (Foucault, *Civilization and Madness* 245). The novel, like Tellson's bank, is a place to "meditate on your misspent life," and attests to the truth of the Marquis St. Evremonde's observation, "Repression is the only lasting philosophy" (153).

NOTES

1. For the relationship between Carlyle's *The French Revolution* and *A Tale of Two Cities*, see Michael Goldberg's *Carlyle and Dickens*, pp. 100–28, as well as Baumgarten, Timko, Vanden Bossche, and Gilbert.
2. Michael Timko makes a similar argument in reference to the importance of the "symbol" of the family and "domestic tranquility" in *A Tale of Two Cities*: "Much of the novel's emotional appeal, Dickens thought, would come from his readers' immediate response to this picture of domestic bliss; they would recognise in it those moral and ethical qualities nurtured in family life that would assure the survival of nations and of mankind itself" (182).
3. As Sander Gilman notes, "Of all the models of pathology, one of the most powerful is mental illness. For the most elementally frightening possibility is loss of control over the self. . . . Often associated with violence . . . the mad are perceived as the antithesis to the control and reason that define the self" (23),
4. In addition to Showalter, see also Scull, Dorner, and Skultans.
5. As James M. Brown notes, "Tellson's functions as a social microcosm and the description of Tellson's building works to suggest the operation of a complex and ominous set of social forces beneath the prosperous middle-class surface" (120).
6. In a letter to Forster in 1856, Dickens attributes a "year of restlessness" to what he calls the "skeleton in his domestic closet" (qtd. in Ackroyd 756, 763).
7. See Fredric Jameson's reading of the "Dickensian paradigm" and the relationship between realism and revolutionary change in *The Political Unconscious*, pp. 188–94.
8. John Conolly maintains that the business of the asylum physician is "to declare the truth." *On Some of the Forms of Insanity*, p. 85.
9. Writing to Forster in 1854 on the composition of *Hard Times*, Dickens declared, "I am three parts mad, and the fourth, delirious, with perpetual rushing at *Hard Times*" (qtd. in Johnson 799).

WORKS CITED

Ackroyd, Peter. *Dickens*. London: Sinclair and Stevenson, 1990.

Armstrong, Nancy. *Desire and Domestic Fiction*. New York: Oxford UP, 1987.

Baumgarten, Murray. "Writing Revolution." *Dickens Studies Annual* 12 (1984): 161–76.

Bowler, Peter J. *The Invention of Progress: The Victorians and the Past*. Oxford: Basil Blackwell, 1989.

Brooks, Peter. *Reading for the Plot*. New York: Knopf, 1984.

Brown, James M. *Dickens: Novelist in the Market Place*. Totowa, N.J.: Barnes & Noble, 1982.

Bucknill, John Charles and Daniel H. Tuke. *A Manual of Psychological Medicine*. Philadelphia: 1858.

Carlyle, Thomas. *The French Revolution*. New York: Oxford UP, 1989.

Castel, Robert. "Moral Treatment: Mental Therapy and Social Control in the Nineteenth Century," *Social Control and the State*. Eds. Stanley Cohen and Andrew Scull. Oxford: Basil Blackwell, 1983.

————. *The Regulation of Madness*. Trans. W. D. Halls. Berkeley: U of California Press, 1988.

Conolly, John. *The Treatment of the Insane Without Mechanical Restraints*. London: 1856.

————. *On Some of the Forms of Insanity*. London: 1849.

Coward, Rosalind and John Ellis. *Language and Materialism*. New York: Routledge, 1977.

de Certeau, Michel. *The Writing of History*. trans. Tom Conley. New York: Columbia UP, 1988.

Dickens, Charles. *A Tale of Two Cities*. New York: Penguin, 1991.

Doerner, Klaus. *Madmen and the Bourgeoisie: A Social History of Insanity*. Trans. Joachim Neugroschel and Jean Steinberg. Oxford: Basil Blackwell, 1981. pp. 20–95.

Donelly, Michael. *Managing the Mind*. New York: Tavistock, 1983.

Fee, Elizabeth. "Psychology, Sexuality, and Social Control in Victorian England," *Social Science Quarterly* 58 (March 1978): 632–46.

Foucault, Michel. *Civilization and Madness*. Trans. Richard Howard. New York: Vintage, 1988.

———. *Discipline and Punish*. Trans. Alan Sheridan. New York: Vintage, 1977.

Gilbert, Elliot L. " 'To Awake from History': Carlyle, Thackeray, and *Tale of Two Cities.*" *Dickens Studies Annual* 12 (1984): 247–66.

Gilman, Sander R. *Differences and Pathology: Stereotypes of Sexuality, Race, and Madness*. Ithaca: Cornell UP, 1985.

Hughes, Linda K. and Michael Lund. *The Victorian Serial*. Charlottesville: UP of Virginia, 1991.

Jameson, Fredric. *The Political Unconscious*. Ithaca: Cornell UP, 1981.

Johnson, Edgar. *Charles Dickens: His Tragedy and Triumph*. New York: Simon and Schuster, 1959.

Marin, Louis. *Utopics: the Semiological Play of Textual Spaces*. Trans. Robert A. Vollrath. Atlantic Highlands, N.J.: Humanities P, 1990.

Miller, D. A. *The Novel and the Police*. Berkeley: U of California P, 1988.

Mort, Frank. *Dangerous Sexualities*. New York: Routledge, 1987.

Nead, Lynda. *Myths of Sexuality*. New York: Basil Blackwell, 1988.

Pritchard, James Cowles. *A Treatise on Insanity and Other Disorders Affecting the Mind*. Philadelphia: 1837.

Scull, Andrew. *Museums of Madness: The Social Organization of Insanity in Nineteenth-Century England*. London: Penquin, 1979.

———. "Moral Treatment Reconsidered: Some Sociological Comments on an Episode in the History of British Psychiatry." In *Madhouses, Mad-doctors, and Madmen*. Ed. Andrew Scull. Philadelphia: U. of Pennsylvania P, 1981. pp. 104–17.

———. "The Domestication of Madness." *Medical History* 2 (1983): 233–48.

Shires, Linda M. "Of maenads, mothers, and feminized males: Victorian readings of the French Revolution," *Rewriting the Victorians: Theory, History and the Politics of Gender*. Ed. Linda M. Shires. New York: Routledge, 1992.

Skultans, Vida. *English Madness: Ideas on Insanity 1580–1890*. Boston: Routledge, 1979.

Timko, Michael. "Splendid Impressions and Picturesque Means: Dickens, Carlyle, and *The French Revolution.*" *Dickens Studies Annual* 12 (1984): 177–96.

Vanden Bossche, Chris R. "Prophetic Closure and Disclosing Narrative: *The French Revolution* and *A Tale of Two Cities.*" *Dickens Studies Annual* 12 (1984): 209–22.

Weeks, Jeffrey. *Sex, Politics and Society*. New York: Longman, 1981.

"Your Love-Sick Pickwick": The Erotics of Service

Brian W. McCuskey

Pickwickian innocence has long been one of our most celebrated critical clichés. Who can help smiling at Pickwick's cheerful blundering through a world full of guileful con men and mercenary widows, or envying the ease with which a pint of porter restores his faith in human nature? Even those critics curmudgeonly enough to argue that Dickens' novel qualifies that innocence by ushering Pickwick through debtor's prison and toward experience never allow him to fall very far from grace. In the closing pages, Pickwickian experience ultimately seems nearly as cozy and comfortable—free of guilt, anxiety, and desire—as Pickwickian innocence.[1]

In most criticism of the novel, Pickwick's specifically sexual innocence has remained unquestioned and even asserted as a precondition for both the novel's humor and its canonical status. Elliot Engel and Margaret King claim that Pickwick's celibacy "allows Dickens to do what no comic English novelist before him had done: to make humor respectable, to banish the vulgarity and bawdiness that was beginning to make pre-Victorian audiences squeamish" (133). In an earlier appraisal of the novel, Steven Marcus argues that "the suppression and elimination of the insistent coarseness—and especially of the low-comedy conventions of open sexuality—in this eighteenth-century tradition may be regarded as a requisite first move which enabled Dickens to urge the novel toward a modern, more complex experience of society" (28–29). According to these critics, *The Pickwick Papers* (1836–37) appropriates the narrative structure of such picaresques as Fielding's *Tom Jones* (1749) and Smollett's *Roderick Random* (1748) without resorting to the broad sexual farce of those earlier and lustier novels.

Readings of *The Pickwick Papers* that insist upon Pickwickian innocence often dismiss erotic energy from the text altogether—as if, in Marcus's terms, a "modern, more complex experience of society" did not include a modern, more complex experience of a sexuality no longer quite so "open." Recently, a few critics—James R. Kincaid, Gail Turley Houston, and John Glavin—have wondered what the experience of Pickwickian sexuality might be. All three conclude that Pickwick's sex life is fundamentally regressive, allowing the bachelor to retreat from the anxieties and conflicts of normative middle-class sexuality and to recover the unalienated sexual ego and voracious oral drive of infancy. Kincaid, in a whimsical essay on fat, flesh, and feasting in the novel, claims, "The reader of *Pickwick* is the erotic reader gliding blissfully backwards into full childhood sexuality" ("Fattening Up" 237); similarly, Glavin argues that the novel rescues Pickwick and his readers from the shame of sexuality by infantilizing him and encouraging us to enjoy vicariously "the eccentric solitary's autoerotic triumph" (12). Houston, leery of the destruction wrought by male appetites (even infantile ones), suggests that "the insatiable fat boy" who waits on the Dingley Dell table "seems to represent displaced Pickwickian sexual desire" that the novel must finally moderate (742).

The shared limitation of these arguments is that Pickwickian regression begins to sound suspiciously like Pickwickian innocence, writ now from the psychoanalytic point of view. The novel either celebrates (according to Kincaid and Glavin) or qualifies (according to Houston) an idealized state of sexual satisfaction, liberated from the social imperatives of class and gender. As a result, the regressive hypothesis—much like the notion of Pickwickian innocence—tends to obscure the construction of sexuality in the novel. Rather than a modern, more complex sexuality that engages in diverse and productive ways with emerging Victorian structures of power, the regressive hypothesis necessarily discovers instead an insular and essentialized sexuality that shies away from such engagement.

I contend that *The Pickwick Papers* responds to certain male anxieties about middle-class heterosexual relations by amplifying the scope of bourgeois sexual experience. The virginity of Pickwick notwithstanding, sexual desire wreaks havoc throughout the novel, upsetting the bonds of friendship and family, destabilizing linguistic meaning, and subverting the patriarchal norms of the Pickwick Club. Again and again in the novel, the expression of sexuality within conventional social channels produces humiliation, frustration, and even violence among the Pickwickians and their friends. For all its regressive fantasies, however, *The Pickwick Papers* does not simply retreat reflexively from the anxieties of courtship and marriage. Instead, the novel seeks out alternative spaces and relations where excessive erotic energy might be contained, explored, and exploited. The relocation of desire outside of middle-class marital relations allows the Pickwickians to satisfy their sexual appetites without compromising their authority as bourgeois men.

In struggling to find a productive place for sex in male middle-class life, *The Pickwick Papers* enlists the help of the many servants who populate the novel, from the dozing fat boy to the flirtatious housemaids at Dingley Dell. Descending from the parlor to the servants' hall, the novel discovers below stairs a place where desire circulates outside the confines of normative bourgeois sexuality and where alternative forms of erotic expression might be conceived and made available to the Pickwickians. The boundaries of sexuality in the novel therefore expand to include elements—not only oral and infantile but also cross-class and homoerotic—that apparently affront middle-class sensibilities. The novel actively encourages such violations of the ideological order below stairs in order to mediate the conflict that arises above stairs between the Pickwickians and their ladyfriends. Far from being simply regressive, Pickwickian sexuality actually involves a complex set of practices and relations that are not only thoroughly implicated within nineteenth-century social structures but also carefully designed to consolidate the social and sexual power of Pickwick himself—who begins to appear somewhat less than innocent.

SEX AND MARRIAGE FROM THE PICKWICKIAN POINT OF VIEW

That Pickwick's world is very much a middle-class male world is apparent in the first scene. The novel opens with the first and last meeting of the Pickwick Club which the reader is privileged enough to attend. The Club is something of a patriarchy-in-miniature, functioning as a private and exclusive men's organization dedicated to the "advancement of knowledge, and the diffusion of learning" (*Pickwick* 67)—that is, knowledge and learning seen from its own "Pickwickian point of view" (72). The Club determines to send its heroic leader Pickwick out into the world so that he may record and publish his observations and insights for the benefit of mankind and, of course, for the prestige of the Club. During Pickwick's self-important acceptance speech, a jealous member rises to his feet and hurls the invective 'humbug,' an offense which causes great commotion and argument. However, order is quickly restored, as the offending member concedes that he was using the epithet "in its Pickwickian sense" (72). Pickwick then graciously allows that his own heated response bore "a Pickwickian construction" (72) and the Club is united again.

Two points about the use of language in this opening scene are particularly important for my argument. First, the authority of the Club depends upon the integrity of its male community. Internal division must be resolved or at least effaced if the Club is to function properly. The most efficient means of achieving that resolution is to recast conflict within the context of the "Pickwickian point of view." The specificity of the adjective creates the illusion that some particular and positive point of view exists in which the word 'humbug' has an inoffensive meaning. However, the "Pickwickian point of view" is in fact a nebulous and negative linguistic frame which allows the male community to control the slippery meanings of words and defuse their potential violence, all in the interests of the solidarity of the men's club.[2]

Second, Pickwick's role as scientific observer and reporter for the Club depends upon an objectivist theory of language in which the representation of experience is immediate and free of distortion, the meanings of words remain stable, and the act of representation itself does not affect or alter its object. Armed with only his portmanteau and notebook, Pickwick ventures into a world where fixed linguistic meaning cannot be so easily assumed. His willingness to take people at their word demonstrates his faith in an objectivist theory of language; the comic misunderstandings that result demonstrate the blind spots of that theory. Furthermore, as J. Hillis Miller points out, Pickwick "goes forth to encounter experience with an apparently unshakeable calm because, again like the scientist, he does not expect what he sees will involve or change himself" (7). Neither, James E. Marlow adds, does Pickwick expect that his seeing and writing will involve or change his object; Pickwick writes "in ignorance that his writing might in some way condition the situation" (945). This assumption is immediately questioned in the novel's second scene, in which a suspicious cabman attacks Pickwick (who has been jotting down the man's tall tales) because he believes the scribbling Pickwick to be an "informer" (*Pickwick* 75). Despite this initial setback, Pickwick throughout the novel demonstrates his faith in the transparency and neutrality of language, a belief which precipitates many of his misadventures.

This objectivist theory of language, in which meaning is always stable, and the Pickwickian point of view, in which meaning is always negotiable, are obviously incompatible; or rather, they are compatible only as long as you are a Pickwickian yourself, and are consistently willing to align linguistic meaning with the self-interest and self-preservation of the men's club. Whether or not linguistic meaning is flexible or fixed depends upon the particular ideological imperatives of the male community as it maintains its own integrity against both internal and external threats. The authority of the community thus depends upon its ability at once to manipulate and to efface that theoretical contradiction. In short, the Pickwick Club is emblematic of the larger middle-class patriarchy that governs the world of the novel and the world outside the novel, with its tightly-knit communal bonds, its exclusively male authority, its objectivist pretensions, and its ideological manipulations of linguistic meaning.

At this point, we can see how sexual desire destabilizes both the social and the linguistic constructions of the patriarchal order and generates a corresponding anxiety. Desire threatens the social constructions when erotic energy works its way into the tenuous network of male bonds that constitutes the patriarchal community, exposing and exploiting the gaps within that network. Repeatedly, the attempt by middle-class men to channel their sexual desire appropriately—toward middle-class women—finally produces only competition and violence among those men, as they engage in the numerous fistfights and duels of the novel. Nearly every middle-class woman in the novel finds herself positioned between two hostile men: Rachael Wardle between Tupman and Jingle; Mrs. Pott between Winkle and Mr. Pott; Arabella Allen between Bob Sawyer and Winkle; Miss Witherfield between Peter Magnus and Pickwick himself; and so on. The expression of male sexual desire, then, ultimately disrupts the integrity of the male community. In this context, we can understand why the flirtations of the romantic Tupman must be judged as "anti-Pickwickian" (81).

Female sexual desire is equally and paradoxically problematic. On the one hand, the sexual desire of a woman for a particular man arouses the jealousy of other men and produces conflict within the male community. On the other hand, those men cannot tolerate a female desire which does *not* fixate upon a single male and which thus cannot be permanently ordered and contained within their community. The anxiety here is best expressed in the novel by Tupman, who wonders of his beloved Rachael: "Had her agitation arisen from an amiable and feminine sensibility which would have been equally irrepressible in any case, or had it been called forth by a more ardent and passionate feeling, which he, of all men living, could alone awaken?" (170). Tupman's lovesick rhetoric masks a repressive double standard that constructs Rachael's sexual desire as equally damnable in either case. Of all the Pickwickians, Tupman has the most faith in women; as a result, Rachael's elopement with Jingle nearly destroys the disillusioned Tupman, and he renounces any further involvement with the once-beloved opposite sex.

Sexual desire, whether male or female, also poses a threat to the linguistic constructions of the patriarchal order, destabilizing meaning and exploiting the blindnesses of the Pickwickian point of view. The subversive operations of desire upon and within language produce the central plot complication of the novel—the breach-of-promise charge brought against Pickwick by his landlady, Mrs. Bardell. Mrs. Bardell misreads Pickwick's request to lodge his manservant, Sam Weller, in the house as the proposal of marriage she has always desired from this very eligible bachelor. Pickwick, however, cannot conceive that his words might signify anything other than what he intends, even once the ecstatic landlady has thrown herself into his arms. The ensuing confusion leads to his arrest for breach-of-promise. At the trial itself, the subversions of language by desire reach comic extremes when Mrs. Bardell's lawyer, Serjeant Buzfuz, rereads and misreads Pickwick's brief and business-like notes to her ("Chops and Tomata sauce") as covert expressions of passion (562–63). Here, Pickwick's faith in his own point of view, his certainty

that he need only speak the truth for the truth to be known, literally impris-
ons him.[3]

The expression of sexual desire thus threatens the novel's patriarchal community either by upsetting the male bonds that ensure its integrity, or by
upsetting the linguistic relations that ensure the preservation of its interests
and the exertion of its authority. The novel therefore views women with
particular distrust and suspicion; whether they are the agents or the objects
of desire, women introduce chaos and violence into the otherwise comfortable
Pickwickian circle. Such anxiety is most evident in the novel's morbid fascination with widows, or as Tony Weller calls them, "widders." Tony himself
has married a "widder," whose shrill voice and shriller Methodism are the
source of much discomfort to him, and he repeatedly warns his son Sam to
"be wery careful o' widders all your life, specially if they've kept a public-
house" (353). Tony insinuates here that women who have entered the world
of business become dangerous, as they assume a measure of authority and
individualism traditionally reserved for men. Furthermore, Tony's paranoid
distrust of widows who remarry suggests an underlying alarm about the tran-
sience and mutability of female desire. Barbara J. Todd has argued that "the
remarriage of any widow confronted every man with the threatening prospect
of his own death and the entry of another into his place" (55). For this reason,
Tupman, fearing that Rachael may be attracted to Jingle, recalls the widow
at the Rochester ball who danced with more than one man, "and his mind
was troubled" (*Pickwick* 178).

The widow, as a sexually experienced and post-menopausal woman, also
represents a female sexuality both aware of its own needs and desires as well
as liberated from the physical constraints of pregnancy and childbearing. Such
a female sexuality is understandably threatening to the Pickwickians; again
and again the novel associates widows with sexual aggression and danger.
The widow Bardell, obviously the most aggressive and dangerous woman of
all, becomes Pickwick's point of reference for all female desire; when Arabella Allen's elderly aunt displays "increasing admiration" for the bespectacled
hero, Pickwick "thought of Mrs. Bardell; and every glance of the old lady's
eyes threw him into a cold perspiration" (773). Widows in the novel wield
a sexual power terrifying to the male community; as Tony Weller concludes,
"I *have* heard how many ord'nary women, one widder's equal to, in pint o'
comin' over you. I think it's five-and-twenty, but I don't rightly know vether
it an't more" (397). Although he is a working-class coachman, Tony Weller
articulates the misogynistic distrust felt primarily by middle-class men; by
suggesting that the fear of widders transcends class difference, the novel
naturalizes the male sexual anxiety that underwrites the Pickwickian community.

While widders are the women most feared by the Pickwickians, the novel
represents relations with any woman as an inherently dangerous proposition,

fraught with potential anxiety and conflict. When recounting the wedding of Mr. Trundle and Isabella Wardle, the narrator somewhat disingenuously claims that "we indulge in no hidden sarcasm upon a married life" (467); this is true only in so far as most of the novel's sarcasm is well out in the open. Without exception, married men in the novel are harried and ordered about by their shrewish wives. Mr. Pott, editor of the *Eatanswill Gazette*, lacks the courage to forbid Mrs. Pott's flirtations with Winkle; Mr. Raddle, husband to Bob Sawyer's landlady, endures the hysterical rantings of Mrs. Raddle; even the magistrate of Ipswich, Mr. Nupkins himself, must indulge the insults and tantrums of Mrs. Nupkins. Dickens' later novels oppose such instances of marital strife against an implicit norm of domestic harmony, but this first novel's celebrations of hearth and home have more to do with male 'conwiviality,' as Sam Weller would say, than with wedded bliss. Weddings do provide occasion for much merrymaking among the Pickwickians, but the novel leaves little doubt that bachelorhood is greatly to be preferred to married life. As Tony Weller warns his son, "If ever you gets to up'ards o' fifty, and feels disposed to go a marryin' anybody—no matter who—jist you shut yourself up in your own room, if you've got one, and pison yourself off hand. . . . Pison yourself, Samivel, my boy, pison yourself, and you'll be glad on it arterwards" (398).

Death before marriage: this is the most forceful articulation of the Pickwickian view of sex and women. It is important to note here that the novel's point of view is not necessarily Pickwickian itself; any sympathy the narrative exhibits for the Pickwickians coexists with an ironic distance from them. The oscillation between irony and sympathy presents the major difficulty in evaluating the politics of *The Pickwick Papers* (indeed, of any Dickens novel). The novel does employ farce to poke fun at the pretensions of the Pickwick Club and the anxieties of the bachelor community, but the models of social power and sexual desire that support patriarchal authority are no less powerful for being caricatured. Despite its self-conscious irony, *The Pickwick Papers* is not a politically radical novel; its parody of male anxieties is less an act of subversion than an offer of catharsis. While Kincaid argues that the novel affords the pleasure of "gliding blissfully backwards into full childhood sexuality," I would argue quite the opposite. *The Pickwick Papers* allows the reader to wallow in all the fear and trembling of adult male sexuality, to indulge in the most gynephobic of fantasies, and to exalt the spirit of eternal bachelorhood, as embodied in the impressive girth of the illustrious Mr. Pickwick.

SERVANT SEX AND PICKWICKIAN DESIRE

In a world where heterosexual desire produces more anxiety than pleasure, how can middle-class men enjoy erotic energy without fear of wives and widows? This is the question that troubles the novel as it explores alternative methods of both expressing and managing sexual desire within the male community. In thinking through these problems of middle-class sexuality, the narrative enters the servants' hall and employs the many housemaids and footmen of the Pickwickians. Servants, of course, are notoriously troublesome figures in nineteenth-century fiction. In *The Servant's Hand: English Fiction from Below*, Bruce Robbins argues that the servants' hall is a volatile site of political resistance in the English novel. Literary servants, according to Robbins, consistently destabilize the ideological structures that support bourgeois authority. The impertinence, exposition, and agency of servants below stairs interrupt the dominant discourse of the parlor above and disrupt the smooth operation of the middle-class master's power. Drawing on Fredric Jameson's theory of the political unconscious, Robbins concludes that servants in the novel collectively harbinger a future social transformation from capitalist alienation to utopian community.

Without question, literary servants initiate various inversions and transgressions of the Victorian cultural order. As Peter Stallybrass and Allon White have argued, socially marginal figures (such as servants) are symbolically central to bourgeois culture: "Points of antagonism, overlap and intersection between the high and the low . . . provide some of the richest and most powerful symbolic dissonances in the culture" (25). The dissonance so produced may expose and even heighten certain tensions and contradictions within the structure of Victorian ideology. However, despite Robbins's claims, the literary servant does not therefore *necessarily* subvert or challenge bourgeois authority. Victorian novels do not always seek to correct the symbolic ambivalence generated below stairs; often, they encourage disorder in one symbolic field as a means of producing order in another. *The Pickwick Papers*, for example, endorses a variety of sexual excesses and transgressions below stairs in order to consolidate male social power above. Far from offending Pickwickian principles, the licentious behavior of servants actually allows the novel to soothe Pickwickian anxieties. *The Pickwick Papers* employs servants to revise the limits of normative middle-class sexuality and thus to resolve the social and sexual conflicts felt by men in the novel.

Servants are consistently eroticized throughout *The Pickwick Papers*—whether in the background, where we glimpse "buxom servants lounging at the side door, enjoying the pleasantness of the hour, and the delights of a flirtation" (171); or in the foreground, as "three or four buxom girls" rush forward with brandy and towels to welcome Pickwick and friends to Dingley Dell (138). Female servants in the novel are repeatedly characterized as 'buxom'; it is interesting to note in this context that the word, whose nineteenth-century usage suggests a plump and large-breasted female body, has its roots in the Old English verb for submission or obedience (*bugan*).

The word thus conflates sex and service even as the novel as a whole does so. The most striking example of this association comes when Sam and Mary shake out a carpet between them:

> It is not half as innocent a thing as it looks, that shaking little pieces of car-pet—at least, there may be no great harm in the shaking, but the folding is a very insidious process. So long as the shaking lasts, and the two parties are kept the carpet's length apart, it is as innocent an amusement as can well be devised; but when the folding begins, and the distance between them gets gradually lessened from one half its former length to a quarter, and then to an eighth, and then to a sixteenth, and then to a thirty-second, if the carpet be long enough: it becomes dangerous. We do not know, to a nicety, how many pieces of carpet were folded in this instance, but we can venture to state that as many pieces as there were, so many times did Sam kiss the pretty housemaid. (640)

As this housework-cum-striptease suggests, servants express their own sexual desire among themselves with a freedom unknown to their middle-class masters. Sam Weller nods, winks, and whistles at any and every servant girl he meets, and his courtship of the pretty housemaid, Mary, is characterized by a long series of bawdy jokes and bodily caresses. Servants remain blissfully unaware of the social and psychological complications of sexual desire, finding only pleasure in what Sam calls "natur" (434).

The sexual freedom of the servant class provides a space in which the novel can relocate and represent libidinal energy without endangering the male middle-class community at its center. It is here, in the corridors and kitchens, that the novel allows desire to surface most openly and to operate most pleasurably. The servant class thus functions as something of an erotic playground for the members of the men's club. Slumming with the servants provides a means of genuinely expending sexual energy outside of socially sanctioned relations with middle-class women. For example, Tupman, having been disappointed in his wooing of Rachael Wardle, resorts to stealing kisses from her chambermaid (139, 465). Bob Sawyer, the spurned admirer of the lovely Arabella Allen, pursues a servant girl in the house of his rival's father, the elder Winkle (803–04). Finding only frustration and denial within the conventional channels of middle-class desire, these men redirect their sexual energy toward female servants, who appear from behind doors and under stairwells with faces flushed and bonnets askew after the furtive fondlings of their masters.

In these scenes, the novel's representation of master-servant erotics seems strangely evacuated of either sexual violence or social oppression. Indeed, the novel goes to great lengths to mask the power differential at the center of cross-class sexual relations. When Bob Sawyer confronts the elder Winkle's servant girl, "stretching forth his arms, and skipping from side to side, as if to prevent the young lady's leaving the room," the narrative makes the initial observation that he is behaving "playfully" (804). Emma responds to Tupman's advances with "half-demure, half-impudent" glances at him, suggesting her own complicity within the erotic exchange (465). However, these flirtations, despite their coy and comic representation, actually conceal an underlying assertion of class distinction and social power. The novel, and its middle-class male characters, construct the servants as expendable and exchangeable objects of desire. Throughout the rambling adventures of the Pickwickians, nameless servant girls appear briefly to bestow smiles and attention upon the men before melting gracefully out of the scene. Tupman happily chases the Wardles' chambermaid because the servant's desire poses little threat to the middle-class male; he has no intention of marrying a servant, and so her fickleness (unlike Rachael's) does not trouble him. When Bob Sawyer's advances are flatly rejected, the maidservant's slap to his face elicits no reaction from him, and the narrative blithely comments that he has merely been "deprived of the young lady's society" (804). The sexual desire of servants has significance only as long as they desire their masters and thus soothe middle-class male social and sexual anxieties. Any refusal to do so is either reconstructed as an exciting and enticing deferral of desire, as when Emma initially "rewarded" Tupman with "sundry pushings and scratchings" (139), or is simply ignored and forgotten, as with Bob Sawyer. The erotics of the master-servant relation thus finally reconfirm the power differential between them; flirtation is as much an articulation of social authority as it is of sexual desire.

As if to anticipate doubts about the exercise of social power, the novel also employs servants to develop strategies for the extra-marital expression of desire that do not involve the Pickwickians in coercive cross-class relationships. Servants help to map out spaces where the normal limits of bourgeois sexuality may be exceeded, although in deliberate and controlled ways. At the midway point of his adventures, Pickwick and his friends find themselves at Dingley Dell for the Christmas wedding of Mr. Trundle and Isabella Wardle. Sexual tension between Snodgrass and Emily and between Winkle and Arabella is running high, fueled by the excitement of another couple's wedding. As a counterpoint to the morning's wedding, the novel describes the evening's festivities in the kitchen, where family and friends gather together with the household servants. The Pickwickians hang a branch of mistletoe from the ceiling, which "instantaneously gave rise to a scene of general and most delightful struggling and confusion" (475). Here, in the servants' territory of the kitchen, the middle class allows unruly erotic energy to be released among its own members; Winkle, Arabella, Snodgrass, Emily, and the rest enjoy a brief but delicious moment of licensed pleasure. However, the sexual pandemonium is only apparently chaotic; in fact, the confusion of the scene is governed by particular rules designed to control the sudden eruption of desire. The rules are visible just beneath the surface of the delightful struggle: the young ladies "screamed and struggled, ran into corners, and threatened and remonstrated, and did everything but leave the room, until some of the less adventurous gentlemen were on the point of desisting, when they all at once found it useless to resist any longer, and submitted to be kissed with good grace" (475). The kissing is at once sanctioned and normalized within the strictly defined social space under the mistletoe.

The servants themselves are not confined within this ritualized space; Sam, "not being particular about the form of being under the mistletoe, kissed Emma and the other female servants, just as he caught them" (475). Against the background of this uninhibited servant sexuality, the novel establishes and asserts an implicit norm of middle-class sexual restraint, even as it provides a strategy of expressing, however fleetingly, middle-class sexual desire. This strategy repeats itself throughout the novel in a variety of forms—in the "snug and pleasant" flirtations of the Pickwickians and their ladies when crossing a stile (464), in the "many jokes about squeezing the ladies' sleeves" when the Pickwickians stow themselves into the Wardles' carriage (124), and so on. The squeezing of sleeves, touching of hands, and glimpsing of ankles are invariably accompanied by the nervous joking and professions of dismay which make erotic energy both conventional and tolerable. Employing the servant class as a foil, the novel articulates a middle-class sexuality characterized by the carefully restrained expenditure of erotic energy—a normalizing strategy that John Kucich has argued becomes the dominant mode of sexual expression in Dickens' work as a whole.

This strategy of containment is effective only so long as erotic energy does not overflow the channels designed for its expression. Pickwickian desire, however, often spills over these channels (witness the groping of housemaids) and requires recuperation elsewhere. With the help of that remarkable servant, Joe the fat boy, the novel constructs an alternative space in which middle-class male sexual desire may be displaced and expressed: the dinner table. Through Joe, the narrative explicitly associates sexual and alimentary appetite; he is frequently to be found "hanging fondly over a capon" or whatever dishes happen to grace the Pickwickian table (124–125). When dining with the pretty housemaid Mary, Joe ogles both her body and the food, apparently unable to distinguish between them; indeed, when he pays her a compliment on her looks, "there was enough of the cannibal in the young gentleman's eyes to render the compliment a doubtful one" (857). As Kincaid points out, Joe "does not distinguish between sexual contact and possession, nor between possession and consumption: to love is to eat" ("Fattening Up" 243).

The association between lust and gluttony allows the Pickwickians to indulge themselves without restraint in the pleasures of food and drink; at the dinner table, they can freely expend and express their own erotic energy without involving themselves in the dangers of sexual relationships. Houston, in arguing that the fat boy represents "displaced Pickwickian sexual desire," suggests that the novel rewrites erotic longings as hunger pangs in order to keep Pickwick innocent. Houston does note that this displacement both allays and enlarges Pickwickian sexual appetite, but she does not attend to the ways in which the rewriting of lust as hunger both alleviates male sexual anxiety and protects male social authority. Gluttony in the novel functions as a subli-mated and idealized sexual desire—a desire which takes food rather than women as its object and thus meets with no obstacle in satisfying itself. Again, we may turn to Joe for illustration of this Pickwickian principle of dis-placement:

> The fat boy, with elephantine playfulness, stretched out his arms [toward Mary] to ravish a kiss; but as it required no great agility to elude him, his fair enslaver had vanished before he closed them again; upon which the apathetic youth ate a pound or so of steak with a sentimental countenance, and fell fast asleep.
>
> (860)

At the very moment of frustration, sexual desire neatly converts itself into alimentary appetite, allowing Joe to satisfy himself without further denial or delay. Through this same principle, the Pickwickians find satisfaction for their own appetites, a satisfaction that excludes women and itself reaffirms the bonds between men, as they push themselves back from the table and light their ritual cigars.

Pickwickian servants are thus inextricably bound up with the erotic lives of their masters; the novel employs servants to develop and explore a variety of alternatives for expressing sexual desire outside of middle-class marital relations. Furthermore, servants are so involved with the sexuality of the middle-class characters that even those marital relations depend upon the intervention of valets and chambermaids. The novel asserts that servants pos-sess a thorough knowledge of their masters' and mistresses' affairs and de-sires: "There were a great many young ladies in a great many houses, the greater part whereof were shrewdly suspected by the male and female domes-tics to be deeply attached to somebody, or perfectly ready to become so, if opportunity offered" (636). Such knowledge allows the servants to act upon the behalf of their masters and mistresses, managing their various flirtations and assignations. As Sam says, he "only assisted natur'," having helped Winkle and Arabella meet secretly in the back garden of her aunt's house (758); for this reason, the old lady later accuses Sam of "skulking about my house, and endeavoring to entrap my servants to conspire against their mis-tress" (770). The happy couple also owes the housemaid Mary a debt of gratitude for arranging their elopement; Winkle acknowledges that "we couldn't possibly have done it without her assistance'' (758). Servants not only help initiate marital relations between their masters and mistresses; once that relation has been established, servants continue to mediate between both parties. Whenever the Potts quarrel, Mrs. Pott enlists her serving maid, Goodwin, "a young lady whose ostensible employment was to preside over her toilet, but who rendered herself useful in a variety of ways, and in none more so than in the particular department of constantly aiding and abetting her mistress in every wish and inclination opposed to the desires of the unhappy Pott" (320). Goodwin understands the sexual politics of marriage enough to manipulate discussion between Mr. and Mrs. Pott and give her mistress the upper hand; here, as throughout the novel, the servant presides over the sexual relations of the middle class.

While *The Pickwick Papers* thus grants servants certain kinds of license and authority in sexual matters, the novel also carefully restricts the power that such license and authority might afford housemaids and footmen. When Joe the fat boy glimpses Tupman and Rachael kissing in the garden, the sexual knowledge of servants becomes a threat to the couple; they fear that exposure of their erotic play will offend the moral sensibilities of the middle-class family. However, Joe does not share his knowledge with old Mrs. Wardle to gain some material advantage over her or the family; instead he informs her that he simply "wants to make [her] flesh creep" (180). This peculiar expression suggests that Joe desires only to communicate the erotic charge of the secret, not to exploit its social implications. His ignorance of the power of sexual knowledge becomes more explicit near the end of the novel, when he catches Snodgrass and Emily embracing. Their efforts to buy his silence initially confuse him, as "he looked rather puzzled at first to account for this sudden prepossession in his favour" (856); at length, he understands the significance of the secret only enough to give it promptly away with his nudges and winks at the dinner table. Joe does not recognize that such secrets can empower him; because his own sensual appetites are so completely satisfied, he fails to comprehend the anxiety and frustration of middle-class desire that would allow him to manipulate his betters. Joe's comic ignorance is only the most extreme example of the novel's blanket refusal to allow servants the social self-consciousness that would enable them to transmute sexual knowledge into material advantage.

Even if servants are less interested in the power than in the pleasure made available by desire, the novel nonetheless imposes one important prohibition on the expression of servant desire. We have already seen that female servants' desire for their masters bolsters certain assumptions central to middle-class male authority. However, the desire of a male servant for his mistress undermines that authority in crucial ways. More than threatening the moral purity and sexual chastity of the middle-class woman, the male servant's desire offers her an alternative outlet for expressing her own sexuality—a humiliating possibility for middle-class husbands. Furthermore, the male servant's desire brings middle-class and lower-class men into direct competition with each other, contact degrading to a middle-class suitor, even if he is ultimately successful. For these reasons, the novel introduces us, along with Sam, to a group of pretentious footmen at a Bath 'swarry', where the menservants divide up a leg of mutton and gossip about the ladies of the house. When one footman comments to another, that the mistress "leans very heavy on your shoulder when she gets in and out of the carriage," the first man agrees and notes that she has "refused one or two offers without any hobvus cause," nodding "as if there were more behind, which he could say if he liked, but was bound in honour to suppress" (613). The novel, however, quickly and thoroughly squelches their social affectations and sexual transgressions with the help of the sarcastic Sam, who muses, "I don't think I can do with anythin' under a female markis. I might take up with a young ooman o' large property as hadn't a title, if she made wery fierce love to me. Not else" (614). Sam's cutting wit throughout this scene deflates the pretensions of the Bath footmen; the novel thus keeps servant desire in its proper place and ensures that sex below stairs continues to serve the interests of patriarchal authority above stairs.

THE SECRET LIFE OF MR. PICKWICK

The Pickwick Papers, then, offers its readers two complementary pleasures: the indulgence in patriarchal anxieties and misogynistic fantasies about middle-class marital relations; and the exploration of alternative structures of desire grounded within the novel's servant class and extended to the Pickwickians. At this point, it should be clear that *The Pickwick Papers*, despite its innocent reputation, is one of the sexiest of Victorian novels; its famously freewheeling narrative and haphazard subplots are held together by an underlying obsession with desire and its effects. What then are we to make of the mysteriously celibate hero at the center of the novel—Pickwick himself? While even he can be guilty of "patting the rosy cheeks of the female servants in a most patriarchal manner" (214), Pickwick's general exemption from both the normalizing courtship rituals and the philandering with servants gives rise to the ideal of Pickwickian innocence expounded by most literary criticism of the novel.

Having described the novel's anxieties about sexual desire and social authority, as well as having outlined the novel's strategies of displacing, containing, and expressing erotic energy, I now want to complicate and challenge the received notion of Pickwickian innocence. There is no doubt that Pickwick remains sexually innocent through the novel; his comically abstract theories of courtship (406), his fear of women who flirt with him (773), and his mortification at being seen in his nightcap (390) all attest to that innocence. Much of the novel's comedy depends upon his ignorance of sexual innuendo and meaning. Nearly all of Pickwick's friends at one time or another comment on their leader's celibate lifestyle; Tupman speaks for all of them when he states that Pickwick is fortunate to be "placed far beyond the reach of many mortal frailties and weaknesses which ordinary people cannot overcome" (212).[4] Free from the burden of desire, incapable of being "suspected of any latent designs" (470), Pickwick himself suggests that his innocence goes so far as to contain and even neutralize the dangers of erotic energy. In defending his decision to assist Winkle and Arabella in their rendezvous, Pickwick claims that "my presence would remove any slight colouring of impropriety that it might otherwise have had" (770). No wonder that Pickwick's innocence has become such a critical cliché; by the end of this nine-hundred-page novel, the reader has been fairly brainwashed into hailing him as a philanthropic eunuch.

In many ways, the figure of Pickwick is the ultimate fantasy of middle-class male subjectivity—an independent bachelor who not only is principled, respectable, and wealthy, but who also remains blissfully free of the dangers and frustrations of bourgeois sexuality. One might argue—following Kincaid and Glavin—that the novel offers us Pickwick's specifically regressive pleasures in exchange for the anxieties of middle-class marriage. The novel, however, does not unequivocally endorse Pickwick's celibacy; his innocence and ignorance are parodied too often for Pickwickian regression to be considered a model of sexual health. Rather than privileging Pickwick's oral and auto-erotic urges as the end of sexuality in the novel, we must locate his idealized celibacy within a broader sexual economy implicated within the social relations of the middle-class community.

The structural significance of Pickwickian innocence becomes apparent when one evaluates the central relationship of the novel—the master and his valet. Side by side, through thick and thin, Pickwick and Sam stand in complementary relation to one another, each serving as a foil on either side of the novel's standard of middle-class sexual behavior. Sam's unruly libido overflows the limits of those normalizing channels, as we have seen, allowing the reader to identify with and sublimate his pleasures. Those pleasures, however, are always only potentially transgressive. Sam's erotic urges never threaten the stolid middle-class community because the novel limits his desire to lower-class female objects; his nods and winks are never directed at the Pickwickians' ladyfriends. For this reason, Pickwick, when hiring Sam, can ignore or at least overlook the one "amiable indiscretion, in which an assistant housemaid had equally participated," in the history of Sam's conduct (236).

Sam's sexuality is always safely expressed and employed; his dalliances pose no threat to Pickwick's middle-class integrity or authority. On the other hand, Pickwick's extreme abstinence at once corrects the excesses of his valet as well as affords protection from jilts and widders. Oscillating between these twin poles of indulgence and continence, the novel locates and maintains an implicit bourgeois norm of libidinal thrift.

From this point of view, Pickwickian innocence (with its regressive pleasures) does not constitute a genuine alternative to orthodox middle-class sexuality so much as it helps to test and define its limits. Houston suggests as much when she argues that the novel confines and subsumes Pickwick's dangerously self-centered appetites safely within the boundaries of other peoples' conventional marriages. Pickwick thus "ends young and wedded—vicariously and voyeuristically—to the sexual desires of all the newlyweds" (Houston 752). Although Pickwick does confess that "the happiness of young people . . . has ever been the chief pleasure of my life" (*Pickwick* 893), Houston's analysis assumes that the novel will tolerate only the expression of an orderly heterosexual desire. We must also ask whether Pickwickian innocence actually camouflages a more enigmatic and complicated sexuality that may exceed the boundaries laid down by bourgeois society.

Pickwick appears sexually innocent only if innocence is conceived in strictly heterosexual terms; by enlarging the field of relations in which desire operates, we may begin to call his innocence into question. Here, I am indebted to Sedgwick's definition and analysis of male homosocial desire in English fiction. Sedgwick genders the Girardian triangle of rivalry and desire, arguing that men express their homosocial desire for one another through their traffic in women. That traffic may take the form of competition or exchange, but in either case, the shared female object allows male heterosexual desire to be recuperated as male homosocial desire, reinforcing patriarchal authority. The strength of Sedgwick's argument is the continuity she demonstrates between male heterosexuality, homosociality, and homosexuality—the places where these categories meet and overlap, the ways in which they determine each other's operations, and the levels on which those operations both cooperate and compete with one another. Thus, she can describe bonds between men as being at once homophobic and homosocial, or erotic and filial, and so on, depending upon the particular, historically determined, ideological constructions of those categories.

Sedgwick is most interested in the Gothic paranoia of the later Dickens, where the conflation of sexual desire and male homosocial bonds produces the extreme homophobia of the text; but even in the sunny world of *The Pickwick Papers*, which according to Sedgwick depicts an "encompassing homosocial love rendered in the absence of homophobia" (165), bonds between men are explicitly and powerfully charged with erotic energy. The erotic undercurrent is most visible within the dynamics of the duel; through the ritual of duelling, the violent sexual tension which arises from competition between two men for a single woman is recuperated as a positive energy that affirms the bonds between the men. The duel itself must be called off at the last moment, of course, before real violence is done, but not before the conflict has brought the two men closer together. There are several such aborted duels in the novel, most of them involving the pseudo-sportsman, Winkle; in each case, the woman drops out of the erotic equation, and the men are left to resolve their differences, converting destructive heterosexual tension into constructive homosocial bonds. Thus, Winkle and Slammer part on terms of good fellowship, as do Winkle and Dowler.[5] The fundamentally erotic nature of the duel is best illustrated by the rules given to Winkle before his contest with Slammer. The duel requires "a secluded place, where the affair can be conducted without fear of interruption" (96), in the interests of mutual "satisfaction" (101)—a description which might equally apply to a lovers' rendezvous. Such an arrangement is the most formal manifestation of the novel's larger economy of eroticized physical violence between men—grabbing each other by the shirt, holding each other around the waist, shoving from behind, and landing punches to the body and face. The erotic energy coursing through these descriptions of physical contact is finally diffused through the frequent shaking of hands among the men, accompanied by "protestations of eternal friendship" (631), a gesture that reasserts the integrity of the male community.

In this context, the male bond between Pickwick and Sam must be reevaluated as the central element within the novel's elaboration of male homoerotics. We have already seen how Pickwick's hiring of Sam is confused with a marriage proposal; from the beginning, then, their relationship depends upon the conflation of heterosexual and homosocial ties. With the help of the servant Mary, the novel ensures that the master-servant bond remains erotically charged; in Sedgwick's terms, Sam's courtship of Mary is not so much an expression of heterosexual desire for her as it is an expression of homosocial desire for Pickwick. When Sam composes a "'walentine' for the pretty housemaid, he signs it, "Your love-sick/Pickwick" (543). Sam's 'werse' doubles and aligns his own desire and interests with that of his master; in becoming a third term between the two men, Mary allows them to assert their bond with each other. This Girardian dynamic surfaces most visibly near the end of the novel, as each man employs Mary to express his devotion and commitment to the other. Pickwick, with a faltering voice, addresses Sam:

> "I wish to free you from the restraint which your present position imposes upon you, and *to mark my sense of your fidelity and many excellent qualities*, by enabling you to marry this girl at once, and to earn an independent livelihood

for yourself and your family.''   (886; my italics)

Pickwick offers Mary to Sam as a means of displaying his own affection for the loyal valet; however, never to be outdone, Sam refuses the offer, declaring that his relationship to Pickwick is more important to him than marriage with the housemaid. In this way, Mary is batted back and forth between the two men as they pledge their devotion to each other.

The erotics of Pickwick's and Sam's relationship surface most startlingly when another servant, Job Trotter, confides to Sam: ''I could serve that gentleman [Pickwick] until I fell down dead at his feet.'' Sam reacts jealously, retorting, ''None o' that, I say, young feller. . . . No man serves him but me'' (734). Sam follows that retort with his famous encomium of Pickwick as an ''angel in tights and gaiters'' and defies Job to ''let me see the man as wenturs to tell me he knows a better vun'' (734). Confronted by a potential rival for Pickwick's attention, Sam displays all the possessiveness of other jealous lovers in the novel and adopts their rhapsodic style of praise. In evaluating this intense emotional bond between Pickwick and Sam, Marcus has outlined the ways in which master and servant exchange filial and paternal roles (30–44); similarly but more significantly, the two men are also alternately feminized within their relationship. Sam serves as the devoted and obedient attendant to his master Pickwick, nursing him through sickness, playing the part of the domestic angel better than any woman in the novel; Pickwick often acts the vulnerable ingenue, depending upon the worldly Sam to negotiate their way through the city and its corruption. The mapping of gender in their relationship becomes so complex that we should not be surprised, finally, to hear an echo of the marriage service in the novel's last few words: ''Every year, [Pickwick] repairs to a large family merry-making at Mr.Wardle's; on this, as on all other occasions, he is invariably attended by the faithful Sam, between whom and his master there exists a steady and reciprocal attachment which nothing but death will terminate'' (898).

Till death do them part: Victorian novels are famous for ending with a marriage, and *The Pickwick Papers* is no exception. The novel concludes with the homosocial marriage of two men whose emotional ties transcend without rejecting the social hierarchy and whose commitment to one another cannot be damaged by rivalry over women. This male bond which affirms class difference even as it neutralizes class conflict and which excludes female desire is *the* patriarchal fantasy at the center of the novel. Having described the threat of sexual desire and detailed the dangers of married life for middle-class men, the novel subsumes the marriage relation within the master-servant relation, allowing Pickwick to enjoy all the benefits of marriage without any of its attendant anxieties or frustrations. Glavin has objected that reading *The Pickwick Papers* ''as a closet homosocial romance tends, ultimately, to

reinscribe the erotic categories on which conventional bourgeois sexual sce-
narios depend" (11). But this is precisely the central strategy of the novel:
to develop alternatives to normative middle-class sexuality without violating
the ideological order—including its erotic categories—that underwrites middle-class social authority. *The Pickwick Papers* represents nothing less than
the struggle to redefine marriage apart from women—to replace that unstable
heterosexual relation with a safer, stronger male homosocial bond. Furthermore, because that bond maintains a power differential in terms of class
(rather than gender), Pickwick and Sam do not engage in the competition for
social status and prestige that generates the violence between middle-class
men in the novel's opening scene. Working-class politics have no place in
Pickwickian England: class difference is a source of social harmony, not
tension.

However, the homoerotic component of the master-servant relation necessarily generates certain anxieties. It is here that Sedgwick's assumption of an
"absence of homophobia" in the novel must be qualified. For in order to
preserve and promote the intensity of the bond between Pickwick and
Sam—an intensity that depends upon erotic energy—the novel must also
protect their relationship from any hint of homosexuality that would immediately and irrevocably subvert the patriarchal homosocial fantasy. Any strong
emotional bond between men is vulnerable to suspicion unless that bond is
carefully articulated within a socially sanctioned and institutional relation,
such as the family, or, in this case, the master-servant relation. Because it is
so difficult to categorize, the bond between Alfred Jingle and Job Trotter
causes a great deal of confusion and anxiety in the novel. No one can be sure
if the two men are master and servant or not; Sam refers to Jingle as "[f]riend
or master, or whatever he is" (308), and Lowten, the legal assistant, similarly
terms Job "that servant, or friend, or whatever he is" (839). As a result of
this confusion, Job's devotion in following Jingle to South America elicits
the derision of Lowten, who calls Job "downright sneaking" (840). Lowten
continues his diatribe:

> "Friendship's a very good thing in its way: we are all very friendly and comfort-
> able at the Stump, for instance, over our grog, where every man pays for
> himself; but damn hurting yourself for anybody else, you know! No man should
> have more than two attachments—the first, to number one, and the second to
> the ladies; that's what I say—ha! ha!"   (840)

Lowten's suspicion of male friendship, his homophobic response to any "attachment" not easily classified as either self-serving or heterosexual, is what
must be deflected away from Pickwick's and Sam's attachment to each other.
For that reason, the novel foregrounds the master-servant dynamics between
the two men. Pickwick is always careful both to rebuke the irrepressible Sam

when he forgets his proper place and to clarify the nature of their relationship when necessary. At one point, Peter Magnus wonders aloud whether Sam is a friend of Pickwick, who replies, "Not exactly a friend. . . . . The fact is, he is my servant, but I allow him to take a good many liberties" (381).

Furthermore, the polarization of Pickwick's and Sam's sexual attitudes also conceals the homoerotics central to the novel's fantasy of male community and homosocial bonds. By emphasizing Pickwick's inviolable celibacy and Sam's rampant heterosexuality, the novel simultaneously locates an implicit heterosexual norm between them *and* diverts attention away from their alternative homoerotic relation. The appearance of "Two sturdy little boys" (897) in Pickwick's back garden at the end of the novel accomplishes precisely these twin objectives. Sam's fruitful marriage to Mary not only affords Pickwick the luxury of vicarious procreation but also camouflages the homoerotic bond between servant and master. Sedgwick's perception of the absence of homophobia in the novel is, in fact, the calculated effect of its homophobic strategies of displacement and effacement.[6]

The critical adulation of Pickwickian innocence attests to the success of those strategies; like Pickwick himself, the novel has long managed to avoid being "suspected of any latent designs." The sexual politics of *The Pickwick Papers* come into focus only once one has descended below stairs and thoroughly interrogated the cozy and comfortable relations between masters and servants. At the close of the novel, the lights go down on a newly chartered Pickwickian community—what J. Hillis Miller calls "Pickwick's little heavenly city" (32) of friends and family. The pretension and violence exhibited by the Pickwick Club in the first chapter has now been tempered by the benevolence and modesty of Pickwick and his followers. No longer does sexual desire threaten the authority or frustrate the members of this kinder, gentler patriarchal order, for at its center resides a bond impervious to any such threat or frustration—the idealized union of master and valet. No wonder that such a union would have held a particular fascination for the young Charles Dickens. The first number of *The Pickwick Papers* was published on March 31, 1836; two days later, on April 2, Dickens himself became a married man.

NOTES

1. Critics who argue that Pickwick's innocent character changes over the course of the novel include James R. Kincaid ("Education"), Robert Patten, and, most famously, W. H. Auden.
2. Garrett Stewart makes a similar point: "So before we learn any other meaning for 'Pickwickian,' we understand it stylistically, so to speak, as a kind of verbal

nullification, a retroactive euphemism under whose aegis words are able to retreat from their own consequences" (26). I am more interested in the political implications of such a gesture than is Stewart.

3. Here, as in other Dickens novels, the authority of the law stands apart from the authority of the patriarchal order; unlike the linguistic mobility of the Pickwickian point of view, the linguistic mobility of the law is employed to perpetuate the legal institution itself, regardless of the damage inflicted upon the male community.

4. See also Winkle's testimony that Pickwick has never considered marriage (569); Perker's and Wardle's amusement at Pickwick's ignorance of sexual intrigue (843, 853); and the ladies' repudiation of the idea that Pickwick might marry at the end of the novel (891).

5. That the duel is an exclusively male enterprise, conducted finally without reference to the individual woman involved, is demonstrated by Miss Witherfield's meddling in the clash between Pickwick and Magnus. In reporting the duel to the authorities, Miss Witherfield violates her passive role within the erotic triangle and upsets its delicate structure, preventing the necessary movement from confrontation to resolution. Significantly, the novel describes such interference as foolish and alarmist; Miss Witherfield's agency here is ultimately less empowering than it is degrading.

6. The last line of the first edition of *The Pickwick Papers* reads, "which nothing but death will *sever*" (my italics)—a more compromising verb than "terminate."

WORKS CITED

Auden, W. H. "Dingley Dell and the Fleet." *Selected Essays*. London: Faber and Faber, 1964. 164–89.

Dickens, Charles. *The Pickwick Papers*. Harmondsworth: Penguin, 1986.

Engel, Elliot, and Margaret King. *The Victorian Novel Before Victoria*. London: Macmillan, 1984.

Glavin, John. "Pickwick on the Wrong Side of the Door." *Dickens Studies Annual* 22 (1993): 1–19.

Houston, Gail Turley. "Broadsides at the Board: Collations of *Pickwick Papers* and *Oliver Twist*." *SEL* 31 (1991): 735–55.

Kincaid, James R. "The Education of Mr. Pickwick." *Nineteenth-Century Fiction* 24 (1969): 127–41.

———. "Fattening Up on Pickwick." *Novel* 25 (1992): 235–44.

Kucich, John. *Excess and Restraint in the Novels of Charles Dickens*. Athens: U of Georgia P, 1981.

Marcus, Steven. *Dickens: From Pickwick to Dombey*. London: Chatto and Windus, 1965.

Marlow, James E. "Pickwick's Writing: Propriety and Language." *ELH* 52 (1985): 939–63.

Miller, J. Hillis. *Charles Dickens: The World of His Novels*. Cambridge: Harvard UP, 1958.

Patten, Robert L. "The Art of *Pickwick*'s Interpolated Tales." *ELH* 34 (1967): 349–66.

Robbins, Bruce. *The Servant's Hand: English Fiction from Below*. New York: Columbia UP, 1986.

Sedgwick, Eve Kosofsky. *Between Men: English Literature and Male Homosocial Desire*. New York: Columbia UP, 1985.

Stallybrass, Peter, and Allon White. *The Politics and Poetics of Transgression*. Ithaca: Cornell UP, 1986.

Stewart, Garrett. *Dickens and the Trials of Imagination*. Cambridge: Harvard UP, 1974.

Todd, Barbara J. "The Remarrying Widow: A Stereotype Reconsidered." *Women in English Society 1500–1800*. Ed. Mary Prior. London: Methuen, 1985. 54–92.

Playing Around With Melodrama: The Crummles Episodes in *Nicholas Nickleby*

Tore Rem

It is a long time since J. Hillis Miller first presented the idea of the Crummles sections of *Nicholas Nickleby* as a sort of parody of the rest of the novel (90).[1] Since then many critics have supported this view but most of them have left it as a general assertion. The only attempt to illustrate what this actually means is by Michael Slater, who uses about fifteen lines of his introduction to the Penguin edition for a couple of examples.[2] No one at all has attempted to explain or describe what such a conception of these parts of *Nicholas Nickleby* adds to the book as a whole.

A couple of critics have, however—in important studies of the theatrical aspects of *Nicholas Nickleby*—made comments touching on what I am about to discuss. Considering whether the Crummles troupe adds a carnivalesque quality to the work or not, Paul Schlicke claims that "the actors do not contribute to an overall design" (86), while Joseph Litvak states that "any argument for the 'carnivalesque' at all is itself misleading" (114). The reasons for these arguments—the "provincial remoteness" (Litvak 115) of the actors and that "Dickens deports Crummles out of England before the novel is ended" (Schlicke 85)—are in my opinion not very convincing. Schlicke's and Litvak's views are based on the idea that plot is the only important structural device in *Nicholas Nickleby*. It might be enough to point to Chesterton's observation that it is characteristic of Dickens that "his atmospheres are more important than his stories" to indicate another approach (xxi), and my central argument here is that the relationship between parody and melodrama constitutes a different sort of organizing principle from a plot- or character-centered one. The Crummles episodes should therefore not be dismissed as unimportant to the novel because of their separateness in the plot or the lack of interaction between the actors and other important characters. There is, however, no room for a treatment of the carnivalesque qualities of the novel in this study.

It seems to be generally acknowledged that theatricality is a central concern or theme in the novel. Slater states that "theatricality and roleplaying are the living heart of *Nicholas Nickleby*" (15) and this point is also important to the studies by Litvak and Schlicke. Theatricality is not limited to Crummles's company, it seems to affect everyone and everything. If this is the case, it must be a matter of course that the most theatrical episodes of *Nicholas Nickleby* should be related to the other parts of the book. *Nicholas Nickleby* is, as I see, permeated by an attitude of self-reflexivity and play-acting. We also come quickly to realize that the theatricality of the actors is not in any way limited to their stage characters. They so conscientiously play the part of being actors that, like the first-tragedy man, they black themselves all over (724). A distinct self-consciousness in the actors as private individuals is present all along, and this strong self-awareness leads to great performances when the company mingles with society such as in the wedding ceremony (401–02) and the farewell scene (478).[3] This theater knows no footlights, to echo Bakhtin's writings on the carnival.

Parody is a theoretical concept which is often used in a confusing way, or misused, by critics. It is not to be employed interchangeably with satire. One distinction has to be made clear to begin with: parody (in literature) always has another literary object—be it another specific text, a style of writing, or a genre—as its target.[4] When I consider the Crummles parts a parody of the rest of *Nicholas Nickleby*, I think of them as a parody of the mode of melodrama or as self-parody (because so much of *Nicholas Nickleby* is melodramatic). This is not to be confused with the satire on the Yorkshire schools through the portrayals of Mr. Squeers and his academic establishment, which is aimed at the "external world".

Through its extravagant play-acting on and off stage, the Crummles troupe constitutes only part of what I find to be an overall pattern of melodrama versus parody in *Nicholas Nickleby*. Parodic alternatives to melodramatic episodes are amply provided throughout the novel. The parts in which the actors perform do, however, supply concentrated examples of parody. My intention in this article is to provide a reading of the Crummles section by pointing to scenes and incidents in the rest of the novel which can be said to be commented on by the parody of the Crummles sections. It must be remembered that this is only one among many possible readings, since I primarily focus my attention on the melodramatic trait which is parodied in a scene with the troupe, and then try to hold up a corresponding serious melodramatic scene from elsewhere in the novel. By parodying melodrama Dickens in fact also parodies other parts and elements of his own novel.

The actors in *Nicholas Nickleby* are introduced when Nicholas and Smike happen to encounter Mr. Vincent Crummles and his two sons at a roadside inn. The very first impression Nicholas receives is of the rehearsal of a combat (352–54) between "a couple of boys, one of them very tall and the other very short" (352). After a long struggle it is "the short sailor" (354) who eventually crushes what seemed his superior. When the proud father asks for the opinion of the spectators, it is interesting to note Nicholas's answer:

> "You won't see such boys as those very often, I think," said Mr Crummles.
> Nicholas assented—observing, that if they were a little better match—
> "Match!" cried Mr Crummles.
> "I mean if they were a little more of a size," said Nicholas, explaining himself.
> "Size!" repeated Mr Crummles; "why, it's the very essence of the combat that there should be a foot or two between them. How are you to get up the sympathies of the audience in a legitimate manner, if there isn't a little man contending against a great one—unless there's at least five to one, and we haven't hands enough for that business in our company."
> "I see," replied Nicholas. "I beg your pardon. That didn't occur to me, I confess."
> "It's the main point," said Mr Crummles.   (355)

In a similar way, the main plot of *Nicholas Nickleby* is constructed so as to "get up the sympathies" of the readers of the novel. The whole combat we witness can be read as a brief and stylized exaggerated version of Kate and Nicholas's encounter with villains in a real and wicked world. In a purely realistic novel, they would have little or no chance of success, and when Nicholas questions the equality of the match he can obviously not imagine that the short sailor in a way is himself. Melodrama, with characters who are "helpless and unfriended" (Vicinus 128) and with unrecognized virtue as a major motif, builds on the David versus Goliath pattern.[5] This trait is brought out when "the short sailor" is said to be "the moral character evidently, for he always had the best of it" (354).The victorious end that both Kate and Nicholas experience is a distinct feature of melodrama (Calhoun-French 492–A).[6] The fact that in this mode those who seem to be the weakest and most unfortunate characters actually perform the greatest and most noble deeds is parodied in an observation made by the narrator during Nicholas's last rendezvous with the company: "It is observable that when people upon the stage are in any strait involving the very last extremity of weakness and exhaustion, they invariably perform feats of strength requiring great ingenuity and muscular power" (725).

Rivalry and duels fuelled on envy and a wish for revenge are motifs as old as Menelaus and Paris in European literature. In the scene we are about to consider, the object of envy is not Helen but Thalia. Because of the clearly polarized structure of such situations, rivalry is very central to melodrama.[7]

The actor Lenville is envious because of Nicholas's unexpected success in the theatrical profession, and challenges him. The parallels between pages 457–59 and dramatic incidents like the confrontation scenes between Nicholas and Squeers (e.g., 220–23) and between Nicholas and Ralph (e.g., 322–28 and 813–19) are, in several ways, striking. The real reason why Mr. Lenville challenges Nicholas and wants to win, is, in Mr. Folair's words, that if he does not, "there wouldn't be any romance about it, and he wouldn't be favorably known" (456). This is also very important to Nicholas's role in his noble "duels" with Squeers, Hawk, Gride, and Ralph: he needs a certain flavor of romance about his actions to be favorably known by the reader as the hero of the work. Lenville receives Nicholas "with his severest stage face" and he is "whistling defiance" (457). When Ralph "receives" Nicholas rather unexpectedly on the sudden return of the latter from the country, the uncle is described in similar terms: "He stood fixed and immoveable with folded arms, regarding his nephew with a scowl of deadly hatred" (322). Lenville "fold[s] his arms" (458) in the same manner.

Mr. Lenville is an experienced villain, and knows what weapons to use. When Nicholas has saluted him, the actor "laughed a scornful laugh, and made some general remark touching the natural history of puppies" (457), and afterwards he exclaims: "They shall not protect ye—boy!" (458). Ralph on his part, "withdrawing his eyes with a great show of disdain," uses the word "boy" to depreciate Nicholas when they first meet, and this is commented on by the narrator: "This word is much used as a term of reproach by elderly gentlemen towards their juniors, probably with the view of deluding society into the belief that if they could be young again, they wouldn't on any account" (84). Like Lenville, Ralph rarely expresses more than "a half smile" (85), and he, too, communicates scorn through "artful insinuation" and "well-considered sarcasm" (326). Lenville's first impression has, however, not made a sufficient impact, and he proceeds to call his antagonist "slave" (457) and to pronounce: "Object of my scorn and hatred [. . .] I hold ye in contempt" (458). As a reaction to this last elevated expression, Nicholas starts to laugh. When comparing this to other situations and examples of melodramatic rhetoric in the novel, it is odd that Nicholas does not laugh more often. Or rather, does he not realize that in a very real sense he is laughing at himself too?

In a confrontation with Hawk, Nicholas renounces him by saying that "you are a base and spiritless scoundrel! . . . and shall be proclaimed so to the world" (496). Ralph, on his part, once states that "I speak plainly . . . because I feel strongly" (715). The rhetoric in scenes of confrontation reflects, in Peter Brooks's terms, "the desire to express all" (4). Nicholas speaks as plainly as Ralph in this respect. This is his exclamation to Ralph and Gride after Mr Bray's death:

"Aye!" said Nicholas, extending his disengaged hand in the air, "hear what he says. That both your debts are paid in the one great debt of nature—that the bond due today at twelve is now waste paper—that your contemplated fraud shall be discovered yet—that your schemes are known to man, and overthrown by Heaven—wretches, that he defies you both to do your worst".   (818)

Nicholas prefers to refer to himself in the third person, which heightens the elevated effect. He even extends "his disengaged hand in the air" just like Lenville is "flourishing his right arm" (457). The actor also makes use of other physical expressions such as "two looks" that "express defiance on the stage" and he takes to the uttermost his expressive vocabulary of grimaces when he "treated Nicholas to that expression of face with which, in melodramatic performances, he was in the habit of regarding the tyrannical kings when they said, 'Away with him to the deepest dungeon beneath the castle moat' " (458). "Nicholas with his eyes darting fire" (815) provides a good equivalent to Lenville's expression, and whereas Nicholas would want to rescue rather than capture people in the claustrophobic settings of the gothic novel, he still uses the same rhetoric as Lenville's tyrannical king when he calls Dotheboys "this foul den" (222).[8]

Unlike Paris, Nicholas does not need to be removed by Aphrodite to get out of the duel. After Lenville has approached him "in a very stately manner," he soon finds himself in a very different state because Nicholas "without the smallest discomposure, knock[s] him down" (458). This actuates the last phase of this parody: Mrs. Lenville, "uttering a piercing scream threw herself upon the body." The exceedingly moving proof of her affection even makes the body exclaim that "this is affecting!" (459). Lenville then proceeds to "draw . . . the back of his hand across his eyes" (459). The effect of this gesture is much the same as that of the scene where the false parent Snawley, in a desperate attempt to mobilize paternal emotion for Smike, "nodded his head, and wiped his eyes; the first slightly, the last violently" (682). Mr. Lenville, "the father that is yet to be" (459), is, however, melted by the screams of the weaker sex and apologizes "scowling upwards" (ibid.). This villain has, like Ralph, been "beaten at every point" (882), and yet shows no true contrition.

When considering Mrs. Lenville's demonstrations of grief, a parallel from another duel in *Nicholas Nickleby* comes to mind. The struggle between the goodness of the Cheeryble brothers and the evil of Mr. Bray concerning Madeline is brought to an end, and Mr. Bray's plans are "overthrown by Heaven" (818) when he falls down dead (an incident as convenient as Mrs. Clennam's house falling down in *Little Dorrit*). Madeline first utters "a most apalling and terrific scream" and then "scream succeeded scream" (815). When Nicholas enters the room he finds Bray's "daughter clinging to the body" (817). My point here is not that this is ridiculous—the young girl has an adequate reason for expressing her grief—but it is nevertheless a conventional melodramatic reaction. These particular situations and stock reactions are parodied in Mrs. Lenville's behavior in the Lenville episode. It is similar to a delightful death scene in Jane Austen's epistolary *Love and Friendship*. Here is Laura's version of what occurred after she and her friend found their husbands dying:

> Sophia shrieked and fainted on the ground—I screamed and instantly ran mad. We remained thus mutually deprived of our senses some minutes, and on regaining them were deprived of them again.
>
> For an hour and a quarter did we continue in this unfortunate situation—Sophia fainting every moment and I running mad as often.   (119)

Dickens was not the first to ridicule conventional over-reactions in popular literature, but alongside his parodies he also depicts how "the insensible girl" Madeline is carried off from the scene by our hero in a strictly "melodramatic" fashion (817). The element of performance in the Lenville episode is finally highlighted by Nicholas "bowing slightly to the spectators as he walk[s] out" after having broken Mr. Lenville's ash stick in a decently melodramatic manner (459). It is as if Nicholas wants to be applauded for his melodramatic performance turned parody.

There are two plays or spectacles in the Crummles sections that are given in detail.[9] The first is "Nicholas' play" as he describes it (375–76) and as it is performed (390–92), the second is fully reported on pages 378–79. I want to follow the order in which different melodramatic elements are introduced into the plays, and point out various episodes from elsewhere in the novel in connection with each trait discussed. Let us start with Nicholas's description of the new play which he simply is to translate from French to English. He receives a clear answer from the manager when being uncertain about his inventiveness in "writing dramas": "Invention! what the devil's that got to do with it!" (371). Still, the outpouring of creative absurdity is so powerful that nothing but a long quotation can do this play justice:

> "What do you mean to do for me, old fellow?" asked Mr Lenville, poking the struggling fire with his walking-stick, and afterwards wiping it on the skirt of his coat. "Anything in the gruff and grumble way?"
>
> "You turn your wife and child out of doors," said Nicholas; "and in a fit of rage and jealousy stab your eldest son in the library."
>
> "Do I though" exclaimed Mr Lenville. "That's very good business."
>
> "After which," said Nicholas, "you are troubled with remorse till the last act, and then you make up your mind to destroy yourself. But just as you are raising the pistol to your head, a clock strikes—ten."
>
> "I see," cried Mr Lenville. "Very good."
>
> "You pause," said Nicholas, "you recollect to have heard a clock strike ten in your infancy. The pistol falls from your hand—you are overcome—you burst into tears, and become a virtuous and exemplary character for ever afterwards."

"Capital!" said Mr Lenville: "that's a sure card, a sure card. Get the curtain down with a touch of nature like that, and it'll be a triumphant success."

"Is there anything good for me?" inquired Mr Folair, anxiously.

"Let me see," said Nicholas. "You play the faithful and attached servant; you are turned out of doors with the wife and child."

"Always coupled with that infernal phenomenon," sighed Mr Folair: "and we go into poor lodgings, where I won't take any wages, and talk sentiment, I suppose?"

[. . .]

"Why, isn't it obvious?" reasoned Mr Lenville. [. . .] "You get the distressed lady, and the little child, and the attached servant, into the poor lodgings, don't you?—Well, look here. The distressed lady sinks into a chair, and buries her face in her pocket-handkerchief—'What makes you weep, mama?' says the child. 'Don't weep, mama, or you'll make me weep too'—'And me!' says the faithful servant, rubbing his eyes with his arm. 'What can we do to raise your spirits, dear mama?' says the little child. 'Aye, what can we do?' says the faithful servant. 'Oh, Pierre! says the distressed lady; ''Would that I could shake off these painful thoughts: '—'Try, ma'am, try,' says the faithful servant; 'rouse yourself, ma'am; be amused.'—'I will,' says the lady, 'I will learn to suffer with fortitude. Do you remember that dance, my honest friend, which, in happier days, you practised with this sweet angel? It never failed to calm my spirits then. Oh! let me see it once again before I die!'—There it is cue for the band, *before I die*,—and off they go. That's the regular thing; isn't it, Tommy?"

"That's it," replied Mr Folair. "The distressed lady, overpowered by old recollections, faints at the end of the dance, and you close in with a picture."

(375–76)

The very first element introduced into the play can be seen as an exaggerated version of what happens later on in the novel if we consider Ralph *in loco parentis* for Nicholas and Kate: "'You turn your wife and child out of doors,' said Nicholas; 'and in a fit of rage and jealousy stab your eldest son in the library' " (375). In the main plot, Ralph does really want to get rid of his family. He makes Kate and her mother move out from Miss La Creevy to a "deserted mansion" (197), and his many attempts at humiliating Nicholas, for instance by sending him to Squeers or by taking Smike away from him (and Ralph's schemes are at least part of the reason for Smike's death), make up attempts at a "stabbing in the library." The melodramatic rage and jealousy involved is evident from Ralph's thoughts:

I couldn't hate him more. Let me but retaliate upon him, by degrees however slow; let me but begin to get the better of him, let me but turn the scale, and I can bear it. (838)

When my brother was such as he . . . the first comparisons were drawn between us—always in my disfavour. *He* was open, liberal, gallant, gay; *I* a crafty hunks of cold and stagnant blood, with no passion but love of saving, and no spirit beyond a thirst for gain. I recollected it well when I first saw this whipster; but I remember it better now.   (524)

Like Ralph, the character in the play also makes up his mind to take his own life in the last act, but otherwise their stories are different: in a powerful emotional scene—caused by the vague memory of a clock striking ten at a crucial moment in the past—the would-be suicide in an instant decides to "become a virtuous and exemplary character for ever afterwards" (375). Our villain is also confronted with his past in the end—the memories of "his own child" Smike flock upon him (903)—but he chooses the destructive solution and hangs himself. The dark cloud that follows Ralph on his way to his death (902) is, however, another example of the "hypersignificant signs" of melodrama (Brooks 126). The absurd links of cause and effect in the play highlight the irrationality of this device. The episode in the main plot in which Brooker turns up at Smike's deathbed has a similar fantastic effect (861). The incredible event creates a blur between dream and reality, and it sums up and rounds off the boy's pitiful life. In his very last hours he sees the person who took him to Squeers's establishment years ago. Through the use of these melodramatic signs a legible universe is displayed. A life that has order and meaning is communicated by showing this structured reality below the surface. An event in the novel that clearly illustrates this melodramatic structure occurs when Nicholas arrives at the hotel where he overhears Sir Mulberry Hawk et co. talking about his sister. He is "strongly attracted to the hotel, in part by curiosity, and in part by some odd mixture of feelings which he would have been troubled to define" (491). There is no doubt that there is a clear and willed meaning attached to the vague feelings: good is to confront evil. Nicholas's emotions are instruments in leading him to what is already determined to happen. A final very explicit example of these signs is Bray's dream foreshadowing his own death (812).

"The faithful and attached servant" (375) is the next character that we are introduced to in Nicholas's play. In the novel as a whole Newman Noggs is certainly the person whom this label fits.[10] The rest of the play is also an excellent parody of the Nickleby family. Acting "Newman's part," Folair asks if he has got it right: "and we go into poor lodgings, where I won't take any wages, and talk sentiment, I suppose?" (376). The poor lodgings have already been referred to, and the gentleman turned beggar (69) does not become richer by assisting the Nicklebys:

> Newman Noggs did not say that he had hunted up the old furniture they saw, from attic or cellar; or that he had taken in the halfpennyworth of milk for tea that stood upon a shelf, or filled the rusty kettle on the hob, or collected the woodchips from the wharf, or begged the coals.   (198)

These self-sacrificing services are not noticed by Mrs. Nickleby, and this is only the beginning of all the help Newman gives the family; eventually he even assists the Cheerybles in arranging the happy ending of the novel (917).

In Mr. Lenville's colorful suggestions of additional material for the play, we also hear of a lady who "talk[s] sentiment." That is an accurate depiction of Mrs. Nickleby's gibberish, and the line spoken by this lady further on also seems to be made for her: "I will learn to suffer with fortitude" (376). There should be no doubt about who "the distressed lady [who] sinks into a chair, and buries her face in her pocket-handkerchief" is, and we are not surprised when she is "overpowered by old recollections" in the end (376).[11] Mrs. Nickleby, although often parodically described *within* the main plot of the melodrama, is also a representative of the serious melodrama. The play can be said to reveal a parody of her as a participant in the suffering little family, while it constitutes a mere description of her as a parodic character within that melodramatic setting. It is, after all, a good characterization of the widow to describe her as continually crying because of her recollections.

Having studied the first version of our young Shakespeare's play in such detail, there is no time to look at the rather unrecognizable performance of the play here. The other play that we encounter in the Crummles section offers a parody which is more hyperbolic and a plot even more intricate than the one we have already looked at. The dramatis personae do, however, at times take up positions very similar to those of characters in the rest of *Nicholas Nickleby*. The comment on this particular plot seems worth quoting: "The plot was most interesting: It belonged to no particular age, people, or country, and was perhaps the more delightful on that account, as nobody's previous information could afford the remotest glimmering of what would ever come of it" (378). If we think of this statement as commenting on melodrama in general, we are made aware of the fact that melodrama, being a hybrid form, is far from fulfilling the demand for unity in classical drama. The indeterminable quality of the plot can be said to expose the extensive utilization of coincidence. Critics who dislike *Nicholas Nickleby* will probably easily adopt the first ironic observation that the plot "was most interesting" for their own assessment of the novel as a whole. Despite what can be felt to be indeterminability, the use of coincidence can also be said to create predictability. We know where a melodrama is supposed to end, and the use of credible events are instrumental in forwarding this. When the heroes experience downfalls, the device of coincidence "intensifies the effect of paranoia" and creates a "projection of 'irrational' fear," whereas the reward of providence must be the result when this unfolding is reversed (Bentley 203).[12]

The faithful servant is this time exchanged with "a page doing duty everywhere and swearing to live and die in the service of everybody" (378). We have already noted Newman's services, but the page seems to resemble Smike even more. Smike promises Nicholas: "To go with you—anywhere—every-where—to the world's end—to the churchyard grave" (226). He lives and dies in the service of the Nickleby family.

Ralph becomes a *pater familias* after his brother's death, although it would be stretching the point to call him a patriarch. In this play, however, he shares certain characteristics with a representative of this Old Testament profession: "This patriarch was the father of several of the characters, but he didn't exactly know which, and was uncertain whether he had brought up the right ones in his castle, or the wrong ones, but rather inclined to the latter opinion" (378–79). Mistaken identity is a typical trait in melodrama, and here the play parallels the main story: that Smike turns out to be Ralph's son is central to the plot of *Nicholas Nickleby*.[13] Newman Noggs can also be said to be commented on through this parody when we are introduced to "the comic fighting-man (who overheard whatever was said all through the piece)" (379).[14] Here, I find that even the name of the part describes Newman well. This is how the comic fighting-man of the main plot is described:

> As the usurer turned for consolation to his books and papers, a performance was going on outside his office-door, which would have occasioned him no small surprise, if he could by any means have become acquainted with it.
> Newman Noggs was the sole actor. He stood at a little distance from the door, with his face towards it; and with the sleeves of his coat turned back at the wrists, was occupied in bestowing the most vigorous, scientific, and straightforward blows upon the empty air.   (451)

There are in *Nicholas Nickleby* many instances of either overhearing or of finding letters (e.g., on pages 42, 703–13, and 769). Ralph has good reason to inform Gride that "clerks and servants have a trick of listening" (707) because Newman hears him from the closet as he utters this suspicion.[15] At the end of *Nicholas Nickleby*, Newman is central in defeating the villains who are "baffled by his skill and bravery" (379), just as the audience is by Lenville's villain.

Behind the actual eavesdropping we find a more fundamental melodramatic trait: coincidences, as I have already noted, abound in the genre, and they are there to expose a "hidden reality" (Brooks 2).[16] To show what the parody pin-points when it makes the comic fighting-man overhear everything that happens, I want to select one series of coincidences out of many. Shortly after Smike has walked into Squeers by coincidence and has been taken captive by him (582), Nicholas visits the boy's rescuer John Browdie and his wife at the Saracen's Head Inn (630–47). It is perhaps not strange that Fanny Squeers, who stays at the inn, overhears their conversation about her (636), but when the two men go downstairs because of a fight there (642), the number of coincidences become overwhelming. One of the men fighting is

Mr. Frank Cheeryble, the nephew of the brothers, who has just arrived from abroad and whom Nicholas is supposed to meet the following day. By coincidence, Frank has overheard some disrespectful remarks about a young lady he knows, and this is the reason for the quarrel (644). The young lady so insolently spoken about downstairs later turns out to be the very girl that the young man upstairs is violently in love with. By coincidence, Nicholas even considers what he would have done if someone had spoken in the same way about his "unknown," and he decides that he would have reacted as Frank did (645). As if this is not enough, the person who insulted the young lady turns out to be "Tom—the ugly clerk" (646). This is the same man who offended Nicholas so much by treating Madeline disrespectfully in the General Agency Office (253).

The number of coincidences that coincide at the inn on this evening is truly astonishing. It even makes the melodramatic hero use the expression "that's odd enough!" (646). Later this device is defended through the words of another character. When Tim Linkinwater hears that Nicholas has met Frank the previous night, he declares:

> "That those two young men should have met last night in that manner is, I say, a coincidence—a remarkable coincidence. Why, I don't believe now," added Tim, taking off his spectacles, and smiling as with gentle pride, "that there's such a place in all the world for coincidences as London is!"   (649)

What has happened is definitely remarkable, but the vast number of people living in London could statistically make the chances to meet acquaintances even smaller. The reader may be tempted to change Tim's statement slightly: "I don't believe now, that there's such a place in all the world for coincidences as melodrama is".

The rest of the play contains episodes we know from other parts of *Nicholas Nickleby* such as "pistolling," wrong identities in the dark (cf. the Bobster scene, 613–14), and "loss of life" (379).[17] The successful outlaw (378) with his exclamation "Beware!" (379) can be seen as a parody of the picaro Nicholas with his melodramatic outcries (e.g., 220 and 322). In the end the patriarch looks more like the Cheerybles when he finds the occasion appropriate "for marrying the young people" (379). He is of course perfectly correct, as are the brothers, because the end is the right place for weddings in melodramas and in *Nicholas Nickleby*. The wedding and the great farewell scene in the Crummles sections—often referred to by critics—are of course parodies of these two common elements of the standard melodrama and of the many farewells and weddings in the book as a whole.

The clear polarization of good and evil is also subject to an excellent parody. On their way from the theater, Mr. and Mrs.Crummles exemplify the clear contrast between light and darkness:

Mrs Crummles trod the pavement as if she were going to immediate execution with an animating consciousness of innocence and that heroic fortitude which virtue alone inspires. Mr Crummles, on the other hand, assumed the look and gait of a hardened despot; but they both attracted some notice from many of the passers-by.   (371)

This polarity is strongly reminiscent of the situation of two other walkers who are probably not as self-conscious in their display of vice and virtue:

> It was a curious contrast to see how the timid country girl shrunk through the crowd that hurried up and down the streets, giving way to the press of people, and clinging closely to Ralph as though she feared to lose him in the throng; and how the stern and hard-featured man of business went doggedly on, elbowing the passengers aside, and now and then exchanging a gruff salutation with some passing acquaintance, who turned to look back upon his pretty charge with looks expressive of surprise, and seemed to wonder at the ill-assorted companionship. But it would have been a stranger contrast still, to have read the hearts that were beating side by side; to have laid bare the gentle innocence of the one, and the rugged villainy of the other.   (187–88)

Both good and evil are personified, and the extremes that are parodied in Mr. and Mrs. Crummles's walk are also evident when Nicholas compares Madeline and Gride by the simile of "the vulture and the lamb, the rat and the dove" (802) and in the narratorial comment when Ralph and Nicholas first meet:

> The face of the old man was stern, hard-featured and forbidding; that of the young man, open, handsome, and ingenuous. The old man's eye was keen with the twinklings of avarice and cunning; the young man's, bright with the light of intelligence and spirit.   (82)

Since an elevated sort of rhetoric is particularly important to melodrama, this aspect must be considered before we end.[18] The exalted rhetoric results in a peculiar stage speech in a novel like *Nicholas Nickleby*. "Not to put too fine a point upon it," to use Mr Snagsby's favorite apology for cautious plain speaking (*Bleak House* 193; Ch. 11), to a modern ear much melodramatic rhetoric sounds less successful or, to use stronger words from Mr. Mantalini's mouth, as if performed in a "private-madhouse-sort of manner" (515). It is probably the impact of the realistic tradition that causes this reaction in us, because it stresses a down-to-earth way of speech where emotionally fraught motifs are revealed little by little. But melodrama is "the quintessence of drama" and is therefore concerned with acting out and expressing all (Bentley 216).[19] Brooks asserts that there is in this mode a will to put pressure on the surface to make it yield an excess of meaning(1, 3). On the occasion of their little party before departing for the new world, Mrs. Crummles returns thanks "in a manner and in a speech which has never been surpassed and seldom equalled" (729). From what we know of her we have no reason to doubt this, and it is characteristic that what is never normally expressed is uttered as a most natural thing in melodrama.[20] Mr. Crummles's realization that "language was not powerful enough to describe the infant phenomenon" (365) is a variation on this theme, of course, and not an indication of his sobriety.

Examples of melodramatic language abound in the novel. We have a true heroine's utterance in Kate's communication to Sir Mulberry: "Unhand me, sir, this instant" (313). *Luke the Labourer*, a conventional melodrama, contains a phrase almost identical: "Unhand me, sir, or I will call for help" (Smith 23).[21] Other classic melodramatic utterances in *Nicholas Nickleby* are such as "I couldn't hate him more. Let me but retaliate upon him" (838), and the "little piece of sound family feeling" Ralph expresses when he says of his nephew: "I'd give good money to have him stabbed to the heart and rolled into the kennel for the dogs to tear" (578).[22]

The imperative is frequently applied, and we take it for granted that Mrs. Crummles must order her dinner with the phrase: "Let the mutton and onion sauce appear!" (372). The mixture of the serious peremptory tone and mutton underlines the parody, but it is the same dramatic form Nicholas avails himself of when he cries "Stop!" (220), "Stand off!" (817), or "Give way!" (818). The dialogue between Mrs. Crummles and Nicholas when he meets the company again in London reveals parodic and genuine emotion present in the same scene:

> "And how is your friend, the faithful Digby?"
> "Digby!" said Nicholas, forgetting at the instant that this had been Smike's theatrical name. "Oh yes. He's quite—what am I saying?—he is very far from well."
> "How!" exclaimed Mrs Crummles, with a tragic recoil.
> "I fear," said Nicholas, shaking his head, and making an attempt to smile, "that your better-half would be more struck with him now, than ever."
> "What mean you?" rejoined Mrs Crummles, in her most popular manner. "Whence comes this altered tone?"
> "I mean that a dastardly enemy of mine has struck at me through him, and that while he thinks to torture me, he inflicts on him such agonies of terror and suspense as—You will excuse me, I am sure," said Nicholas, checking himself. "I should never speak of this, and never do, except to those who know the facts, but for a moment I forgot myself".   (725–26)

Mrs. Crummles's syntax is stilted and her vocabulary archaic, but Nicholas is not far from her in manner of speech when he has "so sudden an explosion" (726). He forgets himself by referring to his "dastardly enemy" as if he was in the middle of a confrontation with the villain. It is interesting to notice the resemblances between the two participants in this conversation when Nicholas for the first time brings Ralph, and thus the main melodramatic plot, into the reality of the theater troupe.

The distance between the language of the melodramatic actress and of the hero of our story is thus not always as great as we might assume. In the clash with Ralph when he wants to "bear [Madeline] hence" (818), Nicholas replies in the following words to his uncle's curses:

> "Whence will curses come at your command? or what avails a curse or blessing from a man like you? I warn you, that misfortune and discovery are thickening about your head; that the structures you have raised through all your ill-spent life are crumbling into dust."   (818)

This equals, if it does not surpass, the old theatrical heroine's language. At times the hyperbolic nature of melodrama in the novel as a whole tends to overshadow the local parody in the Crummles chapters. Exclamations such as "the time for any palliation and concealment is past" (500), "there is but one step to take, and that is to cast him off with the scorn and indignation he deserves" (504), "I do not know that man. I cannot breathe the air that he corrupts" (677), "you make this house a hell, and visit these trials upon yonder wretched object" (referring to Smike, 686), "base hound" (805), "obstinate dog," and "I spit upon your fair words" (879) abound, particularly in the speeches of Nicholas and Ralph. Nothing is spared in expressing the fundamental conflict between good and evil.

I have examined how the scenes involving the theater company parody melodramatic episodes in the main plot of *Nicholas Nickleby* and elements of melodrama in general. The two different approaches to these situations and this rhetoric, the comic and the serious, stand side by side and do not eliminate each other.[23] Parody is dependent on a norm. In *Nicholas Nickleby* this norm is melodrama. The inherent value of melodrama must, as Peter Brooks has demonstrated so well in his excellent study of the mode, be taken seriously and emphasized according to its own criteria. Self-parody does, just like carnival, only supply a "temporary liberation from the prevailing truth and from the established order" (Bakhtin 10). In our reading of the novel we are provided with alternative portrayals of the same phenomena. Because we are supplied with parodic descriptions alongside the melodramatic ones, we start to see an interaction between the various alternatives. A farewell is not just a farewell, it can be sentimental *or* parodic, or both. In this way more possibilities and a richer picture of life are created for us in our reading.

The feeling of these sections is, like the effects of other kinds of parody in the book, displayed through what Bakhtin calls the festive laughter of the people. It is an expression not only of pure satirical mockery, but of a deep, warm, penetrating sort of self-consciousness. It does not destroy or undermine the other parts of the novel because "the people's ambivalent laughter ... expresses the point of view of the whole world; he who is laughing also belongs to it" (12). By this I mean that the existence of the one does not destroy the value of the other. One version gives life to the other and makes the overall picture more dynamic and complex. Dickens is actually capable of a constructive self-critique. The advice that Nicholas receives from his manager is worth noting: " 'You shall study Romeo when you've done that piece ... Rover too;—you might get up Rover while you were about it, and Cassio, and Jeremy Diddler. You can easily knock them off; one part helps the other so much' " (373). The parts of the young lover Romeo, the hero Jack Rover, the farcical character Jeremy Diddler, and the thoroughly villainous Cassio are said to help each other.[24] Implicit in the advice one senses a conviction that these parts are very similar, which is absurd, but in our reading of the novel it makes sense that we benefit from completely different approaches. The best, even if the most demanding, way of reading *Nicholas Nickleby* is to apply a sort of double vision. This, however, is not always easy in concrete instances. For us this final quotation is most probably outrageous parody, but for Mr. Vincent Crummles it is simply broad truth:

> "He is quite one of us. His mother was on the stage."
> "Was she, indeed?" rejoined Nicholas.
> "She ate apple-pie at a circus for upwards of fourteen years," said the manager;
> "fired pistols, and went to bed in a nightcap; and, in short, took the low comedy entirely. His father was a dancer."
> "Was he at all distinguished?"
> "Not very," said the manager. "He was rather a low sort of pony. The fact is, that he had been originally jobbed out by the day, and he never quite got over his old habits. He was clever in melodrama too, but too broad—too broad."
> (361–62)

NOTES

1. "The scenes of the provincial theater thus act as a parody of the main plot, and of the life of the chief characters in the main story. In spite of himself Dickens reveals the fictive nature of his own novels and the vacuity of his characters." We here note an observation of a sort of self-reflexivity, a statement on the unintentional character of this self-critique, and a negative view of the melodramatic characters in the novel's main plot.
2. George J. Worth uses the term "mock melodrama" about the Lenville episode and some other material in the novel, but he seems to consider these parts as just another form or nuance of melodrama. I find his observations valuable, but he does not look at the Lenville episode in relation to scenes from the "serious"

melodrama in the rest of the novel, 56–57. All further references to *Nicholas Nickleby* in this article are to the Penguin edition.

3. Jean Ferguson Carr has touched on this self-consciousness in *Dramatic Dickens*, ed. Carol Hanberry MacKay 27–44 (p. 41). She claims that the value of theater as metaphor lies "in its emphasis on the artistry and artfulness of projects of self-knowledge." In *Little Dorrit* we can observe that even the door of the theater is self-conscious (278). This is a negative self-consciousness, but still with an element of vanity, I think: "[The door] appeared to be ashamed of itself and to be hiding in an alley."

4. Hutcheon distinguishes between parody and satire by calling the former "intramural" and the latter "extramural" 25.

5. See Brooks on unrecognized virtue, *The Melodramatic Imagination: Balzac, Henry James, Melodrama, and the Mode of Excess* (26). Wolgang Herrlinger also emphasizes the "stoic strength in the weak" and mentions the "*active* little crutch" of Tiny Tim in *A Christmas Carol* as an example of this phenomenon, *Sentimentalismus und Postsentimentalismus: Studien zum Englischen Roman bis zur Mitte des 19. Jahrhunderts* 252 (my translation).

6. She states that "the typical social melodrama ends 'happily'; the evil are punished, the good rewarded."

7. John Kucich is concerned with this in *Excess and Restraint in the Novels of Charles Dickens*, and he has devoted a chapter on villains (59–104) and another one on heroes (105–32).

8. In Ann Radcliffe's *The Mysteries of Udolpho*, Emily has to stay in a gloomy castle, sleeping in a deserted apartment where it is only possible to bolt the door from the outside (242). This situation of confinement is a frequently employed device in the novels of terror. See Edith Birkhead, *The Tale of Terror: A Study of the Gothic Romance*, 47–51.

9. This is in addition to the short description of the "Indian Savage and the Maiden" (363–64). Even if the maiden in this short pantomime or ballet has "a dirty white frock" (363), she still fights in the struggle of light against a dark world. Northrop Frye has touched on this when stating that "the dance of the savage and the Infant Phenomenon . . . mirrors the Dickensian theme of the girl-child in the monster-world," "Dickens and the Comedy of Humor," in *Charles Dickens: Modern Critical Views*, ed. Harold Bloom, 71–91 (p. 87).

10. Margaret Ganz mentions some of the ways in which Newman functions as Nicholas's assistant, 131–48 (p. 136). Michael R. Booth claims that in melodrama "it is the comic man who keeps an eye on the heroine, insults the villain, and overhears and frustrates his plots" when the hero is away, *English Melodrama* 17. Lewis Horne stresses that Nicholas is dependent on Newman's assistance, but in a somewhat larger way: he needs the help of Newman Noggs to become a new man himself (165–77).

11. James L. Smith asserts that in melodrama "aged parents always bemoan their present miseries, recall the happy days gone by and implore heaven to look with mercy upon their children far away" (32).

12. Bentley 203.

13. Anette Doblix Klemp notes this "secrecy surrounding a character's birth" as a melodramatic characteristic 3636–A. Brooks calls "mysterious parentage" an "element . . . from the melodramatic repertory" (3).
14. Slater has observed this in his introduction to *Nicholas Nickleby*: "The way in which Mr Lenville's villainy in a Crummles melodrama is baffled by the comic fighting-man 'who overheard whatever was said all through the piece' is echoed in the main plot by the way in which Newman Noggs helps to baffle the schemes of Ralph and Gride by contriving to eavesdrop at vital moments' (8).
15. Eavesdropping is a frequently used element in melodrama, and I here again want to refer to the melodramatic novel *Old Goriot*. The situations where Rastignac discovers some of the secrets of both Vautrin and Goriot are dependent on his eavesdropping and peeping through key-holes, and are central to the plot. Schlicke calls eavesdropping a "stock play-acting situation" (49).
16. Klemp calls "the reliance upon coincidence" a melodramatic characteristic (3646-A), and Eric Bentley mentions the "notorious" melodramatic "device: outrageous coincidence" (202). It is worth noting that Taylor Stoehr states about Dickens' novels that "there seems to lurk behind the facade of normal occurrences some secret meaning" and that the "apparently disconnected elements are in fact related." This is actually a good description of the mode of melodrama (11–12).
17. Violence is an important element of *Nicholas Nickleby*. Even the hero's faithful friend Newman has to admit that "he is a violent youth at times" (778). Carol A. Bock is concerned with this aspect of the novel (87–102).
18. Bentley has devoted pages 206–10 in *The Life of the Drama* to the treatment of melodramatic language. Brooks states that "[melodrama's] typical figures are hyperbole, antithesis, and oxymoron: those figures, precisely, that evidence a refusal of nuance and the insistence on dealing in pure, integral concepts" (40). Worth claims that "melodramatic speech . . . rises well above the casualness of ordinary talk. Not just its diction but also the syntactic and figurative devices that are employed in it are literary rather than colloquial, showing evidence of greater learning and greater linguistic calculation than either the kind of characters who use it or the situations in which they find themselves seem to warrant" (16).
19. Bentley earlier mentions that "the exaggerations will be foolish only if they are empty of feeling" (204).
20. According to Brooks, "Nothing is spared because nothing is left unsaid; the characters stand on stage and utter the unspeakable, give voice to their deepest feelings, dramatize through their heightened and polarized words and gestures the whole lesson of their relationship" (4).
21. James L. Smith (23).
22. A representative expression of revenge taken from the melodrama *The Woodman's Hut* is "Tremble, dastards, the day of retribution will arrive," in Smith, 19. The kennel mentioned in Ralph's outcry is, by the way, "not a dog-kennel but the gutter in the street," endnotes, *Nicholas Nickleby* (968).
23. Slater is of the same opinion in expressing: "Parodies as devastatingly funny as this derive not from scorn but from love" (16). By his statement he places this parody in the "respectful" end of the range of "ethos" that Hutcheon as suggested.

24. For the two less known plays see footnotes in *Nicholas Nickleby* (964).

WORKS CITED

Austen, Jane. "Love and Friendship," in *The Juvenilia of Jane Austen and Charlotte Brontë*. Harmondsworth: Penguin, 1986:99–128.

Bakhtin, Mikhail, M. *Rabelais and His World*, trans. Helene Iswolski. Cambridge, MA: M.I.T. Press, 1968.

Bentley, Eric. *The Life of the Drama*. London: Methuen, 1966.

Birkhead, Edith. *The Tale of Terror: A Study of the Gothic Romance*. New York: Russell, 1963.

Bloom, Harold, ed. *Charles Dickens: Modern Critical Views*. New York: Chelsea House, 1987.

Bock, Carol A. "Violence and the Fictional Modes of *Nicholas Nickleby*," *Massachusetts Studies in English* 10 (1985): 87–102.

Booth, Michael R. *English Melodrama*. London: Jenkins, 1965.

Brooks, Peter. *The Melodramatic Imagination: Balzac, Henry James, Melodrama and the Mode of Excess*. New York: Columbia UP, 1985.

Calhoun-French, Diane M. "Mr. Popular Sentiment: A Study of the Novels of Charles Dickens at Best-selling Social Melodramas." *DAI* 44 (1983): 492–A. University of Louisville.

Chesterton, G. K. *Chesterton on Dickens*. Rutland, VT: Dent, 1992.

Dickens, Charles. *Bleak House*. Harmondsworth: Penguin, 1985.

———. *Little Dorrit*. Harmondsworth: Penguin, 1985.

———. *Nicholas Nickleby*. Harmondsworth: Penguin, 1988.

Ganz, Margaret. "*Nicholas Nickleby*: The Victories of Humour," *Mosaic* 9.4 (1976): 131–48.

Herrlinger, Wolfgang. *Sentimentalismus und Postsentimentalismus: Studien zum Englischen Roman bis zur Mitte des 19. Jahrhunderts*. Tübingen: Niemeyer, 1987.

Horne, Lewis. "Covenant and Power in *Nicholas Nickleby*; or, the Guidance of Newman Noggs," *Papers on Language and Literature* 25.2 (1989): 165–77.

Hutcheon, Linda. *A Theory of Parody*. New York: Routledge, 1991.

Klemp, Anette Doblix. "Dickens and Melodrama: Character Presentation and Plot Motifs in Six Novels," *DAI* 45 (1985): 3646-A. Pennsylvania State University.

Kucich, John. *Excess and Restraint in the Novels of Charles Dickens.* Athens: U of Georgia P., 1981.

Litvak, Joseph. *Caught in the Act.* Berkeley: U of California P., 1992.

Mackay, Carol Hanberry, ed. *Dramatic Dickens.* Basingstoke: Macmillan,1989.

Miller, J. Hillis. *Charles Dickens: The World of His Novels.* Cambridge, MA: Harvard UP, 1958.

Radcliffe, Ann. *The Mysteries of Udolpho.* London: Oxford UP, 1966.

Schlicke, Paul. *Dickens and Popular Entertainment.* London: Hyman, 1985.

Slater, Michael. *Introduction to Nicholas Nickleby.* Harmondsworth: Penguin, 1988.

Smith, James L. *Melodrama (The Critical Idiom).* London: Methuen, 1973.

Stoehr, Taylor. *Dickens: The Dreamer's Stance.* Ithaca, NY: Cornell UP, 1966.

Vicinus, Martha. "Helpless and Unfriended: Nineteenth-Century Domestic Melodrama," *New Literary History* 13.1 (1981)127–43.

Worth, George J. *Dickensian Melodrama: A Reading of the Novels.* Lawrence: U of Kansas Publications, 1978.

The Perfect Murder: Patterns of Repetition and Doubling in Wilkie Collins's *The Woman in White*

Shirley A. Stave

Part way into Wilkie Collins's *The Woman in White*, Marian Halcombe reveals in a journal entry a discussion held among the residents of Blackwater Park concerning the possibility of escaping apprehension after committing a serious crime. Marian dutifully records her own and her sister Laura's remonstrances that "Murder will out," as well as Sir Percival and Count Fosco's disdain at what they consider the naiveté of the young women. Later, Walter Hartright's narrative reveals Sir Percival's disdain as stemming from his own audacious—and hithertofore undetected—crime, a forgery which establishes him as the legitimate heir to his father's lands and title. While the murder discussion serves to reveal the nefarious characters of the charlatan and his cohort, it also, of course, foreshadows the revelation concerning Sir Percival's claims to legitimacy. Seemingly, then, Laura and Marian's idealism prevails—once again, crime is brought to light and the criminal punished, through divine intervention, one might argue, the villain burning to death during his attempt to destroy the evidence of his forgery. The moral order is restored and nothing is rotten in the state of England.

Or perhaps such a reading is too innocent. Perhaps the reader is beguiled by Walter's assembled narratives into accepting him as a legitimate hero who rescues Laura and Marian from poverty and obscurity, re-establishing Laura's right to her title and inheritance. However, if one were to employ a hermeneutics of suspicion in approaching the text, one might argue that Sir Percival's crime is re-enacted by Hartright himself, that the two characters parallel each other, functioning as psychological doubles of each other. Just as the earlier crime involved the manipulation of a text to authenticate Sir Percival in the eyes of English society, so Hartright manipulates the texts he assembles to

287

justify his behavior toward Laura and Marian and to legitimize his status in society.

Walter's situation as the historical section of his narrative begins is far from ideal. Suffering from the sort of ennui that suggests depression, Walter describes himself as "out of health, out of spirits, and, if the truth must be told, out of money as well" (2). The death of Walter's father left Walter's sister and mother well-provided for; however, Walter, who followed his father's profession of drawing-master, inherited no money but rather was bequeathed his father's students and clients. However, Walter's irresponsibility has left him financially dependent on his mother and sister, a situation which must rankle someone as obsessed with stereotypical notions of masculinity and femininity as Walter's narrative repeatedly reveals him to be.

The source of Walter's gender anxiety warrants speculation. On the one hand, maleness/masculinity is typically associated with authority, with the power to speak and act, with Law, with reason, with the establishment of civilization—in essence, with the power of the Phallus. On the other hand, it is identified with physical strength, brute force, that which is untamable and uncontrollable, the antithesis of civilization. The problem with this definition of maleness is not simply that it is dually articulated, but that its terms are self-contradictory. However, Walter's situation is further complicated by his class status. For the upper-class Victorian male, access to the machinery of culture—to the courts of law, to the benches of justice, to the pulpits and lecterns—bestowed a sense of maleness, of empowerment. For the lower-class male, the physicality of his job, the knowledge of his superior strength, his ability to fight and win, defines him as male/masculine. Walter exists in a world between. His refinement, his education, his speech, would identify him with the upper classes, in whose homes he is a fixture, yet always as a social inferior, never as a peer. At the same time, Walter is not portrayed as being particularly strong and his profession as drawing master would likely appear to working-class men as something dandified, unmanly. Walter has no access to male authority, hence his obsessions with it.[1] Peter Caracciola, in a discussion of the scene in which Walter pulls his friend Pesca out of the water, describes Walter as "life-giving" and sees the entire situation as "embryonic" (397). In other words, Walter has become identified with the mother, with lack, and what he has birthed is his "son," a diminutive, eccentric man who is a social embarrassment, Walter's projection of his own sense of/lack of self.

When Walter acquires a splendid position—that of drawing-master to two young women, at a generous salary plus all living expenses, in addition to being accepted within the family as a social equal—his pride does not permit him to relish the experience. Mr. Fairlie's social condescension unravels Walter's image of himself as a peer to Laura and Marian, and forces an unwelcomed awareness of class difference; Walter finds himself speculating on whether he is acting "too much in the character of a guest, and too little in the character of a drawing-master" (45). In addition, as Walter finds himself attracted to both women, he must face the fact that his position allows him access to "beautiful and captivating women, much as a harmless domestic animal is admitted among them" (55); essentially, he must confront his own sense of himself as castrated. When the innocent Laura returns his affection and Marian intervenes to prevent the social calamity that would occur were the younger woman to throw over her titled intended for a poor drawing-master, Walter's pride is once again wounded by Marian's castigation as well as by her demand that he leave Limmeridge House. Marian's directness, strength, and resourcefulness, which Walter continually cites as evidence of Marian's masculine nature, must be opposed and Marian herself must be punished, her authority crushed, her voice silenced; essentially, she must be returned to the realm of the feminine, to the role of angel in the house, a role she has emphatically and shockingly denounced, claiming, "[Laura] is an angel; and I am——Try some of that marmalade, Mr. Hartright, and finish the sentence, in the name of feminine propriety, for yourself" (27). While Marian possesses authority, Walter, entangled in his internal drama of gender anxiety, will feel he has none.

However, Walter's relationship with Marian is complicated by his attraction to her. According to his narrative, which was written well after the fact, Walter's initial impression of Marian is that while her body is stunningly proportioned and exquisite, a perception the confident Marian herself apparently shares, she does not wear stays but rather moves with a sexual suggestiveness that disconcerts Walter, "[t]he lady is ugly!" (25). Enough critical attention has been devoted to Marian's face to convince the reader that Walter's claim need not be accepted as true. Nina Auerbach shows how the description we are given of Marian also describes a woman much of England regarded as a stunning beauty—Jane Morris, a "similarly uncorseted Pre-Raphaelite idol" (137). Suffice it to say that no other character in the novel expresses alarm over Marian's appearance (or her moustache) and Count Fosco reveals himself to be entranced by her to the point that he acts against his own better judgment, the result being his exile and death. However, the last words of Pesca, the character who can be read as Walter's alter ego/interior self, need to be considered: "Marry one of the two young Misses; become Honourable Hartright, M.P." (13). For all of her bodily appeal and her comfortable, engaging manner, Marian is poor and marrying her will do significantly little to alter Walter's state, even though a marriage between the two would not be considered socially inappropriate. Rather, Walter must secure the heart (and wealth) of Laura if he is to take Pesca's advice.

Although Walter is on the one hand attracted to Marian and on the other "almost repelled by the masculine form and masculine look" (25) of Marian's

features, which suggest to him that she is "altogether wanting in those feminine attractions of gentleness and pliability" (25), he also enjoys Marian's
sharp mind and biting humor; not surprisingly, a camaraderie develops between them. While Laura represents to him all that is feminine and "pliable,"
he is troubled by the "something wanting" (42) in her and speaks of her
"quaint, childish earnestness" (43), hardly a term of praise for an adult
woman. That the narrative reveals Walter as engaging in far more conversation with Marian than with Laura is telling. The paradigm for the triangulation
of their friendship is the extended discussion between Walter and Marian of
the supposed identity of the mysterious woman in white, which Marian insists
Laura not share, for fear that it will distress her. In spite of all Walter's
objections to Marian's "masculinity," she becomes his confidant, his friend,
and his ally, while Laura becomes more and more childish and quaint as the
novel progresses.

   If Walter experiences doubts about his manhood as a result of his encounters with Marian, the young woman's perception of her own positionality
regarding gender is not without problems either. While she self-confidently
assumes her own worth as a human being, she can only do so by defining
herself in opposition to other women. She consistently demeans the behavior
and ability of women in general, presumably to mark her lack of affiliation
with them and their proscribed role in society. For example, when she first
meets Walter, she speaks in very disparaging terms about the recent visit of
two women friends, claiming that the absence of "a flirtable, dancable, small-
talkable creature of the male sex" (26) left the woman with nothing to do
but quarrel with one another. She adds, "We are such fools, we can't entertain
each other at table. You see I don't think much of my own sex. . . . [N]o
woman does . . . although few of them confess it as freely as I do" (26). Here,
and in the numerous other similar passages in her journal, Marian is being
dishonest. She clearly does not regard herself as a fool, and her esteem for
Laura is amply demonstrated throughout the text. However, in articulating
the cultural stereotype of woman, Marian presumes she can separate herself
from participation in that stereotype. Shortly afterward, Marian explains to
Walter that "Women can't draw—their minds are too flighty, and their eyes
are too inattentive" (28). Marian's tactics have become more subtle. Drawing
was a culturally sanctioned activity for women, hence Walter's position at
Limmeridge. In affirming her lack of talent, Marian again distances herself
from the limitations her society imposed upon women; however, in attributing
drawing to the realm of the "masculine," Marian flatters Walter's ego and
ministers to his wounded sense of his own manhood.

   In her narrative treatment of other women, however, Marian is less kind.
While she consistently articulates, in words and in actions, her full admiration
and love of Laura, she is at times scathing toward other women, particularly

toward Eleanor, wife to Count Fosco. Admittedly Eleanor proves herself to be an unworthy character and Marian's uncontrollable fascination for the hefty count suggests jealousy may lie beneath her castigation of the countess. Nevertheless, Marian's vituperative description of Eleanor remains surprising, especially given the nature of the characteristics she attacks. She claims that prior to her marriage, the countess "was always talking pretentious nonsense," that she dressed inappropriately, revealing "the structure of the female skeleton, in the upper regions of the collar-bones and the shoulder-blades" (194), and that she "advocated the Rights of Women" (210), particularly the right of women to express their opinions independent of men. Coming from a woman who on more than one occasion demonstrates her ability to talk at great length, who flaunts conventional "decency" in her own dress by refusing to wear a corset, and who clearly embodies a sense of feminism in her being, these comments again indicate Marian's refusal to claim sisterhood with any woman. While she scorns conventional women as silly, she also scorns an unconventional one as ridiculous. In attempting to carve out a space for herself, as a woman in a time when womanhood and personhood appear as mutually exclusive categories, Marian feels the need to define herself in antithesis to all other women. Much later, when the combined assaults of Fosco and Walter render her helpless, she has no allies to whom to turn, and she is defeated.

To add to the complication, Marian herself grows attracted to Walter, an attraction which he reveals without comment, as though he seemingly were unaware of her feelings for him.[2] Initially, Marian is clearly attracted to Laura and one can argue that the older woman's feelings for the younger never diminish. However, whatever her deeper feelings may be, Marian finds herself also attracted to Walter. After she discovers that Walter loves Laura (or plays at loving Laura), as she insists that he leave Limmeridge, she vehemently demands that he "Crush [the love]," adding, "Here, where you first saw her, crush it! Don't shrink under it like a woman. Tear it out; trample it under foot like a man" (61). The intensity of her language undercuts the sound advice she offers and hints at feelings of jealousy. The question then is raised whether Marian is jealous that someone else loves Laura or jealous that Walter loves someone else—or whether both alternatives are true. Similarly, her words suggest a familiarity with eradicating an unwanted passion. Has Marian had to "trample underfoot" her love for Laura, who is soon to marry Sir Percival, or her love for Walter, who apparently prefers someone else in spite of his intimacy with Marian? Again, both readings may be equally valid. When their seemingly final leavetaking occurs, Walter makes a point of mentioning Marian's "sisterlike" touch and kiss, as well as her words, "I had better not stay for both our sakes" (110). That a Victorian woman would draw to her to kiss a man with whom she is not in any way connected in itself reveals the depth of Marian's feelings, as do her words, which suggest not simply that, were she to stay, she would cry, but also that she would reveal love to Walter. Her own journal reveals her continued obsession with the absent Walter, as does her prophetic dream, which indicates the depth to which her soul is bound up with his. Much later, when she and Walter are caring for the emotionally disabled Laura while passing themselves off as brother and sister, it is understandable that Marian begins to feel like Walter's helpmate. When Walter then suggests to Marian that his relationship with the women "ought to be a stronger one than it is now" (510), the narrative suggests that Marian assumes he is going to propose marriage to her: "She leaned near to [Walter], with a look of surprise" (510). When he reveals his true intent, to marry Laura instead, Marian's "face grew pale. For a while, she looked at [him] with a sad, hesitating interest" (510) before clasping his hand and abruptly leaving the room. Since Walter's narrative reveals these details to the reader, presumably Walter knows of Marian's feelings and chooses not to acknowledge them to her. However, in revealing them at all, he empowers himself as the attractive, desirable hero, at the same time that he appears both innocent and honorable in not speaking of what is obvious.

Walter chooses Laura as the object of his "affections" before he is aware of her connection to Sir Percival Glyde. Marian's revelation of the virtual engagement stuns Walter, whose hopes for financial security and social status are thereby crushed. At this point in the narrative, Walter is completely unable to act in his own interests. He has no choice but to obey Marian's injunction that he leave Limmeridge. However, Walter's narrative reveals that during the lengthy emotional discussion, the image of Anne Catherick haunts Walter: "[the memory of her] remained there throughout the interview—remained, and not without a result" (60). On the surface, the "result" to which Walter alludes is his suspicion, at the interview's end, that the nobleman to whom Laura is informally engaged is the same one who terrorized the mysterious woman in white. What enters the narrative at this point is coincidence, particularly coincidence that is privileged as participating in the uncanny. In and of itself, the fact that Laura and Anne resemble each other is not as remarkable as Walter's extreme agitation at the recognition of their resemblance, along with his inclination to read one of the women as a copy, a repetition, of the other, rather than perceiving them as two discrete beings who happen to look alike. In a discussion of repetition, John T. Irwin comments, "Yet it is not every repetition that evokes the feeling of the uncanny, it is only certain events whose repetition reminds us of that inner compulsion to repeat, and the specific character of those events, according to Freud, is that they all represent the recurrence of something that has been repressed" (83). Our hermeneutics of suspicion would suggest that what Walter represses is the knowledge that it might be possible to swap the two women, that it might be possible to circumvent Marian's protectiveness and come by a fortune. From this point on, Walter and Sir Percival Glyde can be seen as mirroring each other, repeating each other's acts even as they both attempt to gain possession of Laura Fairlie and her money. As rivals for Laura's love (and money), Walter and Sir Percival differ from each other not merely in their social status, but also in age. Walter makes much of the 25-year-age difference between Laura and Sir Percival; we learn as well that Sir Percival and Laura's father were good friends. Effectively, Sir Percival can be read as a father figure—to Laura, but also to Walter, whose own father is also dead and whose quest for social legitimacy parallels that of the younger Sir Percival. Walter's desire for Laura, then, can be read as a violation of the incest taboo, whether Laura is perceived as the mother figure that the son desires to possess in the stead of the father, or whether she is seen as the sister whom both the father and the son unlawfully desire.

Significantly, at this point, Walter lacks all power. While Walter's narrative construes his lack of authority as class-linked to some degree—he cannot expect Laura to abandon Sir Percival for him, since he is in no position to provide for her—in a greater sense, the matter is simply one of agency. Laura intends to obey her dying father's last request regardless of her own feelings. At this time of Walter's greatest helplessness, he is at greatest remove from the narrative. Even though in assembling the texts he can edit them as he sees fit, he omits any first-hand accounts of his days from the time he leaves Limmeridge until he returns to England after his journey to the jungle. Irwin, in a discussion of male passivity, suggests its origins lie in "a kind of helplessness—helplessness in the grip of fate, in the flux of time, helplessness in the face of death, helplessness at the hands of the all-powerful father" (96). One can argue that it is Walter's fear of the father—specifically a fear of castration by the father—that sends Walter packing. Since Walter's narrative has already betrayed his castration anxiety, we can speculate that he adopts a "feminized" role as a protective mechanism. Sir Percival, on the other hand, assumes full authority as the all-powerful father. Therefore, once Laura is legally bound to him in marriage, and he thereby controls much of her money, he no longer feels compelled to feign any affection for her. Laura's revelation to Marian about her one attempt to establish a romantic intimacy with her husband suggests that were he to have continued his courtship attentions to her, Laura would have fairly quickly switched her affections from Walter to her husband. However, Sir Percival's moodiness, along with his underestimating Marian's strength of will and determination (a mistake Walter never makes), turns Laura against him, making it necessary for him to swap Anne for Laura to have access to Laura's entire fortune. Hence Laura is imprisoned in the asylum and a befuddled Ann is paraded as Laura, Lady Glyde.

Or so Walter would have us believe. However, the "canonical" version of the events that occur over those mysterious days indicates that Laura comes to Count Fosco's house, takes ill, and dies (perhaps the victim of the count, whose medical knowledge is amply demonstrated and who had suggested to Percival that Laura's death would be financially advantageous to the baronet). The courts do not question the evidence. When Walter and Marian attempt to present the "real" Laura as alive, her own servants do not recognize her. "Laura" herself has no memories that allow her to claim her title and her money. Although Walter obtains documents from the mysterious woman's attending physician, the woman who assisted in preparing the body for burial, the cook, even the tombstone, the piece of evidence that "proves" that the living woman is Laura and not Anne is simply an entry in the record of a livery stable's business transactions. However, as the text has already demonstrated, records can be forged, entries can be added after the fact. The paralleling of the form this portion of the narrative takes—that of an entry in a book—with Sir Percival's forgery, again revealed as an entry in a book, in his case, the church marriage register, calls attention to the earlier forgery. Walter's discussion with the carter emphasizes the connectedness of the two incidents. The carter who "recalls" taking Lady Glyde to Fosco's house remembers her name because it was his own wife's maiden name. In and of itself, this information is no more than trivia, but it echoes an earlier scene in which Walter, on perusing the marriage register, remarks that his given name appears on the same page as the baronet's forged entry. If bribery can effect a woman's removal from an asylum, which it does, it can most certainly cause someone to remember an event which may not have taken place. The carter's narration also calls to mind the bribed nurse, who accepts Marian's money so that she can be married; the carter mentions having recently been married. Presumably his financial situation could also stand to be improved. One final bit of narrative play suggests that Walter's wife may be Anne Catherick rather than Laura Fairlie, Lady Glyde.[3] In their attempt to find someone to identify Laura, Walter and Marian overlook the one person, besides Marian, who knew her best—her nurse, governess, and companion, Mrs. Vesey. Mr. Fairlie rarely saw his niece; the servants only saw her formally; Mrs. Vesey knew Laura well. It is unthinkable that the desperate Walter would overlook such an opportunity—unless he deliberately meant to overlook it. In his reconstruction of his first day at Limmeridge, Walter comments, upon meeting Mrs. Vesey: "Surely a mild, a compliant, an unutterably tranquil and harmless old lady? But enough, perhaps, for the present, of Mrs. Vesey" (39). The words insinuate that the reader will learn Mrs. Vesey's true nature by and by—that her mild, compliant appearance is misleading. However, Mrs. Vesey never deviates from her "cabbage"-like demeanor and never poses a threat to anyone, except perhaps, in Walter's mind. Were Mrs. Vesey to speak, would she identify Walter's wife as Anne Catherick and Walter as a schemer? Must she then also be silenced, as are all the women in the novel?

Walter's desire to possess "Laura" remains complicated by his mixed motives. On the one hand, he needs the money and status she can give him. On the other hand, Walter needs the reassurance that he possesses the agency of the Phallus and to acquire it, he must possess the father's woman. Irwin speaks of the three stages of Oedipal fantasy in the male child:

> first, to supplant the father; second, to establish his priority to the father, to efface his father's seniority, so that as the mother's lover the son would come before the father; and third, to establish the son's originality by affirming the mother's virginity so that the son does not merely come *before*, he comes first.
>
> (146)

Walter accomplishes all three stages. He obviously supplants the father by winning Laura's affections; when Sir Percival conveniently dies while trying to hide evidence from Walter, the younger man marries the "father's woman." Additionally, even when Laura is married to and living with Sir Percival, it is Walter she truly loves, so that here the son can be said to "come before the father." The third stage of the Oedipal fantasy would initially appear to be more problematic, given that Percival and Laura live together for some months after their marriage. However, in a conversation supposedly recorded by Marian in her journal (a journal that has been edited by Walter), Fosco speculates that Laura is likely to bear a child, assuming logically that Percival and his wife engage in the act of sex. Sir Percival's vehement response, that Laura is "not in the least likely to" (298) bear a child, along with Marian's assessment of Laura as not having experienced the "usual moral transformation which is insensibly wrought in a young, fresh, sensitive woman by her marriage" (180), suggest that the marriage goes unconsummated, and therefore that Walter is Laura's first lover. That Walter would desire that Percival had never made love with Laura makes psychological sense; if, however, Walter did indeed find his bride a virgin, it lends credence to the idea that Walter's wife is Anne rather than Laura.

Ultimately, though, whether Walter's wife is Anne or Laura is inconsequential—the two have become interchangeable by this point in the text, their identities fused. The two women are even narratively recorded to use language in the same way. Both women lead into an act of communication with the words, "Do you believe in dreams?" followed by an elaboration of a dream sequence, which allows the two women to again be paralleled. In a discussion of the scene in which Walter realizes that the lack he senses in Laura is filled by his remembrance of Anne, D. A. Miller claims that "the Laura Walter most deeply dreams of loving proves to be none other than the Anne who has been put away. It is as though, to be quite perfect, his pupil must be taught a lesson: what is wanting, what Laura obscurely lacks and Walter obscurely wishes for, is the sequestration in the asylum" (113). He further argues that "[t]he same internment that renders Laura's body docile, and her mind imbecile, also fits her to incarnate the norm of the submissive Victorian wife" (112). Along similar lines, Pamela Perkins and Mary Donaghy point out Walter's narrative "vagueness" in his early descriptions of Laura and add, "Laura thus functions from her first appearance in the story merely as a heroine to be loved, a blank to be filled in by male desire" (393). The Laura Fairlie Marian knows and loves is irrelevant to Walter's narrative—and to Walter. Laura is an attractive, pliable, young heiress who will do nicely in Walter's plans to advance himself; she will be a good match. However, Anne, with her childlike dependence and her intellectual weakness, would be an even better match—still attractive, still pliable, but even more readily controlled. That it becomes in some ways impossible to ascertain the identity of the woman who marries Walter suggests that, whoever she is, her identity has been consumed by male desire and male narrative. Laura/Anne does not exist except as the body/land, that over which the male rules to ascertain his authority. Whether she is confined in the house or the asylum by Sir Percival, or confined through pregnancy in her marriage to Walter, Laura/Anne in essence does not exist narratively except as a cipher or a lack, an empty symbol that points to male authority, the agency of the Phallus.

Such is not the case with Marian, however. When Walter meets Marian, she is a confident, assertive young woman who, while far from independently wealthy, has a modest income that permits her to live comfortably as Laura's friend and companion. By the novel's end, she is poverty-stricken and completely dependent on Walter (and the obedient Laura), having spent her small fortune in the attempt to prove Laura's identity. While Walter also spends his money in the same effort, he is rewarded by marriage to the presumed heiress, while Marian must live off the charity of the couple. But the cooptation of Marian's identity could never happen through financial means alone. Throughout her early days at Limmeridge and later at Blackwater Park, Marian is resourceful and empowered; significantly, she not only acts but she also writes. She seizes control of the pen, keeping a journal, writing letters, under the control of no man. When she receives a letter from Walter, she reinscribes it into her journal, but burns the actual document, so that his voice only reaches the reader through her text. Much has been made of Fosco's seizure of her journal and his inscribing himself within it, an act tantamount to rape, but the challenges to Marian's authority as writer begin earlier, when Fosco and his tamed wife tamper with the mail she writes, opening the letters to destroy pages of her text. After her audacious act of eavesdropping, which results in a serious illness, Fosco pries into her private papers to appropriate her journal; after this point, she never is shown writing again. However, Fosco is not the only villain here. As Tamar Heller points out, "The colonization of Marian's voice is particularly villainous, but it is only a more obvious version of Hartright's own strategy for containing Marian's narrative energy'' (134). Walter not only edits Marian's journal, retrieving only the parts he considers significant, but he also inscribes himself within it, significantly placing his entry before Fosco's. It is, after all, Walter's editorial comment that explains how the journal ''ceases to be legible'' and which contextualizes Fosco's comments. The silencing of Marian has begun. Later, when Walter recounts a time to which he had no direct access, the months after the death of ''Lady Glyde,'' during which time Marian steals a woman out of the asylum, he explains that he will ''relate both narratives, not in the words (often interrupted, often inevitably confused) of the speakers themselves, but in the words of the brief, plain, studiously-simple abstract which I committed to writing'' (381). The articulate, self-possessed Marian is now portrayed as ''confused,'' her language equated with that of the addled Laura/Anne. Later, Walter will write letters ''[making] the inquiries in Marian's name'' (512); he presumes to appropriate not only her pen, but also her name. To align himself with the Law of the Father, from which Walter has felt excluded, he must seize complete narrative authority; hence by this point in the text, any pretence of a multiplicity of voices has vanished and Walter's voice is the only one that speaks. Significantly, during this time, he also forbids Marian to leave the house, eventually even refusing to confide in her his plans concerning Laura. Although Marian regards Walter as her friend and protector, in terms of her ability to move and speak freely, her situation is in no way different from what it was at Blackwater Park, when she was controlled by Sir Percival and Count Fosco.

The echo that exists between the scenes of Marian imprisoned at Blackwater and again imprisoned at the text's end, in a situation that simulates freedom, recurs throughout the novel, particularly in Walter's relationship with both Sir Percival and the Count. In the former relationship, the paralleling takes the form of action and circumstance. Reading suspiciously, we see both men in dire financial straits; both men marry Laura Fairlie for her money and then imprison her within the house; both men commit forgeries which legitimize their position within society. In Sir Percival's case, his actions are clear, his crimes documented; in Walter's echo of Sir Percival, Walter *appears* to be the noble hero (just as Marian *appears* to have free agency). More subtle textual clues link the men. As I mentioned before, when Walter comes upon the marriage register in which Sir Percival has forged the names of his parents, he discovers his own name written in the book; in the *copy* of the marriage register, his name appears *in place of* Sir Percival's name. Sir Percival's parents' marriage ''exists'' as a blank, a gap, much as Walter's own marriage to Laura goes narratively unrecorded. On the night of Sir Percival's death, Walter is mistakenly addressed by the other man's name. When the burned body is removed from the church, Walter confides in the reader that ''as [he] had never seen the dead man, in his lifetime . . . there was no hope of identifying him'' (481); immediately after this confession, he affirms with complete certainty that the body is that of Sir Percival. Essentially, Walter and Sir Percival fuse just as Laura and Anne do; both are unnecessary to the narrative, since the one is merely an echo of the other. Walter has succeeded in killing the father to become the father, so just as an imprisoned Laura is indistinguishable from Anne, so an empowered Walter is indistinguishable from Sir Percival.

Walter's identification with Count Fosco is more directly tied to narrative style, but also to desire. Both men are attracted to Marian (an attraction Sir Percival does not share), although Fosco speaks and acts out what Walter only hints at. However, what strikes the reader most powerfully is the similarity in the form of self-address both men use. When Fosco writes in Marian's journal, he begins a pattern that he will repeat throughout his later documents, that of referring to himself as ''ME'' (all upper-case letters). When Walter first speaks with Mr. Kyrle, he responds to the attorney's query by whom Fosco and Percival will be forced to confess to their crimes with the words, ''By me'' (lower case letters) (409). At this point, while Walter sounds like Fosco, visually his words do not mirror Fosco's writing. Later, however, when Walter records Marian's account of her conversation with Fosco, he transcribes Fosco's use of the word ''ME'' in all capital letters, and then immediately refers to himself in the same way. Walter is obviously intent on identifying himself with the power of the Italian expatriate. Given that Fosco's power is repeatedly spoken of in terms of his power over women, shown both in his ''taming'' of the feminist Eleanor and in his emotional conquest over Marian, Walter's desire takes on a psychological dimension. Walter wishes to subdue Marian in the same way Fosco controls Eleanor, who is essentially enslaved to her husband through her worship of him. Marian describes the Countess Fosco: ''On the few occasions, when her cold blue eyes are off her work, they are generally turned on her husband, with the look of mute submissive inquiry which we are all familiar with in the eyes of a faithful dog'' (195). Marian goes on to claim ''He looks like a man who could tame anything. . . . If he had married *me*, I should have made his cigarettes as his wife does—I should have held my tongue when he looked at me, as she holds hers'' (195). Yet Marian reveals that the Count is obsequious to his wife in public, that he flirts with her and plays with her. She adds, ''The rod of iron with which he rules her never appears in company—it is a private rod, and is always kept up-stairs'' (200). Fosco's control of his wife is associated with his sexual prowess, that which fascinates Marian and that which Walter lacks and hence desires. Walter's identification with Fosco can be read as his attempt to gain sexual ascendancy over Marian. He intends her response to him to parallel Eleanor's response to Fosco—and he essentially succeeds. At the novel's end, the Laura/Anne-Marian-Walter triangulation strikes one as a form of group marriage. Perkins and Donaghy suggest that Walter's marriage to Laura is not successful, pointing out that "[n]ot only does Walter continue to turn to Marian for help and for intellectual companionship, but also the relationship between Marian and Laura remains far stronger than that between Walter and Laura" (396). Essentially, Walter has two wives—Laura/Anne to bed, and Marian as cowed friend/domestic servant. In spite of all his claims that Marian be the one to "end our Story" (584), it is his pen that transcribes her words and his editorial comment that steals those last words from her. His final act is to refer to Marian as "the good angel of our lives" (584). The demon has been chained, the free woman restrained, the speaking woman silenced. Walter has succeeded where Percival has failed.

But if Walter essentially parallels Percival, how does Fosco enter the equation? Fosco's parallel in the text can be seen to be Pesca, Walter's tiny Italian friend. Walter reveals that he once saved Pesca, a would-be Englishman who is locked forever into "otherness," from drowning, earning the eternal gratitude of the little man, who longs to repay Walter and thereby secures the drawing-master his position at Limmeridge. However, Pesca never appears as anything more than a caricature—the exaggeration with which he is portrayed makes his intrusions into the novel appear disjunctive. Described as the tiniest human being Walter has ever seen, Pesca appears in obvious counterdistinction to Count Fosco, the fattest human being anyone has ever seen, and an Italian expatriate as well. If the text opens with the narration of Walter's saving Pesca from drowning, it ends with Fosco's drowned body on display in the morgue. The echo that has repeatedly marked this text recurs here, but one must ask why. How do these two Italians, or caricatures of Italians, play into Walter's narrative? We notice that Walter and Sir Percival, already mirrored in each other, each is associated with one of the Italians, Walter with the tiny Pesca, Sir Percival with the corpulent Fosco. The Italians enable the two Englishmen, providing avenues of action for each. Hence, Pesca, as I have already shown, obtains Walter the position at Limmeridge and Fosco hatches the scheme to substitute Anne for Laura and come by Laura's inheritance in the process (or to murder Laura for her money). In this way, the Italian characters figure as alter-egos, as the part of the psyches of the Englishmen that pushes them toward their goal, which in both cases is social legitimacy. The "otherness" of the Italians is then appropriate, since they reveal the degree to which Walter and Sir Percival each perceives his own incorporation into society. The absurd little Pesca can never pass himself off as English, in spite of his endless attempts to perfect his speech and to acquire English mannerisms. Walter's condescending descriptions of Pesca, which mock the speech of the little Italian, reveal his *self*-contempt, his sense of his *own* ridiculousness. In her discussion of the miniature and the gigantic, Susan

Stewart claims that "[t]he miniature, linked to nostalgic versions of childhood and history, presents a diminutive, and thereby manipulatable, version of experience, a version which is domesticated and protected from contamination" (69). Walter's narrative focus on Pesca's size is then appropriate given Walter's narrative's dishonesty, a dishonesty which stems from its nostalgia in telling a "love" story of villains overthrown and true love overcoming all obstacles, and which attempts to manipulate and domesticate its tale of the will to power of one determined man, disguising the manipulation and domestication of Marian and Laura as heroism.

The character of Fosco, however, is another matter. Although he, too, possesses his eccentricities, Marian reveals that "[t]here are times when it is almost impossible to detect, by his accent, that he is not a countryman of our own" (197). Since Sir Percival is convinced his crime has gone undetected, his alter-ego also "passes" in society; furthermore, while Percival at times reveals himself to be frustrated with Fosco, overall he respects and is dependent on the figure who represents his interior self. That Percival's alter-ego appears as a count, a nobleman, reveals the strength of Percival's sense of his own authority as well as Walter's anxiety in the face of the father-figure who, presumably, possesses the Phallus. The corpulent Fosco can be read as an inflated Pesca, as the inverse of the bumbling, embarrassing, social failure. As Stewart points out, "The gigantic is viewed as a consuming force" (86); within this novel, regardless of the ending Walter would have us read, the character we recall as possessing the greatest force, the greatest magnetism, the greatest authority, is clearly Fosco.

At Sir Percival's death midway through the narrative, Walter, who has merged with the baronet, identifies himself with Fosco, just as Sir Percival has done. But as I have already shown, what Walter specifically admires in Fosco in his mastery over women, his sexual potency. It becomes possible, then, to read the two Italians as phallic signifiers, as Walter's perception of his own and Sir Percival's power, specifically the power of the phallus, which is linked to maleness, to the ability to write, and to cultural legitimacy. Initially, Walter is befriended by the tiny Pesca, but the association embarrasses the Englishman obsessed with definitions of manhood. When we are introduced to Pesca, we are told he "appeared in the servant's place" (3), again an indication of Walter's own self-assessment. Walter then recounts the day he saved Pesca's life; his language is telling. He speaks of "the poor little man [who] was quietly coiled up at the bottom . . . looking many degrees smaller than I had ever seen him look before" (4). The tiny, coiled up "little man" bespeaks Walter's sense of his own manhood. Having become financially dependent on his mother, unable to find adequate employment, Walter's "manhood" is drowning, shrunken. The name of this little Italian, Pesca, significantly means "fishing" or "fisherman," while, as Peter Caracciola points out, the name Walter comes from the word "water" (397). Additionally, in Sicilian dialect, "lu pesciu," the fish, is a vulgar term for the penis. When, then, Pesca announces the Limmeridge position he has obtained for Walter, the drawing-master is frustrated and reluctant to accept the situation. Unable to act, he has become passive, feminized, in his own eyes a mirror of the contemptible Frederick Fairlie, whose company Walter detests and whose "manhood" in any conventional sense is mocked throughout the text. Significantly, when Walter enters Mr. Fairlie's bedchamber, he finds himself surrounded by pale sea-green silk, drowning once more, the image of his debilitated manhood prostrate on the bed before him, unable to speak loudly or move quickly. When the interview between the two is ended, Walter describes leaving the room as "coming to the surface of the water, after deep diving" (37), an echo again of Pesca's drowning. Little wonder that the audacious Marian, with her "horrid heavy, man's umbrella" (191) strikes Walter as masculine.

The corpulent Fosco is, of course, another matter. I have already mentioned Marian's discussion of his "rod of iron" and subsequent taming of Eleanor (not to mention of Marian). Reading Fosco as phallic does not require a great leap of imagination. However, to add to the imagery, Collins calls attention to Fosco's pet white mice, which on several occasions are shown "pop[ping] in and out of his waistcoat" (198) or being stroked "reflectively with [the Count's] chubby little-finger" (210). However, even the forceful Count's gender identity is revealed as ambiguous. In discussing Fosco's love of pastry, Marian comments that he "devours [it] as I have never yet seen it devoured by any human beings but girls at boarding-schools" (202), associating him with feminine activity and feminine desire. His love of sartorial finery similarly links him with the feminine. Specifically, his "pale sea-green silk" waistcoat associates him with the effeminate Frederick Fairlie, the walls of whose bedchamber are hung with sea-green silk. From Walter's position of gender uncertainty, no one can ever be manly enough—no one truly possesses the Phallus; all claims to authority are, at base, illegitimate. However, Fosco remains the most legitimate character; Walter reveals that his name "was really his own" (582). Therefore, as Walter transforms himself into Percival, he begins his identification with the Italian count, as I have shown. Once he has succeeded in marrying Laura, securing her fortune, and imprisoning Marian, his authority is certain. He no longer needs his alter-ego as enabler or as representative of the phallic order to which he wishes access. Hence, Fosco leaves the narrative in the same way Pesca entered it, through water. However, the little Pesca does not die, but re-enters the narrative, as godfather to Walter and Laura's son.

The re-emergence of the semiotic indicator of gender anxiety problematizes the novel's ending. Heller sees in the novel's final words "the lingering

instability of masculine identity'' (139) and suggests Walter's insecurity in
the presence of his upper-class son as the source of the anxiety. I would
suggest that the situation is more complicated. On the one hand, Walter's
problems with his own masculinity stem from his awareness of his—and his
wife's—lack of legitimacy. Having married ''Laura'' and silenced Marian,
Walter's desire for both women has vanished, since desire is always forward-
looking; the sexual potency and control that Fosco represented to Walter is
something that he has achieved. However, Walter's anxiety about his ''otherness,'' about his knowledge of how he came by Limmeridge, is not eased,
but continues to haunt him. His assembled narratives, which both attempt to
fix in the reader's mind a sense of the justness of his actions at the same time
that they provide all the evidence for distrusting Walter as narrator, grow out
of his desire to prove his rightful place in society. However, Walter himself
understands that his claims to status are not legitimate. As Regis Durand
points out in a discussion of doubling and repetition, ''The doubles, the
duplication itself, never return to an origin, but only to empty places, other
copies'' (70). He goes on to speak of ''the impossibility of a return to an
origin and a legitimacy'' because ''[t]he secret of the absent father is that he,
too, is a lost son'' (70). In other words, having achieved the authority of the
father, Walter realizes there is no authority; Sir Percival was never Sir Percival. Having achieved what Sir Percival was amounts to very little. Having
killed the figure of the double, Walter is doomed to the uncertainty that
characterized him. As Otto Rank writes, ''The . . . slaying of the double,
through which the hero seeks to protect himself permanently from the pursuits
of his self, is really a suicidal act'' (79). Hence Pesca, the indicator of Walter's
dis-ease, reappears. To return to the discussion that opened this article, I would
claim that while Fosco's point about brilliant criminals escaping detection is
true some of the time, it does not take human psychology into account.
Criminals do not escape detection if their sense of guilt would have them
wish to be punished. The problem with Walter is not his mind, even though
he has repeatedly revealed himself to be less than brilliant. Rather, his problem
is with his heart. Even his desperate gesture of naming himself ''Hartright''
cannot efface the sense that he is a conniving imposter who has taken advantage of an opportune situation. Hence his narrative betrays him into providing
the clues that allow a careful reader to unmask him.

NOTES

1. One could argue, of course, that Walter's problem is the universal human one of
   realizing his own impotence. As Jane Gallop states, ''Lacan's message [is] that
   everyone, regardless of his or her organs, is 'castrated' '' (20).

2. Oddly enough, I found no other critics who commented on Marian's feelings for Walter.
3. Another obvious avenue of identity is also overlooked. Anne Catherick is documented to have a severe heart ailment. If Walter's wife were indeed Laura Fairlie, a medical examination would reveal her heart to be sound; significantly, Walter's wife is never subject to such an examination.

WORKS CITED

Auerbach, Nina. *Woman and the Demon*. Cambridge: Harvard UP, 1982.

Caracciola, Peter. "Wilkie Collins' 'Divine Comedy': The Use of Dante in *The Woman in White*." *Nineteenth-Century Fiction* 25 (1971): 383–404.

Collins, William Wilkie. *The Woman in White*. Oxford: Oxford UP, 1989.

Durand, Reges. " 'The Captive King': The Absent Father in Melville's Text." *The Fictional Father: Lacanian Readings of the Text*. Ed. Robert Con Davis. Amherst: U of Massachusetts P, 1981. 48–72.

Gallop, Jane. *Reading Lacan*. Ithaca: Cornell UP, 1985.

Heller, Tamar. *Dead Secrets: Wilkie Collins and the Female Gothic*. New Haven: Yale UP, 1992.

Irwin, John T. *Doubling and Incest/Repetition and Revenge*. Baltimore: Johns Hopkins UP, 1975.

Miller, D. A. "Cage aux Folles: Sensation and Gender in Wilkie Collins's *The Woman in White*." *The Nineteenth-Century British Novel*. Ed. Jeremy Hawtorn. London: Edward Arnold, 1986. 95–124.

Perkins, Pamela and Mary Donaghy. "A Man's Resolution: Narrative Strategies in Wilkie Collins' *The Woman in White*." *Studies in the Novel* 22 (Winter, 1990): 392–402.

Rank, Otto. *The Double: A Psychoanalytic Study*. Trans. Harry Tucker, Jr. Chapel Hill: U of North Carolina P, 1971.

Stewart, Susan. *On Longing: Narratives of the Miniature, the Gigantic, the Souvenir, the Collection*. Baltimore: Johns Hopkins UP, 1984.

Thackeray and Becky Sharp: Creating Women

John Watson

"I don't think Thackeray likes women." The comment from an extremely intelligent young woman, a teacher returning to university for higher qualifications, startled me at the end of my customary impassioned defence of Thackeray's treatment of women in *Vanity Fair*. Implied is the notion that a writer is essentially bound to his work, so that a critic might approach the work to know the life, as Freud does with Leonardo Da Vinci: "in these figures Leonardo has denied the unhappiness of his erotic life and has triumphed over it in his art, by representing the wishes of the boy, infatuated with his mother, as fulfilled in this blissful union of the male and female natures" (XI: 118). Doubt is cast on the objective validity or truth to be found in it, as though a work of art "can be analyzed in terms of the poet's repressions" (Jung 193–94), or limits, or prejudices. A sub-textual river runs through it, leading from the work back to the author. Jung thought the reverse, that "what is essential in a work of art is that it should rise far above the realm of personal life and speak from the spirit and heart of the poet as man to the spirit and heart of mankind" (194).

Critics have been divided over the question of objectivity or subjectivity, in their accounts of Becky Sharp. Some find Thackeray hiding behind her skirts, using her as a Shavian mouthpiece, a "shield behind which to take refuge" (Ennis 142), the "chief projection of the author" (Barickman et al. 184), even the product of "his own compensatory relations with his mother and his daughters" (McMaster 220). Others find a firmly maintained ironic distance between author and character: "not only could she have chosen a way of life morally better than the one she did, but she ought to have chosen it" (Hagan 502). Ultimately, the question of whether or not Thackeray likes women leads into questions of the nature of artistic creation, and of the effects of pursuing a subjective or an objective line of connection between the life

305

and the art. My argument will be that Thackeray's personal ambivalence towards women prompts him to respond to the "conscious outlook of his time," so that he rises "above the realm of personal life" (Jung 191); but that this is a less than transcendent position, shifting variably between the subjective and objective ends of a continuum. Becky Sharp is my focal point, because she seems furthest from Thackeray's own life and "shaped herself in Thackeray's mind from his observation of many women and his reading of many books" (*Letters*, I: clvii).[1] But of course, Amelia, too, is essential for the emerging view of Thackeray's ambivalence towards women in this novel.

Of the external sources for Becky, Theresa Reviss is the only one specifically acknowledged by Thackeray, though clearly his knowledge of her was only superficial (*Letters*, I: clvii–clx). W. G. Elliot remembers how his mother was asked by Thackeray, "So you knew Theresa Reviss. Tell me of her." After telling what she knows, Mrs. Elliot asks in return, "Did you have her in your mind when you wrote the character of Becky Sharp in *Vanity Fair*?" Thackeray merely "nodded his head, said nothing, and left the sofa" (27–28). This adopted daughter of the Bullers, the "only legitimate child of a beautiful young 'improper female,' " as Jane Carlyle snorts magnificently after a difficult week as hostess (II: 144), was however only fifteen years old in 1847, so that her subsequent career as the countess de la Torre could not be used here. Her outrageous refusal of £5,000 a year in marriage came well after Becky's unwilling refusal of Sir Pitt in chapter 14.[2] Thackeray knew her from about 1840 (aged eight) when he describes how Mrs. Buller "is ruining her and killing her with physic—it was really melancholy to see the airs and selfishness of the child."[3] She thus becomes a type of childish vanity for the beginning of the novel; though Thackeray has made Becky not a spoiled pet but an unloved outcast whose "airs" are used exhilaratingly as weapons against the greater selfishness of people like Miss Pinkerton. Dislike is less apparent in the writing than sympathetic understanding; certainly, the creation is more ambivalent for Thackeray than the source.

At the other end of her career, Becky could be linked to Lady Morgan, as Lionel Stevenson has shown (547–51). Various letters show Thackeray's personal acquaintance with this garrulous Irish adventurer, ex-governess and novelist, who achieved rank by refusing to marry without it.[4] Certainly, her writing would have stirred his satiric sense with its garrulity and romantic effusiveness: "Her voice faltered as she spoke—her fingers seemed unconsciously to stray over the chords of the harp—her eyes, her tearful, beautiful eyes, were thrown up to heaven, and her voice" . . . and so on (*The Wild Irish Girl*, 65). The musician is Glorvina, the heroine of *The Wild Irish Girl*, who supplied the name for Glorvina O'Dowd. Becky, too, sings affectingly; of course, she has to sing for a husband at the Sedleys' and so she lays on the pathos as her " 'deep toned voice falter[s]' " in the best drawing-room manner (XI: 42).[5] The wetness of Thackeray's source is used for comic effect:

the "simple appeals to the affections" in the songs become artful appeals in the singer (XI: 41). Thackeray's response to Lady Morgan's writing is certainly sardonic: "I am concerned to see in the Morning Chronicle that Lady Morgan's eyes are so weak that her ladyship is obliged to forego all literary occupation."[6] Presumably also he followed the deflating reviews and parodies of her work in *Fraser's Magazine for Town and Country*. In the "Gallery of Literary Characters No LX" (1835), her knowledge of affairs in France is ridiculed: "A connexion with a quack French clique of the most ignorant and pretending praters in the world has been a great misfortune to Lady Morgan; for on the strength of that acquaintance she thinks herself entitled to pretend to know gentlemen and ladies on the continent" (529).[7] Thackeray reverses this with Becky to show up the ignorant aristocracy around her: "it was only from her French being so good, that you could know she was not a born woman of fashion" (XI: 356). So, Lady Morgan's career and literary efforts provide Thackeray with a satiric stimulus to create a character whose accomplishments he respects much more than those of her source. But then, unexpectedly, in a letter to his mother, Thackeray shows an ability to take Lady Morgan's political earnestness seriously: "why is it that one does not like women to be too smart?—jealousy I suppose: a pretty selfish race we are truly: and Lady Morgan has shown how cruelly the ladies are kept down."[8] He acknowledges his own sexism; the cause; and the consequences of it as she argues them. If anything this suggests a capacity to get beyond his own limits and helps to explain the greater respect for Becky: she is a woman whose refusal to be "kept down" is a sign of her creator's awareness of his own "jealousy."

Thus, apart from providing a stimulus for the child Becky and the later Becky on the Continent, these characters prompt Thackeray to respond to the position of women kept down or denied the usual social powers of privileged girls.

French-born governesses of Thackeray's acquaintance further intensify the Frenchness of his conception of Becky. In his essay, "Shrove Tuesday in Paris" (1841), Thackeray describes his encounter with "Madam or Mademoiselle Pauline," aged "about five-and-thirty years" (*Works*, III: 500–01).[9] He had known her previously as a governess in England, living a life sufficiently pleasant with its "comfortable hot joint every day with the children" (and hence unlike Queen's Crawley). But her reversion to type is what takes his fancy on this reunion. She had left her comfortable life in England to return to France to make shirts for young men like Thackeray: "a grisette she was, and a grisette she would be." "Cheerful in poverty," "lax in . . . morals," she represents a "type quite unknown in England." Specifically, she foreshadows Becky's production of yet another artless story for Jos up the back stairs: Pauline, too, conducts the young Thackeray up a "damp, mouldy staircase" to a room where she imparts "secrets" which would probably offend his present readers (III: 501–03). More generally, she shows Thackeray's interest in broadening his social history, to get beyond English prudery with a character who enjoys being a "perfect Bohemian . . . , herding with people whom it would make your hair stand on end to meet" (XI: 822). True, by this stage in the novel, Thackeray's moral clamps on Becky are rather tighter, as in his siren/monster imagery of slimy tails at the beginning of the same chapter (XI: 812); but his emphasis on her cheerful reversal to type, with the comedy of the brandy bottle clinking against the plate of cold sausage, reflects his more ambivalent attitude to grisettes like Pauline: "to rightly judge the woman's character, we must take the good and the bad together" (III: 502).

The Praslin tragedy in Paris may also have taken Thackeray's attention, being a report of the murder of the duchess of Praslin by her husband, after a period of estrangement intensified by his attentions to the family governess, Mlle Deluzy-Desportes. She too has Becky's eyes, as appears in the duchess's letter to her husband: "Before the steps of the carriage were let down I read in your icy looks—in the faces of my children—in the little green eyes that glittered behind your shoulder, that I should have to undergo treatment so painful and humiliating that I cannot express it in language" (Roughead 282). In the account of the trial, what stands out clearly is the contrast between the governess's protestations of vulnerability ("I am a poor abandoned creature, without other resources than an old grandfather, who is severe") and other accounts of her power, recorded for example in the duchess's diary:

> April 23—. . . Mdlle. D—is mistress of the house. . . . A young woman of twenty-eight to be allowed to enter at all hours the room of a man of thirty-seven, and to receive him at all hours in her own apartment.[10]

Certainly, Jos, after believing in Becky's vulnerability (Rawdon "trampled upon me, and deserted me"), finds out how powerful she is: Dobbin "must go now. Becky might come in," he wails (XI: 833,874).

These morally outrageous and politically radical women show how Thackeray's social and emotional range is broadened to include French manners and morals, and how relatively simple attitudes towards them (mainly negative) have become complex as the artist takes "the good and the bad together" in creating his imaginary society.

Literary forerunners, sources, and influences are more difficult to pin down and different critics have their own preferences. What strikes a reader of the literature available to Thackeray is always the mixing of attitudes in his work, as opposed to the wide range of simply good women or simply bad women in the surrounding literature. On 18 January 1840 Isabella Thackeray went "to the play with the Kembles" (Letters I: 413). This was The Clandestine

Marriage (1766), with a big scene in which Lord Ogleby mistakes Fanny's sighs for signs of tenderness towards himself and declares his passion for her: "Thou amiable creature, command my heart, for it is vanquished!" To which she replies, being already married in secret, "I cannot, my lord—indeed I cannot." She then exits in tears, without divulging her marriage to Lovewell, and leaves someone else to clear up the mess (Garrick and Colman, 702).Thackeray adds immeasurably to the comic effect in his scene between Becky and Sir Pitt: "Oh sir—I—I'm *married already*" (XI: 178). But this "clandestine marriage" (Thackeray picks up the phrase when Briggs tells Mrs. Bute, XI: 196) has all the additional moral ironies of Becky's "genuine tears" over this lost chance to scramble in among the landed gentry. The virtuous eighteenth-century heroine is reflected in Thackeray's Restoration comedy mirror.

A similar process affects Thackeray's response to novels with conventional heroines moving upwards in society, whose quivering virtue he parodies.[11] Fanny Burney's Evelina and Cecilia are conventionally virtuous, Evelina quite spirited in her resistance to the boorish Sir Clement. She is sensitive to music, but wary of indelicate plays like *Love for Love*; and full of admiration for Lord Orville and his elegant manners. Becky's letter shows Thackeray's reaction against such by seeing Sir Pitt in these terms: "anything less like Lord Orville cannot be imagined" (XI: 89). Whereas Evelina characteristically "hesitate[s] between fear and indignation" (93), Becky tackles boorish male attention with zest and inventiveness: "It's a false note," she tells Miss Crawley after depositing Rawdon's missive in the fire (XI: 129). Thackeray elsewhere shows his affection for Burney's "old perfumed, powdered D'Arblay conversation" by quoting from Lord Orville's talk and adopting his own characteristically nostalgic response.[12]

Similarly with Lady Blessington's "Femme de Chambre": Selina the governess moves upwards, but is besieged by wicked noblemen and others until finally she marries "the curate of a neighboring parish, a young man highly esteemed" (386). Thackeray derides the literary Lady Blessington: "Miss Landon, Miss Mitford, or my Lady Blessington, writes a song upon the opposite page, about water-lily, chilly, stilly, shivering beside a streamlet. . . ."[13] But this does not stop him from pursuing a friendship in correspondence and arranging with her to contribute "a little story" to *The Keepsake*, which she edited (*Letters* I: 420). Such examples show Thackeray resisting the perfumed unrealities of literature rather than yielding to any misogynist desire to undermine female motives.

Nevertheless, Thackeray does seem to be drawn towards bad women in literature. Miss Matthews in Fielding's *Amelia* draws from him a critical response that could be applied exactly to Becky: "The Matthews is a wonderful portrait, and the vanity which inspires every one of the actions of that passionate, unscrupulous lady . . . is touched with a master's hand.''[14] Like Becky, she comes between husband and wife, as when she seduces Captain Booth in prison into passing the evening ''in a manner inconsistent with the strict rules of virtue and chastity'' (*Amelia* I: 178). And of course she makes a dark contrast with the heroine Amelia. Like Becky also, she has ''starts of kindness,'' because Fielding ''paints the good part'' of his ''equivocal'' characters.[15] But unlike Becky she is genuinely passionate, in her sexual response to Booth, and in her jealous revenge upon her de facto husband Hebbers when he ''marries'' the widow Carey.

Becky is much more dispassionate and adroit in her intrigues and manipulations, a characteristic rather of Thackeray's French reading. Maria de Flammareil, de Bernard's ''woman of a certain age,'' has a high old time manipulating a variety of lovers present and former, until she responds to pressure from her husband and subsides with a new lover, almost a toy-boy, Léon Boisgontier. She, like Becky with General Tufto, has to deal with attentions from the superannuated M. de Pomenars. The darker strands of sexual menace in the French are reflected in the later intrigues of Lord Steyne and his new mistress, and in the veiled threats to Becky to keep away because ''Rome is very unwholesome'' (XI: 827). Thackeray's delight in the ''exquisite fun and sparkling satire'' of this French novel, his joy in the extravagance of a ''husband and *three* lovers,''[16] finds a muted counterpart in Becky's European wanderings among students and other unsavory characters.

In spite of his evident drawing back from Balzac's ''horrors'' ''not fit for the *salon*,''[17] Thackeray read several of the novels,[18] and the links of imagery and episode suggest a knowledge of *La Cousine Bette* (1846), in particular of Valérie Marneffe, behind the characterization of Becky. Valérie, married to Marneffe, but the mistress of a growing assortment of barons and counts and deputy mayors, uses Cousin Bette as her ''sheep-dog (118)''; is ''an engaging, as a siren'' in persuading Baron Hulot of her undivided attention (207); poses as Delilah for her Polish sculptor Wenceslas (260); shows all the skill of an actress in writing to Hulot that her husband is a tyrant who threatens her: ''You see my tears; they are dropping on the paper and soaking it'' (295); and is disturbed in bed twice with a lover. When Baron Montès finds her with Wenceslas she responds with a ''cackle of forced laughter'' before confronting him boldly (448). These details are all echoed: in Briggs the ''sheepdog''; in the protestations to Lord Steyne that Rawdon is a cruel tyrant; in her letter of ''headache'' and ''heartache'' sent to him in the sponging house; in her ''horrid smile'' at the climactic discovery; and in the frequent siren/Delilah imagery: '' '*I'll* make your fortune', she said; and Delilah patted Samson's cheek.'' ''Don't we see every day in the world,'' asks the narrator, ''great whiskered Samsons prostrate in Delilah's lap?'' (XI: 473, 664, 672, 675, 199, 190). Balzac's hostility towards Valérie is undisguised—she is ''that

shameless slut, as treacherous, but as lovely and as engaging, as a siren"
(207). Thackeray's implied attitude, also harsh, is, however, warmed by his
continual interest in his siren's psychology: she admires Rawdon when he is
roused out of his torpor to attack Lord Steyne, even though she is about to
lose him; and she conducts a vigorous and entertaining offensive to "make
[Rawdon's] fortune," before shifting her attentions elsewhere (XI: 676, 199).
Thackeray respects her. Balzac loathes Valérie Marneffe whose "heart is a
cashbox" and he finally concocts a hideous death for her "after dreadful
sufferings" (165, 464); but Becky ends her days smiling from a respectable
booth in the fair, a sort of settled Clytemnestra, all passion spent.

One has the sense of Thackeray's responding to women in literature with
delighted parody. He draws French manners into his circle and leavens black
French pessimism about the female heart with an interest in female responses
at a time of crisis. The femme fatale, whom he enjoyed in his own "Legende
of the Rhine" (1845), with its Keatsian Lady of Windeck, has progressed,
by way of French intrigues and English silver forks, to the point where Thackeray can answer his own admission of "jealousy" towards clever women by
creating one whom he fears, but also respects. Details of borrowed episodes
and character contrasts flood the narrative, particularly in the continental
chapters. If it be true that we could not "conceive of anyone but a German
writing *Faust*" (Jung 197), it is by no means true that only an English writer
could write parts of *Vanity Fair*.

But these are really only the periphery of the character, the mannerisms
and predicaments off-loaded by her creator. They have little to reveal about
the creation of Becky's inner life and its possible relation to Thackeray's
inner life. Indeed, Becky's inner life is much more shadowy than Amelia's.
Take her reception at Court and subsequent interview with Lord Steyne about
Miss Briggs (ch. 48). These are her performances watched by someone
else—by Rawdon admiring her jewels, or by Lord Steyne wanting to get rid
of Miss Briggs. Her inner life is implied rather than given: she blushes a little
when Rawdon questions her about the diamonds, and then after Lord Steyne
leaves she rises "with the queerest expression of victorious mischief" (XI:
608). What *is* actually given serves the purpose of the moral fable: she feels
"as if she could bless the people out of the carriage windows" on the way
to court (XI: 600). This affectation and elation is not particularly female in
content: others blush around her and attempt their own performances; Georgy,
for instance, is elated at going to grandfather's to live. Thackeray is keeping
his distance, whether from tact or uncertainty.

Amelia, on the other hand, shows what Thackeray has himself experienced
of female responses. She feels "alarm and jealousy" when Georgy brings
back toys after visiting the Miss Dobbins, and then "look[s] out feverishly"
for old Mr. Osborne's proposal (XI: 583). Her scuffle with Mrs. Sedley over

the books for Georgy is followed by the realization that she will have to part with her son: she "[sinks] down in despair and utter misery" (XI: 587). This inner precision comes from the three models who sat for Amelia: "You know you are only a piece of Amelia—my mother is another half: my poor little wife *y est pour beaucoup*."[19] Jane Brookfield, with whom Thackeray was falling in love during the writing of *Vanity Fair*, was his "beau-ideal,"[20] full of "innocence, . . . angelical sweetness and kindness," which filled him with "a spiritual sensuality so to speak."[21] She behaved as he thought a woman should, though she also showed the teasing quality which nearly destroys Dobbin: "you make gentle fun of us all! . . . You see I am making you out to be an Ogre's wife and poor William [sc. Brookfield] the Ogre to whom you serve us up cooked for dinner."[22] Mrs. Carmichael-Smyth provides the motherly femaleness of Amelia, somewhat stifling in its effects: "it gives the keenest tortures of jealousy and disappointed yearning to my dearest old mother . . . that she can't be all in all to me" (*Letters* III: 13). Isabella Thackeray, by now under private care in England, provides the passive, depressive melancholy of Amelia, and also her worship of George. Isabella plays Amelia to William's Georgy in the matter of his wish to go to Belgium without her. She writes sadly to her mother-in-law about her failure to prevent this: "I tried to persuade him not to go but it seems as if I was always to damp him." (*Letters* I: 462) Later, she behaves in such a way that Thackeray, with something of the sultan in himself, plays George to her Amelia, and concludes that she "felt she was unworthy of having such a God of a husband." "God help her," he adds smugly to his friend Edward FitzGerald (*Letters* II: 3). "What magnanimity to stoop to such a humble Cinderella," thinks the narrator on Amelia's behalf (XI: 139).

Becky seems quite unlike these three women whom Thackeray knew intimately.They are not sexy, witty, ebullient social climbers with a cash-box in their heart. Perhaps Thackeray merely gathers his materials as already seen, and in the creation of Becky Sharp keeps a discreet distance from an inner life little known to him. This is not my view of the case: it would diminish her into a collection of tics, of received social and male attitudes handed on, or female attitudes parodied; a sort of cross-channel stereotype borrowed for stirring up English prudes.

Lambert Ennis claims that Thackeray puts himself into Becky, in her mimicry and hatred of pompous authority: "Thackeray understood the rebel's psychology because he was himself a secret rebel; he knew the trickster's [psychology] because he dreaded it" (145). Similarly, Bernard Paris finds in Becky "the aggressive trends that [Thackeray] repudiates but longs to express" (87). This line of approach makes Becky a disguised Thackeray, rebelling against her awful school as Thackeray would have liked to rebel against Charterhouse, and releasing her creator's satirical tendencies; in which case the character of Becky would pose no problem about Thackeray's "liking" women. She satirizes affairs at Queen's Crawley in her first letter to Amelia, nailing up the uncertain status of governesses in her description of Miss Horrocks the butler's daughter who "was very much overdressed, and who flung me a look of great scorn as she plumped down on her knees." The narrator distances himself ironically: "she might, when on her knees, have been thinking of something better than Miss Horrocks's ribbons . . ." (XI: 94, 95). Clearly, both layers of satire reflect Thackeray himself; though equally clearly he finds Becky limited and can see beyond her. Her raging against pedigree—"I am as well-bred as the earl's granddaughter" (XI: 19)—is of a piece with Thackeray's own pique at being snubbed in Grand Cairo by a prince in mufti to whom he spoke: "It is our fault, not that of the great, that they should fancy themselves so far above us."[23] Her heartless response to "some old tenant" who has been sent to the workhouse (XI: 89) reminds one of the younger Thackeray's own admission of Irish beggars that "I have never yet had the slightest sentiment of compassion for the very oldest or dirtiest of them, or been inclined to give them a penny"—though he does wonder how they survive without his help.[24]

Taking these psychological links a bit further, we can see Thackeray using Becky for situations that were affecting him at the time of writing. In 1845, Isabella was placed in the care of Mrs. Bakewell, and by 1846 Thackeray had moved with his daughters to 13 Young St. Kensington. He writes sadly to Isabella's brother Arthur Shawe on 21 June 1847 that "she doesn't want to see me or the children" (*Letters* II: 306); and so dedicates himself to be a solo parent, as he tells his mother: "now God Almighty grant I may be a father to my children" (*Letters* II: 255). So, when Rawdon, not Becky, parents their son, Thackeray relives his own chaste bachelor fatherhood during Isabella-Becky's absence: "For Rawdon minor he had a great tenderness then, which did not escape Rebecca, though she did not talk about it. . . . [He] had begun to think of his bachelorhood with something like regret" (XI: 478). All the loneliness in *Vanity Fair*, from Dobbin reading the *Arabian Nights* or thinking his midnight thoughts about Amelia; to Rawdon minor listening on the stairs to his mother's singing or Rawdon major feeling "scared" at Becky's social triumphs (XI: 653)—all of this reflects Thackeray's personal circumstances, in which he admits he "should like a wife . . . very much" (*Letters* II: 351).

To this extent, then, Becky stands as an Isabella-Thackeray substitute. As Jung says, "Nor is there anything new in the statement that personal factors largely influence the poet's choice and use of . . . materials" (193). One would go on to qualify this by noticing that the "personal factors" are hidden: Becky is not insane and Rawdon is not totally responsible for the domestic arrangements. Becky can be blamed to an extent that Isabella obviously cannot. Thackeray's earlier moral exhortations to Isabella to exert herself and perform her "duty of affection" properly (*Letters* I: 311), have to be abandoned when she slips beyond the range of such boy scout advice. There had been hope, after her suicide attempt in the Irish sea, that Mrs. Carmichael-Smyth might have helped her keep well by "[putting] her mind into healthful train" so that she would be "able to perform the duties w^h. she will be called on to fulfill."[25] But now, in 1848, "the poor little wife seems gradually sinking lower I think."[26]

But still the creation of Becky teases us further. She is not Thackeray, not a transvestite figure, not really grounded on Isabella; in particular, Thackeray *blames* her, for reasons that reach beyond morality, society or literary conventions.

To consider the source of this "blame" is my next point. The narrator of *Vanity Fair* finds women to be irresistibly fascinating match-makers, who are "like the beasts of the field, and don't know their own power" (XI: 34). At their worst (like Rose Dawson) they lack "character enough to take to drinking"; at their best (like Amelia) they cannot "reach up to the height" of an attachment like Dobbin's, being yet tyrannical in their power to deceive honest army officers (XI: 98, 853, 862–63). If, like Becky, they desert their child and betray their husband, it is appropriate that both should reject such a siren, Circe and roving Arab (XI: 812, 843, 856). Tyrants or sirens, deceivers or destroyers, they are vain and limited of accomplishment—except, in this last respect, for Becky. Consequently, he blames them. As the book develops, the vision of the ideal beauty of womanhood shifts in the eye of the beholder, so that the boy Rawdon's attachment to his mother fades: "the beautiful mother-vision had faded away after a while" (XI: 561). At the end, Rawdon "has declined to see his mother, to whom he makes a liberal allowance" (XI: 877).

This attitude of blame is not emphatic in Thackeray's attitudes at the time of writing the novel, apart from his exasperated response to his mother-in-law Mrs. Shawe who withholds the promised money for her daughter: "I wish she would show some sign of recognition of poor Isabella's claims upon her, that the formality of enmity might be given up" (*Letters* II: 324). Otherwise, Isabella's slide into "unintelligible inanity" is balanced (in the same letter) by the delights of the new romantic relationship with Jane Brookfield his "beau-ideal" (*Letters* II: 231). Loneliness is tempered by the delights of parenting his two daughters again after their sojourn in Paris with the Carmichael-Smyths. Some tussles with his mother over the children were inevitable but were handled effectively enough. The proposal that the children live with him now is "best," he writes to her, because there "can't be two first principles in a house" (*Letters* II: 255). The dispute over the "governess question," on which he "intend[s] to have [his] own way," and does so by dismissing the unsuitable Bess Hamerton, drags on in relation to the various candidates who succeed Bess (*Letters* II: 324); and over whether Mrs. Carmichael-Smyth's man Quinn should be sent for to look at Anny's toe (*Letters*

II: 349). But he flatters his parents—"I have never seen finer gentlefolks than you two—or prouder'; and they flatter him: "All my dearest old mother's praises alarm me" (*Letters* II: 334, 355).

Influence from the life in 1847–48 appears in the novel's elegiac perspectives, of happiness remembered in a "brief prime of love" before the failure of marriage (XI: 846); and in the emphasis on the care of children, particularly motherless boys. But not in the blame attached to predatory women who emasculate men by reducing them to a "torpid submissive" state (XI: 578); not in much of the Becky material, in fact. A clue for this blame appears in the letter acknowledging "my dearest old mother's praises": he goes on to write that such praises are "so very undeserved"; which suggests a depressive temperament uneasy under the stroking of praise (*Letters* II: 355). Another clue appears in the letter proclaiming Mrs.Brookfield as his "beau-ideal": "she always seems to me to speak and do and think as a woman should." Then follows (in the letter) a little scene describing some of the things a woman "should" be doing: "You should have seen the three Camberwell ladies the other day, my wife, Mrs Gloyne and Mrs Bakewell—one mending the right hand breeches pocket another the left the third a hole in my coat-tail!" (*Letters* II: 231). Women should mend a man's inexpressibles—in triplicate even. But Becky refuses to do what a woman should—except for her one symbolic shirt-making gesture "for her dear little boy" (XI: 557). Such clues lead us further back into Thackeray's life.

In his early childhood, after being shipped back to England from India without his parents (by which time his widowed mother had married Captain Carmichael-Smyth), Thackeray went for a time to Mr. and Mrs. Arthur's unpleasant school, where at bed-time he would yearn "Pray God, I may dream of my mother."[27] In 1819, when Thackeray was eight, she returned to England, to a rapturous reunion on both sides: "he could not speak, but kissed me and looked at me again and again."[28] She was his protective angel, his ideal of femaleness who returned after a separation to save him and idolize him as her little hero, her "Billy Boy."[29] When she went "splendidly dressed" with him to a concert,[30] she assumed a stature similar to young Rawdon's image of Becky: Rawdon "gazed with all his eyes at the beautifully-dressed princess opposite to him" (XI:477). Thackeray saw his youth as "dark and sad and painful with my dear good mother as a gentle angel interposing between me and misery" (*Letters* II: 361).

Out of this alternation between misery at school and protection at home, a sense of interconnection developed between mother and son. He wonders why she has not written to him on his twenty-fourth birthday, admitting his own remissness but reiterating that "a man does not forget his best friend & his greatest consolation"; certainly, he continues, she would not hurt him "with bad words" as his grandmother Mrs. Butler has been doing (*Letters* I: 289).

He himself shows a similar attitude later to poor Isabella Shawe who had not written for a week during their difficult engagement; he urges her to say to herself of her husband-to-be, "I am sure that he thinks of me daily & hourly, that he feels hurt at any conduct of mine w^h. may bear an appearance of neglect, and elated by the smallest & most trivial mark of my affection." It is, he rounds off with a flourish, "the duty of affection" (*Letters* I: 310–11). The emotional ties between mother and son extend even to the next life, so that Thackeray assures his mother he will not go to Hell, "for if I went you in Heaven w^d. be miserable" (*Letters* I: 464).

She is a strong-principled woman, whose severe religion her son spent some time counteracting, and who did not shrink from administering to others for their own good her strong views of duty. Her son felt called on to remonstrate with her, not for blaming Isabella's failures in duty but for choosing the wrong time for this (she was about to be confined): "Mrs P. repeated to Isabella . . . every word you said, about her faults not doing her duty & so on. . . . It was an unlucky time to lecture her that's all: when she is better talk away and amen" (*Letters* I: 469). The difficulties of choosing a wife sufficiently independent of his mother (and of her own mother, the formidable Mrs. Shawe) become apparent in his tendency to confess Isabella's fault to his mother. A month after his marriage he confesses, "I am sorry to tell you we are the laziest people in all Paris, my wife has fairly beaten me and we never breakfast before eleven o'clock". Further on in this letter he reassures his mother, "I love you better since I was married than before. . . . I am grown a little more *good*" (*Letters* I: 320, 322). Thus, he sides with mother against wife in matters of duty and work. Writing to his mother after Isabella's emotional collapse, he even accepts Isabella's sense of her unsuitability to be his wife: "She . . . thinks she has entailed <all kinds of misfortune on> me, and that she was never fit to be a wife. The old story, & alas partly the <truth."[31]

Amelia is, therefore, an expression of Thackeray's strong views, inherited from his mother, of the dutiful behavior of a good wife. She sits across Russell Square waiting for George to come from his billiards; later, after the grand ball at Brussels, though she knows something has gone wrong, she still waits in bed for him to return: "she had kept her eyes closed, so that even her wakefulness should not seem to reproach him" (XI: 360). Even after his death, she still obeys his silhouette: "she could not bear the reproaches of the husband there before her" in the picture hanging over the chest of drawers (XI: 846). She is a mere appendage of her husband. Yet she is something less than a "beau-ideal": she keeps Dobbin dangling until he is disillusioned (a state Thackeray himself had yet to reach with Jane Brookfield); her humorless weepiness (derived from both Isabella and Mrs. Carmichael-Smyth) is finally exasperating "work" (XI: 866); and her worship of her son does not save him from being sacrificed at the Osborne temple. The final effect of all her devotion to duty is that her son and her husband are likely to be drained by her attentions. Amelia may be a "real gentlewoman" (XI: 708), but William is required to save Georgy from the gambling tables and to fend off Major Loder and Captain Rook. Even this most desirable wife, delicious to kiss under William's cloak, meets with an ambivalent response from her creator: "Farewell, dear Amelia—Grow green again, tender little parasite, round the rugged old oak to which you cling!" (XI: 871)

Becky, on the other hand, is a dangerously independent woman, as far removed as possible from the Thackeray notion of a desirable wife who sits mending inexpressibles. Religious practices for her are a charade, a ceremony to go through with the "gravest resignation" (XI: 469). Far from idolizing her husband she feels barely concealed scorn for him, and finally indifference: "He was allowed . . . to come and go when he liked, without any questions being asked" (XI: 578). Thus, she exhibits everything Thackeray's idealized image of his mother led him to disapprove of. He tends to preach over Becky as he had done over Isabella: "It may perhaps have struck her that to have been honest and humble, to have done her duty, . . . would have brought her as near happiness" as her chosen path, intones the narrator in a fair imitation of Pitt Crawley's manner (XI: 533). And thus he blames Becky and prompts my student's sense of an antagonism towards women, in particular towards a woman who refuses to do her duty and accept her dependence on a man. Whether dependent and dutiful or independent and subversive, women draw the narrator's judgment. Something more than the acceptance of an ideal, and the parody of it for purposes of the moral fable, is, however, involved.

In fact, Thackeray's relations with his mother were not simply ideal. The sense of oneness, that he "can't bear to think of . . . Mother living beyond [him]",[32] has slightly unhealthy aspects, as when he sees her bed years later and feels "very queer" (*Letters* II: 361); or when he disguises his jealousy towards the major, his stepfather: "How disgusted I have felt at hearing my old GP snoring in my mother's room."[33] When others come near, for example his cousin Mary Carmichael who had married the major's younger brother Charles, friction develops because it is soon clear that, as Thackeray admits, "My dear old mother with her imperial manner tried to take the command of both of them, and was always anxious to make them understand that I was the divinest creature in the world, whose shoe-strings neither of them were fit to tie" (*Letters* II: 506). The ironic John the Baptist allusion indicates his uneasy sense of the excessiveness of such favoritism. His sense of her strong-willed desire to dominate undoubtedly contributes towards his own depressive turn of mind: "It gives the keenest tortures of jealousy and disappointed yearning to my dearest old mother . . . that she can't be all in all to me, mother sister wife everything but it mayn't be—There's hardly a subject on w[h]. we don't differ.'' To Thackeray it seems that their connections supersede even those of her own marriage: "she lives away at Paris with her husband . . . who loves nothing but her in the world, and a jealousy after me tears & rends her" (*Letters* III: 12–13).

Like young Rawdon, Thackeray feels the loss of the ideal image in his developing ambivalence: "when I was a boy at Larkbeare, I thought her an Angel & worshipped her. I see but a woman now, O so tender so loving so cruel" (*Letters* III: 13). Her punitive evangelical Christianity and her entire absence of humor gave her, or expressed themselves in, a melancholy personality, which Thackeray recognized in himself: "I suppose she inherits from me rather a gloomy temper" he writes of his mother late in life, reversing the normal sequence as if to intensify it and even take the blame (*Letters* IV: 233). He writes to reassure Anny, quailing under their grandmother's harsh interpretations of the Bible: "When I was of your age I was accustomed to hear and read a great deal of the Evangelical (so called) doctrine and got an extreme distaste for that sort of composition" (*Letters* III: 93), thus paving the way for her hoped-for assertion of independence with maturity. Humorless, evangelical Lady Southdown is his literary revenge.

Thus at the time of writing *Vanity Fair*, Thackeray can refer to his dispute over the "governess question," as well as to his grandmother's death, and conclude, "I grow as melancholy as an owl" (*Letters* II: 324). But the melancholy reaches further back in his life, which explains his difficulty in accepting praises from his mother: "All my dearest old mother's praises alarm me and everybody else's indeed: They are so very undeserved" (*Letters* II: 355). Lady Ritchie writes of the lasting effects on her father of this powerful authority's judgments: "she used to make him unhappy by her reproofs & she always treated him as if he was a little boy."[34]

This ambivalance, this experience of women as both angelic and imperious, jealous, cruel, wanting to dominate in male-female relations, is what takes the authorial "blame" of Becky beyond mere comfortable moral tut-tutting. Becky destroys instead of protecting; she attaches herself to a man and sucks the life out of him, perhaps even kills him literally. Many a marriage in the fair bears the imprint of her interference, from old Sir Pitt and Lady Rose, who is merely contemptible ("I need not be afraid of *that* woman," (XI: 92), to Amelia and George, where the sneers are open: "Another woman was laughing or sneering at her expense, and he not angry" (XI: 354). Only Dobbin manages to hear the siren without turning into a swine; whereas other men are entangled in green silk bonds, or find their heavy cavalry routed. Noticeably often, they regress to a boyish state: Jos weeps childishly over her possible displeasure; Sir Pitt comes to depend on her to keep his rooms tidy; and Rawdon becomes her "errand-man" to whom she says "go and have ginger-beer and sawdust at Astley's" (XI: 659, 662).

Thackeray's own ambivalent experiences of women lie behind the various ambivalences in *Vanity Fair*. Amelia and Becky are contrasted as good and bad; but also, Amelia the good mother has a parasitic effect on men and Becky the bad mother is charming and witty and even contributes to a rake's reform. The difficulties of achieving emotional independence in the life are reflected in the creations of an extremely clinging woman and an extremely independent woman. Both have their delights and dangers. Moments when a woman simply takes a man in her arms and caresses him—as Mrs. Sedley does with her bankrupt John, or Lady Jane with Rawdon in the sponging house—are a rare and "inexpressible delight and anguish" (XI: 213).

The limits of this biographical approach to literature are, first, that the answer to my student's question about whether Thackeray likes women is arguably to be found without reference to Thackeray's life. Evidence for moral and emotional disapproval can be found actually in the novel he wrote; though we cannot prove conclusively an authorial dislike from inside a novel, since it might be putting a special case, as here—a moral fable designed to argue the negative for the question, "Which of us is happy in this world?" (XI: 878).

Further, such biographical questions do not demonstrate that the art of the novel is great or otherwise. Even Freud modestly disclaims any aesthetic intent in his discussion of Leonardo: "Pathography does not in the least aim at making the great man's achievements intelligible" (130). Certainly we must remain mindful of Wimsatt and Beardsley's 1954 caveat: "The poem is not the critic's own and not the author's (it is detached from the author at birth and goes about the world beyond his power to intend about it or control it). The poem belongs to the public" (5).

The biographical approach to literature has two virtues. First, it helps us to enjoy the creative process behind art—the limits, shape and emphasis of this particular creation, coming at this particular point in Thackeray's life and at this particular point in literary and social history; an art created by a man with certain attitudes, coping with certain formative experiences. In particular, Thackeray gets beyond the difficulties of his own domestic life with his innate sense of humor, which is what enlivens the characterization of Becky and draws people towards her with reckless condonation. As he himself recognized: "I inherit from her [sc.his mother] this despondency I suppose—but have the pull over her of a strong sense of humor" (*Letters* IV: 264).

Second, it provides a perspective on the question of subjectivity versus objectivity. As if to illustrate Jung's "objective and impersonal" artist,[35] Barickman, MacDonald and Stark have developed A. E. Dyson's view that Thackeray reflects his culture as "fundamentally rotten."[36] Everything in the novel that appears critical of women is seen to have an objective moral purpose: the "stereotype of tireless feminine devotion" originates in "a male doctrine that women have been made to subscribe to'' (156). Apparent agreement between narrator and male readers is didactic, to ''show them the barbarousness of the gentleman's easy assurance'' (156). The result is that in the view of these critics our gaze is continually directed outwards towards society in a process that is noble and moral, and objective: Becky's ''attraction [for the reader] is based upon rebellion against a system that subjugates the oppressors as well as the victims, and it causes a *human* fellow feeling'' (189). That is, the ''real shoddiness is in the ideals themselves, not in the women who embody them'' (173).

Thackeray is thus larger than his experiences—the subjective element is diminished as the characters begin to have a life of their own which diverges from their creator's life. Amelia does not collapse into madness like Isabella, or remain inaccessible like Jane Brookfield, or overwhelm her child like Mrs. Carmichael-Smyth, or leave a grieving bachelor/husband. When Thackeray writes privately about Becky's life subsequent to the novel he subsides into a merely moral mode and punishes her by, for example, specifically depriving her of her title (which in the novel she still uses): ''it turned out that Colonel Crawley . . . had died of fever three months before his brother, whereupon Mrs. Crawley was obliged to lay down the title which she had prematurely assumed'' (*Letters* II: 376). In the novel, however, Becky faces them out with a smile and they scuttle away from her booth. Thus, she resists her creator's wish to allegorize her (like Spenser's Malbecco who becomes Gealosie). The creative imagination gets beyond personal and moral limits; or, as Thackeray says, ''I don't control my characters . . . I am in their hands, and they take me where they please'' (*Jeaffreson* I: 196). Thackeray himself was scornful of the activities of ladies: ''a woman who occupies herself all day with her house and servants is frivolous, ditto she who does nothing but poonah-painting and piano forté, also the woman, who piddles about prayer-meetings, and teaches Sunday schools'' (*Letters* I: 317). Becky's hostility to all these occupations reflects the novel's sense of the powerlessness and triviality of the lives of women.

The defect of this objective approach is that it softens the focus and blurs the gaps between author and character and reader. If Becky is ''the chief projection of the author'' and we as readers experience ''*human* fellow-feeling,'' there is a closing of these gaps and a romanticizing of Becky into a colorful victim (Barickman et al. 184, 189). But as John Hagan shows, Thackeray maintains his critical distance from Becky, particularly in developing his religious fable: ''once we grant this religious perspective, not only the argument from circumstance but all the others too which have been used to urge our sympathy for Becky must crumble'' (502); because from a religious point of view an individual must ultimately take responsibility for her choices: ''It may perhaps have struck her that to have been honest and humble, to have done her duty, and to have marched straightforward on her way, would have brought her as near happiness as that path by which she was striving to attain it" (XI: 533).

That is, Thackeray's profound criticism of society's construction and suppression of women does not absolve them from personal responsibility or protect them from their creator's judicious hostility, permeated as it is with "bleeding" and "regret" (XI: 561, 478) from his private experiences of an absent mother and wife.

Further, the "objective" critics imply that Thackeray somehow transcends his culture, or cuts himself loose from its restrictions, to offer "profound insights . . . about Victorian culture" (Barickman et al. 193). But these insights are clearly not absolute. Thackeray is a man of his time, subjectively involved with women, ambivalent about the social roles they adopt. When Rawdon minor gasps out his rage and grief to the kitchen staff after Becky boxes his ears, the narrator comments that "the beautiful mother-vision had faded away" (XI: 561). Is this because Becky refuses to play the ideal role demanded of her by male society? Certainly. But also, the narrator himself bleeds with the boy's "bleeding" heart. Becky *should* have let him hear her singing. There is more than just the kitchen inquisition sitting in judgment upon this fading of the mother-vision. Thackeray himself believes in the role of mother, about which he has become doubly disillusioned in his own life.

Less than fully objective, then; but less than fully subjective as well. Thackeray himself continued to write lovingly to his mother, "so cruel" as she was, while in his fiction the boy Rawdon (in the episode quoted) engages in hostility with Lord Steyne's hat (XI: 562) until all the servants know about it and the narrator then develops his own consideration of "guilt" underneath appearances, preparatory to his great question about Becky's "guilt" (XI: 677).

In this great novel, then, there is a complex balance between objectivity and subjectivity. From either end of the continuum, my student's sense of "blame" might have been picked up. Her remark might be modified: Thackeray personally dislikes female power and its social causes; but still cries "Un biglietto" with his incorrigible creation.

NOTES

1. Ray's book *The Buried Life* gives his fullest account of "the relation between Thackeray's fiction and his personal history" (sub-title), but Becky is not examined there in any detail.
2. Letter from Thackeray to Mrs Carmichael-Smyth, 5 June 1848 (*Letters* II: 382).

3. Letter from Thackery to Mrs Carmichael-Smyth, 18 January 1840 (*Letters* I: 413).
4. See *Letters* III: 373, IV: 123, 343.
5. Quotations here and following refer to the Oxford Thackeray. Page numbers from *Vanity Fair* (the same as those in the World's Classics edition) are given in the form XI: 42. Other references are given in the form *Works* XIII: 147.
6. Letter to B. W. Procter, 29 December 1838 (*Letters* I: 376).
7. Thackeray does express his own view in his *Paris Sketch Book* (1841): "Authors such as Lady Morgan and Mrs Trollope, having frequented a certain number of tea-parties in the French capital, begin to prattle about French manners and men—. . . ; they speak to us, not of men, but of tea-parties" (II: 97).
8. *Letters* I: 447. He refers to *Woman and her Master* (1840), Lady Morgan's history of women, in which she asks, "Is woman still a thing of sufferance and not of rights, as in the ignorant infancy of early aggregation, when the law of the strongest was the only law acted on?" (I: 9).
9. See also Colby, 239–40.
10. *Complete History of the Praslin Tragedy*. The two quotations are taken from the sections in English, 5(a), 7(a).
11. For example Fanny Burney: *Evelina* (1778) and *Cecilia* (1782). See also Moler, 171–81.
12. "On a Peal of Bells." *Works* XVII: 605.
13. "A Word on the Annuals." *Works* II: 337–8.
14. "Fielding's Works." *Works* III: 391. See also Rogers, 141–57.
15. "Fielding's Works." *Works* III: 392, 391.
16. "On Some French Fashionable Novels." *The Paris Sketch Book. Works* II: 109.
17. *Paris sketch Book. Works* II: 99; "Jerome Paturot." *Works* VI: 320.
18. *Les Chouans, Le Peau de Chagrin. Letters* IV: 483.
19. Letter to Mrs Brookfield. *Letters* II: 394.
20. Letter to Mrs Carmichael-Smyth, 6 March 1846. *Letters* II: 231.
21. A provocative confession from Thackeray to Rev. William Brookfield, 3 February 1847. *Letters* II: 271–72.
22. Letter to Jane Brookfield, 14 October 1848. *Letters* II: 439.
23. *The Book of Snobs. Works* IX: 274.
24. *The Irish Sketch Book. Works* V: 42.
25. Letter to Mrs Carmichael-Smyth, 21–23 September 1840. *Letters*, I: 478.
26. Letter to Mrs. Carmichael-Smyth, 7 January 1858. *Letters*, II: 334.
27. "On Letts's Diary." *Works* XVII: 554.
28. Lady Ritchie, *St. Nicholas* XVII: 107, quoted in *Letters* I: 9–10n.
29. Mrs. Charmichael-Smyth, letter to Mrs Graham. *Letters*, I: 10.
30. Ray, *The Uses of Adversity* 109.
31. *Letters*, I: 480. The pointed brackets indicate Ray's "conjectural restoration" of "mutilated" words (*Letters* I: lxvi).
32. Transcript of manuscript letter, quoted in Ray, *The Uses of Adversity* 109.
33. Manuscript letter, 6 December 1856, quoted in Ray, *The Uses of Adversity* 113.
34. Lady Ritchie's manuscript reminiscences, 1878, quoted in Ray, *The Uses of Adversity* 110.

35. "He is objective and impersonal—even inhuman—for as an artist he is his work and not a human being" (Jung 194).
36. See also Dyer: Becky represents "women who confront the demands of society aggressively" (216). Micael Mary Clarke adopts a similar approach to Thackeray as a proto-feminist: "he enabled his readers to visualize the sufferings of women like Norton, circumventing any prejudice against her scandal-ridden past or against the feminist movement itself" (350).

WORKS CITED

Balzac, Honoré de. *La Cousine Bette*. Paris, 1846. Tr. James Waring. London: Everyman's Library, 1991.

———. *Les Chouans*. Paris, 1829.

———. *Le Peau de Chagrin*. Paris, 1831.

Barickman, R., S. MacDonald, and M. Stark. *Corrupt Relations: Dickens, Thackeray, Collins and the Victorian Sexual System*. New York: Columbia UP, 1982.

Bernard, Charles de. *La Femme de Quarante Ans*. Paris, 1836: Tr. as *The Woman of a Certain Age*. Ed. Mrs. Gore. London, 1841.

Blessington, Marguerite, Countess of. *The Memoirs of a Femme de Chambre*. Leipzig, 1846.

Burney, Fanny. *Evelina*. Dublin, 1778. London: Everyman's Library, 1958.

———. *Cecilia*. Dublin, 1782.

Carlyle, Jane Welsh. *Letters and Memorials*. Ed. Thomas Carlyle and J. A. Froude. 3 vols. London: Longmans, Green, 1883.

Clarke, Micael M. "William Thackeray's Fiction and Caroline Norton's Biography: Narrative Matrix of Feminist Legal Reform." *DSA* 18 (1987): 337–51.

Colby, Robert. *Thackeray's Canvass of Humanity*. Columbus: Ohio State UP, 1979.

A Complete History of the Praslin Tragedy. France: Cour des pairs, 1847. Tr. (unknown) "The Praslin Tragedy at Paris."

Dyer, Gary R. "The 'Vanity Fair' of Nineteenth-Century England: Commerce, Women and the East in the Ladies' Bazaar." *Nineteenth-Century Literature* 46 (1991): 196–222.

Elliot, W. G. *In My Anecdotage*. London: Philip Allan, 1925.

Ennis, Lambert. *Thackeray: the Sentimental Cynic*. Evanston: Northwestern UP, 1950.

Fielding, Henry. *Amelia*. London, 1751. 3 vols. Oxford: Basil Blackwell, 1926.

Fraser's Magazine for Town and Country. Vol XI: May, 1835.

Freud, Sigmund. "Leonardo Da Vinci and a Memory of His Childhood." 1910. *The Complete Psychological Works of Sigmund Freud*. Ed. James Strachey. 24 vols. London: Hogarth Press, 1953–74. XI: 63–137.

Garrick, David, and George Colman the Elder. *The Clandestine Marriage*. London, 1766. *Plays of the Restoration and Eighteenth Century*. Ed. D. MacMillan and H. M. Jones. New York: Holt, Rinehart and Winston, 1931.

Hagan, John. "*Vanity Fair*: Becky Brought to Book Again." *Studies in the Novel North Texas State University* 7 (1975): 479–506.

Jeaffreson, J. C. *A Book of Recollections*. 2 vols. London: Hurst and Blackett, 1893.

Jung, C. G. *Modern Man in Search of a Soul*. Tr. C. F. Baynes. London: Kegan Paul, 1933.

McMaster, Juliet. *Thackeray: The Major Novels*. Toronto: U of Toronto P, 1971.

Moler, Kenneth L. "Evelina in *Vanity Fair*: Becky Sharp and Her Patrician Heroes." *Nineteenth-Century Fiction* 27 (1972): 171–81.

Morgan, Lady, *née* Sydney Owenson. *The Wild Irish Girl*. London, 1806. London: Pandora, 1986.

———. *Woman and her Master*. 2 vols. London, 1840.

Paris, Bernard J. *A Psychological Approach to Fiction*. Bloomington: Indiana UP, 1974.

Ray, Gordon N. *The Buried Life*. London: Oxford UP, 1952.

———. *Thackeray: The Uses of Adversity, 1811–1846*. London: Oxford UP, 1955.

Ritchie, Anne I. Thackeray, Lady. *St. Nicholas*, XVII.

———. manuscript reminiscences (see Ray, *Thackeray: The Uses of Adversity*).

Rogers, Winslow. "Thackeray and Fielding's *Amelia*." *Criticism* 19 (1977): 141–57.

Roughead, William. *The Seamy Side*. London: Cassell, 1938.

Stevenson, A. Lionel. "*Vanity Fair* and Lady Morgan." *PMLA* XLVIII (1933): 547–51.

Thackeray, William Makepeace. *The Letters and Private Papers of William Makepeace Thackeray*. 4 vols. ed. Gordon Ray. Cambridge: Harvard UP, 1945–6.

———. *The Oxford Thackeray*. 17 vols. ed. George Saintsbury. London: Oxford UP, 1908.

————. *Vanity Fair*. London, 1848. Ed. John Sutherland. Oxford: Oxford UP, 1983.

Wimsatt, W. K. Jr. and Monroe C. Beardsley. "The Intentional Fallacy." *The Verbal Icon: Studies in The Meaning of Poetry*. Lexington: U of Kentucky P, 1954. 3–18.

Acknowledgement: to my colleague Lawrence Jones, for reading the manuscript and making a suggestion which helped to change the direction of the last pages.

Recent Dickens Studies: 1994

Joel J. Brattin

Critical and popular interest in Dickens continues unabated; this essay, like its predecessors, treats a great many books and articles. I have omitted dissertations, audio and video tapes, items published in any language other than English, and a host of other peripheral or ephemeral items, though I cannot claim to have been entirely systematic in these decisions; despite these omissions, and the exclusion of several items appearing in on-line bibliographies or published checklists which proved not to have actually been published in 1994, the number of treated items—for the first time in the history of *Dickens Studies Annual*—extends well beyond one hundred. I note with regret and dismay that, due to circumstances beyond my control, several texts which were in fact published in 1994 were not made available to me. Other works have, no doubt, eluded my notice; I apologize for any books or articles I have unintentionally overlooked.

Though no system for treating this mountain of titles is ideal, I have chosen in this essay to treat scholarly and popular editions of Dickens' works first, followed by casebooks and notes, adaptations, fictional works treating Dickens, and children's books. The largest portion of this review article, that devoted to studies of individual works, is next; I work chronologically from *Sketches by Boz* to *Edwin Drood*. Next come biographical studies of individuals in Dickens' circle, general approaches to Dickens' career, and surveys of criticism. I conclude by treating studies of Dickens that focus on more than one title; I group similar approaches when possible. This brief introduction (and judicious use of the index at the back of the volume) should help readers find those sections of this review of greatest relevance to their own interests.

I have attempted to offer fair summaries of the arguments in the various books and articles I treat here, as well as evaluative comments; though my summaries are by no means intended as a substitute for the original works, I hope they will be useful in helping readers determine which items published in 1994 will be of greatest interest and value.

The finest scholarship on Dickens published in 1994 deserves special mention here. Of the articles focusing on Dickens' earlier works, Robert Newsom's essay on affinities between *Pickwick* and the utilitarians, Nancy Weston's exploration of an original for *Oliver Twist*'s Bill Sikes, Paul Schlicke's historical note on the song and supper-clubs alluded to in *The Old Curiosity Shop*, and Robert M. Polhemus's exploration of the religious impulses behind that same novel are most revealing. Of the articles treating later works, Stanley Friedman's historical work on a source for Uriah Heep in *David Copperfield*, Lynette Felber's feminist analysis and Daniel H. Lowenstein's legal analysis of *Bleak House*, and Razak Dahmane and Barry Thatcher's considerations of metaphor and language theory in *Hard Times* are especially rewarding. Each of these essays repays close attention. More wide-ranging books, including Gail Turley Houston's *Consuming Fictions* and Harry Stone's *The Night Side of Dickens*, (despite significant limitations) are also provocative and insightful. In the end, however, the two finest works of 1994 are Malcolm Andrews's *Dickens and the Grown-Up Child* and Anny Sadrin's *Parentage and Inheritance in the Novels of Charles Dickens*. Both books combine attentive readings of Dickens with a strongly developed historical sense, lively and imaginative original thinking, sensitivity to Dickens' language, and grace and style in presentation. Both represent the scholarship that I believe will be most enduring; we can only hope as many excellent works on Dickens will be published every year.

EDITIONS

Though editions of some fifteen individual titles reached me in time for inclusion in this essay, others did not, including editions reportedly published by Barnes and Noble, Bracken, Chancellor, Ebury, Longman, W. Murrow, Oxford University, Penguin, and St. Martin's presses. Of the editions under review here, Michael Slater's edition of *Sketches by Boz and Other Early Papers, 1833–39*, as the first volume of "The Dent Uniform Edition of Dickens' Journalism," may be the most important. Unfortunately, it is incomplete, and textually unsophisticated. Slater fails to consult Dickens' texts in the form in which they were originally published; the text, evidently deriving from an early twentieth-century source, and published without textual apparatus, is unreliable, failing to reflect either Dickens' original intentions or his final ones. However, the book does include a useful glossary and index; the headnotes and annotations will make the book useful for students.

The Everyman's Library editions of *Martin Chuzzlewit, Dombey and Son*, and *Our Mutual Friend* derive their texts from the New Oxford Illustrated edition. All three provide a select bibliography and chronology, Dickens' prefaces or postscripts, and G. K. Chesterton's introduction to the original 1907 Everyman's Library edition. The books offer no explanatory annotations, but provide all of the original illustrations; they are reasonably-priced and attractive hardbound volumes. The introductions to *Martin Chuzzlewit, Dombey and Son*, and *Our Mutual Friend*, by William Boyd, Lucy Hughes-Hallet, and Andrew Sanders respectively, are considered in the section devoted to criticism below.

The Everyman Paperback Classic editions (not to be confused with the Everyman's Library editions) are an energetic competitor with the popular Penguins. Nineteen ninety-four saw the publication of Steven Connor's *Oliver Twist*, David Parker's *Nicholas Nickleby*, Michael Slater's *Martin Chuzzlewit*, Andrew Sanders's *Bleak House*, Grahame Smith's *Hard Times*, Norman Page's *A Tale of Two Cities*, and Robin Gilmour's *Great Expectations*, under the general editorship of Michael Slater. This edition is intended to include, eventually, not just the novels and Christmas books, but all of Dickens' short fiction, journalism, travel writings, and children's books as well; *A Holiday Romance and Other Writings for Children* was published in 1995, so I do not treat it here, but its contents afford evidence of the scope General Editor Slater has in mind. The texts of the novels derive from the 1867–1868 Charles Dickens Editions, on the theory that this edition will include the author's latest revisions; the volumes include Dickens' prefaces and all the original illustrations, plus introductory essays (treated individually in the section devoted to criticism, below), biographical material about Dickens, a chronology, annotations, surveys of criticism and suggestions for further reading, and one or-two-sentence summaries of the contents of each chapter. Some volumes include historical appendices; for example, *Nicholas Nickleby* offers materials on Yorkshire schools, *Hard Times* includes materials on utilitarianism, and *Great Expectations* includes commentary on the variant endings. The prices are extremely low—*Martin Chuzzlewit*, for example, is just $5.99, and *Great Expectations* only $3.95—and these texts will undoubtedly find a wide readership.

The World's Classics edition of *Great Expectations* reproduces Cardwell's flawed text from the Clarendon, omitting the editorial apparatus. Unlike the Clarendon edition, however, this paperback is inexpensive, and with Kate Flint's fine introduction, 13 pages of explanatory notes, and whatever reflected glory the paperback gains from spinning off from the Clarendons, the World's Classics edition may compete with the popular Penguin editions for classroom use. The World's Classics edition of *Hard Times* is no better, textually, than the edition of *Great Expectations* in the same series; this text simply reproduces a 1924 Oxford University Press setting based on the 1868 "Charles Dickens" edition. The real virtues of this edition are its low price, and the useful introduction and the twenty pages of helpful explanatory annotations Paul Schlicke provides.

The Dover Thrift edition of *The Cricket on the Hearth and Other Christmas Stories* includes "The Holly Tree" and "The Haunted House." The texts are reportedly reprinted from an undated New York publication of *Christmas Books* and *Christmas Stories* by The Booklover Press, and thus have no claims to any textual authority. This edition offers no notes or illustrations—but it costs only a dollar, quite a bargain in the 1990s.

Some might consider Robin Waterfield's abridgement of *Oliver Twist* for Puffin books more of an adaptation than an edition, but since Waterfield attempts to retain "the atmosphere of the original" and preserve "Dickens's own words throughout," I mention it here. The book, published without any explanatory annotation, is 346 pages in length, with only moderately larger type than most other paperbacks. Sikes's flight after his murder of Nancy, and the chapter treating "Fagin's Last Night Alive," are wholly omitted.

Though 1994 brought us no new edition of the letters, nor any new scholarly edition of Dickens' texts, there were three review articles treating scholarly editions. In his review essay on Volume 7 of the Pilgrim edition of Dickens' letters, Joel J. Brattin delights in the publication of many previously unknown letters that illuminate Dickens' life, work, and concerns, and praises the erudite and concise annotations to those letters, but notes that omitted letters, overlooked manuscript sources, and errors in transcription, as well as inaccuracies in identifying the locations of letters, leave room for improvement in this essential research tool. Alexander Welsh's review essay on the same volume focuses on Dickens' letters to women, especially Angela Burdett Coutts and Maria Beadnell Winter, but also touches on Dickens' letters about politics. Welsh argues that the letters "provide some of the best reading one can hope for on the novelist and his times." In a review essay on the latest volume of the Clarendon Dickens, Margaret Cardwell's edition of *Great Expectations*, Brattin finds little to praise, lamenting Cardwell's choice of copytext, her acceptance of regularized spelling and punctuation, and her failure to provide a complete and accurate textual apparatus, and arguing that the Clarendon does not provide what readers expect of an authoritative scholarly edition.

The Bureau of Electronic Publishing produced a multimedia CD-ROM in 1994: *Like the Dickens: Complete Works*. This CD-ROM includes the texts of Dickens's novels, short stories, and other works, including such things as *Sketches by Boz* and *American Notes*; unfortunately, there is no indication of the source for these texts. The disk includes a few critical works, including Forster's biography of Dickens, and also a gallery of illustrations and photographs—though the original illustrations to the novels are lacking, and documentation for those illustrations that are included is weak or nonexistent, as it is for the texts themselves. The multimedia effects are unimpresssive; though there are evidently some narrated bits, I found it impossible to access them. The on-line glossary, while a fine idea, is substandard; clicking on James Emerson Tennent, I got a note on Ralph Waldo Emerson, and similarly wrong-headed notes appeared for the highlighted words "rate" and "monthly." Though the quality of the texts themselves is untested (and I doubt anyone would choose to read a Dickens novel off a computer screen), this CD-ROM is certainly the cheapest way I know of to purchase Dickens' complete works. Furthermore, the ability to search all of Dickens' major works (and most of his minor ones) by word is of some potential use to scholars.

CASEBOOKS AND NOTES

Only one critical casebook devoted to Dickens was published in 1994: Roger Sell's collection of contemporary critical essays on *Great Expectations*. Designed primarily for undergraduates, the volume reprints a dozen essays, originally published between 1974 and 1989, that illustrate psychological, sociological, structuralist, post-structuralist, and reader-response approaches; Sell also provides a useful introduction that traces the history of critical response to the work, emphasizing the approaches of the last twenty years or so. The book contains no original essays, beyond the editor's introductory one; the fact that these essays are all printed recently enough that they are readily available elsewhere, and that they are no longer up-to-the-minute "contemporary," diminishes the value of this anthology slightly.

Jeffrey Karnicky and Judy Clamon provide the first two Dickens volumes (for *A Tale of Two Cities* and *Great Expectations* respectively) in an appalling new series of "Literature Study Guides" called MAXnotes. (Dr. Max Fogiel, the "Program Director," urges readers to use the notes "as a companion to the actual work, not instead of it"—but the short chapter-by-chapter summaries, of course, urge students to do quite the opposite.) These shabbily illustrated books (evidently written by college graduates, as B.A. and M.A. follow the author's names on the title pages) offer a great deal of plot summary and generalization, with a fair amount of misinformation and inaccuracy. Karnicky informs his readers that "Dickens could be verbose," characterizes the innocent seamstress of the antepenultimate chapter only as "a condemned woman," and lists only the Signet Classic edition of *A Tale of Two Cities* in his bibliography; he omits all mention of *Martin Chuzzlewit, Dombey and Son, Little Dorrit, Great Expectations*, and *Our Mutual Friend* from his introductory comments on Dickens' life and works. Clamon claims that Victoria ruled for "nearly 60 years," and offers, in her five "sample" essays, conclusions that are invariably restatements of theses, with one or the other always in the passive voice; her section on Dickens' life and works names only

Pickwick Papers, David Copperfield, and *Great Expectations*. The analyses, study questions (and answers), and sample essay topics (with outlines) offer nothing of value to students, who should certainly avoid wasting their time with these volumes.

Reneé Swanson's brief article, noting that dead white males remain an essential part of the curriculum at most universities, has little to do with Dickens, despite its title; I mention it here only because Swanson lists *A Tale of Two Cities* as #9 and *Great Expectations* as #16 in the top 25 bestselling titles in the Cliffs Notes series. Swanson also asserts, erroneously, as it turns out, that the Norton Critical edition of *Great Expectations* will be published "in spring 1994."

ADAPTATIONS

Most of the 1994 adaptations of Dickens are, predictably, of the *Christmas Carol*. David Holman's adaptation for the stage is reasonably successful, if nowhere near as faithful to Dickens' text as Holman suggests. Holman claims that "almost all" of what we read is Dickens' words, but he has Scrooge saying things like "Drat the cheese!" and "You damn puppy"—and dancing the conga. This adaptation appears to be designed for gradeschool children; nine of this book's 77 pages are devoted to "Questions and Explorations," and to a glossary defining such words as "beloved," "stingy," "wombat," and "Satan." A far more interesting treatment of the same book is John R. Carroll's *A Carol for Tiny Tim*, a sequel set 15 years after Scrooge's conversion. Tim Cratchit has grown into a greedy, manipulative young man who extorts money from his father and his uncle Scrooge by pretending that his leg hurts, even though he is now fully recovered. It takes a return visit from the spirits to bring about the happy ending: Tim, who begins the play by swigging from a bottle and exclaiming to his rowdy friends "Well, God bless me, everyone!", ends up recognizing the true meaning of generosity, giving presents to Scrooge and his family, and working as a ditch-digger on Christmas day for the benefit of the poor. Finally, Laurence Maslon provides not one but four adaptations of the *Christmas Carol*, though they are each but a single page in length: witty, satirical scenes in the styles of Samuel Beckett, August Wilson, Wendy Wasserstein, and Bertolt Brecht. These short sketches are amusing, though not surprisingly they shed little light on Dickens' work.

Leonard Hughes offers an interesting report about *A Community Carol*, an adaptation of *A Christmas Carol* set in 1993 in Anacostia, a largely African-American neighborhood in southeast Washington D.C. The cast was to include a large number of non-professional members of that community. Hughes says that the updated adaptation was to retain much of Dickens' original language, though Scrooge's secretary, Penny Cratchit, replaces Bob, and "T.T." (Tiny Tim) is "confined to a wheelchair after being caught in crossfire out on the street." Hughes' article is itself neither an adaptation nor a review; rather, it is the report of an innovative production in process.

Robert Johanson's dramatic adaptation of *Great Expectations*, from the same publisher as John R. Carroll's *A Carol for Tiny Tim*, is somewhat less successful than that sequel, though it is impressive how many strands of plot Johanson retains in a script of under 100 pages. Johanson attempts to use Dickens' language in the dialogue and even in the stage directions; by utilizing old and young Pips simultaneously in some early scenes, he even retains some of the effect of the first-person narration. But there is, obviously, much that is lost; Pumblechook brings wine to the Christmas dinner, but does not hog it, nor is there time for either gravy or tar-water. Mr. Hubble becomes Fudd-like, saying not only "naterally wicious" of Pip, but "naterally dewicious" at the prospect of pork pie. Other innovations are equally distracting: Drummle trying to borrow money of Herbert and calling Pip "Pipsqueak," Pip proposing to Biddy a week before she marries Joe, and Pip bringing Biddy's son with him to Satis House for the final scene accurately forecast that we will get yet another ending to Dickens' work. Johanson includes production notes that include suggestions for costuming, props, and set design.

FICTIONAL WORKS TREATING DICKENS

William J. Palmer's *The Highwayman and Mr. Dickens: An Account of the Strange Events of the Medusa Murders: A Secret Victorian Journal, attributed to Wilkie Collins*, a detective novel set in the shadier parts of London of 1852 and featuring Dickens, Collins, Inspector Field, and other Dickensian characters, was originally published in 1992; fans of historical fiction and mysteries will welcome its appearance in paperback in 1994. Readers should be aware that the book treats what Hollywood calls "mature subject matter," and that the book employs "adult language" that would bring many a blush to the cheek of The Young Person.

CHILDREN'S BOOKS

Kathleen Trull's children's book *Lives of the Writers* tells colorful stories and anecdotes about twenty literary luminaries, from Shikibu Murasaki and Shakespeare to Langston Hughes and Isaac Bashevis Singer. In the four-page chapter devoted to Dickens, Trull emphasizes Dickens' move from rags (and the blacking factory) to riches (and Gad's Hill Place). The story of Dickens' life is told more colorfully than accurately, with an emphasis on peculiarity and eccentricity—I'm not sure, for example, that Dickens was "set for life" with the publication of *Pickwick*, nor that when Dickens was not writing well, he invariably "doodled or picked fights with his wife [or] his ten children," nor that he attended hangings whenever possible. The illustrator Kathryn Hewitt portrays Dickens posing with a giant steel-tipped pen, and offers another picture of bottles, paste, and some "Ebenezer's Boot Blacking" labels.

STUDIES OF INDIVIDUAL WORKS

Sketches by Boz

Takao Saijo's article points out that many annotators have been led astray with respect to a reference to "Tom King and the Frenchman" in the "Seven Dials" sketch: T. W. Hill made mistakes in the identification of these two, and others have uncritically adopted Hill's annotation, but Saijo clears up all misunderstandings.

The Pickwick Papers

Mara H. Fein examines "The Politics of Family in *The Pickwick Papers*," and finds, beneath the obvious affirmations of home, hearth, and domesticity, a strong undercurrent: Dickens often presents bachelors who destabilize the family. Fein pays particular attention to the cannibalistic valentine Sam Weller views in a shop-window, to the gendered threat women like Mrs. Bardell and her friends Mrs. Cluppins and Mrs. Sanders pose to middle-class family values, and to the "commodification of affection" Mr. Pickwick himself represents. Fein intentionally over-reads the "Chops and Tomata Sauce" note, demonstrating that Buzfuz may indeed be right. Here and elsewhere, Fein is less than wholly convincing, but the essay remains one of the most provocative articles of 1994, reevaluating the relationship between sex, class, and the hegemony of middle-class values affirmed at the end of the novel.

Like Fein, Robert Newsom also takes a controversial position in his essay on *Pickwick*: he argues, seriously and quite convincingly, that Pickwick has important similarities to Jeremy Bentham, and that Pickwick and Dickens are far closer to utilitarian in spirit than they (or we) recognized. Bentham, Pickwick, and Dickens value happiness and pleasure as the ultimate basis for "utility," and the popular vision of utilitarians as selfish is not, Newsom

argues, a fair representation of Bentham's thought, which is "radically egalitarian." Pickwickian ethics ultimately reduce to a utilitarian ethics of "pleasure shared," despite the fact that Dickens himself never seem to have
"discover[ed] the goodness in Bentham." Newsom presents his argument
with wit and insight; even the erudite footnotes are funny.

Oliver Twist

In his short introduction to the Everyman paperback, Steven Connor suggests that *Oliver Twist* is "mythic," and usefully points out that, although
the novel depends on a strict moral and geographical isolation of good and
evil, nevertheless "almost against its own interests, the novel comes gradually
to reveal the manifold connectedness of details that it might otherwise wish
to keep distinct." This connectedness ultimately delivers Oliver, but it also
rules out the possibility of finally segregating the different social worlds of the
novel, making Oliver's history far more complex, rewarding, and memorable.

Cervantes's *Rinconete y Cortadillo* is a source for *Oliver Twist*, according
to Pamela H. Long; unfortunately, her argument hinges on rather flimsy evidence. She cannot demonstrate that Dickens read *Rinconete y Cortadillo*, and
thus she can only note parallels: both books treat thieves and prostitutes, both
have settings that feature shabby furniture, both Monipodio and Fagin are ill-
looking villains, and so on.

Fifteen-year-old Angela Marie Priley may be the youngest Dickensian to
publish anything in 1994; her essay contrasting *Oliver Twist* with the movie
musical *Oliver!* suggests that the movie botches the plot, distorts the character-
izations, and scants Dickens' criticism of social institutions.

Ridgway K. Foley, Jr., cites *Oliver Twist* and other Dickens novels to
establish that Dickens felt "contempt and concern" for law and lawyers.
Foley's real argument, legal rather than literary, is that the law is now "an
ass of gargantuan proportions."

Nicholas Nickleby

David Parker's introduction to the Everyman paperback edition of *Nicholas
Nickleby* admits weaknesses in the organization and plotting of that novel,
but argues that the novel is valuable not only for the energy of Dickens' style,
but for Dickens' tightly-focused concentration on theme: the relationship between money and love. Considering not only the Nicklebys but the Squeerses,
Cheerybles, and Crummleses, Parker suggests that a scornful reaction to Nicholas and Kate's renunciations is in some sense a failure to understand or fully
appreciate laudable nineteenth-century values.

John J. Fenstermaker claims that the ads found in the 1838–1839 *Nickleby*
"Advertiser," particularly the ads for reading material, are an attempt to

"market morality": the advertisements tend to reflect attitudes about religion, patriotism, and familial responsibility that are "anchored by respectability and duty." Fenstermaker says that these advertisements "reveal much of the value system being carefully planted and vigorously nurtured" in the early years of Victoria's reign.

Nineteen ninety-four's only separately-published essay focussing on *Nicholas Nickleby* itself is Sylvia Manning's exploration of parody. In this rather dark essay, Manning sees Dickens obsessively offering parody and self-parody virtually everywhere in the novel, and argues that "the perversion of parody" "keeps the story from achieving shape." Manning argues also that *Nickleby* is "a novel of the excluded subject," and that beneath the high comedy lurks the fear that "inclusion is always factitious." Smike cannot be excluded, nor included, in the happy ending, so he must be killed; the novel raises questions about whether marriage can really be a happy ending, and equally troubling questions "about the delusional nature of inclusion." Manning suggests, finally, that "the narrator, the reader, and Mrs. Nickleby see the same way." Manning's approach is certainly original, but her grim vision of *Nicholas Nickleby* may not attract many converts.

The Old Curiosity Shop

In an energetic and fascinating historical note, Paul Schlicke examines Dick Swiveller and the song and supper clubs that flourished in the early 1800s. Schlicke provides generous examples of the songs and activities characteristic of these clubs, the ancestors of the music hall, and convincingly demonstrates that some of what may appear to be personal eccentricities of Swiveller in fact pertain to his social role as "Perpetual Grand of the Glorious Apollers."

Michael Steig considers Quilp, and to a lesser extent Nell and her grandfather, in his *Dickens Quarterly* piece. Steig points out that not everyone delights in Quilp; some readers respond to him as a realistic (and horrible) character, rather than a mythic or grotesque (and delightful) one. Steig rightly points out that these three characters call up a "wide and personal" range of response.

In a rich and thought-provoking essay, Robert M. Polhemus argues that *The Old Curiosity Shop* has a great deal to do with the religious impulse: the need to find and show faith in a fallen world. Extending the arguments he put forth in *Comic Faith* (1980) and *Erotic Faith* (1990), Polhemus likens *The Old Curiosity Shop* to a "secular, popular, literary cathedral"—a "big-top circus kind of cathedral" displaying the characteristics Ruskin found in Gothic architecture. Polhemus devotes particular attention to faith in the child, pointing to Nell's role as Virgin and redeemer, and to Quilp as a figure that "breaks down the categories and barriers between child and adult." In his conclusion, Polhemus convincingly places Dick Swiveller "at the crossroads of Christian, comic, and erotic faith, and faith in a child."

Martin Chuzzlewit

Treating both *American Notes* and *Martin Chuzzlewit* in his article about "Topographical Disaffection," Rodney Stenning Edgecombe suggests that these works reflect " 'scenic tapinosis'—the landscape of belittlement," common in colonial literature. Edgecomb argues that Dickens' harsh judgments of the American landscape derive from three fused elements: the obvious failures of American society, Dickens' disappointed psyche, and the American landscape itself, neutral but charged and configured by Dickens' disappointments. Arguing that Dickens' vision was shaped by both American landscape and American culture, Edgecombe notes that Dickens criticized both the primeval swampy forest and "the tenuous, half-established agrarian culture that has tried to displace it." By criticizing and diminishing the foreign landscape, Dickens necessarily enlarges and valorizes London, smoky and grimy though it may be.

Robert E. Lougy also considers the American episodes in *Martin Chuzzlewit*. Referring to Rousseau and Marx, but drawing still more heavily on Freud and Lacan, Lougy says that "we are born into a network of signifiers," and suggests that we are also implicated, as members of the human family, in Dickens' narrative. Lougy argues that in *Martin Chuzzlewit*, Dickens focuses on "the question of human nature itself," and that Dickens' quintessential American is "a violent and angry male child," resisting Oedipally the legitimacy of old-world authority and engaging in repetitive patterns of voracious orality and excremental activity, pursuing "a kingdom of nature rather than a kingdom of culture and thus engag[ing] in a cycle of repetition and return that is, Dickens suggests, death-ridden and death-haunted." Lougy's argument is clearly stated, and perhaps of greater intrinsic interest than Edgecombe's, though it is not, finally, any more convincing.

In his introduction to the Everyman's Library edition of *Martin Chuzzlewit*, William Boyd argues that the book is badly titled, suggesting that no one cares about Martin, and that, to the extent that Dickens was attempting a more self-consciously structured and sophisticated novel than his previous books, he failed. On the other hand, Boyd argues (as many have before him) that the novel is a comic masterpiece, bubbling with virtuoso wordplay. Despite the sentimentality and melodrama, and the concluding "triumph of decency" which Boyd sees as virtually formulaic, the novel is a great one, because of its "fierce accuracy and intoxicating humour."

Michael Slater's introduction to the Everyman paperback edition emphasizes the influence of Dickens' visit to "the Yahoo-nation of America" on *Martin Chuzzlewit*, and emphasizes the centrality of Dickens' design in this novel, which nevertheless treats the same world as that of the earlier novels. Slater notes Dickens' linguistic versatility, and discusses his care in planning this novel, as well as his interest in "the process of character and personality change"; Slater devotes special attention to Gamp and Pecksniff, and also to Tom Pinch, demonstrating clearly his great importance to Dickens.

James Spedding, in an 1843 issue of *The Edinburgh Review*, argued that Dickens' primary purpose in coming to America was to lobby for international copyright law, and that his silence (in both *Martin Chuzzlewit* and *American Notes*) on his failure to accomplish his task is remarkable. Gerhard Joseph argues that "within a context of the positive of Dickens's speech and negative of his silence," perhaps Dickens did address this issue obliquely in *Martin Chuzzlewit*: he suggests that Seth Peksniff's appropriation of young Martin's architectural design for a grammar school raises some of the issues of intellectual property rights, plagiarism, and piracy that Dickens intended to settle through international copyright law. Joseph also argues, interestingly, that the issue is not one-sided; perhaps young Martin's insistence that the architectural plans were "all" his own reflects an all-too-Chuzzlewitian corrupting selfishness, and in any case, Dickens "was hardly a stranger to Pecksniffian hypocrisy, rampant egoism, and mercenary calculation himself." Though the argument is not wholly convincing in every particular—the claim that Mark Tapley "anticipate[s] a major thrust of postmodernist theory" in his "insistence upon the 'intertextuality' and therefore the inter- or transpersonal nature of all intellectual enterprises," for example, seems dubious at best—this lively essay is of genuine value.

Nancy Aycock Metz offers another valuable look at *Martin Chuzzlewit* and architecture, tying the novel to contemporary debates about the professional status and identity of architects and to topical controversies about architectural apprenticeships and competitions. Metz shows that Dickens was well aware of these controversies, and that he chose architecture as the rascally Pecksniff's profession with his eyes wide open.

Taking a reader-response approach to the novel, Michael Greenstein argues that connections between characters (on both physical and psychological levels), and connections between author and reader, are of great importance to Dickens' theme of selfishness in *Martin Chuzzlewit*. Greenstein then looks at connection and coincidence, paying particularly close attention to doors, windows, rooms, crossroads, and watches. The theme is large and the article short, but Greenstein's close reading offers some useful insights.

In his article on *Martin Chuzzlewit* and money, Raymond L. Baubles, Jr., begins with the familiar critical position that characters such as Montague Tigg and Seth Pecksniff dehumanize themselves through excessive greed and financial speculation. Eventually, Baubles puts his case a bit too strongly, arguing that the characters in *Martin Chuzzlewit* "sacrifice their humanity on the altar of mammon," asserting that "there is no one who merits the reader's respect or admiration" in this novel, and stating that Dickens' characters

repudiate "'all things human.'' Baubles suggests that eventually all the characters lack authentic personalities, and become, like Tigg and Pecksniff, mere
commodities.

In a two-part article in *Dickens Quarterly*, Michael Swanton examines the
readership patterns of a "dividing book-club" in Cornwall in 1843–44 that
circulated the serial installments of *Martin Chuzzlewit*. By examining the
circulation-sheets in each monthly number of the novel, Swanton determines
patterns of circulation and readership. He notes, for instance, that 84% of
those in the club wanted to read *Chuzzlewit*, and that the average length of
time to finish the final double number was four days. Swanton's observations
are, perhaps, of greater sociological than literary interest.

A Christmas Carol

One might have thought that after Michael Patrick Hearn's *The Annotated
Christmas Carol* and Paul Davis's *The Lives and Times of Ebenezer Scrooge*
there was little work left to do in terms of studying the *Carol* as a cultural icon.
But Brian Sibley's *The Unsung Story*, profusely illustrated and attractively
designed, proves otherwise: Sibley devotes nearly 200 double-columned pages
to the first of Dickens' Christmas books, treating biographical and historical
contexts, offering contemporary comments and reviews, and considering a
great many adaptations: from stage and film to comic books and comedy
recordings. Sibley writes for a popular audience, but the book, which somewhat unnecessarily includes the complete text of *A Christmas Carol*, is carefully done and includes a surprising amount of unfamiliar material, including
some fine illustrations.

Paul Sammon's *The Christmas Carol Trivia Book* is far less satisfying.
The book is poorly written and edited, and Sammon's intrusive chattiness is
all the more annoying because he insists on referring to himself as "Ye
Author." Sammon's book is not so much about Dickens or Dickens' book
(dismissed in two short chapters) as it is about various film and television
adaptations (these take up the remaining 14 chapters). Much of the trivia in
this book is exceedingly trivial; we learn, for example, the exact place and
date of birth of the director of makeup for the Metro-Goldwyn-Meyer production of 1938. Sammon provides trivia questions at the end of his chapters,
such as "where is Magoo the second time he sings 'All Alone in the World'?"
There are far too many sentence fragments, typographical errors, and errors
of fact in the book, and Sammon's bibliography omits Paul Davis' fine book
on *The Christmas Carol*, which should have been a basic source. Nevertheless,
Sammon's listing of distributors for the various videotapes he touts will serve
a utilitarian purpose for any *Carol* adaptations fans.

In an article for *The Gerontologist* about representations of aging in Shakespeare, Balzac, and Dickens, among others, Herbert S. Donow argues that

Scrooge is the quintessential example of an exploitative old man, greedy and egocentric, noting that where Aristotle thought that the conditions of old age were immutable, Dickens offers the possibility of redemption. Though the article has a great deal to say about aging, it sheds little light on Dickens.

Arthur P. Patterson turns away from economic and psychological interpretations of *A Christmas Carol*, urging that instead the story must be understood by integrating the psychological and spiritual messages: memory and imagination must together lead to transformation and rejuvenation. Patterson suggests that if we read the story rightly, we may, no less than Scrooge himself, be reborn.

Audrey Jaffe's *PMLA* article about the *Carol* takes a far more theoretical approach. Building on Althusser's concept of "interpellation," Jaffe argues that *A Christmas Carol* allegorizes the subject's relation to culture; the text encodes reality as spectacle and manipulates the reader's visual sense in "what is, in effect, the mass marketing of an ideology about sympathy." Jaffe feels that "the story turns its readers into spectators and positions them outside everything"; unfortunately, Jaffe fails to show why this is particularly true of the *Carol*, and her conclusion that what Scrooge particularly needs to learn is a type of gift-giving that is "defined as the purchase and exchange of commodities" that will provide him with "improved business prospects" seems willfully to pervert Dickens' intent.

Dombey and Son

In her introduction to the Everyman's Library edition of *Dombey and Son*, Lucy Hughes-Hallet argues that the novel is, in effect, many novels: comic, sentimental, satiric, and so on. Ultimately, however, she sees the book as not a social novel, nor a commercial one, nor a novel of the city, but as a novel of "domestic, familial, and sexual relationships," focusing on only a few people, especially on Mr. Dombey and "his own true lover," Florence. Although she finds "major structural flaws," Hughes-Hallet nevertheless admires this "brilliantly unrealistic" novel, appreciating Dickens' ability to dissolve the borders between animate and inanimate.

Mary G. McBride urges that, in considering the imagery of waves in *Dombey and Son*, readers not neglect the economic resonances; she finds the wave-like fluctuations in the market of particular significance.

In a more substantial essay, Patricia Marks suggests that through Mr. Dombey Dickens criticizes imperialistic, patriarchal, and commercial models and valorizes (for both men and women) nurturing and mothering ones. Marks's essay is valuable both for its firm grounding in the text of the novel and for its connections to the economic, social, and political world Dickens inhabited.

Susan Nygaard's lengthy essay on upholstery in *Dombey and Son* is argumentative and provocative, even if less than fully convincing. Nygaard takes a statue of an Amazon on display at the Crystal Palace (which Dickens may or may not have seen) as a central metaphor, arguing that Dickens fills the novel with angry amazons who endanger the whole patriarchal system that fosters the firm of Dombey and Son. Nygaard suggests that ultimately Dickens (and Dombey) learns nothing, merely padding or "upholstering" Dombey, rather than offering a searching critique of the patriarchal domesticity that the House of Dombey embodies. Nygaard takes an interesting look at the history of upholstery, and at some Victorian sculpture and furniture design, on her way to her conclusion that upholstery "helped disguise male resistance to change."

The late Roger B. Henkle's essay on "The Crisis of Representation in *Dombey and Son* starts from the position that the novel seems to "abort itself" at Paul Dombey's death—that this point (not just in the novel, but in Dickens' career) marks a recognition that the "old novelistic strategies" can "no longer serve to represent the new experience of the mid-Victorian period," and that this moment in fact represents a "crisis of representation." Henkle links Paul to "oceanic feeling," sentimentality, and the fairy tale, contrasting the auratic with the "detailed and grounded social text" tied to "the world of experience." Dickens transforms the subjectivity of his readers, rids himself of debased Romanticism, and plunges into a new era, symbolized by the steam engine train, that is "dreadfully real." Characterizing Dombey, a failed patriarch, as both empty and stiff, offering no base on which to construct subjectivity, Henkle notes that Carker and Edith Granger, "the only 'artists' in the novel," seethe with energy and desire, and suggests that perhaps they represent the way that new fiction will make "art out of the ravaged and corrupted conditions of the new urban environment."

"The Haunted Man"

Wendy K. Carse's essay on "Domestic Transformations in Dickens' 'The Haunted Man' " focuses primarily on the power of Milly, the working-class "domestic woman," to transform Redlaw, the protagonist of Dickens' 1848 Christmas book. Carse emphasizes issues of gender, class, and the supernatural. While domesticity holds a central place in Redlaw's memories and desire, and Milly, the "domestic Angel," is in fact "the very source of Redlaw's transformation," still Dickens ultimately turns away from the implications of that power, simultaneously natural and supernatural. In the end, Dickens must contain and diminish Milly's power and assert the prerogatives of Redlaw, male and of a higher social class than Milly.

David Copperfield

Stanley Friedman suggests, in a well-argued and convincing article in *The Dickensian*, that Dickens may have based some of Uriah Heep's villainy on the character and actions of Thomas Powell, a man who Dickens had trusted but who was later convicted of forgery and embezzlement. Examining the serial instalments of the novel, Friedman carefully traces the development of Heep's character, linking it meticulously with the chronology of Dickens' relations with Powell, and shedding real light on the ways Dickens transmuted life into art.

Kerry McSweeney addresses important issues (memory, imagination, time, and the formation of identity among them) in his essay "*David Copperfield* and the Music of Memory," but the essay suffers from loose organization and a lack of focus. McSweeney wants to offer a "fresh examination of the operation of memory in *David Copperfield*," but much in the essay inspires instead a sense of déjà vu. As background, McSweeney first examines (perhaps somewhat predictably) the autobiographical fragment, and then (more valuably) looks at *The Haunted Man* and *Oliver Twist*. He attempts to distinguish between "two kinds of memory, one of which relates to the representational aspect of the narration, the other to the expressive aspect." But just a page later, he struggles with another distinction, between "literary-rhetorical memory" and "what is tempting to call the real thing"; McSweeney never really clarifies the relationships between (or among) these two (or four) kinds of memory. Perhaps the most interesting part of this essay is McSweeney's consideration of "lost sisters': Dickens', Redlaw's, Oliver Twist's and Mr. Dick's, as well as Wordsworth's, Coleridge's, and David Copperfield's. Finally, McSweeney insists that David does not transcend past pain, but makes it into "a source of the music of memory that enhances his life experience."

The most ambitious essay on *David Copperfield* published in 1994 fails to mention David, or Dickens, in its title. Michael H. Levenson attempts to trace a path from fantasy to art, and from private, secret desires to public expression, doing so by means of an unabashedly psychoanalytic approach. Levenson argues that fantasy stands between experience and art, and that "the great thematic labor of *David Copperfield* is the overcoming of fantasy." After examining Freud's essay "A Child is Being Beaten," Levenson concludes (with characteristically Freudian logic) that being beaten "is at once a disguised form of sexual satisfaction, and a guilty retribution for that action." Levenson ultimately relates life with Dora to "the reality principle" and life with Agnes to "fancy," arguing that "our most persistant images can keep changing their terms."

Bleak House

In an article treating Dickens and George Henry Lewes's views about Krook's striking death, John B. West denies the possibility of spontaneous combustion. West notes, however, that Lewes was himself mistaken about the nature of tissue metabolism, and that Dickens points out one of the vital issues in nineteenth-century physiological debate: the relationship between metabolism and fire.

Graham Benton's essay on illness in *Bleak House* is expressed in theoretical jargon, but offers little of value that has not been said more clearly before. Benton sees that disease is "a 'real' entity" (and a "force") "to be negotiated," but he also sees it as a pervasive metaphor; Dickens "inscribes" illness to articulate (or deconstruct) decay, justice, and progress. Finally, in a perhaps unintentionally gruesome metaphor, disease "transcends the boundaries of its significance to encompass the textual representation of society."

The final chapter in Beth Fowkes Tobin's Foucault-influenced *Superintending the Poor: Charitable Ladies and Paternal Landlords in British Fiction, 1770–1860* treats "The Cottage Visitor, the Housekeeper, and the Policeman: Self-Regulation and Surveillance in *Bleak House*." Tobin argues that Dickens ridicules and trivializes charitable activities by middle-class women with his portrayals of the ineffective Mrs. Pardiggle and Mrs. Jellyby, and that Ada Clare's upper-class tears are equally ineffective; for Dickens, paternalism, an "outmoded form of social control," cannot ameliorate contemporary social ills. In the novel, Esther Summerson and Mr. Bucket represent the solution to social problems: Esther's combination of system and feeling and Bucket's combination of "surveillance and intimidation" are "complementary," bringing "order to the lives of the people they touch." Tobin usefully links Pardiggle and Jellyby to their historical context, but she oversimplifies and reduces Ada, Esther, and Bucket. Though Tobin's writing is lucid, her critical position with respect to Esther and Bucket is not; a formal conclusion spelling these issues out more clearly would make this book more valuable.

Carrol Clarkson's analysis of "Alias and Alienation in *Bleak House*" focuses primarily on Nemo and Esther. Relying on Derridean concepts of "différance," Clarkson seems to neglect the rather large gap between the law-writer and the law-giver; she seems to find it remarkable that "Esther's polyonomy . . . paradoxically links her to her father and his many names." Clarkson's conclusion that "language can, and does[,] obscure personal identity" offers little.

Of the three explicitly feminist examinations of *Bleak House* under review, Dona Budd's is the least satisfactory. In "Language Pairs in *Bleak House*," Budd argues that the male and female narrators are only the most prominent of many gendered pairs of readers and writers, and she gives special attention to Mr. and Mrs. Bagnet, Mr. and Mrs. Jellyby, Caddy and Prince, Grandfather and Grandmother Smallweed, and Sir Leicester and Volumnia Dedlock. These and other "gendered language couples" reveal the sexual politics of Dickens' novel. Female language correlates with female sexual power, but the ideology of the novel suggests that female speech (or silence) must be dedicated to preserving patriarchal power, which in turn leads to important paradoxes. For example, Budd asserts that "Esther's voice escapes subordination as it is being appropriated, as it reveals, in its woundedness, the violence of the appropriation and subordination it endures." Dickens simultaneously denies women their own voices and "exposes the failure of patriarchy to empower its own biological constituency." Budd's argument, while at times ingenious, is not ultimately compelling.

Barbara Gottfried, also employing a feminist approach, examines "Household Arrangements and the Patriarchal Order in *Bleak House*." Interestingly, she argues that the separation of public and private spheres in the novel "is more apparent than real": that in fact public and private, "legalistic and domestic, are inextricably linked." Gottfried pays special attention to the patriarchal Smallweed household as paradigmatic. Gottfried's argument that "even the most apparently uncorrupted households are implicated in the interdependence of love and money, familial relations and the law" is startling, and not wholly convincing: she eventually suggests that Jarndyce (and presumably Allan Woodcourt) buy Esther's love.

Perhaps the richest of the three articles is Lynette Felber's, published in *Victorian Newsletter*. Analyzing "the gendered qualities of narrative and discourse," Felber finds Esther's narration a prefiguration of what French essentialist feminists have labeled *écriture féminine*, subverting the "masculine" suspense plot which "thrust[s] forward to a climax" in favor of an alternative feminine order characterized by multiplicity, irregularity, profusion, recursion, and a fluid, "discursive, conjunctive style." Felber presents her case most convincingly, and without recourse to unnecessary jargon; she carefully considers many related and relevant issues, including what some have seen as Dickens' "anti-feminist platform in his representation of Mrs. Jellyby," and the significant differences between essentialism and a naive biologism in feminist theory. She concludes that *Bleak House* reprivileges and valorizes women's bodies and values, and that through Esther's non-teleological narrative, Dickens "demonstrates a strategy to destabilize male hierarchy." Her exploration of the conclusion of the novel is particularly intriguing; she finds that Esther's narration resists "the male trajectory of discovery and the closure imposed by the third-person narrator by providing an open, ambiguous antiending." Here as elsewhere in the essay, Felber's exploration is itself multifaceted (though neither open nor ambiguous); she considers many possibilities, and discriminates among them carefully, leading to provocative and valuable conclusions.

Less successful is Miguel M. Mota's attempt to explore Dickens' "Christian vision" in *Bleak House*. With some nods toward contemporary theory, Mota argues that Dickens enacts ontological and transcendental elements of

Christianity in the narrative structure of *Bleak House*: that this novel becomes "a framework of discourse in which a multitude of voices are brought together for dialogical intermingling." This bringing together leads, in Mota's view, to Christian community. Readers predisposed to this position may be willing to grant that in this novel Dickens "displays a marked preoccupation with the possibility of salvation through Christian means." Mota, however, offers little textual evidence to support this view. Considering the scene of Jo's death, Mota argues that the Lord's Prayer "remains as 'Jo's Will' " and that the silence at the moment of Jo's death is "the silence of the Word, silence as the sound of possibility."

Rodney Stenning Edgecombe offers a brief (but nevertheless rather muddled) note on the first paragraph of *Bleak House*, asserting that "the waters" there mentioned are "clearly" those of Genesis 1:9.

Daniel H. Lowenstein's lengthy article "The Failure of the Act" in the *Cardozo Law Review* treats Shakespeare and Hugo, as well as Dickens, but over one-third of its 104 pages focus on the law and lawyers in *Bleak House*. Lowenstein takes Richard Weisberg's 1992 book *Poethics* as the occasion for his essay, noting his own differences with Weisberg, especially with respect to Lady Dedlock, Tulkinghorn, and Bucket. In the section devoted to Dickens, Lowenstein carefully explains that Lady Dedlock's real moral failure is "her unwillingness to tell the truth to her husband," and notes that Tulkinghorn is not the root cause of her distress; Lowenstein argues that Tulkinghorn is neither monstrous nor (particularly) unprofessional, but that he fails to separate professional and personal perspectives, and treats people as "means rather than ends." Clearly and convincingly, Lowenstein demonstrates Bucket's ruthlessness, characterizing him as "a good-natured, charming Tulkinghorn." Lowenstein offers useful insights into Dickens' representation of the law, and in his conclusion differs from Weisberg by voicing doubts that "law and literature" should be "a theoretical discipline." Instead, Lowenstein suggests that "the function of criticism is to give readers ideas and suggestions that may enhance the immersion in the text." Lowenstein packs his own clearly-written essay with many such ideas and suggestions; this essay is both thoughtful and valuable.

In his introduction to the Everyman paperback edition of *Bleak House*, Andrew Sanders draws attention to the historical background of the novel, especially to the political, economic, and technological context: a static and stagnant London which is, paradoxically, in transition. Sanders suggests that though the novel is complex, multi-layered, and perplexing, it is also progressive, unwinding and unraveling mysteries; despite Esther's insecure and inconclusive conclusion, we must not read *Bleak House* as circular: "there can be no turning back in either the private or the public spheres delineated in *Bleak House*."

Hard Times

Two of the year's best articles look closely at the metaphors in *Hard Times*. Barry Thatcher's fine essay on Dickens' contributions to the debate between radical utilitarian language theorists and the more conservative philologists focuses most insistently on *Hard Times* (though he also considers a series of articles on philology and language published in *Household Words*). Thatcher may be going a bit too far when he says that *Hard Times* "is based on these linguistic issues," but he makes a compelling case that the language theory debate was of great importance to Dickens. Thatcher shows how closely Gradgrind's language, in the early chapters of the novel, reflects and exemplifies Jeremy Bentham's theory of language, and how the narrator's language, reflecting Richard Trench's theory, "becomes an antidote for Gradgrind's Benthamite language." Thatcher's historical work is valuable, as is his stylistic analysis; he demonstrates, for example, that Gradgrind uses only about one-tenth as many adjectives as the narrator. Ultimately, Thatcher argues that *Hard Times* is not a Bakhtinian heteroglossic novel; though Dickens intentionally heightens bipolar or oppositional structures in the novel, the narrator is a "clear victor" in the ideological battle being waged and "makes monologic order out of heteroglossic chaos" at the end of the novel.

In the same issue of *Dickens Studies Annual*, Razak Dahmane presents another valuable article on *Hard Times* that works from a surprisingly similar perspective. "A Mere Question of Figures: Measures, Mystery, and Metaphor in *Hard Times*" examines closely the way Dickens has his utilitarian characters (especially Gradgrind and Bounderby) "literalize": these characters, lacking metaphorical proficiency, often unwittingly take imaginative characters literally, thereby betraying their own literal-mindedness. Dahmane's analysis of this phenomenon is patient and perceptive; the double meaning of the word "figures" in his title accurately forcasts the cleverness of his analyses. Dahmane skillfully avoids oversimplification, making his points without denying Mrs. Sparsit's and Mr. Harthouse's metaphors, Dickens' own personal fondness for factual accuracy, the sometimes destructive powers of a "wicked imagination," and the delightful "literalizations" of such attractive characters as Boffin in *Our Mutual Friend*. Dahmane concludes by emphasizing the importance of "seeing the mystery . . . at the living heart of human reality," suggesting that before we can reform society, we must ourselves "re-form" and "re-imagine" it.

Somewhat less satisfying is the third essay on *Hard Times* in *Dickens Studies Annual*, Katherine A. Retan's analysis of "Lower-Class Angels in the Middle-Class House." Retan focuses primarily on *Hard Times* and Elizabeth Gaskell's *Ruth*, but considers *Oliver Twist, Dombey and Son*, and *Bleak House* too; she looks at the way domestic females learn to manage desire through a ritualistic contact with transgressive female sexuality. In earlier Dickens novels, the sexually-degraded lower-class woman (Nancy) transforms the middle-class woman (Rose Maylie) into a domestic Angel. In *Hard Times*, these relations are somewhat different, in that the middle-class Louisa is herself sexually tainted, and then redeemed by contact with the pure but lower-class Angel Sissy Jupe. Retan argues that Gaskell initiated this pattern of a lower-class domestic angel in *Ruth*, though in Gaskell's novel, it is the lower-class angel, not the middle-class woman, who comes into direct contact with "sin." Retan argues that ultimately Sissy Jupe is powerless to heal the "social ills which produce gender and class unrest" in *Hard Times*; she is inadequate partly because she is in fact "untouched by the shame associated with transgressive sexuality." Retan identifies the transformation of a rebellious middle-class daughter into a domestic Angel as *Ruth*'s "central project," and evidently sees both *Ruth* and *Hard Times* as (wittingly or not) serving a conservative agenda.

Paul Schlicke's concise introduction to the World's Classics paperback traces the novel's origins, considering both the business decisions that prompted Dickens to launch a weekly serial and the "urgent social problems" —especially utilitarianism and political economy—that Dickens wanted to address. Schlicke presents *Hard Times* as dramatizing Dickens' "most mature convictions about the value of entertainment," and argues for the value of entertainment, imagination, leisure, "Fancy," and fellow-feeling, all embodied in Sleary's circus. Noting that *Hard Times* lacks the abundance and exuberance of Dickens' other works, Schlicke praises the economy, intensity, and coherence of Dickens' shortest novel, finding that Dickens' method and technique admirably suit his theme.

Grahame Smith's introduction to the Everyman paperback edition of *Hard Times* notes that Dickens' return to weekly serialization results in an allegorical or even "skeletal" quality, but that the novel has a symbolic power that results from the material conditions of its production: Dickens' focus on the destructive powers of industrialization, utilitarianism, and a stifling "education" are only to be resisted or penetrated by "fancy," and "intuition rooted in loving sympathy."

Little Dorrit

In *Critical Theory and the Novel*, David Suchoff uses the critical theory of Theodor Adorno and Walter Benjamin to examine the critical force that problems of mass culture bring to the works of Dickens, Melville, and Kafka. Suchoff's chapter on Dickens focuses primarily on *Little Dorrit*. Suchoff explores many paradoxes, such as the ways in which "Dickensian radicalism contest[s] the commodifiable forms, even those Dickens himself helped to create, in which the people's will could be coerced." Suchoff also asserts that Dickens' public positions frequently controvert "the culturally critical force his novels often assert," with respect, for example, to imperialism. Many of the conclusions that Suchoff reaches are provocative, but few are really convincing: the possibility that the Clennams were involved in the opium trade is interesting, though there is no textual evidence for it beyond Dickens' naming of "China," but many readers will wish for more evidence before accepting that Dickens "challenge[s] the limits of Victorian taste" by linking Amy Dorrit, Maggy Arthur's true mother, Affery, and Mrs. Clennam as victims of unspeakable sexual abuse, or that Miss Wade's judgments are properly characterized by "accuracy," or that "male violence and its supression are the paternal secret of the plot," or that Mrs. Clennam is truly actuated by "compassion."

Piya Pal Lapinski offers an interesting comparison between LeFanu's story "Carmilla" and *Little Dorrit*, examining images of female vampirism. While not, strictly speaking, a vampire, Miss Wade does anticipate Carmilla in her inarticulate and tormented rage; furthermore, Lapinski argues, Wade and Carmilla share a physical resemblance,a demonic energy, and a near-obsessive desire for control.

A Tale of Two Cities

The only separately-published article published in 1994 to treat *A Tale of Two Cities* is James F. Hamilton's "Terrorizing the 'Feminine' in Hugo, Dickens, and France," and it is not a strong one. Hamilton "reinterpret[s]" (or, more accurately, misinterprets) matricide as "killing of the feminine," and argues that in *A Tale of Two Cities*, "the feminine side of life is repressed, rejected, or killed by a cold, mechanical reasoning." In order even to begin defending this strange claim, Hamilton must distort the meaning of "feminine" until it includes "the primary one of gender, the secondary contra-sexual potential of men in the anima, [and] the all-embracing archetype of human regeneration—the great mother." Even so, Hamilton's task is not easy. Hamilton mentions that (the presumably "feminine") Charles Darnay adopts his mother's name, devotes a substantial amount of his critical discussion to Lucie Mannette's regenerative and transformative power, and then gives Madame DeFarge and the "sharp female called La Guillotine" short shrift, saying that they represent the "negative anima." One wonders if this is code for saying that these females are "masculine," or that they—and the Vengeance, who goes unmentioned—embody "cold, mechanical reasoning." Hamilton says that Carton gets in touch with his "feminine" self, and that the poor seamstress of the final chapter is Carton's true double, "his reborn anima.'' Ultimately, Hamilton claims, Dickens's view of the Terror is ''romantic and optimistic,'' and *A Tale of Two Cities* ''reaffirms the supremacy of bourgeois values—class structure, gender roles, and absolute moral values.''

Norman Page's brief introduction to the Everyman paperback edition of *A Tale of Two Cities* emphasizes the ways that Dickens encodes his own personal experience into his second historical novel, asserting that Dickens' own life was itself in revolution. Page tells us that Dickens, although fascinated by violence, suggests here that ''violence can never be justified since it leads to anarchy.'' Page admits that the novel is experimental, and not always successfully so, but finds that many of Dickens' new moves in this work are of great interest.

Great Expectations

Bibliographic research has revealed a new first American edition of *Great Expectations*: John M. Dundek has discovered that the two-volume James G. Gregory edition (New York, 1861) was deposited at the copyright office on 26 August 1861, six weeks before T. B. Peterson's one-volume edition. The 1861 Harper book edition noted in Wilkins's 1910 bibliography is evidently spurious.

James P. Crowley argues that *Great Expectations* is far more meditative than the typical *bildungsroman*, and claims that Pip's ''act of narration follows the stages of Christian spiritual inquiry given by St. Ignatius Loyola in his *Spiritual Exercises*,'' including memory, understanding, and will, and concluding with an embrace of humility. Crowley feels that Pip ''will move toward the future as a better man'' with Estella, ''having conquered himself through a continuous and living meditative process.''

John Cunningham offers a more sophisticated Christian interpretation of the novel, using biblical typology to support his claim that metaphors of baptism and redemption are among the ''controlling symbolic structures'' of *Great Expectations*. Cunningham argues that the novel opens with a parody of baptism—Pip and Magwitch being ''born'' into guilt and death—and that only in the final third of the novel does Dickens transform corrupted figures of baptism into genuine ones. Exploring Christian emblems, references, and allusions carefully, Cunningham makes a strong case, linking themes of suffering, repentance, forgiveness, and regeneration to Dickens' ''pattern of baptism and of comedy.''

Mary Galbraith examines the first chapter of *Great Expectations* closely, looking at how Dickens uses first-person narration to present childhood experience. Galbraith argues that the chapter progresses through three phases: before, during, and after Pip's contact with the convict Magwitch. In the first section, the narrator separates himself from the child, though probing the childhood experience deeply. In the central section, the narrator identifies with the child, but presents experience dramatically, rather than psychologically. In the final phase, the narrator identifies with and enters into the child's experience. Galbraith is cautious and precise, and raises interesting questions about Dickens' construction of subjectivity.

Rodney Stenning Edgecombe explores "Violence, Death and Euphemism in *Great Expectations*," noting examples of euphemism (or periphrasis, or litotes) in the speeches of Joe, Jaggers, and Miss Havisham, as well as in the language of the narrator, and arguing that by such means, Dickens "secures the tragi-comic colour of his novel." Edgecombe asserts that euphemisms transpose suffering and humor, distancing death and violence and effacing traditional generic distinctions.

Kate Flint offers a fine introduction to the World's Classics paperback, surveying the reactions of Dickens' contemporaries, considering the origins of *Great Expectations* in Dickens' own experience, and discussing Dickens' explorations of the influence of heredity and environment in shaping character. Flint also examines issues of identity, guilt, and work in the novel.

Robin Gilmour's concise introduction to the Everyman paperback focuses attention on the quiet authority of the narrative voice, and links this to Dickens' purchase of the house at Gad's Hill; Gilmour thinks the house has everything to do with "expectations," and the relationship between past and present. Gilmour identifies *Great Expectations* as a beautifully plotted *bildungsroman*, and sees "crime, guilt and gentility" as key themes. Gilmour devotes particular attention to Jaggers as one of Dickens' "most mature and brilliant creations."

Our Mutual Friend

Andrew Sanders begins his introduction to the Everyman's Library edition of *Our Mutual Friend* by arguing that, though Henry James was wrong to identify Dickens' writing as tired, Dickens himself was physically exhausted, straining under the difficulties of living a double life. Sanders also suggests that many of his Dickens' characters are fatigued, subdued, and "scrunched"; this "self-consciously 'modern' " novel "undermines expectations," dwelling on dust, money, alienation, and social dislocations. Sanders concludes, however, with Dickens' affirmations of love, of fairy-tale, and of magic, which hint at how the alienated characters in *Our Mutual Friend* are "blessedly transformable"; he notes that with the final word of the novel, "an exhausted world seems to brighten too."

Howard W. Fulweiler argues that Darwin's *The Origin of Species* and Dickens' *Our Mutual Friend* share a common vision and treat similar sets of issues, including predation, inheritance, sexual selection, survival, and the complex interrelationship of the individual and the environment. Darwin, however, takes a capitalist, competitive, and Malthusian approach; Dickens endorses generosity and love, enabling the novel to transcend Darwinian constructs in favor of a teleological and designed evolution. Fulweiler does well at pointing to both the similarities and differences between Darwin and Dickens.

Using a stylistic and linguistic approach, Mary Jane Chilton Curry contrasts *Our Mutual Friend* with James's *The Golden Bowl*, arguing that Dickens is more prone to use anaphora (references back to something previously mentioned) and James is more likely to use cataphora (references that point forward). Furthermore, Curry finds Dickens to be more referentially explicit than James; Dickens' use of anaphora creates "syntactic links that, in turn, create semantic, mystery-solving links," whereas James's novel taxes our analytic abilities more strongly with open-ended and ambiguous references. Curry concludes that "because epistemological uncertainties are resolved," Dickens' novel is essentially a work of realism, in contrast with *The Golden Bowl*, which approaches postmodernism in its raising of ontological questions.

The allusions Rodney Stenning Edgecombe spots in "Two Oblique Allusions in *Our Mutual Friend*" are oblique, at best: Edgecombe senses submerged connections between Podsnap's language and a passage from James Thomson's "The Seasons," and further connections between a later Podsnap passage and I Corinthians 13:12.

Though *Our Mutual Friend* makes it into the title of Robert Ter Horst's article, Ter Horst is primarily interested in discussing a novel by José Eustasio Rivera. In the lone paragraph of Dickensian relevance, he claims that *Our Mutual Friend* "is a kind of father of Dickensian waters," and a "fully tidal novel that marks its tributaries and its main stream on the map of jealousy and misconception."

"The Signalman"

Graeme Tytler's brief article in *The Explicator* argues that Dickens' 1866 ghost story is in fact about a man afflicted with a type of partial insanity known in Dickens' day as lypemania or monomania, and that "the ghost's unmistakenly [sic] human utterances and gestures are . . . merely expressions of a partially insane signalman's unconscious." Tytler also argues that we accept "language," "narrative," and "society" as "signalling systems," and finally suggests that Dickens may be "hinting that the supernatural experience is somehow inseparable from the idea of society qua signalling system."

The Mystery of Edwin Drood

Elsie Karbacz and Robert Raven offer imaginative but somewhat implausible speculations about the plot of *The Mystery of Edwin Drood*, suggesting that the Princess Puffer may have had a child by "Eddy" Drood (our Edwin's father), and that, though she named this child Edwin, he's not our Edwin, but Edwin's half-brother. They also think that John Jasper may have murdered the *other* Edwin, leaving ours to return triumphantly in the end. Well, perhaps.

Don Richard Cox's article about some newly-discovered page proofs for *Edwin Drood* is much more solid—but it does not, finally, solve any real mysteries; these page proofs, not known to Margaret Cardwell when she prepared the text for the Clarendon edition, are part of a set Dickens sent to Boston to be published in *Every Saturday*, and are identical to the proofs at Yale. The corrections Dickens marked on these early proofs do not seem, ultimately, to shed much light.

Charles Forsyte's two paragraphs in *Notes and Queries* answer, at least partially, some questions relating to Charles Dickens Junior's introduction to an 1896 American edition of *Drood*, reprinted in London in 1923, but offer no insight into the novel itself.

In his essay on muscular Christianity in *Edwin Drood*, David Faulkner argues that Dickens' portrait of Septimus Crisparkle's "Christian manliness" engages pressing issues of the 1860s: "the causes and cultural implications of England's accelerated global expansion." Despite the fact that Crisparkle is "an exemplary muscular Christian," Faulkner treats Crisparkle and John Jasper as doubles and not as simple opposites, and asserts that in *Drood* Dickens was moving away from those representational conventions he had earlier helped to shape; now, Faulkner argues, "schizoid addiction and muscular Christianity" are interdependent and mutually permeable. Faulkner holds that "Dickens's opium den function[s] as a destabilizing node within Victorian culture, a fictional space in which all boundaries (of gender, of race or culture, of the self) [a]re put in question."

BIOGRAPHICAL STUDIES

Robert Vine offers a biographical sketch of John Augustine Overs, a working-class poet and cabinet maker Dickens helped from 1839 until Overs's death in 1844 at the age of 36. In a second portion of the same article, Sheila Smith describes the contents of a manuscript book of poetry by Overs, lent, with a trinket box Overs made for his wife, to the Dickens House Museum.

In the same issue of *The Dickensian*, Sidney P. and Carolyn J. Moss consider the case of Frederick Dickens, Charles's brother, adding details of his courtship and marriage to Anna Weller (1848), his improvidence, adultery (1857), divorce (1859), bankruptcy, and death (1867) to the story as it had been known previously. The Mosses argue that Dickens' publication of an essay on "Debt" in *All the Year Round* in 1864 may well have been inspired by Frederick's experience.

The Mosses also published a book, *Charles Dickens and His Chicago Relatives: A Documentary Narrative*, treating Charles Dickens only peripherally and focusing on his youngest brother Augustus, who, in 1857, deserted his blind wife Harriette in England and fled to the United States with his pregnant mistress Bertha Phillips, with whom he lived until his death in 1866. Though the book treats Charles's relationship with his brother (the original "Boz"), and includes a great deal of information about the response of the Chicago papers when Charles manifested no great eagerness to support the mistress they erroneously identified as Charles's "sister-in-law," the book is finally of little real relevance to those who study Charles Dickens, and of even less relevance to those who study his novels.

Claire Tomalin notes a recently discovered photographic portrait of Ellen Ternan, and offers evidence suggesting that it may have been ordered and paid for by Dickens himself.

GENERAL TREATMENTS OF DICKENS' CAREER

In *Charles Dickens*, Brian Murray offers a brief survey of Dickens' life and works, refreshingly free of arcane jargon. The book, designed for undergraduates and the general reader, will likely be of use for those audiences, though specialists and scholars will probably find little of value. The book offers generous quotations from Dickens' works, and interesting comments from some influential Dickens critics. Unfortunately, none of the quotations are documented. Strangely, Murray omits both *Barnaby Rudge* and *A Tale of Two Cities* from his critical discussion of the novels, and fails to list *Great Expectations* in his "select," one-page bibliography of Dickens' works. Many may find Murray's taste congenial; Robin Williams, Preston Sturges, and the Marx Brothers all appear in the index, where Foucault and De Man do not.

John Kucich offers a brief and lucid overview of Dickens' career in the *Columbia History of the British Novel*. (Unfortunately, "British" appears as "Btritish" in the running heads.) Kucich writes clearly and colorfully, emphasizing Dickens' appeal to the "lower orders," his populism, and his "middle-class identifications." Kucich usefully considers Dickens' relationship to "Englishness," and to the individualist ethos of the Victorians; he also considers Dickens' attitudes toward politics, domesticity, women, religious ideas, psychology, literary influences, and "the death wish," among other topics. Anyone who attempts to treat so many topics in so few pages must of necessity be quite general; nevertheless, Kucich offers several fresh perspectives, and a useful vision of Dickens' accomplishments. Kucich quotes at least a dozen critics who do not appear in his brief, eleven-item bibliography; the eight-sentence biographical blurb on Dickens in the appendix overlooks *Dombey and Son*.

Far less significantly, in 1994, the *Contemporary Review* reprinted an article by Amelia Edwards, originally published in 1894, on Dickens, Thackeray, and Trollope. Dickens gets short shrift; all we learn is that he was "essentially a caricaturist" and that he "depicted his fellow-men as they are not."

CRITICAL SURVEYS

In the first of his articles in *Dickens Quarterly* tracing the history of critical response to Dickens, Simon Trezise looks at biography and biographical criticism. Trezise says that early Dickensian biography is essentially fiction, given how much is omitted and distorted, but that contemporary biographers, faced with the task of presenting a life objectively, may well retreat from such a difficult task and create fictions too. Trezise devotes some special attention to the difficulties of psychoanalytic biography, and offers a useful bibliography of biographical critics from Forster and Sala to Ackroyd, Allen, and Tomalin. In the second such article, Trezise examines the evolution of Marxist criticism, noting the increasingly sophisticated contributions from Shaw and T. A. Jackson through Raymond Williams to Terry Eagleton, Frederic Jameson, Pam Morris, and Edward Said. In his concluding pages, Trezise notes that however oversimplified the arguments of the early Marxists, they could communicate more effectively than many modern theorists; Trezise poses the valuable question, "What purpose is served by addressing the problems of oppression in a language that is likely to alienate the oppressed?" He concludes that Dickens' "simple, direct and accessible literary images" like poor Oliver Twist "will continue to entertain some readers and trouble the conscience of others."

Ella Westland also contributes to the *Dickens Quarterly* series, offering a critical overview of "Dickens and Women." In the first portion of her essay, Westland examines the strategies and motivations of critics who approach Dickens' treatment of women, including Michael Slater's "methodologically pre-feminist" book of 1983, various works of feminist scholars in the 1970s, and several works with psychoanalytic approaches to Dickens and women. The second portion of Westland's useful survey traces mainstream feminist approaches to Dickens, including the work of Nancy Armstrong and Mary Poovey. Westland concludes with words of praise for Ellen Ternan's biographer, Clair Tomalin, for quietly "shifting . . . the center of gravity" and insisting "that the peripheral is political."

Stanley Friedman's "Recent Dickens Studies: 1992," published in the 1994 volume of *Dickens Studies Annual*, notes sixteen books and over 60 articles published in 1992. Friedman's wit and perceptiveness make this survey very useful; Friedman goes into greater depth in his review essay than I do in this one, rarely offering less than a full page to a book.

STUDIES FOCUSING ON MORE THAN ONE WORK

—Reflexive delight

Sharon Kubasak's valuable appreciation "Reflexive Delight" in the *Dickensian* focuses on imaginative literature's power to delight. To this end she considers what she calls Dickens' " 'fictional dream' miniature," which simultaneously immerses us in the world and distances us from it. In the "fictional dream" miniature, the reader experiences an extinction of self, a renewal, and a restoration—and this produces a special delight. Through his art, Dickens inspires a kind of collaborative creative activity in his readers. Kubasak's article serves as a reminder of some of the most important reasons we read Dickens.

—The grown-up child

One of the year's most important, interesting, and well-written books is Malcolm Andrews's *Dickens and the Grown-Up Child*. Andrews notes that Dickens' interest in children and maturity had at least as much to do with "metaphysical-historical" reasons as with autobiographical ones, and, focusing on these former reasons, Andrews looks at the tensions in the adult-child relationship. Andrews first considers the eighteenth-century notions of childhood that were Dickens' inheritance, looking at the ways the notion of the Noble Savage became transformed into the cult of the child, and also considering the ways Dickens sought to amalgamate "past and present, childhood and maturity, fancy and reality." Andrews considers these themes with respect to two articles Dickens wrote for *Household Words*, "Dullborough Town" and "Where We Stopped Growing," and then, in the later part of the book, gives special treatment to three works from the late 1840s: *A Christmas Carol*, *Dombey and Son*, and *David Copperfield*. Andrews identifies a great variety of different types of the "grown-up child"; examples from *David Copperfield* include Clara Copperfield, Dora, Em'ly, Agnes, Ham, Mr. Peggotty, Traddles, David, and even Dickens himself. But these many and varied examples are not due to sloppy thinking on Andrews's part; he carefully discriminates between the various sorts of grown-up child, and patiently and carefully pursues the ways Dickens treats crucial issues of childhood, childishness, maturity, and responsibility in his works of "romantic realism." Ultimately, Andrews argues that the grown-up child functions as a kind of critique of nineteenth-century society and culture; the book is convincing and consistently thought-provoking.

—Women

Natalie McKnight argues that Dickens' own conscious resentment of his mother, combined with subterranean hostility against women in general, led him to beat, batter, and otherwise torture mothers in his novels. McKnight's psychological approach includes some examples that are less than wholly convincing (e.g., Mrs. Joe and Miss Havisham, neither of whom are actually mothers); her conclusion, that Dickens may have feared "the earthy force represented by women in general and mothers in particular," remains unproven.

Juliet John gives special attention to Edith Dombey in her article about "Dickens' Deviant Women," but also considers Rosa Dartle, Lady Dedlock, Miss Wade, and others, arguing that such characters are "much maligned yet much neglected." John feels that critics who see these characters as too melodramatic do not recognize that Dickens is using melodrama in "an ambitious and sophisticated way" to reveal character. John insists that, despite Edith's role-playing, she is "ultimately sincere": "true to a hidden self." John also considers deviant women as art objects, claiming that Dickens' "good" women are not likened to works of art, and as sex objects, claiming that Dickens' "wayward women consistently focus his investigation of adult sexual relationships and the perverted and inhibited form they took in the patriarchal world of Victorian England."

Anne M. Skabarnicki's article in *Carlyle Studies Annual* considers Dickens' habit, in common with Carlyle's, of "down-sizing the feminine": diminishing women in stature. Skabarnicki finds little in the letters and works of either writer to comfort a feminist critic; she examines Dickens' condescending treatment of his wife (manifest in his letters to her), and notes that Dickens finds the horrors perpetrated by women in *A Tale of Two Cities* more chilling than those perpetrated by men. Though the sexism of writers like Dickens and Carlyle is more subtle than that of, say, Coventry Patmore, Skabarnicki suggests it may ultimately be more pernicious.

The chapter on Dickens in Tom Winnifrith's *Fallen Women in the Nineteenth-Century Novel* is unsuccessful. Winnifrith attempts to interweave biography and criticism, but his understanding of either is minimal. Winnifrith gets many details wrong, substituting "Fascinating" for "Fascination" Fledgeby, "Peg Neagles" for Pet Meagles, "Rev. Noodle" for Mr. Moddle. His interpretations of the novels are equally suspect; he seems somewhat overeager to discover "sin" and "guilt" in sexuality, and to find "indelicate references" and "lurid language" in Dickens' writing. At times, the chapter seems to be not so much about "fallen women" as about sexuality itself; Winnifrith apologizes for having so few fallen women to talk about, and instead talks about Kate Nickleby, Little Nell, and the Miss Pecksniffs. Winnifrith feels that Dickens would be "likely to associate sex with dirt and degradation," and that he probably "began to hate the sexual instinct" after his difficulties with his wife; he concludes that "Dickens did not treat woman fairly" in his life or his fiction.

—*Disease*

Miriam Bailin's book on the sickroom in Victorian fiction devotes special attention to Charlotte Brontë, George Eliot, and Dickens; her chapter on Dickens treats many of the novels, though she gives particular emphasis to *The Old Curiosity Shop* and *Our Mutual Friend*. Bailin sees the sickroom as a kind of escape or retreat from the conflicts of the Victorian era, and argues that "fictional representations of illness serve to resolve both social conflict and aesthetic tension." She says that in the rest, repose, and therapy the sickroom offers, Dickens images a glimpse of heaven. Though Bailin's book was first published in 1994, I give no extended treatment of it here, as interested readers can consult Barry V. Qualls's discussion in a previous volume of *Dickens Studies Annual*.

J. E. Cosnett's short article, "Charles Dickens and Epilepsy," quotes from several novels, especially *Oliver Twist, Bleak House*, and *Our Mutual Friend*, to demonstrate that Dickens accurately represented the symptoms, causes, and consequences of epileptic seizures. Cosnett speculates as to the specific type of epilepsy suffered by Monks, Guster, Headstone, and others.

Clearly written and theoretically sophisticated, Gail Turley Houston's *Consuming Fictions* combines close readings with the insights of historical analysis and gender studies, examining consumption (medical, alimentary, and economic) in ten of Dickens' novels. Houston finds anorexia nervosa a significant disease both literally and metaphorically, as "a sign of the gender conflicts and the economic and social dynamics of Victorian England." Though Houston admits that only a dozen cases were diagnosed in the nineteenth century, and that the disease was named only after Dickens' death, she argues that many Victorian writers were probably undiagnosed victims of anorexia nervosa. Houston offers a range of clever readings, often with surprising conclusions—her identification of Tom Pinch as the hero of *Martin Chuzzlewit* and her appreciation of the "bold, sexual, appetitive, and appetizing Ruth," not always highly valued by readers, are but two examples.

—Cannibalism, passion, and necessity

Anthropologist Anne Keenleyside's article in *The Explorer's Journal* also treats consumption—but of another sort entirely. Her discussion of cannibalism among members of the Franklin party of Arctic explorers (1819–22) would not normally have merited discussion here, but given its relevance to Harry Stone's book (treated below), and the fact that Keenleyside discusses Dickens' horror at Dr. John Rae's 1854 report of cannibalism in the Franklin party and Dickens' spirited defense of the Franklin explorers, I note that in 1993 Keenleyside discovered a previously unrecorded site on Erebus Bay that provides "the best evidence of cannibalism to date": nearly 400 human bones, with 92 of these bones bearing cut marks made by removing flesh from them.

For a more extended treatment of Dickens and cannibalism, one must turn to Harry Stone's book *The Night Side of Dickens: Cannibalism, Passion, Necessity*. The book is over 700 pages long, and may be best understood as three different books packaged as one: Stone treats cannibalism, passion (especially obsessive sexual passion), and necessity (particularly with respect to the question of free will) in three separate sections, and though he offers many cross-references, these sections are finally rather loosely linked together, as representing different aspects of Dickens' "night side," a hidden, secret, and dark side of Dickens' life and art.

The section on cannibalism, as long as the other two sections put together, is clearly the least satisfactory. Stone sees cannibalism virtually everywhere: finger-biting and baby-nursing are cannibalistic, and Stone often wanders from true cannibalism into discussion of that which is merely gory, morbid, or disturbing (e.g., riots, dismemberment, decomposing bodies, threats, cruelty, and martyrdom), without considering whether or not anyone actually eats anyone else. Stone identifies undertakers (Sowerberry), resurrection-men (Cruncher), and watermen (Hexam and Riderhood) with cannibals, since they make their living (and thus take their nourishment) from death. Before reading Stone, I could not name a single cannibal in *Great Expectations*; now I know that Magwitch, Orlick, Miss Havisham, the Pockets, and even Pip are all cannibals. (Come to think of it, even Jaggers, who is not in the index, bites his finger.) Part of the problem is that Stone often seems to confuse the literal with the metaphoric, using the word "literally" (especially in the phrase "quite literally") far too often, and inappropriately; for example, a nursing infant is "quite literally, consuming its mother." Silliness like this is often a distraction, and may make readers less likely to consider seriously many of Stone's claims, like the rather insulting one that Dickens is "of the cannibal species, and hungry." Stone is very interested in Dickens' articles in *Household Words* about the Franklin party, and states that "Dickens proved to be quite right in his conviction that Franklin and his main party had not succumbed to cannibalism"; Keenleyside's work suggests that if Stone is right, it can only be technically (the new site may not have been manned by Franklin's "main party").

Fortunately, the other sections of Stone's book are more rewarding. Stone uses many different approaches in the book, but the biographical, psychological, and historical ones dominate; the index lists 50 pages on which Stone discusses the blacking factory, and 83 on which he discusses Ellen Ternan. Sometimes the psycho-biographical speculations wear thin, but often they are provocative and insightful. Stone devotes a great deal of attention to a few little-read pieces of Dickens' fiction: more than forty-five pages, for example, to a short story in *The Lazy Tour of Two Idle Apprentices* which Stone calls "The Bride Chamber." Stone most convincingly shows the relevance of this story, and of *The Frozen Deep*, and of an essay called "Please to Leave Your Umbrella," to a study of Ellen Ternan and passion, and demonstrates that Dickens' portrayals of passion change qualitatively after the publication of "The Bride Chamber." Stone's analysis of this story is perhaps the best part of the book. The final section, on necessity, focuses primarily on *George Silverman's Explanation*, which Stone feels is a neglected masterpiece. Stone applies insights from his analysis of this book to Dickens' other fiction, arguing, for example, that Pip has important affinities with Silverman. Stone offers the most sophisticated manuscript analysis of 1994, considering Dickens' letters, manuscripts, and number plans at various points in the book; with 145 illustrations, many of them unfamiliar and relevant, Stone's book is also one of the most richly illustrated.

—Crime

Cranky and idiosyncratic, crime novelist Nicolas Freeling's treatment of Dickens' three major crime novels (*Bleak House, Little Dorrit*, and *Great Expectations*) sheds surprisingly little light on either these novels or on crime fiction. Freeling writes colorfully, and feels free to express his opinions without citing those of earlier critics. Perhaps not many readers will agree that *David Copperfield* is "tosh," or that *Great Expectations* is Dickens' greatest work because "[t]here is no fussy crowd of minor figures, tiresome subplots, bravura tear-jerking, nor that restless manic quality"—but there is something appealing in Freeling's freely-voiced (if not always well-argued) opinions. Freeling claims to enjoy, but nevertheless dismisses, Dickens' early and mid-career work, and rejects *A Tale of Two Cities* as soppy and *Our Mutual Friend* as "sad bosh." Freeling likes Mrs. General in *Little Dorrit*, but seems to miss Dickens' main point by diminishing her rank: he always refers to her as "Mrs. Major," as if she were the widow of Major Major Major Major in Joseph Heller's *Catch-22*. Though the book is amusingly vivid, it is not wholly accurate, nor clearly argued.

—Time

Another book focusing on the late novels is Soultana Maglavera's *Time Patterns in Late Dickens*, which treats the novels from *Bleak House* through *Our Mutual Friend*. Maglavera is admirably clear about her goal: she wants to use theory (in this case, "functionalist thematic narratology" examining issues of temporal sequence) not for its own sake, but to reveal meaning. She claims that the "temporal anachronies" in the novels elucidate a number of key themes in Dickens, especially about interconnectedness, reality and appearances, and a "Christian view of time where past and present are joined" and shaped by love, forgiveness, and sacrifice. Unfortunately, the rather cheaply-produced (and very expensive: $50 for a 251-page paperback which includes 45 pages of narratological tables) book delivers little: in one of the strongest chapters, a narratological analysis of *Bleak House*, Maglavera demonstrates that Dickens uses temporal sequence to heighten both mystery and suspense and to emphasize the themes of interconnectedness, time, and "the power of true love and concern for others." In the *Hard Times* chapter, a ten-page consideration of Bounderby's recurring lies about his childhood yields only the conclusion that this shows us something about appearances and reality not always matching. Maglavera's fault in this book is not her method, nor her goals, but the unfortunate gap between the two: she would like to make significant points, but too often resorts to unearned conclusions about the importance of love, sacrifice, and "the Christian version of time." Her other conclusions are, unfortunately, rather obvious: that temporal dislocations make readers reflect on "the nature of linear time," for instance. The design and copy-editing are weak; the many extra spaces seemingly added inadvertently make the pages unpleasant to look at, and I noted more than forty references to a "Hillis-Miller," alphabetized in the bibliographies under H, before I stopped counting half way through the book.

James E. Marlow's book *Charles Dickens: The Uses of Time* also considers time, but from a somewhat less rigid theoretical position. His book is loosely structured, and ranges quite freely: he associates issues such as revenge, memory, causation, guilt, poetic justice, and determinism with the past; hunger, cannibalism, and food with the present; and revenge (again), great expectations, imagination, work, domesticity, and duty with the future. Marlow's book offers little sustained argument, and many of his best points have little real connection with time, but nevertheless Marlow does provide some insights of great interest: his treatment of the meaning of Estella's true parentage makes clear Dickens' thematic intentions for *Great Expectations*, for example, and he has valuable points to make about *Nicholas Nickleby* and "the world," and about the true value of Eugene Wrayburn's marriage to Lizzie Hexam. That Marlow moves from *Great Expectations* on one page to *Pickwick* on the next suggests the loose organizational scheme of this book—but Marlow's notion that Pickwick "retires not from life but from a naive vision that conceives of life as static" is genuinely thought-provoking, and the book is often rewarding, if somewhat frustrating, to read. The index is weak, omitting over a dozen of Marlow's references to Carlyle; cannibalism is a most important topic to Marlow, but in order to find any references, one must look under "E," for "English cannibalism."

—Art

In one of 1994's most challenging, but ultimately least satisfying, explorations of Dickens and the visual arts, Tim Dolin takes a look at "Companion Pieces: Dickens's Sister-Travellers," considering Victorian photography and painting as well as Dickens' fiction. Using a sometimes bewildering feminist jargon—as when he states that "the unregarded glass presents a particularly coercive instatement of 'patriarchal/ideological/pornographic motives' "—Dolin examines the "sexual collusions . . . present in the image of two identical women looked at by a man." Dolin argues that "substitute sisterhood" exposes "the way in which narrative colludes in the operations of gender in Victorian culture." By substitute sisterhood, Dolin seems to mean women who look like sisters but are not; his main examples, drawn from *Little Dorrit*, are Amy/Minnie and Miss Wade/Tattycoram. Dolin is not, evidently, a careful reader of Dickens; he offers Emily and Rosa Dartle as an example of "the good woman placed beside and usually redeeming a fallen version of the domestic ideal," and claims, strangely, that Mr. Carker is "slaughtered by the very powerlessness of his glance." Criticizing Dickens' "pathological expansiveness" and "haphazard spontaneity and expediency,' Dolin feels that Dickens' failure to resolve the stories of Wade and Tattycoram ("the novel's annihilation of their voices") places Dickens' "imperative of connection" at risk.

Murray Roston's article "Dickens and the Tyranny of Objects" focuses not on paintings, but on furniture and domestic decoration. Demonstrating the increasing diversity of types of couches, door-knockers, and inkstands in the mid-Victorian era, Roston argues that Dorothy Van Ghent and her many followers (including J. Hillis Miller) are mistaken in suggesting that Dickens invests inanimate objects with life and dehumanizes his characters. Roston argues that mistaken view is based on a misunderstanding of Victorian attitudes toward material objects: the Victorians were not overwhelmed by, but welcomed, the proliferation of goods; members of the middle class were at last able to purchase items that reflected, matched, or even extended their individual personalities. Objects became animated not by drawing life from persons, but by serving as projections of their owners; Dickens' use of metonymy lends richness and vitality to his characters, and does not "de-animate" or rob characters of their souls. Roston's provocative argument is illustrated with fascinating examples of Victorian design, and with apposite quotations from Dickens' novels.

Catherine Griffey, David Parker, and Jane Ramsey offer information about two long-lost portraits of Catherine Dickens by Daniel Maclise, painted ca. 1846–1847. The article reveals that these paintings are in the possession of California collector William P. Wreden, who plans to bequeath them to the Dickens House Museum on his death. (Note: Mr. Wreden died shortly after the publication of this article in the *Dickensian*.)

J. J. Dennett sees many links between Dickens and the painter J. M. W. Turner, but focuses primarily on their treatment of "mighty waters": ship-wrecks, tempests, and Niagara Falls. Dennett argues that both artists intended to communicate, through their representations of mighty waters, an attitude about "spirituality, religion, God and Jesus." Ultimately, Dennett argues, the two depict nature as forgiving and redemptive, not retributive.

Nancy Weston notes that Dickens' friend Daniel Maclise, an Irishman who painted a portrait of Francis William Sykes in 1837, had an affair with Lady Sykes, and that Sykes behaved abominably; Weston offers a fascinating and entirely convincing argument (based, in part, on a most attentive reading of Maclise's painting) that Dickens modelled Bill Sikes in *Oliver Twist* on Francis William Sykes, and that Sikes provides a kind of coded commentary on Sykes's behavior and personality. Furthermore, Weston effectively points to some larger social and political implications of Dickens' fictionalized portrait, suggesting that Dickens criticizes the base soul of the Englishman Sykes, while standing up for "art, friendship and love."

—Expulsion and the Scapegoat

Michiel Heyns writes with clarity, wit, and sophistication in his chapter on expulsion and the scapegoat in Dickens. Heyns argues that characters in Dickens tend to attach to one another with an almost obsessive attraction; the marriage of the heroine is essential business for Dickens, and more generally, "Partnerships are at the centre of Dickens's design." But the lonely and excluded characters, the scapegoats of the narrative who are the "unacknow-ledged energants of the plot," "challenge the novel's resolution." Focussing primarily on the middle and later novels, Heyns sheds light on solitary or excluded figures such as Dombey, Uriah Heep, Hortense, Miss Wade, Orlick, and John Jasper, devoting particular attention to Bradley Headstone, Dickens's most fully-drawn scapegoat. Heyns argues that, especially in *Our Mutual Friend*, Dickens carefully balances the "expulsive" and the "redemptive," and that Headstone, himself both an "unacknowledged structural principle" in the novel and a dark embodiment of the destructive potential of partnership and love, is "the active principle of the plot."

—Law, Property, and Inheritance

Larry M. Wertheim offers an extended treatment of "Law, Literature, and Morality in the Novels of Charles Dickens" in the *William Mitchell Law Review*. Examining Dickens' portrayal of the law and of lawyers in *The Pickwick Papers, David Copperfield, Bleak House, A Tale of Two Cities*, and *Great Expectations*, and also applying the literary theory of Stanley Fish to legal texts in *Pickwick Papers* (Mitchell examines only Pickwick's incriminating conversation with Mrs. Bardell and Buzfuz's address to the jury about Pickwick's "Chops and tomata sauce" note), Wertheim concludes that morality and legality are not the same thing, and that the law is an adequate means to achieve moral ends. Wertheim offers adequate summaries of some of the legal issues in the novels he treats, and effective sketches of several legal characters, though he fails to offer anything as closely argued as Lowenstein's treatment of *Bleak House*, discussed above.

Less successful are the two chapters devoted to Dickens in Jeff Nunokawa's *The Afterlife of Property*. The purpose of Nunokawa's work seems to be primarily cultural analysis rather than literary study, and reading these chapters requires great effort; Nunokawa fills his pages with opaque and obscure abstractions, and though his sentences are neither jargon-filled nor ungrammatical, they have little solid grounding in Dickens' text. In "Domestic Fictions: *Little Dorrit* and the Fictions of Property," Nunokawa claims that possession equals appropriation and that all acquired property is "haunted"; a representative sentence tells us that "*Little Dorrit* restores the compromised realm of inheritance not only by reproducing versions of ownership that are defined by their distance from the work of acquisition, but also by constructing a realm of domestic relations that furnishes the object for such an owner." At times, Nunokawa stretches the boundaries of meaning too far, claiming, for example, that "As acquisitive capacity, the feminine ceases to be good, or merely false, and becomes instead a form of genitalia that scars and 'stick[s].' " The chapter entitled "For Your Eyes Only: Private Property and the Oriental Body in *Dombey and Son*" is equally unconvincing. Nunokawa argues that capital and sexuality are "a form of exhibition" and that Walter Gay's fortunes are "Orientalized," but Nunokawa's admission that the minor character known as Cleopatra "constitutes *Dombey and Son*'s most extended treatment of an Oriental figure" suggests that the topic is not, finally, of central importance.

One of the finest publications of the year is Anny Sadrin's book, *Parentage and Inheritance in the Novels of Charles Dickens*. The book is Sadrin's own elegant translation of the first portion of her 1980 doctoral thesis, and it is most persuasively written. Sadrin considers the inheritance of both patronymic and patrimony, focusing particular attention on *Oliver Twist, Dombey and*

Son, Bleak House, Little Dorrit, Great Expectations, and *Our Mutual Friend*. With grace, wit, and intelligence, Sadrin explores the complex meanings surrounding the inheritance of name and money in these and other novels. One of her central contentions, and one which I have long resisted, is that Dickens' plots are of great interest and importance, and that Dickens organizes those plots with great skill; Sadrin argues so convincingly that I now see this aspect of Dickens' artistry with new eyes. Sadrin does not shy from controversy, writing, for example, of Estella and Pip in *Great Expectations* that "this love-story is of such limited significance to the novel as a whole that Dickens could rewrite its conclusion at will . . . without damaging or improving the book." Instead of focusing on Estella and Pip, Sadrin argues that *Great Expectations* is "first and foremost the novel of a son,"'"the son of Philip Pirrip." Sadrin's use of evidence from the text to support her views is masterful; she earns the right to make strong statements by her ability to back them up with appropriate citations, and her close analysis (often considering grammar, rhetoric, and style) is admirable. Though every chapter contains riches, perhaps the one devoted to *Little Dorrit*," 'Nobody's Fault' or the Inheritance of Guilt," may be the most valuable, containing penetrating discussions of self-negation, forgiveness, vindictiveness, parricide, patriarchy and matriarchy, guilt, and grace.

ACKNOWLEDGEMENTS

I am very grateful to the staff of Gordon Library, particularly Diana Johnson in ILL, for their help in locating many sources *Dickens Studies Annual* was unable to obtain. I am also thankful to Mr. Robert Googins for his assistance with articles in law journals, to James P. Hanlan for his help with technical issues, and to Steven C. Bullock for his many valuable suggestions. I owe my biggest debt to Libby Westie, Kate Brattin, and John Brattin, who helped me overcome the loss of a great deal of computer data, and who are always able to set me in the right direction, no matter what.

WORKS CITED

Andrews, Malcolm. *Dickens and the Grown-Up Child*. Iowa City: U of Iowa Press; Basingstoke: Macmillan, 1994.

Bailin, Mariam. "Charles Dickens: 'impossible existences.' " In *The Sickroom in Victorian Fiction*. Cambridge: Cambridge UP, 1994. 79–108.

Baubles, Raymond L., Jr. "Displaced Persons: The Cost of Speculation in Charles Dickens' *Martin Chuzzlewit*." In *Money: Lure, Lore, and Literature*. Ed. John Louis DiGaetani. Westport, CT: Greenwood, 1994. 245–52.

Benton, Graham. " 'And Dying Thus Around Us Every Day': Pathology, Ontology and the Discourse of the Diseased Body. A Study of Illness and Contagion in *Bleak House*." *Dickens Quarterly* 11 (1994): 69–80.

Brattin, Joel J. "Frustrated Expectations." *Dickens Quarterly* 11 (1994): 138–47.

———. "The Latest Letters from Dickens." *Dickens Quarterly* 11 (1994): 36–44.

Budd, Dona. "Language Couples in *Bleak House*." *Nineteenth-Century Literature* 49 (1994): 196–220.

Carroll, John R. *A Carol for Tiny Tim*. Woodstock, IL: Dramatic Pub., 1994.

Carse, Wendy. "Domestic Transformation in Dickens' 'The Haunted Man.' " *Dickens Studies Annual* 23 (1994): 163–81.

Clamon, Judy. *Charles Dickens' Great Expectations*. MAXnotes. Piscataway, New Jersey: Research & Education Association, 1994.

Clarkson, Carrol. "Alias and Alienation in *Bleak House*: Identity in Language." *Dickens Studies Annual* 23 (1994): 121–35.

Cosnett, J. E. "Dickens and Epilepsy." *Epilepsia* 35 (1994): 903–05.

Cox, Don Richard. "The *Every Saturday* Page Proofs for *The Mystery of Edwin Drood*." *Dickensian* 90 (1994): 95–101.

Crowley, James P. "Pip's Spiritual Exercise: The Meditative Mode in Dickens' *Great Expectations*." *Renascence* vol. 46, no. 2 (Winter 1994): 133–43.

Cunningham, John. "Christian Allusion, Comedic Structure and the Metaphor of Baptism in *Great Expectations*." *South Atlantic Review* 59 (May 1994): 35–51.

Curry, Mary Jane Chilton. "Anaphoric and Cataphoric Reference in Dickens's *Our Mutual Friend* and James's *The Golden Bowl*." In *The Text and Beyond: Essays in Literary Linguistics*. Ed. Cynthia Goldin Bernstein. Tuscaloosa: U of Alabama P, 1994. 30–55.

Dahmane, Razak. "A Mere Question of Figures: Measures, Mystery and Metaphor in *Hard Times*." *Dickens Studies Annual* 23 (1994): 137–62.

Dennett, J. J. "Mighty Waters in the Work of Dickens and Turner." *Dickensian* 90 (1994): 179–88.

Dickens, Charles. *Bleak House*. Everyman Paperback Classics. Ed. Andrew Sanders. London: J. M. Dent; Rutland, Vermont: Charles E. Tuttle, 1994.

———. *The Cricket on the Hearth and Other Christmas Stories.* Dover Thrift edition. Ed. Thomas Crofts. Mineola, New York: Dover, 1994.

———. *Dombey and Son.* Everyman's Library edition. Introd. Lucy Hughes-Hallet. New York: Knopf, 1994.

———. *Great Expectations.* World's Classics edition. Ed. Margaret Cardwell. Introd. Kate Flint. Oxford: Oxford UP, 1994.

———. *Great Expectations.* Everyman Paperback Classics. Ed. Robin Gilmour. London: J. M. Dent; Rutland, Vermont: Charles E. Tuttle, 1994.

———. *Hard Times.* World's Classics edition. Ed. Paul Schlicke. Oxford: Oxford P, 1994.

———. *Hard Times.* Everyman Paperback Classics. Ed. Grahame Smith. London: J. M. Dent; Rutland, Vermont: Charles E. Tuttle, 1994.

———. *Like the Dickens: Complete Works.* Parsippany, NJ: Bureau of Electronic Publishing, 1994.

———. *Martin Chuzzlewit.* Everyman's Library edition. Introd. William Boyd. New York: Knopf, 1994.

———. *Martin Chuzzlewit.* Everyman Paperback Classics. Ed. Michael Slater. London: J. M. Dent; Rutland, Vermont: Charles E. Tuttle, 1994.

———. *Nicholas Nickleby.* Everyman Paperback Classics. Ed. David Parker. London: J. M. Dent; Rutland, Vermont: Charles E. Tuttle, 1994.

———. *Oliver Twist.* Everyman Paperback Classics. Ed. Steven Connor. London: J. M. Dent; Rutland, Vermont: Charles E. Tuttle, 1994.

———. *Oliver Twist.* Abridged by Robin Waterfield. London: Puffin, 1994.

———. *Our Mutual Friend.* Everyman's Library edition. Introd. Andrew Sanders. New York: Knopf, 1994.

———. *Sketches by Boz and Other Early Papers, 1833–39.* The Dent Uniform Edition of Dickens' Journalism, Vol. 1. Ed. Michael Slater; with illustrations by George Cruikshank. London: Dent; Columbus: Ohio State UP, 1994.

———. *A Tale of Two Cities.* Everyman Paperback Classics. Ed. Norman Page. London: J. M. Dent; Rutland, Vermont: Charles E. Tuttle, 1994.

Dolin, Tim. "Companion Pieces: Dickens's Sister-Travellers." *Word & Image* vol. 10, no. 2 (April–June 1994): 107–18.

Donow, H. S. "The Two Faces of Age and the Resolution of Generational Conflict." *Gerontologist* 34 (1994): 73–78.

Dundek, John M. "Note 551. A New First American Edition of *Great Expectations.*" *The Book Collector* 43 (1994): 298–99.

Edgecombe, Rodney Stenning. "The 'Waters' in *Bleak House*, Chapter 1." *Notes & Queries* n.s. vol. 41 (September 1994): 353.

———. "Topographical Disaffection in Dickens's *American Notes* and *Martin Chuzzlewit.*" *Journal of English and Germanic Philology* vol. 93, no. 1 (1994): 35–54.

———. "Two Oblique Allusions in *Our Mutual Friend.*" *Notes and Queries* n.s. vol. 41 (September 1994): 352–353.

———. "Violence, Death and Euphemism in *Great Expectations.*" *Victorians Institute Journal* 22 (1994): 85–98.

Edwards, Amelia. "From a Past Contemporary: Three Victorian Novelists." *Contemporary Review* (August 1994): 102–04.

Faulkner, David. "The Confidence Man: Empire and the Deconstruction of Muscular Christianity in *The Mystery of Edwin Drood.*" In *Muscular Christianity: Embodying the Victorian Age.* Ed. Donald E. Hall. Cambridge: Cambridge UP, 1994, pp. 175–93.

Fein, Mara H. "The Politics of Family in *The Pickwick Papers.*" *ELH* 61 (1994): 363–79.

Felber, Lynette. " 'Delightfully Irregular': Esther's Nascent *écriture féminine* in *Bleak House.*" *The Victorian Newsletter* 85 (Spring 1994): 13–20.

Fenstermaker, John J. "Using Dickens to Market Morality: Popular Reading Materials in the *Nickleby* 'Advertiser.' " *Journal of Popular Culture* 28 (1994): 9–17.

Foley, Ridgway K., Jr. "Mr. Dickens Was Right." *The Freeman* 44 (1994): 8–12.

Forsyte, Charles. "Charles Dickens Junior, Harold Macmillan, and *Edwin Drood.*" *Notes and Queries*, n.s. vol 41 (September 1994): 353–54.

Freeling, Nicolas. "Charles Dickens." In *Criminal Convictions: Errant Essays on Perpetrators of Literary License.* Boston: David R. Godine, 1994. 26–57.

Friedman, Stanley. "Heep and Powell: Dickensian Revenge?" *Dickensian* 90 (1994): 36–43.

———. "Recent Dickens Studies: 1992." *Dickens Studies Annual* 23 (1994): 337–401.

Fulweiler, Howard W. " 'A Dismal Swamp': Darwin, Design, and Evolution in *Our Mutual Friend.*" *Nineteenth-Century Literature* 49 (1994): 50–74.

Galbraith, Mary. "Pip as 'Infant Tongue' and as Adult Narrator in Chapter One of *Great Expectations.*" In Elizabeth Goodenough, ed., *Infant Tongues: The Voice of the Child in Literature.* Detroit: Wayne State UP, 1994. 123–141.

Gottfried, Barbara. "Household Arrangements and the Patriarchal Order in *Bleak House.*" *Journal of Narrative Technique* 24 (1994): 1–17.

Greenstein, Michael. "*Martin Chuzzlewit*'s Connections." *Dickens Quarterly* 11 (1994): 5–13.

Griffey, Catherine, David Parker, and Jane Ramsay. "The Maclise Portraits of Catherine Dickens." *Dickensian* 90 (1994): 165–70.

Hamilton, James F. "Terrorizing the 'Feminine' in Hugo, Dickens, and France." *Symposium* vol. 48, no. 3 (Fall 1994): 204–15.

Henkle, Roger B. "The Crisis of Representation in *Dombey and Son.*" In *Critical Reconstructions: The Relationship of Fiction and Life.* Eds. Robert M. Polhemus and Roger B. Henkle, eds. Stanford: Stanford UP, 1994. 90–110.

Heyns, Michiel. " 'Oh, 'tis love, 'tis love . . .': Privileged Partnership in Dickens." In *Expulsion and the Nineteenth-Century Novel: The Scapegoat in English Realist Fiction.* Oxford: Clarendon Press, 1994. 90–135.

Holman, David. *The Play of Charles Dickens' A Christmas Carol.* Heinemann Plays series. Oxford: Heinemann, 1994.

Houston, Gail Turley. *Consuming Fictions: Gender, Class, and Hunger in Dickens's Novels.* Carbondale and Edwardsville: Southern Illinois UP, 1994.

Hughes, Leonard. "Dickens in the 'Hood." *American Theatre* vol. 11, no. 1 (January 1994): 14–19.

Jaffe, Audrey. "Spectacular Sympathy: Visuality and Ideology in Dickens's *A Christmas Carol.*" *PMLA* vol. 109, no. 2 (March 1994): 254–65.

Johanson, Robert. *Charles Dickens' Great Expectations.* Woodstock, IL: Dramatic Pub., 1994.

John, Juliet. "Dickens' Deviant Women: A Reassessment." *The Critical Review* 34 (1994): 68–84.

Joseph, Gerhard. "Charles Dickens, International Copyright, and the Discretionary Silence of *Martin Chuzzlewit.*" In *The Construction of Authorship: Textual Appropriation in Law and Literature.* Eds. Martha Woodmansee and Peter Jaszi. Durham and London: Duke UP, 1994. 259–70.

Karbacz, Elsie, and Robert Raven. "The Many Mysteries of *Edwin Drood.*" *Dickensian* 90 (1994): 5–18.

Karnicky, Jeffrey. *Charles Dickens' A Tale of Two Cities.* MAXnotes. Piscataway, New Jersey: Research & Education Association, 1994.

Keenleyside, Anne. "The Last Resort: Cannibalism in the Arctic." *The Explorer's Journal* vol. 72, no. 4 (Winter 1994/95): 138–43.

Kubasak, Sharon. "Reflexive Delight." *Dickensian* 90 (1994): 25–35.

Kucich, John. "Dickens." In *The Columbia History of the British Novel.* Ed. John Richetti. New York: Columbia UP, 1994. 381–406.

Lapinski, Piya Pal. "Dickens's Miss Wade and J. S. LeFanu's Carmilla: The Female Vampire in *Little Dorrit.*" *Dickens Quarterly* 11 (1994): 81–87.

Levenson, Michael H. "The Private Life of a Public Form: Freud, Fantasy, and the Novel." In *Critical Reconstructions: The Relationship of Fiction and Life.* Eds. Robert M. Polhemus and Roger B. Henkle. Stanford UP, 1994. 52–70.

Long, Pamela H. "Fagin and Monopodio: The Sources of *Oliver Twist* in Cervantes's *Rinconete y Cortadillo.*" *Dickensian* 90 (1994): 117–24.

Lougy, Robert E. "Desire and the Ideology of Violence: America in Charles Dickens's *Martin Chuzzlewit.*" *Criticism* 36 (Fall 1994): 569–94.

Lowenstein, Daniel H. "The Failure of the Act: Conceptions of Law in *The Merchant of Venice, Bleak House, Les Miserables,* and Richard Weisberg's *Poethics.*" *Cardozo Law Review* 15 (1994): 1139–1243.

Maglavera, Soultana. *Time Patterns in Late Dickens: A Study of the Thematic Implications of The Temporal Organization of* Bleak House, Hard Times, Little Dorrit, A Tale of Two Cities, Great Expectations, *and* Our Mutual Friend. Costerus New Series 94. Amsterdam; Atlanta GA: Editions Rodopi B.V., 1994.

Manning, Sylvia. "*Nicholas Nickleby*: On the Plains of Syria." *Dickens Studies Annual* 23 (1994): 73–92.

Marks, Patricia. "Paul Dombey and the Milk of Human Kindness." *Dickens Quarterly* 11 (1994): 14–25.

Marlow, James E. *Charles Dickens: The Uses of Time.* Selingsgrove: Susquehanna UP, 1994.

Maslon, Laurence. "A Christmas Goose, or God Help Us, Everyone!" *American Theatre* vol. 11, no. 10 (Dec. 1994): pp. 22–25.

McBride, Mary G. "Contemporary Economic Metaphors in *Dombey and Son.*" *Dickensian* 90 (1994): 19–24.

McKnight, Natalie. "Making Mother Suffer, and Other Fun in Dickens." *Dickens Quarterly* 11 (1994): 177–86.

McSweeney, Kerry. "*David Copperfield* and the Music of Memory." *Dickens Studies Annual* 23 (1994): 93–119.

Metz, Nancy Aycock. "Dickens and 'The Quack Architectural.' " *Dickens Quarterly* 11 (1994): 59–68.

Moss, Sidney P., and Carolyn J. Moss. "Frederick Dickens: From Courtship to Courtroom." *Dickensian* 90 (1994): 102–12.

Moss, Sidney P., and Carolyn J. Moss. *Charles Dickens and His Chicago Relatives: A Documentary Narrative.* Troy, NY: Whitson, 1994.

Mota, Miguel M. "The Construction of the Christian Community in Charles Dickens' *Bleak House.*" *Renascence* vol. 46, no. 3 (Spring 1994): 187–98.

Murray, Brian. *Charles Dickens.* New York: Continuum, 1994.

Newsom, Robert. "*Pickwick* in the Utilitarian Sense." *Dickens Studies Annual* 23 (1994): 49–71.

Nunokawa, Jeff. *The Afterlife of Property: Domestic Security and the Victorian Novel.* Princeton, NJ: Princeton UP, 1994.

Nygaard, Susan. "Redecorating Dombey: The Power of 'A Woman's Anger' versus Upholstery in *Dombey and Son.*" *Critical Matrix: The Princeton Journal of Woman, Gender, and Culture* 8 (1994): 40–80.

Palmer, William J. *The Highwayman and Mr. Dickens.* New York: Ballantine, 1994.

Patterson, Arthur P. "Sponging the Stone: Transformation in *A Christmas Carol.*" *Dickens Quarterly* 11 (1994): 172–76.

Polhemus, Robert M. "Comic and Erotic Faith Meet Faith in the Child: Charles Dickens's *Old Curiosity Shop* ('The Old Cupiosity Shape.')" In *Critical Reconstructions: The Relationship of Fiction and Life.* Eds. Robert M. Polhemus and Roger B. Henkle. Stanford: Stanford UP, 1994. 71–89.

Priley, Angela Marie. "An Analyis of *Oliver Twist* and *Oliver!*" *Children's Literature Association Quarterly* 18 (1993–1994): 189.

Retan, Katherine. "Lower Class Angels in the Middle Class House: The Domestic Woman's Progress in *Hard Times* and *Ruth.*" *Dickens Studies Annual* 23 (1994): 183–204.

Roston, Murray. "Dickens and the Tyranny of Objects." *Dickens Studies Annual* 23 (1994): 1–16.

Sadrin, Anny. *Parentage and Inheritance in the Novels of Charles Dickens.* European Studies in English Literature series. Cambridge: Cambridge UP, 1994.

Saijo, Takao. "T. W. Hill and 'Tom King and the Frenchman.' " *Dickensian* 90 (1994): 113–116.

Sammon, Paul. *The Christmas Carol Trivia Book: Everything You Ever Wanted to Know About Every Version of the Dickens Classic.* Secaucus, NY: Carol, 1994.

Schlicke, Paul. "Glorious Apollers and Ancient Buffaloes." *Dickensian* 90 (1994): 171–178.

Sell, Roger D., ed. *Great Expectations*. New Casebooks series. New York: St. Martin's P, 1994.

Sibley, Brian. *A Christmas Carol: The Unsung Story*. Oxford: Lion, 1994.

Skabarnicki, Anne M. "Dear Little Women: Downsizing the Feminine in Carlyle and Dickens." *Carlyle Studies Annual* 14 (1994): 33–42.

Steig, Michael. "Abuse and the Comic-Grotesque in *The Old Curiosity Shop*: Problems of Response." *Dickens Quarterly* 11 (1994): 103–14.

Stone, Harry. *The Night Side of Dickens: Cannibalism, Passion, Necessity*. Columbus: Ohio State UP, 1994.

Suchoff, David. "Dickens." In *Critical Theory and the Novel: Mass Society and Cultural Criticism in Dickens, Melville, and Kafka*. Madison: U of Wisconsin P, 1994. 40–88.

Swanson, Reneé. "The Living Dead: What the Dickens are College Students Reading Today?" *Policy Review* no. 67, Winter 1994. 72–73.

Swanton, Michael. "A Readership (and Non-Readership) for *Martin Chuzzlewit*, 1843–44." *Dickens Quarterly* 11 (1994): 115–26 and 161–71.

Ter Horst, Robert. "From *Lazarillo de Tormes* to Dickens's *Our Mutual Friend*—The European Topography of *La Voragine*." *Revista de Estudios Hispánicos* 28 (1994): 25–41.

Thatcher, Barry. "Dickens' Bow to the Language Theory Debate." *Dickens Studies Annual* 23 (1994): 17–47.

Tobin, Beth Fowkes. "The Cottage Visitor, the Housekeeper, and the Policeman: Self-Regulation and Surveillance in *Bleak House*." In *Superintending the Poor: Charitable Ladies and Paternal Landlords in British Fiction 1770–1860*. New Haven: Yale UP, 1994, pp. 129–52.

Tomalin, Claire. "Ordered by Boz? Life of Charles Dickens—An Undiscovered Portrait of Nelly Ternan." *TLS* no. 4736 (7 Jan 1994): 11.

Trezise, Simon. "Dickens and Critical Change: The Making of Dickens: Aspects of Biographical Criticism." *Dickens Quarterly* 11 (1994): 26–35.

———. "Dickens and Critical Change: The Making of Dickens: The Evolution of Marxist Criticism." *Dickens Quarterly* 11 (1994): 127–37.

Trull, Kathleen. "From Raisin Pudding to Oysters and Champagne: Charles Dickens." Illustrated by Kathryn Hewitt. In *Lives of the Writers: Comedies, Tragedies (and What the Neighbors Thought)*. New York: Harcourt Brace, 1994. 38–41.

Tytler, Graeme. "Dickens's 'The Signalman.'" *Explicator* vol. 53, no. 1 (Fall 1994): 26–29.

Vine, Robert, and Sheila Smith. ''John Overs: Family Tradition, Poetry and Memorabilia.'' *Dickensian* 90 (1994): 85–94.

Welsh, Alexander. ''Dickens and Certain Women.'' *Yale Review* 82 (1994): 143–51.

Wertheim, Larry M. ''Law, Literature, and Morality in the Novels of Charles Dickens.'' *William Mitchell Law Review* 20 (1994): 111–54.

West, John B. ''Krook's Death by Spontaneous Combustion and the Controversy between Dickens and Lewes: A Physiologist's View.'' *Dickensian* 90 (1994): 125–29.

Westland, Ella. ''Dickens and Critical Change: Dickens and Women.'' *Dickens Quarterly* 11 (1994): 187–96.

Weston, Nancy. ''Dickens, Daniel Maclise and the Real Bill Sikes.'' *Dickensian* 90 (1994): 189–96.

Winnifrith, Tom. ''Dickens.'' In *Fallen Women in the Nineteenth-Century Novel.* New York: St. Martin's P, 1994. 93–112.

Index

373